RETHINKING
EUROPEAN JEWISH HISTORY

THE LITTMAN LIBRARY OF
JEWISH CIVILIZATION

Dedicated to the memory of
LOUIS THOMAS SIDNEY LITTMAN
who founded the Littman Library for the love of God
and as an act of charity in memory of his father
JOSEPH AARON LITTMAN
and to the memory of
ROBERT JOSEPH LITTMAN
who continued what his father Louis had begun

יהא זכרם ברוך

Get wisdom, get understanding:
Forsake her not and she shall preserve thee

PROV. 4: 5

The Littman Library of Jewish Civilization is a registered UK charity
Registered charity no. 1000784

RETHINKING EUROPEAN JEWISH HISTORY

◆

Edited by

JEREMY COHEN

and

MOSHE ROSMAN

London

The Littman Library of Jewish Civilization
in association with Liverpool University Press

The Littman Library of Jewish Civilization
Registered office: 4th floor, 7–10 Chandos Street, London W I G 9DQ

in association with Liverpool University Press
4 Cambridge Street, Liverpool L69 7ZU, UK
www.liverpooluniversitypress.co.uk/littman

Managing Editor: Connie Webber

Distributed in North America by
Oxford University Press Inc., 198 Madison Avenue,
New York, NY 10016, USA

First published 2009
First published in paperback 2014

© *The Littman Library of Jewish Civilization 2009*

Catalogue records for this book are available from the
British Library and the Library of Congress
ISBN 978-1-906764-54-8

Publishing co-ordinator: Janet Moth
Proof-reading: Kate Clements
Index: Tom Broughton-Willett
Designed by Pete Russell, Faringdon, Oxon.
Typeset by Hope Services (Abingdon) Ltd

Printed and bound in Great Britain by
CPI Group (UK) Ltd., Croydon, CR0 4YY

Acknowledgements

THIS book represents the second in a new series of conferences and publications entitled New Perspectives on European Jewry, a series recently launched by the Goldstein-Goren Diaspora Research Center at Tel Aviv University. The conference convened in Tel Aviv early in January 2005, and this thematically designed collection of essays, though not the proceedings of our meetings, has taken shape in their aftermath.

As the field of Jewish history positions itself at the beginning of a new century and a new millennium, 'New Perspectives' will grapple afresh with the theoretical, topical, and methodological issues that nourish the relationship between the Jewish present and the Jewish past. We hope that *Rethinking European Jewish History* will assume a significant place in this venture—that, in questioning old assumptions, it will engage a broad range of readers in a new, imaginative, and fruitful discussion.

The editors express their profound thanks to Tel Aviv University's Goldstein-Goren Diaspora Research Center and its dedicated staff—above all, Ora Azta, Aviva Rosental, Daphna Schnabel, and Haim Cohen—and to the editors and officers of the Littman Library of Jewish Civilization for their good-natured, unflinching commitment in moving this project forward from beginning to end. We thank Shulamit Volkov for her help in planning the 2005 conference. And we gratefully acknowledge the generous support of the Goldstein-Goren family foundation in facilitating our conference and the volume that follows here in its wake.

Erev Shavuot 5767   J.C.
May 2007   M.R.

Contents

Note on Transliteration

THE transliteration of Hebrew in this book reflects consideration of the type of book it is, in terms of its content, purpose, and readership. The system adopted therefore reflects a broad approach to transcription, rather than the narrower approaches found in the *Encyclopaedia Judaica* or other systems developed for text-based or linguistic studies. The aim has been to reflect the pronunciation prescribed for modern Hebrew, rather than the spelling or Hebrew word structure, and to do so using conventions that are generally familiar to the English-speaking reader.

In accordance with this approach, no attempt is made to indicate the distinctions between *alef* and *ayin*, *tet* and *taf*, *kaf* and *kuf*, *sin* and *samekh*, since these are not relevant to pronunciation; likewise, the *dagesh* is not indicated except where it affects pronunciation. Following the principle of using conventions familiar to the majority of readers, however, transcriptions that are well established have been retained even when they are not fully consistent with the transliteration system adopted. On similar grounds, the *tsadi* is rendered by 'tz' in such familiar words as barmitzvah, and so on. Likewise, the distinction between *ḥet* and *khaf* has been retained, using *ḥ* for the former and *kh* for the latter; the associated forms are generally familiar to readers, even if the distinction is not actually borne out in pronunciation, and for the same reason the final *heh* is indicated too. As in Hebrew, no capital letters are used, except that an initial capital has been retained in transliterating titles of published works (for example, *Shulḥan arukh*).

Since no distinction is made between *alef* and *ayin*, they are indicated by an apostrophe only in intervocalic positions where a failure to do so could lead an English-speaking reader to pronounce the vowel-cluster as a diphthong—as, for example, in *ha'ir*—or otherwise mispronounce the word.

The *sheva na* is indicated by an *e*—*perikat ol*, *reshut*—except, again, when established convention dictates otherwise.

The *yod* is represented by *i* when it occurs as a vowel (*bereshit*), by *y* when it occurs as a consonant (*yesodot*), and by *yi* when it occurs as both (*yisra'el*).

Names have generally been left in their familiar forms, even when this is inconsistent with the overall system.

Introduction

JEREMY COHEN

THE FIELD OF JEWISH HISTORY has always developed in relation to the experiences of the Jews: not only their past experiences, which determine the *matter* that historians study, but also their present experiences, which determine the *manner* in which they study it—their motivations, their methods, and their perspectives. As an academic subject, the history of the Jews originated in the political, social, and cultural agenda of enlightened, nineteenth-century Jewish intellectuals. Dispassionate, scientific study of the Jewish past, they believed, would help to rehabilitate their classical heritage—and thus to secure equality and acceptance for their co-religionists in European states and societies. As Yosef Hayim Yerushalmi concluded a quarter of a century ago in his groundbreaking study of Jewish history and Jewish memory, *Zakhor*, 'Modern Jewish historiography . . . originated, not as scholarly curiosity, but as ideology, one of a gamut of responses to the crisis of Jewish emancipation and the struggle to attain it.'[1] While the essential nexus between scholarly discipline and contemporary reality has persisted, much has changed since then, both in the field of Jewish historical studies and in the contemporary experience that nurtures it. As Western society has entered the third millennium in Christian history, and as European Jewish historical scholarship prepares to enter the third century in its development, this book comes to grips with various aspects of that change.

During the last forty years, Jews, the cultures of the Jews, and the cultural and historical scholarship of the Jews have entered an age that many now call 'postmodern'. Postmodernism has ushered the study of the Jewish past into a new world of discourse, filled with terms, categories, ways of thinking, and, above all, challenges that had rarely shaped the conversations of Jewish historians in prior generations. Present-day historians cannot evade the postmodern realization that their research testifies to their own cultural orientation no less than the past that they set out to understand. They do not recover the unadulterated, factual truth of past events so much as construct, or interpret, those events in accordance with who they are. As anthropologist Clifford Geertz, one of the chief players in this postmodern or

[1] Yosef H. Yerushalmi, *Zakhor: Jewish History and Jewish Memory* (Seattle, 1982), 85.

'cultural' turn, proposed, because 'man is an animal suspended in webs of significance he himself has spun', we must take 'culture to be those webs, and the analysis of it to be therefore not an experimental science in search of law but an interpretive one in search of meaning'.[2] Given such an appreciation of culture, historians in our own day, exactly like writers of earlier periods on whose works we typically rely as primary sources, do not simply relate past events and their meaning; they fashion them. Some would go so far as to argue that 'historiography is not merely literary'; rather, it is 'always at least as fictional as it is factual'.[3]

For Jewish historians, however, the postmodern challenge extends further, not only to the fruits of their labour but to the heart of their subject matter. If our reading of the past depends above all on the ideological postures and interpretative models of our own culture, how, as Moshe Rosman has put it, can we legitimately define an academic field on the basis of 'a unitary, continuous, coherent Jewish People with a distinct culture and history?'[4] Who and what rightly belong in such a story? What do Jewish identity, Judaism, and 'Jewishness' entail? Jewish historians of the last decades have therefore begun to focus, for instance, on multiple and variegated 'cultures of the Jews', rather than more monolithic projects such as 'the Jews' history, culture, and religion'.[5] They have recognized the need to map Jewish identities in whatever manner such identities express themselves, rather than measure just how Jewish they are (or were).[6] They have grown increasingly self-conscious of the metanarratives—overarching, ideologically grounded plans or 'scripts'—that have typically framed our appreciation of the past, predicting the way things *should* develop and serving as a standard for evaluating *how* they have developed.[7] Jewish historians now shy away from the older *bipolar* appreciation of the Jewish past, whereby the Jewish people's survival has owed itself to the victory of its internal solidarity, faith, and creativity over hostile forces of change and assimilation that triggered processes of 'inexorable erosion' and self-destruction. Bipolarity has since yielded to diversity in our reading of Jewish cultural history; there remain no norms or rules to which we can rightly

[2] Clifford Geertz, *The Interpretation of Cultures: Selected Essays* (New York, 1973), 5.

[3] Patrick Brantlinger, 'A Response to *Beyond the Cultural Turn*', *American Historical Review*, 107 (2002), 1506.

[4] Moshe Rosman, *How Jewish Is Jewish History?* (Oxford, 2007), 1. Rosman's new book lurks in the background of other points raised in this introduction, but, in the absence of direct quotations, I have refrained from citing it repeatedly.

[5] Contrast David Biale (ed.), *Cultures of the Jews: A New History* (New York, 2002), with Louis Finkelstein (ed.), *The Jews: Their History, Culture, and Religion*, 2 vols. (New York, 1949).

[6] See Laurence J. Silberstein (ed.), *Mapping Jewish Identities* (New York, 2000).

[7] Among others, see the instructive observations in Joseph Dan, 'Chaos Theory, Leotard's History, and the Future of the Study of the History of Ideas', *Jewish Studies Quarterly*, 3 (1996), 193–211.

expect past (or present) experiences to conform. 'Every place, every time, every group, could manifest different results in different permutations. Order has been replaced by flux; one law of motion by a myriad of contexts, and by a multiplicity of responses.'[8] More and more, Judaic scholars now deplore 'essentialism'—what literature scholar Diana Fuss defines as 'a belief in the real, true essence of things, the invariable and fixed properties which define the "whatness" of a given entity'[9]—in discussing Judaism and Jewish identity. And yet one cannot help but wonder: in decrying essentialism, have we done away with whatever Jewish factor gives coherence (legitimacy) to the field that we study? Have we discarded the proverbial baby of *Jewish* civilization with the bathwater of ideological construction?

The postmodern turn has also led many to lament the privilege and status traditionally enjoyed by dominant, hegemonic, and colonizing cultures in our study of the past. And, in the history of Western culture, what exemplifies the dominant, the hegemonic, and the colonizing better than the European? Postmodernism has made it fashionable to avoid Eurocentrism in cultural studies. We now promote the study of the non-Western, the marginal, and the disenfranchised. And we applaud multiculturalism, a perspective that recognizes the importance of the cultural spaces shared by different, often rival, groups, not just the well-defined boundaries between them. Multiculturalism, in turn, leads us to appreciate the cultural minority as a *hybrid* component of the surrounding majority culture. Popularized by the Indian critic Homi Bhabha, this notion of hybridity suggests that the cultural identity of the subjugated, colonized minority does not erode when it clashes with the (attractive and/or oppressive) culture of the colonizing majority. Rather, minority cultures emerge afresh in the spaces where they encounter the dominant cultures in which they reside. This encounter is a highly fluid one, riddled with ambivalence, the blurring of boundaries, cooperation as well as resistance, and a creative responsiveness to the 'other' that has implications for both colonizer and colonized alike.[10]

Beyond their relevance for the academic discipline of history, such tendencies certainly shed light on the collective identity crisis confronting Europeans today, as the continent reconstitutes itself along demographic, political, sociological, and cultural lines. Since the fall of the Iron Curtain two decades ago, the grand divisions between East and West—along with the master-narratives that they nourished and that nourished them—have shrunk,

---

[8] Jonathan Frankel, 'Assimilation and the Jews in Nineteenth-Century Europe: Towards a New Historiography?', in Jonathan Frankel and Steven J. Zipperstein (eds.), *Assimilation and Community: The Jews in Nineteenth-Century Europe* (Cambridge, 1992), 4–5.

[9] Diana Fuss, *Essentially Speaking: Feminism, Nature and Difference* (New York, 1989), pp. xi–xii.

[10] Among others, see Homi K. Bhabha, *The Location of Culture* (London, 1994).

if not disappeared. Political boundaries have been redrawn: Germanies reunited, the Soviet Union disbanded, central European and Balkan states redivided and reconstituted. Europe now includes nearly a score of independent countries that did not appear on the map half a century ago. In some respects, political borders have assumed new significance, especially in so far as they realize the collective aspirations of previously disenfranchised national and ethnic groups. Yet in other respects, the European Union, which celebrates its fiftieth birthday as this book goes to press, has minimized the significance of many of these borders, and one can often cross them virtually unawares, without having to present a passport or change currency. Immigration to this new world of opportunity has swelled. Ethnic diasporas have proliferated throughout Europe, asserting their cultural distinctiveness and aspirations more than ever before. And a transnational perspective has gained prominence in historical and cultural studies, often eclipsing the traditional Western emphasis on distinct national entities, properly ensconced in their respective nation-states, where their separate national cultures grow and develop in keeping with their unique national characters.

How does all this bear upon European Jews and the study of their past? The new Europe presents its Jews with both challenge and opportunity. European Jewries must now find their niche—and express their identity—not only in relation to an ever more amorphous and nondescript European majority but also alongside many other increasingly outspoken ethnic and religious minorities. As we know from other periods in European Jewish history, having to find one's place amidst an array of other 'others' can prove no less problematic than salutary.[11] Moreover, while nineteenth- and twentieth-century Jews understood (rightly or otherwise) that the price of admission into the 'established' societies and cultures of Europe amounted to at least a partial repression of their Jewish identity, today's multiculturalism has rendered calls for conformity unfashionable, impractical, and politically incorrect. The basic convictions of those who struggled for Jewish enlightenment and emancipation—that acceptance into the polities, societies, and cultures of Europe would mark the fulfilment of Jewish history—no longer appear appropriate in a European society struggling with the legacy of the Holocaust, a society in which, on the one hand, traditional forms of Christianity have lost the allegiance of the majority, and, on the other, cultural and ethnic diversity has become the norm. The attractive European world that, in the nineteenth and twentieth centuries, induced Jews to redefine their social and religious identities so as to become modern but somehow remain Jewish has largely disappeared. Once again, the Jews of Europe must exert

[11] See, for example, Jeremy Cohen, *Living Letters of the Law: Ideas of the Jew in Medieval Christianity* (Berkeley, Calif., 1999), pt. 3.

themselves to determine precisely where they stand within the larger non-Jewish world around them. And renewed self-definition for the present and future, as we know, typically entails a rethinking of the past.

Yet Jews have frequently turned new worlds of opportunity to their advantage more than other minority groups, and, challenges notwithstanding, the new Europe could prove conducive to a revival of Jewish culture and communities. Diana Pinto has, in fact, proposed a 'Jewish paradigm' for the cultural renewal of contemporary Europe. Jews, she argues, can serve as a prototype of the new European: committed to their own ethnicity on the one hand and their full-fledged membership in a diverse civil society on the other, ever conscious of their place in a world-wide Jewish diaspora and the transnational cultural experience that it generates, and proud of their multiple loyalties (to a specific country, to Europe in general, to the Jewish people, and to Israel), Jews can contribute roundly to a 'place where cultural, political and historical contradictions are freely expressed . . . not a tranquil place . . . but a place where full acceptance of the "other" is possible'.[12]

Confronting this blend of challenge and opportunity, Jews of Europe must also look inward as they seek to define precisely what distinguishes them and binds them together as Jews, the perils of essentialism notwithstanding. As British anthropologist Jonathan Webber has noted, without some 'overriding concept of *kelal yisrael* and a long view of the spiritual requirements of Jewish survival, is there not a danger in seeing the diversity of the contemporary Jewish experience as being little more than of exotic, ethnological, or antiquarian curiosity?' The world-wide dispersion of Jews from the former communist bloc, and the former Soviet Union above all, only adds weight to the problem. For here is a Jewish population of millions largely lacking in any substantively *Jewish* way of life. And so Webber sharpens his point: 'All Jews are equal, it could be said; but some, in the final analysis, are perhaps more equal, more central than others.'[13]

Such collective soul-searching invariably leads European Jews to situate themselves and their Judaism on a map now dominated by two non-European centres of Jewish life and creativity: North America and Israel. If, in previous centuries, the heart of Jewish civilization lay in Europe, the destruction of European Jewry during the Holocaust, the establishment of the Jewish state, and the burgeoning of Jewish life in the United States and Canada have since moved European Judaism from the centre to the periphery. The primacy of these American and Israeli centres depends not only on demography and

---

[12] Diana Pinto, *A New Jewish Identity for Post-1989 Europe*, Institute for Jewish Policy Research/Policy Paper 1 (1996), esp. p. 5.

[13] Introduction to Jonathan Webber (ed.), *Jewish Identities in the New Europe* (London, 1994), 26.

socio-economic prosperity but also on metanarratives for understanding the Jewish past, on 'schools' of historical interpretation that find expression both on and off academic campuses. The Zionist metanarrative views the European Jewish experience primarily as one of displacement, alienation, and conflict with the non-Jewish majority; indeed, the persecution of Jews under the Nazi and communist regimes of the last century intensifies the foundational contrast between Jewish life in *galut* (exile) and in the *moledet* (the national homeland). An alternative, increasingly assertive American Jewish metanarrative might read Jewish history as progressing irreversibly from its origins as an ancient tribal kingdom to its climax in modern, Western democracies of the diaspora—especially the United States, where Jews have remained largely unscathed by antisemitic prejudice and persecution. Ironically, both of these metanarratives first crystallized in the ideas and writings of European Jewish intellectuals—among them Reform rabbis, proponents of Jewish nationalism, and some of those very scholars responsible for the birth of Jewish historical studies as an academic field. Will a revival of Jewish life and cultural institutions reinstate Europe as a centre on the map of world Jewry? Will the pan-European preoccupation with the Holocaust, the flowering of Jewish studies at European universities, and Europe's 'current turn towards democracy, pluralism, multi-culturalism, multiple-identities, and the legitimization of diasporas'[14] nourish a viable 'third way' of forging a Jewish civilization in today's (post)modern world? Historians, European and non-European alike, may not have the answers to these questions, but they surely have a stake in them.

The impact of the postmodern cultural turn on the historian's craft and mindset, the critical importance of the European past for any understanding of the modern Jewish experience, and the reawakening of Jewish culture in Europe today—these are but some of the issues that render a rethinking of European Jewish history a timely venture for students of history everywhere. The editors of and contributors to this volume are not European. They have all been trained and employed at universities in North America and Israel. We have no programme or agenda for the rehabilitation of a European civilization. But we do have a shared commitment to understanding the history of that civilization, and we share in an awareness of the symbiotic relationship between historical scholarship and contemporary culture.

*

Our collection divides into four parts, the first two dedicated to program-matic and methodological concerns, the latter two to scholarly conver-

---

[14] S. Ilan Troen, 'The Post-Holocaust Dynamics of Jewish Centers and Peripheries', in id., (ed.), *Jewish Centers and Peripheries: Europe between America and Israel Fifty Years after World War II* (New Brunswick, NJ, 1999), 21.

sations that exemplify processes of rethinking at work. Part I, 'Reorienting the Narrative', considers issues of perspective and terminology that bear directly on both recent and future developments in the study of European Jewish history. In 'Jewish History across Borders', Moshe Rosman advocates balancing accepted chronological, temporal rubrics for organizing the study of the Jewish past with spatial or geographical categories. Not only would a spatial perspective yield new insight into the subject at hand, it might also help avoid the drawbacks of the temporal approach. For temporal periodization was 'an attempt to capture in shorthand the "essential nature" of a historical era. Such essentializing implied a teleology for each period, a sense of inevitable movement in a certain direction towards a defined goal.' Projecting beyond studies defined by the political boundaries of European states, Rosman calls for a more flexible transnational approach, one that would define spatial context in a manner less artificial and more appropriate for the Jews under study. Why not recognize, for example, that German and east European Jews all 'acted as "citizens" of a Jewish "country" called Ashkenaz, with its own language, Yiddish, its own laws and customs, its collection of autonomous Jewish administrative and social institutions and its civic, kinship, business, educational, intellectual, and religious networks'? Likewise, might not 'Europe' today serve as a spatially defined context for new and productive study of the Jewish past?

Highlighting the pitfalls of yet another instance of essentializing, David Engel explores the hazards of imprecise—and irresponsible—terminology in 'Away from a Definition of Antisemitism: An Essay in the Semantics of Historical Description'. Engel uses medieval historian Gavin Langmuir's oft-discussed *Toward a Definition of Antisemitism* and *History, Religion, and Antisemitism* as a reference point in this illuminating case study of the reification of an influential historical descriptor, one that he sees as ultimately counterproductive. 'Throughout the centuries many people have behaved violently towards Jews. Many have depicted them verbally or artistically in derogatory fashion, agitated publicly for their subjection to legal discrimination, discriminated against them socially, or privately felt varying degrees of prejudice towards or emotional revulsion from them. However, no necessary relation among particular instances of violence, hostile depiction, agitation, discrimination, and private unfriendly feeling across time and space can be assumed. Indeed, none has ever been demonstrated.' Their protestations of rational empiricism notwithstanding, Engel argues that self-declared historians of antisemitism have assumed such a relation on the basis of socio-semantic convention, one created in the nineteenth century and sustained since then for reasons more ideological than scholarly.

Alongside antisemitism, the popular notion of Jewish assimilation appears also to have lost its clarity—and perhaps its utility—in the eyes of various contemporary scholars. As Maud Mandel demonstrates in 'Assimilation and Cultural Exchange in Modern Jewish History', the term assimilation certainly requires more nuanced appreciation than it has often received, either among those who have condemned the secularizing acculturation and integration of Jews into Western societies or among others who have highlighted the distinctly Jewish cultural creativity that modern Jewish civilization has fostered. Have cultural assimilation—and the political emancipation that it sought to facilitate—proved good or bad for the Jews? To what extent ought one to deem them destructive or constructive processes in recent Jewish experience? Mandel offers no simplistic answers to these questions but, with particular attention to research on the Jews of modern France, she considers how profoundly the 'reconceptualization of assimilation' has penetrated present-day scholarly discourse. Above all, she invokes the work of Yuri Slezkine (*The Jewish Century*), Andrew Heinze (*Jews and the American Soul*), and others to advocate subsuming assimilation within a model of cultural exchange, a model that highlights the contributions of modern Jews to the very aspects of European cultures that transformed them, 'an interpretative move that situates Jewish historical actors as central rather than peripheral to mainstream cultural change'.

Among its most welcome and significant contributions to our understanding of the past, postmodern criticism has attributed vital importance to women as a historical subject and to gender as a category of critical analysis. Paula Hyman's essay, 'Does Gender Matter? Locating Women in European Jewish History', offers a valuable assessment both of inroads already made by women's history and gender analysis into Jewish historical research and of pressing needs for further investigation. Hyman invokes distinctions drawn several decades ago by Gerda Lerner, 'the doyenne of women's history', to categorize both achievements and desiderata in the field: 'compensatory history' that now focuses on women previously ignored; gender-based adjustment and refinement in interpretation in areas ranging from the Conversos to the shtetl and from the Holocaust to the family; and areas where women's and gender-sensitive history actually have the power to transform, to reshape the fundamental assumptions of European Jewish history, from the substance of Jewish theology and ritual to the processes of assimilation and identity-construction among modern European Jews. As Hyman laments, scholars of Judaica have lagged behind colleagues in other fields in attacking such questions, and she challenges Jewish historians, herself included, to rise to the challenge. Simply put, 'if we seek gender-sensitive scholarship on Jews that puts Jews at the centre . . . then scholars of Jewish history have to assume responsibility for writing it'.

Part II of the collection, 'From the Middle Ages to Modernity', presents three fresh perspectives on how historians can fruitfully confront a monumental transition that everyone agrees occurred, but that few can define or pinpoint to the satisfaction of others. Where, how, at what rate, and with what results did the change take place? In 'Jewish Culture in Early Modern Europe: An Agenda for Future Study', David Ruderman hails the innovative call of Jonathan Israel to recognize an 'early modern age' in sixteenth- and seventeenth-century European Jewish history, distinct from the Middle Ages that preceded it and the modern period that followed. Ruderman provides a useful survey of the recent flurry of historical research into this transitional period, and, offering his own rethinking of Israel's thesis, identifies five markers of a newly emerging transnational European Jewish cultural experience: unprecedented social mobility, mixing, and migration; a surge in the development of powerful Jewish communal structures coupled with the growing laicization of communal authority; an explosion of knowledge, facilitated above all by the onset of printing; a crisis of religious authority, accompanied by the related threats of heresy and enthusiasm, and epitomized in the contemporaneous phenomena of Spinozism and Shabateanism; a mingling of social and religious identities, in which Conversos and their descendants, Jewish converts to Christianity, Christian Hebraists, and 'Shabatean syncretists intent on forging a Jewish–Christian identity' all helped to blur previously sharper boundary lines between Jews and their Christian neighbours.

Complementing Ruderman's take on this early modern phase in European Jewish history, Miriam Bodian calls for a systematic rethinking of the Protestant Reformation and the Jews. She surveys the pioneering articles and chapters devoted by earlier historians (Jacob Katz, Salo Baron, Haim Hillel Ben-Sasson) to the subject, explains the significance of the issues at stake, and justly bemoans the absence of any book-length investigation. From confessionalism to lay piety and superstition to cross-confessional discourse in which orthodox and heterodox Jews participated alongside Christians of varying persuasions—in Italy, in Spain, and even in northern and eastern Europe—Jews contributed more to the fervent religious discourse of the age than has been appreciated. Stressing the Reformation's contribution to 'the emergence of modern Western social and political structures', this essay is also a programmatic one, mapping out the central features of the comprehensive investigation that Bodian persuasively advocates.

Part II concludes with 'Re(de)fining Modernity in Jewish History', in which Gershon Hundert parts company with other historians by refusing to locate the defining characteristics of the modern Jewish experience in the culture of western and central Europe. Hundert insists that, if 80 per cent of world Jewry lived in Poland and Lithuania during the eighteenth and early nineteenth centuries, we must de-Westernize and 'de-teleologize' the

modern period in Jewish history, ridding ourselves of the view that modernity for the Jew necessarily entails movement (or return) from East to West.
Rather, he defines the modern era simply as that spanning the last several
hundred years. Braving the critiques of the anti-essentialists, he understands
the vitality of contemporary Jewishness as embodied in the '"magmatic"
level of Jewish experience which is somehow beneath or beyond cultural,
religious, and political change'. Moreover, the source of this inner core
of Jewish identity, 'a continuing positive self-evaluation as Jews', derives
from eastern, not western, European Jewry; indeed, he deems it 'the most
important ingredient in modern Jewish history'.

The remainder of the volume spotlights two scholarly conversations, case
studies for application of the critical and programmatic categories considered
thus far. Together they frame the chronological period that has concerned us,
from the end of the Middle Ages to the present, and we hope they will prove
suggestive as readers reflect on their own particular areas of research. Part
III, 'On the Eve of the Spanish Expulsion', considers the complex web of
relationships between Jews, Christians, and Jewish converts to Christianity
(Conversos, New Christians, 'Marranos') during the generations following
the massacres and mass conversions of Iberian Jews in 1391. In 'Spanish
"Judaism" and "Christianity" in an Age of Mass Conversion', David
Nirenberg proposes to enrich a 'genealogical' approach to determining
religious identity in fifteenth-century Spain with a 'dialogical' perspective,
rooted in the re-evaluation of self and other that inevitably accompanied the
traumatic events of the period. Thousands of Conversos now living alongside
and between Jews and Christians obfuscated the traditional boundaries
between their communities. And even before the anti-Converso backlash in
the middle of the century, Christian theologians, poets, and politicians joined
in 'hypermarking' Jews and Judaism as a means of clarifying *for themselves*
what it meant to be Christian. 'Precisely because the space between
Christianity and Judaism had for so long been important to many areas of
Christian culture that had little to do with living Jews, the energy released by
the bridging of that space [by the new converts] proved productive' in ways
that transcended the interaction between majority and minority. Almost
despite themselves, Jews and Christians reconstructed themselves and each
other during the century preceding the expulsion, and their new constructions ultimately reshaped the realities of their relationship and environment.
'Christianity and Judaism were in some sense reborn out of one another in
Spain between 1391 and 1492, but both spent the century trying to repress
the pangs of birth.'

In 'The Social Context of Apostasy in Fifteenth-Century Spanish Jewry:
Dynamics of a New Religious Borderland', Ram Ben-Shalom approaches
the same triangular matrix of relations from a different perspective. If

Nirenberg explored the ramifications of Jewish alterity in Spanish poetics and politics of the fifteenth century, Ben-Shalom seeks to ground individual expressions of the new rhetoric (whether in poetry, religious polemic, or political propaganda) in concrete details of the social context that spawned it. Jews no less than Christians—along with the Conversos themselves—engaged in the construction and reconstruction of their respective identities in response to the mass conversions. Citing many of the same sources analysed by Nirenberg, Ben-Shalom insists that neither the Christian nor the Jewish idea of the Jew was 'a general and vague one; it could not represent a negative value in and of its own right. That is, in fifteenth-century Castile it was an entirely contemporary concept, representative of real Jews and Conversos', and firmly rooted in the realities of social interaction among them. Separating the two scholars, perhaps, is a traditional divide between intellectual and social historian, the emphases and interests that each manifests in confronting identical sources—from their linkage to age-old ideas and thought patterns to the details of their own particular socio-cultural context. No less important here, however, is a common denominator in their approaches: recognition of the elusiveness and mutability of ethnic and religious identity, and appreciation of the role of the other in formulating the essential characteristics of the self.

Returning to the contemporary context, Part IV, 'From Europe to America and Back', balances the prevalent westward-moving narrative of modern Jewish history with a look back in the opposite direction. In 'Transnationalism and Mutual Influence', Daniel Soyer explores the interdependence of American and east European Jewish communities during the inter-war years of the twentieth century. Social historians and historians of immigration have for too long allowed the Americanization of the east European Jewish immigrant to the United States to overshadow diverse and continued forms of involvement with her or his previous homeland—in its politics, in international business ventures, in philanthropic support, in travel, and in communication with those who remained behind. Such interaction, in turn, worked its impact on the culture and self-consciousness of immigrant communities in the New World. Soyer accordingly calls for a transnational perspective, which 'focuses on the ways in which migrants negotiate complex interactions across borders and develop an identity that transcends those of both host and home society'. Perhaps the very categories of emigrant and immigrant need to be replaced, or at least counterbalanced, by that of transnational migrants, who 'participate in two societies in two places at once, even if they spend most or all of their time in only one of them'. Not only must this perspective offset an undue emphasis on Americanization in an understanding of the (im)migrant, but it also demands the incorporation of American influence into the narrative of twentieth-century European Jewish history.

Finally, in 'Transplanting the Heart Back East: Returning Jewish Musical Culture from the United States to Europe', Judah Cohen ponders the cultural significance of performances of American Jewish music and musical artists—ranging from the liturgical to the secular, all of them expressive of a European Jewish heritage—in contemporary European Jewish communities. Such performances could nourish the ongoing 'liberal Jewish renaissance' in Germany, as in the appearances of the Reform cantor Rebecca Garfein in Berlin in the late 1990s. They could awaken enthusiasm among Jewish youth and resentment among their non-Jewish neighbours, as did the 'Klezmaniacs' in Poland and Ukraine in 2000. And they could blend various genres and symbolic backgrounds (from the seventeenth-century Salamone Rossi, to the choral settings of Viktor Ullmann in Theresienstadt, to the distinctly American compositions of George Gershwin) into a present-day Jewish medium, as in the 1999 European tour of Boston's Zamir Chorale. As Cohen demonstrates, in every case the performers were both ambassadors and pilgrims, importers of American Jewish culture who recognized in no small measure that they were returning home to their roots. Thus 'did late twentieth-century American Jewry use sound to build bridges across the Atlantic, from West to East', bridges that facilitated a transnational Jewish exchange in both directions, bridges that continue to nourish the revival of European Jewry today.

*

As it focuses on select historical moments and movements from the fifteenth century to the present, we offer *Rethinking European Jewish History* in part as a retrospective on past developments in the field, in part as a programmatic guide for future research, in part as a bibliographical resource. While no particular ideological or interpretative stance unites the contributors or their contributions to this volume, they do share in their readiness to challenge regnant opinions and experiment with new approaches in their stead. From grappling with the temptations of essentialism in definitions of Jewish identity, to redrawing the traditional boundaries—spatial, temporal, and otherwise—in the study of European Jewry, to questioning the value of categories as commonplace as antisemitism, the essays collected here address the paramount importance of questions academic investigators have long asked and those they should now ask, and of the critical assumptions underlying them. Such questions, in the present context, reach far beyond a disinterested reconstruction of the past. As we approach the end of the first decade in a new millennium, we realize that they extend to the ultimate concerns of modern Jews and the historians who study them.

PART I

REORIENTING THE NARRATIVE

ONE

Jewish History across Borders

MOSHE ROSMAN

PERIODIZATION has been a standard subject for Jewish historians at least since the birth of modern Jewish historiography in the nineteenth century. All of those who set out to write about the Jewish past, explicitly or implicitly defined historical periods. In parallel to European history, in general, these were three: ancient, medieval, and modern, a tripartite division that was canonized in textbooks and curriculum plans at all levels of education. However, despite general agreement on the number and names of periods, there was no consensus regarding the dates of each one. Did the ancient period begin with the Davidic Kingdom, the split between Judea and Israel, the Babylonian Exile or the Return to Zion? Did medieval Jewish history begin with the reign of Emperor Theodosius and the rise of Byzantium, the Arab conquest of Erets Yisra'el, or the end of the gaonate and the establishment of Ashkenazi communities *circa* 1000 CE? Is the modern period in Jewish history to be dated from the dislocations of the mid-seventeenth century, the rise of absolutism, the Berlin Haskalah in the late eighteenth century or the emancipation of French Jewry in the wake of the Revolution? Does the modern period continue in our own time or did the modern period end in the late 1940s with the Holocaust and the establishment of the state of Israel?

The lack of consensus concerning the dating of periods follows from the fact that periodization is a coarse form of historical interpretation. The various proposed starting and concluding dates for the periods reflected differing interpretations of what typified each one. The outstanding feature of a modern period begun in 1700 with the migration of a group of some three hundred Jews to Palestine (that betokened—according to some—the first modern 'mass *aliyah*') was Jewish nationalism. The main theme of a medieval period that came to its climax in 1492, with the Spanish Expulsion, was persecution. An ancient period beginning with the return of the Jewish exiles from Babylonia was 'about' the dynamics of Jewish diaspora and the interaction of the Jewish community in Erets Yisra'el with communities elsewhere. In picking a certain date or event as indicative of the beginning or end of a historical period, scholars tried to identify what to their minds was the most significant feature, theme, or process of that period. Periodization was an attempt to capture in shorthand the 'essential nature' of a historical era. Such essentializing implied a teleology to each period, a sense of inevitable movement in a certain direction towards a defined goal.[1]

In the 1960s teleology fell out of favour in Jewish historiography (as it had in other historiographies) because it required fitting the facts into a procrustean bed. Champions of a particular teleology felt obligated to subsume nearly 'everything' that happened in a given period to that period's purported overall direction or momentum—a task necessarily entailing nipping and tucking various developments. Somewhat later, essentializing came to be regarded as simplistic at best and ideologically coloured presentism at worst. Consequently, periodization was relegated to a more minor role and scholars endeavoured to keep it as technical and non-interpretative as possible: delineating conventional breakpoints simply because one has to start *somewhere* when teaching or writing.[2]

More recently, renewed attention has been paid to the question of the periodization of Jewish history. As long ago as 1985 Jonathan Israel proposed adding a fourth period, the early modern, making the traditional division quadripartite.[3] In 2005 I suggested that there is now a fifth period, the postmodern one, beginning around 1950.[4] That same year the prestigious Stern Lectures sponsored by the Israel Historical Society, delivered by Professor Yosef Hayim Yerushalmi, were devoted to periodization, and the Shazar Center for Jewish History published a collection edited by Yosef Kaplan whose Hebrew title translates as 'Fins de siècle—Ends of Ages'.[5] In 2006 a major international conference entitled 'Reconsidering the Borderlines between Early Modern and Modern Jewish History' was held at the Simon Dubnow Institute of Leipzig University. Given periodization's role as emblematic interpretation, this flurry of newfound interest is probably a signal that major reinterpretation of the Jewish historical experience is in gestation.

Curiously, to my mind, while the temporal aspect of Jewish history has gained considerable attention and detailed analysis, the spatial dimension has barely been examined. The geography of Jewish history has been an unacknowledged assumption underlying Jewish historical narratives, rarely raised as an analytical issue in its own right.[6] Here I propose to begin a

---

[1] See M. Rosman, 'Defining the Postmodern Period in Jewish History', ch. 2 in id., *How Jewish Is Jewish History?* (Oxford, 2007); this essay is a revised version of one originally published in E. Lederhendler and J. Wertheimer (eds.), *Text and Context: Essays in Modern Jewish History and Historiography in Honor of Ismar Schorsch* (New York, 2005).   [2] Ibid.
[3] Jonathan I. Israel, *European Jewry in the Age of Mercantilism, 1550–1750* (Oxford, 1985; 2nd edn. 1989; 3rd edn. 1998).   [4] See Rosman, 'Defining the Postmodern Period'.
[5] Kaplan, *Shilhei me'ot: kitzam shel idanim* (Jerusalem, 2005).
[6] For treatments of the question of Jewish geography see Harold Brodsky (ed.), *Land and Community: Geography in Jewish Studies* (College Park, Md., 1998); *Shofar*, 17/1 (1998): a collection of articles devoted to examining issues of Jewish geography. See also n. 7 below.

process of re-evaluation of two of the leading—albeit tacit—geographical axioms of Jewish historiography (the transgeographical one and the geo-political one) and to posit that historical reinterpretation can be approached in spatial terms no less than temporal ones. It is not only periodization that requires reconsideration; Jewish historical geography also might profitably be reconstrued.

The authors of the great multi-volume surveys of Jewish history that began to be published in the nineteenth century (as well as many of the pre-modern chronicles and other historical works) conceived of their subject as transgeographical, that is, transcending the details of geographical diversity.[7] They set as their task the integrated study of the lives of Jews everywhere in the 'Jewish world'. This transgeographical 'territory', inhab-ited by the Jews, included the entire world—or at least those parts of it that 'mattered'.[8] These historians assumed that there was an immanent connection between all Jews no matter where they lived. The links between Jews overrode much of the difference that resulted from being located in disparate geographical locations.

In Heinrich Zvi Graetz's *History of the Jews*[9] the geography of the Jews is almost incidental. There are some chapters that hew to a geographical framework, exploring the history of the Jews in certain regions or countries, such as the Arabian peninsula, Turkey, Holland, Spain, Poland, and England in specific, limited periods. For the most part, however, the book is

---

[7] These historians' 'transgeographic' notion contrasts with both the 'ageographic' concept of some Zionist ideologues and the idea of a Jewish 'normal geographicity' (albeit based on culture) paralleling that of any 'normal nation' espoused by certain non-Zionist nationalists; see Neil G. Jacobs, 'Introduction: A Field of Jewish Geography', *Shofar*, 17/1 (1998), 1–18; Max Weinreich, 'Ashkenazi Jewry within the General Jewish Framework from the Tenth to the Thirteenth Centuries' (Yiddish), *Di goldene keyt*, 50 (1964), 172–82; cf. Adam Teller, 'Hasidism and the Challenge of Geography: The Polish Background to the Spread of the Hasidic Movement', *AJS Review*, 30 (2006), 1–29: 4.

[8] The difference between the whole world and the parts inhabited by Jews was considerable. According to the classification of Gordon W. Hewes, the early modern world was composed of seventy-six distinct cultural spaces. Ranking these by population density, technological development, and degree of urbanization, he called the thirteen most developed areas 'civilizations'. The large majority of Jews were to be found in six of those civilizations: Ethiopia (cultural space no. 65), Islamic territories (no. 66), south-western Europe (no. 67), the eastern Mediterranean (no. 68), eastern Europe (no. 69), and north-western Europe (no. 70). While such ranking expresses cultural bias, this classification does imply that, with the exception of Ethiopia and the eventual addition of the Americas, the Jews were concentrated in the areas that also happened to be the primary stages of 'Western' history. See Gordon W. Hewes, 'A Conspectus of the World's Cultures in 1500 A.D.', *University of Colorado Studies*, 4 (1954), 1–22, and cf. Fernand Braudel, *The Structures of Everyday Life: The Limits of the Possible* (New York, 1981), 56–64.

[9] I quote here from the American edition (Philadelphia, 1891–8), which is abridged but contains additional material not found in the original German, *Geschichte der Juden von den ältesten Zeiten bis auf die Gegenwart* (Leipzig, 1870–1908).

organized so as to tell how Jews originated, cultivated, and articulated a great culture that did more than its share in 'rais[ing] humanity from the slough of barbarity and savagery', as well as how 'they struggled much, and suffered severely . . . during more than three thousand years receiv[ing] many shocks and injuries'.[10] Accordingly, most chapters are not organized by geography, but by trends, events, personalities, movements, or episodes. They typically fit one of three patterns. Many speak of some intellectual or spiritual giant or movement and its transgeographical effect over the Jewish world and beyond: 'Survey of the Epoch of Maimuni (Maimonides)', 'The Age of Solomon ben Adret and Asheri', 'Cultivation of the Kabbala, and Proscription of Science', 'The Mendelssohn Epoch'. Others scan the struggles and sufferings of the Jews the world over in a given period: 'Results of the Expulsion of the Jews from Spain and Portugal: General View', 'Strivings of Eastern Jews for Unity; Suffering in the West', 'General Demoralization of Judaism', 'Light and Shade'. Each chapter falling into one of these categories represents a geographical potpourri, including in its survey Jews located in numerous countries. The third type of chapter focuses on a specific incident or personality of great cultural import, or a particular episode of serious persecution: 'The Black Death', 'The Inquisition in Spain', 'Reuchlin and the Talmud', 'Spinoza and Sabbatai Zevi'. Each of these was a milestone on the great march of Jewish history; its geographical context was of little consequence.

For Graetz, geography was a backdrop, not a cause. It lent atmosphere; it did not determine destiny. While the details surely differed from place to place, the essential fate of the Jews—to create and to suffer—was the same everywhere. The history of this creativity (*Literaturgeschichte*) and suffering (*Leidensgeschichte*) transcended geographical divisions. It was these categories and their subcategories, rather than geography, that provided the organizing categories of Graetz's work.[11]

Graetz's perspective on Jewish history as unfolding on a world-wide stage was also adopted, and made even more explicit, by Simon Dubnow, who actually titled his classic multi-volume history 'The *World* History of the Jewish People'.[12] In practice, Dubnow did tend to survey his subject country by country or region by region. However, he considered the Jews to be one, integral, whole nation spread out over a large area, each part of which happened to fall under the political jurisdiction of some other nation. Dubnow attempted to emphasize the transgeographical unity of the Jews no matter what their physical location, in two ways.

---

[10] Graetz, *History of the Jews*, v. 705–6.

[11] See Michael Meyer, *Ideas of Jewish History* (Detroit, 1987), 229–30.

[12] In German, *Weltgeschichte des jüdischen Volkes* (Berlin, 1925–9), published in English as *History of the Jews* (New York, 1967).

First, he believed that the periodization of Jewish history must be 'in accordance with the shifting hegemony of the various centers of Judaism. . . . At every epoch the scattered people had a major center of some sort, and at times even two such centers, which . . . acquired hegemony over other parts of the Diaspora.'[13] In other words, in every period the Jewish world revolved around one or two hegemonic centres that determined 'changes in the destiny of [the] nation as a whole and not merely in this or that area of its life and development'.[14] By making his story one of shifting centres that, at least culturally, governed (each in turn) a diffuse periphery, Dubnow, like Graetz before him, largely neutralized geography as a divisive factor in Jewish history. The location of the hegemonic centre was significant for understanding the 'destiny of the nation as a whole'; the precise locations of the parts of this whole were incidental. Local influences were of secondary import—or less.

A second expedient Dubnow used to de-emphasize the significance of Jewish geographical diversity was to define some sub-periods according to an event or process that he considered to overshadow everything else: 'The Age of the Crusades', 'The Epoch of the Second Emancipation'. For the post-1789 period, he included a special introduction that supplied the thematic paste that would hold together the separate stories about individual communities told in the final three volumes. This introduction explained how emancipation, reaction, assimilation, and nationalism were the grand processes that were destined to transform modern Jews whatever their geographical position.[15]

Salo W. Baron also discounted the geographical fragmentation of the Jews and affirmed their world-wide unity based on things they shared in common other than territory.[16] Numerous passages in his work functioned to minimize the importance of local factors such as geography. A sampling:

As the Jewish religion developed away from any particular locality, the Jewish people . . . also detached itself more and more from the soil. Common descent, common destiny and culture—including religion—became the uniting forces.[17]

The Jewish community and its religious, social and legal institutions . . . were pliable enough to allow for infinite *local variations in detail, while maintaining unbroken continuity and unity in fundamentals*. (emphasis added)[18]

Such kaleidoscopic variety of legislation, state-wide, provincial or local, as was reflected in our geographic-chronological review of the last two volumes seems to

[13] Dubnow, *History of the Jews*, 34. [14] Ibid. 33.

[15] See Jonathan Frankel, 'Assimilation and the Jews in Nineteenth-Century Europe: Towards a New Historiography?', in J. Frankel and Steven J. Zipperstein (eds.), *Assimilation and Community: The Jews in Nineteenth-Century Europe* (Cambridge, 1992), 1–37.

[16] Salo W. Baron, *A Social and Religious History of the Jews*, 18 vols. (New York, 1952–83); cf. Rosman, *How Jewish Is Jewish History?*, ch. 1, 'Some a priori Issues in Jewish Historiography'.

[17] Baron, *Social and Religious History of the Jews*, i. 17. [18] Ibid. v. 54.

defy generalization. . . . Yet . . . the *basic similarity of institutions governing Jewish life throughout medieval Europe* becomes manifest to any observer. (emphasis added)[19]

In short, sophisticated analysis makes the apparent variety of geographical diversity yield to underlying identities.

Baron's presentation oscillated between thorough country-by-country descriptions of the various Jewish communities throughout the world and thematic chapters and even volumes (volume v: *Religious Controls and Dissensions*; volume vi: *Laws, Homilies and the Bible*; volume xi: *Citizen or Alien Conjuror*; volume xii: *Economic Catalyst*) that attempted to portray the essential similarity both of Jewish communal life and of the political-legal policies and cultural-social practices relating to the Jews wherever they lived. Both the internal dynamics of and external pressures on the Jews were basically the same everywhere. Baron highlighted situations, conditions, concepts, status, and themes that cut across geography.[20]

No one has dared to undertake a single-author multi-volume history of the Jews since Baron. While he was still in the process of writing his magnum opus there appeared a three-volume collective work edited by Hayim Hillel Ben-Sasson. Like its predecessors, this general history of the Jews sought to subordinate Jewish geographical diversity to Jewish cultural unity. Written by scholars who were, like Ben-Sasson, from the Hebrew University in Jerusalem, these volumes grew out of Israeli culture and they are often referred to as the voice of 'the Jerusalem school' of Jewish historiography.

The first volume, with four authors covering the period from the biblical Patriarchs until the Muslim conquest of Erets Yisra'el (640 CE), some twenty-five centuries, was entitled *The Ancient Times*. It conceived the Jewish geographical pattern throughout that period to be that of centre and periphery, with Erets Yisra'el as the main focus and the diaspora in a supporting role. The second volume, *The Middle Ages*, written by Ben-Sasson himself, attempted to have each chapter define how a central process, development, or phenomenon affected Jews or characterized them wherever they lived: 'Effects of Religious Animosity on the Jews'; 'The Flowering of a Centralized Leadership and the Rise of Local Leadership'; 'Changes in the Legal Status and the Security of the Jews'; 'Jewish Autonomy from the Black Death to the Reformation'.[21] Ben-Sasson's conception of Jewish geography

[19] Baron, *Social and Religious History of the Jews*, xi. 3.

[20] Cf. Salo W. Baron, *The Jewish Community: Its History and Structure to the American Revolution* (Philadelphia, 1942), where vol. i gives a chronological-geographical survey of the development of the various Jewish communities, while vol. ii analyses institutions common to Jewish communities throughout history and all over the map of Jewish settlement. Vol. iii is bibliographical.

[21] Titles are taken from the English edition (London, 1976); the Hebrew original was published in Tel Aviv in 1969.

as composed of individual cells (communities) linked in a transgeographical network is neatly implied in a chapter title in another one of his books: 'Poland–Lithuania: A *Province* of Jewish Autonomy' (emphasis added).[22] Wherever Jews lived they constituted a province of the world-wide Jewish 'territory'.

Shmuel Ettinger's final volume, *Modern Times*, flaunting a Eurocentric bias, chose two overarching themes: (*a*) Jewish integration and acculturation into non-Jewish society; and (*b*) the Jewish struggle against destruction through the development of Jewish nationalism. Ettinger tried to show how the opposing trends of Jewish integration into the 'host society and culture' and Jewish national resistance to social absorption and cultural effacement played out in each region or country where Jews lived. No less than Graetz, Ettinger insisted that Jews everywhere were subject to a common destiny and endured a fundamentally similar historical experience.

The idea that Jewish history is transgeographical has been roundly criticized; most famously in a review of the Ben-Sasson book by Jacob Neusner. Neusner thought it preposterous to attempt to 'draw together into one cultural, economic and social continuum all the doings of Jews everywhere at any one time'. Treating Jews in various countries and regions together as part of one integral whole and as one unitary subject, Neusner asserted, led to narrative chaos, with the 'The Economic and Social Crisis in Christian Spain' juxtaposed to 'Jewish Settlement in Eastern Europe and the Barrier of Muscovite Russia'.[23] For Neusner there was no world-wide context for Jewish history, only separate local contexts. Elsewhere I have argued that this approach anticipated a new Jewish metahistory, a multicultural one, which views the non-Jewish context of a Jewish community's life as generally more significant than its links to other Jewish communities or to some common Jewish past. Such a metahistory threatens to dissolve the entire subject of 'Jewish history'.[24]

Even before the development of the multicultural conception of Jewish history, however, many of the Jewish historians who came to maturity in the 1970s and 1980s eschewed the effort to write a world-wide or even regional

---

[22] Hayim Ben-Sasson, *Trial and Achievement: Currents in Jewish History* (Jerusalem, 1974).

[23] Jacob Neusner, review of Hayim Ben-Sasson (ed.), *History of the Jewish People*, *American Historical Review*, 82 (1977), 1030–1.

[24] For a critique of Neusner's view and its implications for the viability of the subject of Jewish history, see Rosman, *How Jewish Is Jewish History?*, chs. 1 and 3. Such a metahistory underlies many of the chapters in the latest attempt at a general history of the Jews, another collective work, David Biale (ed.), *Cultures of the Jews: A New History* (New York, 2002), which has appeared in both one- and three-volume editions. As the plural in its title implies, this book reversed the bias towards world-wide Jewish unity and similarity of historical fate, emphasizing how embedded Jews were in the context of whatever culture and society they happened to be located in. However, in this work, too, geography, while providing a central framework for organizing the book, is left largely unexplored as a factor in history.

history of the Jews and hewed closely to the national model of history-writing exemplified by modern European historiography. Convinced that Jewish historiography suffered from a dearth of consciousness and knowledge of the context within which Jewish life was lived, they were determined to be fully conversant with the history of the particular geopolitical entity (England, Spain, Poland, the Habsburg empire, etc.) where the Jewish community they were researching resided. Their books contextualized Jewish history in every place. As qualified historians of these countries in addition to their credentials in Jewish history, they exploited both Jewish and non-Jewish sources, juxtaposing and comparing them and using them to illuminate each other. This range of sources and propensity for contextualization has lent their work much authority.[25]

The result has been a bounteous harvest of well-researched, rather dense monographs that probe Jewish life in a particular place.[26] These have been characterized by in-depth description of the society, economy, culture, and politics of the country in question in the period under study followed by a portrayal of the Jewish community there and then, with the bulk of each exposition being a careful analysis of how the Jewish community developed in the context of the larger society and interacted with it.

This wave of narrowly focused monographs has certainly been a boon to Jewish historiography, supplying a wealth of information as well as many fruitful and challenging interpretations. However, one of its most profound modifications of the Jewish historical master-narrative was unconscious. The older, multi-volume general histories had downplayed geographical differences between Jewish communities and promoted a transgeographical view of Jewish history. These new monographs were based on the unspoken, unexamined presumption that the fundamental organizing principle of Jewish history should be political geography. The older histories discounted political geography; the newer ones privileged it.

Without reflection, the large majority of these monographs took as their point of departure that the most significant context for writing Jewish history was the geopolitical one. It was the political country that offered the best means for identifying distinctive, separate Jewish communities: Yemenite, French, Polish, Egyptian, etc.[27]

[25] It also belies the canard, still current in some quarters, as to the 'insularity' or 'parochialness' of Jewish historians. Being double specialists, most active Jewish historians are in control of a wide range of both primary and secondary materials reaching beyond Jewish history per se. They also typically take a broad perspective.

[26] These works are too numerous to detail here. A 'Jewish History' subject search in any major catalogue will produce a long list.

[27] Sometimes this political-geographical definition was even anachronistic. For example, politically speaking there was no 'Germany' and no 'Italy' before the second half of the 19th century. The geography of 'German Jewish' history or 'Italian Jewish' history is therefore

Granted the impressiveness of the monograph corpus, the question still needs to be asked. Virtually no one today would challenge the importance of contextualizing Jewish history. However, is the context demarcated by the political-geographical borders that a particular community happened to reside within the only relevant, or even always the most appropriate, one?

Defining a Jewish community according to the political power that rules it admittedly has attractions. It bears the apparently obvious logic of a simple correspondence: the Jews who live in a place are properly part of the history of that place. It supplies a strong link between Jewish history and history, easily making the Jews part of the larger human story.[28] It negates age-old prejudice positing the 'Jew as alien' or 'Jew as the enemy of civilization', asserting that Jews were in fact *of* their countries and not just *in* them. Jews are—on the whole—productive, contributing, progressive members of the societies and states they live in.

For post-Zionist Jews seeking to dissociate themselves from what they regard as the embarrassment, mistake, or tragedy that is Israel, allowing political geography to determine the framework of the Jewish historical metanarrative has the virtue of relieving them of responsibility for or loyalty to Israel. A Jewish state may make sense in the context of a transgeographical and supranational definition of the Jewish people. On the basis of a Jewish people linked perhaps by religion, but separated by political loyalties, cultural affinities, social institutions and—most important—differential historical experiences, it might seem problematic.

Not least, a political-geographical framework has research advantages. It usually keeps the number of major non-Jewish research languages (and travel visas!) required to a manageable minimum and presents a circumscribed set of archives that need to be visited.

These attractions can, however, blind a researcher to connections that may compose other contexts that might be more important and prompt a different overall view of the relations between Jews, non-Jews, and other Jews. For example, readers of prominent early modern chroniclers and auto-biographers—Yosel of Rosheim, Asher Halevi, the anonymous seventeenth-century Bohemian Jewish autobiographer, Glikl bas Judah of Hameln, Jacob Emden, Ber of Bolechow, and Solomon Maimon—can easily see how unimportant political borders were in the economic, cultural, and social life of these protagonists. Whether visiting family, making marital matches, doing business, lobbying government officials, or seeking educational

difficult to define. 'Holy Roman Empire Jewry' or 'Habsburg Jewry' have the advantage of not being politically anachronistic, but the disadvantage of not necessarily including all of the communities that were part of the same cultural, social, economic, and religious sphere, even if they were politically separate; while perhaps implying some non-existent links between some communities.   [28] See Rosman, *How Jewish Is Jewish History?*, ch. 1.

opportunities, these people, and the others portrayed in their accounts, seemed to cross borders virtually at will. In their telling, they could easily travel between Holland, Denmark, the various Germanic states, Hungary, and Poland without the feeling of alienness that travellers to 'foreign' countries often feel.[29] They barely noted the political and legal regime they happened to be under (except when it brought the force of the law to bear against them). They were constantly moving between states, but usually did not seem to be leaving their 'country'.

They acted as 'citizens' of a Jewish 'country', called Ashkenaz, with its own language, Yiddish, its own laws and customs, its collection of autonomous Jewish administrative and social institutions, and its civic, kinship, business, educational, intellectual, and religious networks. It was an integrated 'civil society' that shared norms, lifestyle, and tacit assumptions as to how to interpret reality and what constituted meaningfulness in life. Relative to the non-Jewish populations in the places where they resided, the Jews were everywhere a semi-enfranchised, subordinate minority group.[30]

As is true of most countries, there were regional differences. For example, some liturgical customs were different in Poland as compared to Prussia. There were differences between western and eastern Yiddish. The differing non-Jewish legal frameworks that impinged on the various sub-regions of Ashkenaz created specific challenges and opportunities for the Jews of those areas. Poland offered some cultural models that differed from those in countries to the west and vice versa. The autonomous Jewish institutions displayed variations reflecting adaptation to local legal, demographic, social, and economic conditions.[31] These differences should not, however, obscure the many traditions, institutions, and cultural constructs that the Jews of the sub-

[29] Yosef Levin, *Historical Writings*, ed. Hannah Frankel-Goldsmidt (Jerusalem, 1996); Asher Levy, *Die Memoiren des Ascher Levy aus Reichshofen im Elsass*, ed. M. Ginsburger (Berlin, 1913); Alexander Marx, 'A Seventeenth-Century Autobiography', *Jewish Quarterly Review*, NS 8 (1918), 269–304; *The Life of Glückel of Hameln, 1646–1724: Written by Herself*, trans. and ed. Beth-Zion Abrahams (New York, 1963); Jacob Emden, *Megilat sefer* [Scroll of the Book], ed. D. Kahana (Warsaw, 1897); *The Memoirs of Ber of Bolechow*, trans. and ed. M. Vishnitzer (London, 1922; repr. 1973); *Solomon Maimon: An Autobiography*, trans. and ed. J. Clark Murray (Boston, 1888; new edn., introd. Marc Shapiro, Urbana, 2001).

[30] This conceptualization of Ashkenaz is a development of the construct first proposed by Jacob Katz in *Tradition and Crisis: Jewish Society at the End of the Middle Ages*, 1st published in Hebrew 1958; trans. and with an afterword by B. D. Cooperman (New York, 1993). See also Israel Bartal, 'The Image of Germany and German Jewry in East European Jewish Society During the 19th Century', in Isidore Twersky (ed.), *Danzig Between East and West* (Cambridge, Mass., 1985), 3–17, esp. pp. 4–5.

[31] For explication of some such regional specificities, see e.g. Moshe Rosman, 'Innovative Tradition: Jewish Culture in the Polish–Lithuanian Commonwealth', in David Biale (ed.), *Cultures of the Jews: A New History* (New York, 2002), 519–70; Chone Shmeruk, *Yiddish Literature in Poland* [Sifrut yidish bepolin] (Jerusalem, 1981), 11–74; Teller, 'Hasidism and the Challenge of Geography'.

regions had in common, as well as the many types of familial, social, cultural, economic, political, intellectual, and religious affinity between them.

Another way to think about this is to ask whether the most important determinants in the relationship between Jews in the German states and those in the Polish–Lithuanian Commonwealth, in the early modern period, were the geopolitical boundaries that contained them, their political allegiances and the political controls on them. The conceptualization of these as two separate communities has perhaps led to a lack of attention to the substantial relations between them in areas where boundaries determined by political realities were not dominant.

For example, economically, Jews in Poland and Jews in what later became 'Germany' were part of the same trade network. We know that German court Jews depended on Polish Jews to supply them with horses, grain, cattle, and other products. German Jews supplied Polish Jewish factors with luxury goods. Polish Jews were the single largest group of attendees at the Leipzig trade fairs and were an important presence at Frankfurt, Breslau, and elsewhere as well.[32]

Similarly, Poland and Germany were also in a close cultural relationship. Rabbis born in Germany might be trained in Poland and then serve in either place. In general rabbis moved easily from positions in Polish cities to ones in German communities and back again, implying that their cultural acuity did not require much adjustment when crossing the political borders. Books published in one area were intended for readers in the other. Many aspects of Jewish law and religious customs were also common to both regions. Communities throughout Europe could be involved in communal controversies such as the Emden–Eybeschuetz dispute.[33]

Over the past fifty years scholars have, however, largely refrained from viewing Jewish communities as interconnected irrespective of political borders. The political boundary between Poland and Germany, for example, has proven to be a research boundary as well. Jewish historians specializing in either Germany or Poland (myself included) have done precious little to probe the contours of the Ashkenazi 'network of networks'. They have added tremendous quantities of knowledge to the known history of the Jews

[32] Israel, *European Jewry*; Selma Stern, *The Court Jew* (Philadelphia, 1950; repr. 1985); Bernhard Brilling, *Beiträge zur Geschichte der Breslauer Juden. Die Begründer der Breslauer jüdischen Gemeinde* (Breslau, 1935–6); Max Freudenthal, *Leipziger Messgäste. Die jüdischen Besucher der Leipziger Messen in den Jahren 1675 bis 1764* (Frankfurt am Main, 1928); Bernard D. Weinryb, *Studies in the Economic and Social History of the Jews in Poland* [Meḥkarim betoledot hakalkalah vehaḥevrah shel yehudei polin] (Jerusalem, 1939).

[33] Moshe Rosman, 'The Image of Poland as a Torah Centre after 1648–9' (Heb.), *Zion*, 51 (1986), 435–48; id., *How Jewish Is Jewish History?*, ch. 5, 'Prolegomenon to Jewish Cultural History'; cf. Yom-Tov Lipmann Heller, *Megilat eivah* [Memoir], ed. J. Wreshner (Jerusalem, 1999).

within each separate country but have shied away from trying to integrate these histories. Whether because of an ideological need to emphasize how much the Jews 'belonged' to wherever they lived or the practical difficulties in conducting intensive research in more than one country, researchers have not moved from the national to the regional plane. Consequently, the geography of Jewish history remains primarily political geography rather than cultural, economic, social, or some other type.

It need not be so. An eminent teacher of many of today's senior Jewish historians did construe Jewish geography on bases other than the political one. Reacting against the earlier tendency to conceive of Jewish geography as global, Jacob Katz asserted that 'in order to describe Jewish society in depth, we must divide the Jewish world territorially into a number of "centers"'.[34] His classic book *Tradition and Crisis* was an attempt to portray one of these centres (Ashkenaz, roughly from the Loire to the Dnieper) as an integral cultural and social—even if not political—region. A weakness of his study was that it was based exclusively on Jewish sources and in recent years some have seen it as an attempt by a Zionist historian to create a national Jewish reality where none existed. His successors, employing rich non-Jewish sources, proceeded to show how 'Polish' or how 'German'—and how different from each other—the Jews of those countries were, virtually abandoning the 'centre' or regional perspective.[35]

The approach need not be dichotomous, however. It is probable that non-Jewish sources can also support a transnational view of Jewry (i.e. a view that considers Jews separated by national political boundaries to be linked in other ways). To discover whether this is so, scholars of Polish Jewry can start using German, Bohemian, or Hungarian archives, scholars of German Jewry, Polish archives, and so forth.

A serious attempt to view Jewish history transnationally, yet not globally, is the aforementioned *European Jewry in the Age of Mercantilism* by Jonathan Israel. Not trained as a specialist in Jewish history and drawing mainly on secondary literature, both Jewish and non-Jewish, he speaks here of

a distinctive Jewish culture within Europe. . . . Hispanization of Levantine, and Germanization of east European Jewry . . . imparted a remarkable degree of cohesion to a people scattered in small groups over vast distances in a score of lands. What is more, the two spheres, the Hispanic and the Germanic, were now brought into a high degree of interaction . . . at a deeper level the two spheres developed intellectually and spiritually largely as one.[36]

[34] Katz, *Tradition and Crisis*, 6.
[35] See e.g. Gershon David Hundert, *The Jews in a Polish Private Town: The Case of Opatów in the Eighteenth Century* (Baltimore, 1992), especially the chapter entitled 'Jews and Other Poles'.   [36] Israel, *European Jewry*, 31, 33.

The term 'European Jewry' in the title of the book, then, was not simply shorthand for the diverse collection of Jewish communities in various countries. It connoted the transnational, integral nature of Jews all over Europe; their belonging together more than to their places of residence: the 'unified and integrated Jewish culture . . . was increasingly remote from that of the peoples among whom Jews lived'.[37] It was the Jews' cultural geography that mattered most, and this was 'European', not determined by political divisions.

Recently there have been signs that some historians of European Jewry may be adding to Katz's and Israel's precedents. New analytical paradigms have moved from a political geographical premise to basing themselves on social, cultural, or economic geography.

Works by Miriam Bodian, Jane Gerber, Jonathan Israel, Yosef Kaplan, Gérard Nahon, Evelyne Oliel-Grausz, and others[38] have identified a Sephardi diaspora linked by kinship, commerce, culture, and religious conundrums. The geography of this diaspora has also been merged with the geography of an early modern Jewish social type, the port Jew of the port cities of the Mediterranean, the Atlantic seaboard, and the New World (mostly Sephardi, but including some Ashkenazim and Italians as well). These Jews were distinctive for having pioneered Jewish communities in new or renewed areas of settlement, for their felicitous and non-traditional legal status, for their large-scale, long-distance commercial activities, and for their syncretistic cultural profile.[39]

Other non-politically based Jewish geographies might relate to the networks of court Jews, maskilim, Mediterranean Jewry, or hasidim. In each

---

[37] Ibid. 184.

[38] Miriam Bodian, *Hebrews of the Portuguese Nation: Conversos and Community in Early Modern Amsterdam* (Bloomington, Ind., 1997); Jane Gerber, *The Jews of Spain: A History of the Sephardic Experience* (New York, 1992), 177–211; Jonathan Israel, *Diasporas within a Diaspora: Jews, Crypto-Jews, and the World of Maritime Empires (1540–1740)* (Leiden, 2002); Yosef Kaplan, *An Alternative Path to Modernity: The Sephardi Diaspora in Western Europe* (Leiden, 2000); Gérard Nahon, *Métropoles et périphéries séfarades d'Occident* (Paris, 1993); and Evelyne Oliel-Grausz, 'La Diaspora séfarade au XVIIIe siècle: Communication, espaces, réseaux', *Arquivos do Centro Cultural Calouste Gulbenkian*, 48 (2004), 55–71, and 'Networks and Communication in the Sephardi Diaspora: An Added Dimension to the Concept of Port Jews and Port Jewries', *Jewish Culture and History*, 7/1–2 (2004), 61–76.

[39] The concept of the port Jew was first proposed simultaneously by David Sorkin, 'The Port Jew: Notes Toward a Social Type', *Journal of Jewish Studies*, 50 (1999), 87–97, and Lois C. Dubin, *The Port Jews of Habsburg Trieste: Absolutist Politics and Enlightenment Culture* (Stanford, 1999). It has been the subject of intensive research under the auspices of the University of Southampton AHRC Parkes Centre for the Study of Jewish/Non-Jewish Relations: Port Jews Project. To date three volumes of collected studies on this topic have been published: *Jewish Culture and History*, 4/2 (2001); L. Dubin (ed.), *Port Jews of the Atlantic* (= *Jewish History*, 20/2 (2006)); and David Cesarani and Gemma Romain, *Jews and Port Cities: Commerce, Community and Cosmopolitanism* (London, 2006).

of these cases political geography was a secondary or tertiary factor in the geography of the Jewish phenomenon under discussion.[40] As Feiner and Zalkin have shown, the 'republic' of the Jewish Enlightenment, the Haskalah, was spread out over many countries, and while its supporters, the maskilim, had to deal with specific local challenges in different places, their relations with each other across borders and the problems they had in common were hardly less significant than their local difficulties. Israel showed how Selma Stern's work on the court Jew should be extended to portray a network that superseded political boundaries and even Europe itself. Mediterranean Jewry was ruled by various political entities yet retained multiple common cultural, economic, religious, intellectual, social, and familial ties. The organization of hasidism seems to have been calculated to overcome the boundaries imposed by politics. All of these cases await historical treatment that will further discuss their geographical dimension in social, cultural, economic, and religious terms.

On a more general level, Jewish historians realized some time ago that, as a factor in determining Jewish historical reality, geography mattered. They no longer attempt to portray a virtually identical Jewish experience everywhere. The problem is, in my view, that in releasing geographical diversity from subordination to purported cultural unity they not only modified the transgeographical conception of Jewish history—they abandoned it altogether. The local context was only one context of the Jewish historical experience. Jewish experience was also contextualized within the frameworks of Jewish history, Jewish tradition, and the mutual influences of Jewish communities in various parts of the world. The transnational perspective— the links between Jews in different countries, the characteristics they shared, their conjoint supralocal experience and the common denominators of their local experience—must also be explored. There is a cultural geography of Jewish history that transcends national political boundaries. It may not reveal a monolithic culture, but it will probably lend insight into one that resembles a rope with multicoloured strands all intertwined.

Historians' overdependence on an organization schema for Jewish history that derives from political boundaries has hindered their thinking about and

---

[40] Stern, *The Court Jew*; Israel, *European Jewry*; Shmuel Feiner, *The Jewish Enlightenment* (Philadelphia, 2004); Mordecai Zalkin, *A New Dawn: The Jewish Enlightenment in the Russian Empire* [Ba'alot hashaḥar: hahaskalah hayehudit ba'imperiyah harusit] (Jerusalem, 1996); Ariel Toaff and Simon Schwarzfuchs, *The Mediterranean and the Jews: Banking, Finance, and International Trade (XVI–XVIII Centuries)* [Hayehudim vehayam hatikhon: banka'ut, mamon umishar bein-le'umi], 2 vols. (Ramat Gan, 1989); Evyatar Friesel, *Atlas of Modern Jewish History* (New York, 1990). Each of these works recognizes the (non-political) geographical dimension of its subject (for example, Friezel includes maps relating to the geography of hasidism), but they represent first steps only in introducing non-political geography as an organizing principle of Jewish historical narratives.

researching networks that were connected in ways that made political boundaries irrelevant, or that actually negated those boundaries. By casting geography in terms of cultural, economic, social, or other networks that criss-crossed different political entities, they will attain an additional valuable tool of historical analysis. They will also probably discover new rubrics that place Jewish history in unconventional perspectives.[41]

[41] For an example of this, see Teller, 'Hasidism and the Challenge of Geography'.

TWO

Away from a Definition of Antisemitism

An Essay in the Semantics of Historical Description

DAVID ENGEL

'—and that shows that there are three hundred and sixty-four days when you might get un-birthday presents.'

'Certainly', said Alice.

'And only one for birthday presents, you know. There's glory for you!'

'I don't know what you mean by "glory"', Alice said.

Humpty Dumpty smiled contemptuously. 'Of course you don't know—till I tell you. I meant "there's a nice knock-down argument for you!"'

'But "glory" doesn't mean "a nice knock-down argument"', Alice objected.

'When I use a word', Humpty Dumpty said, in rather a scornful tone, 'it means just what I choose it to mean—neither more nor less.'

'The question is', said Alice, 'whether you can make words mean so many different things.'

'The question is', said Humpty Dumpty, 'which is to be master—that's all.'

READERS MAY RECOGNIZE in the title of this essay an allusion to Gavin Langmuir's oft-cited volume, *Toward a Definition of Antisemitism*. That book presented a series of 'efforts from different angles to answer the same basic question: What is antisemitism, when did it start, and why?'[1] Langmuir was not the first to pose this set of questions, nor has his answer put an end to scholarly discussions of it. Works purporting to relate the 'history of antisemitism' date to the late nineteenth century, and exploring the scope and bounds of that presumed history, the continuities and discontinuities within it, and the factors governing its course continues to be widely regarded as a constructive endeavour for historians to undertake.

What follows engages neither Langmuir's particular answer nor that of any other scholar. In fact, it does not confront Langmuir's question directly at all. Instead, by tracing a hidden assumption that underlies the question, it seeks to demonstrate not only that all previous attempts to answer it have been barren but that all future attempts at an answer will likely be so as well. Even more, it undertakes to show how constituting 'antisemitism' as an

---

[1] Gavin Langmuir, *Toward a Definition of Antisemitism* (Berkeley, Calif., 1990), 1.

object of historical study, in whatever form and according to whatever parameters, has diverted and will likely continue to deflect historians from potentially fruitful ways of investigating the specific incidents, texts, laws, visual artefacts, social practices, and mental configurations that that rubric customarily subsumes. No definition can rectify the damage such deflection invariably brings. Only a thorough rethinking of what the study of 'antisemitism' is supposed to reveal can rid historians of the blinders that the concept has imposed upon them.

*

The argument against constituting 'antisemitism' as an object of study and expending effort upon defining it rests upon certain fundamental notions concerning the semantics of historical description. As employed here, the phrase refers to two activities in which not only historians but all human beings routinely engage: analysing large quantities of information into conceptual categories and endowing the various categories with names. Enquiry into the semantics of historical description involves reflection upon the ways in which historians perform these activities as they ply their discipline, and upon the consequences of their performance for their professional practice.

The starting point for any such enquiry is the self-evident observation that the volume of empirical data that historians acquire in the ordinary course of their work is too enormous to be comprehended without dividing the data into smaller, more manageable blocks. The division is routinely accomplished through a process of abstraction that can conveniently be described in three stages. First, historians notice that certain bits of data share particular characteristics with certain other bits. Next, they decide that those shared characteristics are more significant for their purposes than any differences that might be perceived among them. Finally, they develop the habit of thinking collectively about all bits of data that display those shared characteristics, no matter what differences may distinguish them. The mental collectivities generated by such habits become the fundamental categories that historians employ to organize and make sense of their data and to talk about them with others inside and beyond their professional circle.

The process can be compared to establishing a filing system. Filing involves creating categories that enable and encourage people to place pieces of data together in a common folder by calling attention to certain shared characteristics among them while diverting attention from any discernible differences. People who have set up filing systems for themselves will attest that such categories do not always suggest themselves obviously. Filers often reach a point where they debate in their own minds whether to place a particular piece of paper into an existing folder or to create a new folder for it, because many things set the paper apart from others belonging to any of the folders they have already opened. A system that favours broad categories may make the paper in question blend together with the others with which it is filed, to the point where it is no longer readily perceived for its particular distinguishing features, and considerable effort must be exerted to locate it when the need arises. On the other hand, a system that draws many fine distinctions between categories requires energy both to establish the large number of classifications and to remember how they are distinguished from one another. In both cases, the efficient retrieval of papers when needed becomes difficult, and the purpose of the filing system is defeated. Designers of filing systems thus tend to search for a middle ground, one that will permit users to make the most effective use of the system for the purposes for which they are most likely to apply it.

Individuals designing personal filing systems often depend entirely upon their own resources to find this middle ground. By contrast, the metaphorical filing systems that enable different human groups, including historians and practitioners of other academic disciplines, to organize the data of life into manageable conceptual categories and to talk about the data meaningfully with other members of their group are produced and transmitted socially. The primary means for the social production and transmission of conceptual categories is language. Indeed, one of any human language's foremost functions is to establish a shared system for ordering and assigning common meaning to individual perceptions. Hence, whereas individuals designing filing systems for their own use alone are free to create whatever folders they wish, to establish rules for including an item in a particular folder that are entirely idiosyncratic, and to label their various folders however they please, human beings who wish to communicate their perceptions of reality to others and to allow others to communicate with them have no choice but to join a language community, to assimilate its particular way of parcelling out the universe, and to adopt its practices for naming the various parcels.

The central role that social groups and language play in establishing and conveying conceptual categories has created particular problems for historical analysis. In the first instance those problems reflect a common confusion over the ontological status of the categories that languages delineate. Linguists, anthropologists, psychologists, and sociologists have spent much effort trying to ascertain the degree to which the various parcelling schemes employed by the earth's different language communities are the result of social convention or inscribed in the natural world—that is, the extent to which a language community is truly at liberty to create and name its own categories (in the way that individuals are free to devise their own personal filing systems), as against that to which certain choices are hard-wired into all human brains, as it were, through a process of Darwinian selection favouring conceptual grids that correspond to universally observable physical or biological facts. The problem remains controversial, no doubt in large measure because the two possibilities have often been framed as mutually exclusive. In the event, it is fairly easy to identify categories of both types. Some concepts have obvious physical referents: substances can be classified according to their chemical composition, living organisms according to their genomes, infectious diseases according to their microbial agents. Small wonder that there is little variation in the deployment of such concepts in different languages; clearly there is something in nature that encourages all humans, whatever language they speak, mentally to group all materials of a certain chemical structure or all creatures sharing certain DNA patterns under a single rubric, even if they are not aware themselves of the natural basis for their classification. On the other hand, cross-language comparisons demonstrate the existence of conceptual categories that are entirely the result of human artifice. For example, some languages assign all man-made objects whose purpose is to indicate the time of day to a single category without further subdivision, and they give that category a single label: speakers of German refer to *Uhr*, of Spanish to *reloj*, of Romanian to *ceas*, of Hebrew to *shaon*. Other communities, by contrast, mentally divide those same objects into more than one category, usually based upon size, function, or site of habitual placement, and endow each category with its own distinct name. Thus English speakers are immediately aware of a fundamental distinction between *clock* and *watch*, Polish speakers between *zegar* and *zegarek*, Dutch speakers between *klok* and *horloge*, and French speakers between three concepts—*horloge*, *pendule*, and *montre*. In other words, speakers of the latter languages have decided to pay attention to particular distinctions within the set of man-made time indicators that speakers of the former languages have chosen to ignore. Those choices appear unconstrained by nature in any way: the prospect that any physical or biological fact will ever be discovered that will compel speakers of one or another language community to abandon their current conceptual grid in favour of some other one seems remote. There thus appears to be no basis except a social one for preferring one way of dividing the set of man-made time indicators over another, no justification beyond group convention for designating one scheme of division correct, another incorrect.

Nevertheless, even though many of them lack an unambiguous foundation in the physical universe, a group's linguistic conventions constitute a powerful force for conformity—so powerful, in fact, that those conventions are often mistaken for natural divisions of reality instead of social ones. Lewis Carroll captured that power vividly when he made Alice confront Humpty Dumpty in the passage quoted in the epigraph to this essay. Humpty Dumpty maintained, in effect, that because there is seldom anything in the material world that compels a person to employ any particular conceptual categories or to name them in a certain way, individuals may use whatever categories and names they please, no matter whether anyone else in their group approves or not. It is not clear whether Alice demurred because she believed that the meaning of a word is naturally determined and intrinsic to it or because she felt too much social pressure to declare herself the sole master of her vocabulary as Humpty Dumpty did. Perhaps she felt the latter but interpreted the feeling as meaning the former. Nonetheless, few readers of *Through the Looking Glass* are likely to find Humpty Dumpty's position more reasonable than Alice's. Indeed, the ordinary discourse of primary language communities—those constituted by speakers of one or another of the world's several thousand identified 'natural' languages—tends to treat virtually all conceptual categories as if they were somehow etched into the fabric of the cosmos, and the proper use of the words that signify them as a matter independent not only of individual but of community will.

Still, Humpty Dumpty's injunction to treat words as servants instead of as masters does appear to have found adherents among more restricted language communities, including those constituted by practitioners of one or another academic discipline. Such specialized language communities often develop their own esoteric filing systems, as it were, and assign names to their folders in an idiosyncratic fashion that does not always chime with the way those same names are employed by outsiders. Astronomers offered a graphic demonstration of this practice in 2006, when the International Astronomical Union officially removed Pluto from the category of 'planets' and placed it in a new category, labelled 'dwarf planets', established especially to contain that object and two others that were similarly removed from their former classifications. In doing so the astronomers explicitly disavowed the conceptual grid through which their primary language communities imposed order on the set of celestial bodies in orbit around the sun and substituted another one in its place—one that evaluated differently the relative significance of the similarities and distinctions between Pluto and the eight other such bodies that common discourse lumped together in a single classification. Their action rested upon the premise that, even though it encompassed a set of tangible cosmic objects, the category designated by the term 'planet' was *not* a part of the cosmos itself, but a human creation that humans could change at will. On the other hand, that very premise appears to have been what most upset many of those who expressed consternation over the astronomers' action.[2] As a result, public discussion in the wake of that action

---

[2] See for example the comment of one passer-by in a railway station whose reaction was randomly solicited by a reporter for a local newspaper: 'What's next? The sun's not the sun? The moon's not the moon?' Emma Stickgold, 'Newton T Patrons Fret over Fate of Science Monument', *Boston Globe*, 25 Aug. 2006.

tended to focus not so much on Pluto's particular characteristics as on the question, 'What is a planet?', as if the term 'planet' possessed some tangible reality outside the minds of those who use it. A substantive conversation (one focused upon a specific object) thus evolved into a semantic one (one concerned with the meaning of words). Astronomers generally understood the difference; the broader public, by and large, did not.

Although professional historians practise an academic discipline, they have tended to treat their own concepts less like astronomers and more like the general public. For the most part they have shied away from creating a specialized language of their own, one that employs terms in a strictly technical sense that deviates from the usage of their broader social surroundings. Some have even asserted that, as a matter of principle, history-writing 'should explain itself in terms accessible to all men, not to experts only'.[3] As a result, they have preferred to permit the conceptual categories into which they analyse their data to be determined, named, and supplied to them ready-made by the primary language communities to which they belong, instead of creating and naming categories of their own to meet the particular demands of their work. Doing so has no doubt enhanced their ability to communicate with a broad public, as compared to practitioners of disciplines like astronomy, who feel free to employ terms esoterically, without regard for ordinary usage. However, their preference for Alice over Humpty Dumpty has also made them vulnerable to Alice's confusion: they have often perceived their categories as naturally given instead of socially constructed and taken the words that label them as intrinsically instead of conventionally meaningful. As a result, many of them have invested considerable energy in debates that are far more semantic than substantive—debates focused more on the applicability of certain words to past events than on the events themselves.

Such debates may aim at clarification, but their result more often than not is analytical muddle. The ongoing attempts to answer the question 'What is antisemitism?' offer a case in point.

*

Actually, the question should not be difficult to answer at all. The stem 'antisemit-' came into common usage in Germany during the early 1880s as a designation for particular individuals and groups demanding an end to recently adopted legal arrangements that had, to their minds, granted Jews undue influence over cultural, social, economic, and political life in their country. Contrary to what is widely believed today, those individuals and groups do

---

[3] G. R. Elton, *The Practice of History* (London, 1967), 140. Cf. Michael Stanford, *The Nature of Historical Knowledge* (Oxford, 1986), 148–9.

not appear to have been united by any common set of ideas beyond a general feeling that the legal arrangements they opposed were liable to cause German society long-term harm.[4] Some came to that feeling out of religiously inspired beliefs concerning the proper role of Jews in Christian society, others from a stereotypical identification of Jews with rapacious capital, still others via notions of racial determinism, and a not inconsiderable number simply because they saw political advantage in attacking alleged Jewish power.[5] They began to attract public attention towards the end of 1879, when such prominent Berlin personalities as the preacher Adolf Stoecker and the historian Heinrich von Treitschke lent their names to the cause. The common parlance of the day quickly dubbed them 'Antisemiten' and their activities 'antisemitisch', and most appear to have adopted the name with little protest.[6] 'Antisemitismus' thus signified something like 'acting like an

[4] In particular, there does not appear to be any basis for the usually unquestioned claim that the word 'antisemitism' was deliberately coined by Wilhelm Marr in order to establish a seemingly scientific justification for his attitude or to indicate that Jews constituted a problem because of their race. For detailed explication and sources, see David Engel, 'The Concept of Antisemitism in the Historical Scholarship of Amos Funkenstein', *Jewish Social Studies*, 6 (1999), 111–29, nn. 2, 38–41. Nor is there any compelling evidence that at the time of its introduction the stem 'antisemit-' was generally understood as implying an attitude towards Jews rooted in race. Actually, there is evidence to the contrary: see below, n. 12.

[5] The literature describing these groups is vast and well known. Among the most prominent works are Paul W. Massing, *Rehearsal for Destruction: A Study of Political Anti-Semitism in Imperial Germany* (New York, 1949); P. G. J. Pulzer, *The Rise of Political Anti-Semitism in Germany and Austria* (New York, 1964); Uriel Tal, *Christians and Jews in the 'Second Reich' (1870–1914): A Study in the Rise of German Totalitarianism* [Yahadut venatsrut bareikh hasheni: tahalikhim historiyim baderekh letotalitariyut] (Jerusalem, 1969); Richard S. Levy, *The Downfall of the Anti-Semitic Political Parties in Imperial Germany* (New Haven, 1975).

[6] It is not clear why the name caught on or what was most responsible for its popularity. The circumstances in which the earliest attested use of the term as a designation for an activity of the type in question appeared in print, and the fact that it was made by a Jewish publication, the *Allgemeine Zeitung des Judenthums* (*AZJ*), suggest that the locution was already familiar in public discourse: 'Streitschriften für die Juden', *AZJ*, 2 Sept. 1879, p. 564: 'We have received anonymous correspondence from Hamburg . . . according to which . . . [Wilhelm Marr] has found friends who will bring the "antisemitic weekly" into being'. See Reinhard Rürup, *Emanzipation und Antisemitismus. Studien zur 'Judenfrage' der bürgerlichen Gesellschaft* (Göttingen, 1975), 102. Indeed, the notion of 'Semitism' or a 'Semitic mind' had been in circulation in both the German- and French-speaking worlds since at least the 1840s: see Christian Lassen, *Indische Alterthumskunde*, vol. i (Bonn, 1847), 414 ff.; Ernest Renan, *Histoire générale et système comparé des langues sémitiques*, 2nd edn. (Paris, 1858), 1 ff. The labelling of views that held such a 'Semitic mind' to be inferior to that of the 'Aryan' or 'Indo-European' as 'antisemitic' has been attested since 1860: Alex Bein, *The Jewish Question: Biography of a Worldwide Problem* [She'elat hayehudim: biografiyah shel be'ayah olamit] (Givatayim, 1986), 84–5. The expression was also used as early as 1865 as a designation for institutions that supposedly did not chime with the 'Semitic spirit' (Rürup, *Emanzipation*, 95). It certainly made sense to apply this label to Marr in 1879, since his writings from that year—in particular his infamous pamphlet, *Der Sieg des Judenthums über das Germanenthum*, which appeared in March of that year, were replete with references to 'Semitismus', employed virtually interchangeably with

"Antisemit" '—that is, engaging in activities aimed at promoting the political goals that the various organizations labelled 'antisemitisch' espoused.[7] In other words, when it first appeared the term 'antisemitism' had a rather well-defined, clearly circumscribed, almost tangible referent: it pointed to a limited set of actions undertaken by a largely self-identified set of people who lived and worked in a particular time and place. The entire problem of definition could thus be obviated were the term used to refer solely to those actions and no others. And indeed, some scholars have explicitly proposed employing the designation 'antisemitism' solely in this geographically, chronologically, and politically delimited sense.[8]

On the whole, though, historians have not accepted such proposals, preferring to employ the term as a label for a broader conceptual category, one that incorporates data from a significantly greater range of places, times, and actions. Not surprisingly, their preference seems to have been dictated largely by common usage. Indeed, a rapid extension of the set of attitudes and behaviours referred to as 'antisemitism' in ordinary discourse is evident in publications dating from shortly after the word first came into currency. That extension, in turn, appears to have been spurred by a series of historical developments that unfolded at the same time, developments that, among other things, created the basic intellectual matrix out of which all subsequent discussions of the word and its meaning were formed.

Those developments were set in motion when the individuals and groups who espoused political measures aimed at curbing ostensible Jewish influence began, probably in early 1880, to speak of themselves and to be spoken of widely as constituting a 'movement'.[9] The primary aim of that movement was to spread the notion that the emancipationist model for adjusting the

'Judenthum' as antitheses of 'Germanenthum'. However, it does not appear to have occurred to Marr's first reviewers to use it; see e.g. 'Gegen W. Marr', *AZJ*, 18 Mar. 1879, pp. 178–80. After it was applied to him, beginning in September 1879, he does not appear consistently to have welcomed the label, especially in light of the manner in which his collaborator Hector de Groussillier, who co-founded the so-called Antisemitic League with Marr the following month, interpreted its meaning: see Moshe Zimmermann, *Wilhelm Marr: The Patriarch of Antisemitism* (New York, 1986), 90–3. Perhaps it was the prominent historian and publicist Heinrich von Treitschke's use of the term 'Antisemitenvereine' in November 1879 to designate groups that had come together in recent months to 'speak fairly and moderately of one or another undeniable shortcoming of the Jewish character' that catalysed the spread of the term: see Heinrich von Treitschke, 'Unsere Aussichten', in Karsten Krieger (ed.), *Der 'Berliner Antisemitismusstreit' 1879–1881. Eine Kontroverse um die Zugehörigkeit der deutschen Juden zur Nation*, 2 vols. (Munich, 2003), i. 10. On the other hand, his designation may have reflected what had already become an unselfconsciously employed common coinage.

[7] Engel, 'Concept of Antisemitism', 120.   [8] e.g. Bein, *The Jewish Question*, 84.
[9] Christoph Cobet, *Das Wortschatz des Antisemitismus in der Bismarckzeit* (Munich, 1973), 222; Jacob Katz, *From Prejudice to Destruction: Anti-Semitism, 1700–1933* (Cambridge, Mass., 1980), 245–6.

relations between Jews and the states under whose authority they lived, which by the early 1870s had been adopted everywhere in Europe west of the Oder river, would inevitably generate unfavourable consequences for the majority societies into which emancipated Jewry sought integration.[10] In this fashion, 'Antisemitismus' came to signify not only a set of activities aimed at promulgation of this belief but the belief itself. Moreover, although initially formulated in reference to Germany, the idea also found an audience beyond that country's borders: initiatives consciously imitating the activities of the German 'Antisemiten' soon appeared in Hungary, Austria, and France, and their instigators looked to the German movement for models to adapt to their own local situations.[11] Like those of their German prototype, their activities were also quickly dubbed 'antisemitisch'—largely, it seems, by the German Jewish press, although for the most part they appear readily to have accepted the label.[12] In autumn 1882 various German and non-German groups that identified themselves with the new anti-emancipationist movement came together in Dresden for an International Anti-Jewish Congress. (Internationaler antijüdischer Kongreß), where the foundations were laid for

[10] The earliest activity of the inchoate movement was the so-called 'Antisemitenpetition', initially formulated in August 1880 and presented to German Chancellor Otto von Bismarck on 13 April 1881. The petition, formulated by a coalition of self-proclaimed antisemites, charged that 'wherever Christians and Jews enter into [unregulated] social relations, we see Jews [becoming] masters, while the indigenous Christian population [assumes] a position of servitude', and set forth four demands: restriction of Jewish immigration from other countries; a ban on appointment of Jews to positions of authority; preservation of the Christian character of schools; and separate registration of Jews in official statistics. Text in Krieger (ed.), *Der 'Berliner Antisemitismusstreit'*, ii. 579–81. Cf. the initial draft, with its assertion that 'the issue is no longer making the Jews equal with us; it is much more the spoliation of our national prerogatives as a result of Jews gaining the upper hand' (ibid. ii. 535–8).

[11] Katz, *From Prejudice to Destruction*, 273–4, 285, 287–8, 292.

[12] For one of the earliest examples, see 'Die "Antisemiten" in Ungarn', *AZJ*, 31 Aug. 1880, p. 545. The article placed the words 'Antisemiten' and 'antisemitisch' in quote marks, most likely indicating either that the term was still thought of as a neologism or that, in referring to groups operating in Hungary, the article was extending usage of the word beyond what was regarded at the time as its proper confinement to Germany. The article did not employ the word 'Antisemitismus' at all; indeed, that form of the stem 'antisemit-' had not yet come into regular usage (it began to appear with regularity in newspapers and journals only in 1881: see 'Wie steht es gegenwärtig um den "Antisemitismus"', *AZJ*, 26 Apr. 1881, pp. 267–8, the publication's first use of the term in a headline). There is also no indication that the article's author understood the stem as referring to activity based upon 'racial' as opposed to 'religious' motifs. On the contrary, the bulk of the article consisted of an extensive refutation of the arguments of August Rohling, Professor of Hebrew at Charles University in Prague, whose 1871 work, *Der Talmudjude*, which the most visible of the Hungarian 'Antisemiten', Győző Istoczy, quoted freely, located the roots of the Jews' purported unsuitability for emancipation squarely within classical rabbinic literature. The article placed Istoczy and Rohling's statements about Jews on the same plane as similar statements about Protestants; it saw them clearly as statements about a religious group, not a 'race' (ibid. 545–50). See G. Wolf, 'Anti-semitische Bestrebungen in Wien', *AZJ*, 24 Apr. 1882, pp. 274–6.

the formation of an 'Alliance Antijuive Universelle' that would fight emancipation in all countries.[13]

To be sure, the Congress eschewed the stem 'antisemit-' in its title in favour of the less novel 'anti-Jewish' (*antijüdisch*). It is not clear why. Whatever the case, though, most of the gathering's moving spirits appear to have had no compunction about labelling themselves 'Antisemiten', to the point where newspaper reports of its proceedings sometimes referred to it mistakenly as the Dresden 'Antisemitenkongress'.[14] Indeed, the Congress offered an early indication that, for those involved in it, at least, the two terms were already being taken as synonymous.[15] For participants, moreover, the amalgamation of labels appears to have been deliberate. The Dresden meeting (together with a second one that took place in Chemnitz in April 1883) demonstrated the considerable differences in the ideas that had brought the various German, Austrian, and Hungarian 'Antisemiten' who attended to their anti-emancipationist conclusions. So great were those differences, in fact, that the Congress proved unable to designate any single set of ideas about Jews as either necessary or sufficient qualifications for becoming part of the movement. All that could be agreed upon was a minimal and vaguely defined set of actions: ostracize Jews socially and economically in each country, join no association of which Jews could become members, read no Jewish-owned newspapers.[16] The 'Antisemiten', it seems, could tolerate no higher common denominator if they wished to keep their movement intact. Hence it was but a short time before prominent figures in the movement began to state explicitly: 'In our case, "Antisemit" means . . . an opponent of the Jews [*Judengegner*]'—nothing more.[17]

But if being an 'Antisemit' indeed meant nothing more to those who accepted the label, then both the 'Antisemiten' and their opponents could, if they wished, readily expand the term's referents not only past the borders of Germany but also beyond the realm of contemporary mass politics in which they had at first been located. As it happened, precisely when the 'Antisemiten' began their campaign to undo what they took to be the ill effects of emancipation in Germany and its neighbours, a series of highly visible acts of 'opposition to the Jews' not directly linked to that campaign—in particular the mass violence in parts of the Russian empire during 1881–2, the restrictive Russian legislation that followed in its wake, and the ritual

---

[13] Pulzer, *Political Anti-Semitism*, 103–4; Katz, *From Prejudice to Destruction*, 279–80.

[14] See e.g. 'Stöcker's acht Thesen auf dem antisemitischen Kongreß in Dresden', *AZJ*, 3 Oct. 1882, pp. 652–4.

[15] Another appeared in the thirteenth edition of the *Großer Brockhaus*, in 1882; it defined 'Antisemit' first of all as 'Judenfeind, Gegner des Judentums' (Cobet, *Wortschatz*, 220).

[16] Levy, *Downfall*, 35–6; Katz, *From Prejudice to Destruction*, 279–80.

[17] Cobet, *Wortschatz*, 221.

murder trial in Tiszaeszlár, Hungary—also caught the attention of observers throughout the continent. Many analysts were struck by what they perceived as fundamental similarities between those occurrences and the activities of the so-called antisemitic movement *stricto sensu*. Those similarities were detected not so much in the surface appearance of the events as in their presumed significance as indicators of general trends in European politics. Not only were all of them, in Russia, Hungary, and Germany alike, widely perceived by Jews as a significant threat to their legal status, material well-being, or physical security; they also called into question a political assumption that until but a short while before had seemed to many an unshakable truth—that the triumphant march of Jewish emancipation and social integration, and with them the liberal political and social order as a whole, could not be stopped. Indeed, it was the challenge that these events posed to the liberal vision that appears to have provided the initial stimulus for grouping them mentally together in a single conceptual category, despite the no less obvious differences among them in, among other things, the social identities of the perpetrators, their modes of operation, and their relation to state power.[18] 'Antisemitismus' already served as a widely accepted designation for the German activities in this grouping; soon it became a synecdoche for the category as a whole.

The ascendancy of this particular conceptual grid was not foreordained, however. Nothing and no one, for example, compelled observers to file, as it were, the April 1881 submission of a petition to Chancellor Bismarck to preserve the Christian character of German elementary schools, on one hand, and the mob attacks on Jewish homes and shops in the Ukrainian city of Elizavetgrad during the same month, on the other, together in a single metaphorical mental folder instead of in two distinct ones (the first labelled, perhaps, 'anti-emancipationist political activity', and the second, 'physical attacks upon Jews'). If the former filing scheme became dominant, those who adopted it must have convinced themselves that it offered certain advantages in relating to both phenomena, advantages that would be lost if the set of 'antisemitism's' rapidly expanding referents were divided and analysed differently. For those who identified with the antisemitic movement or wished it well, the most obvious benefit was the integrative function that such a broadly drawn category could serve: it helped self-described *Judengegner* in different locations, who acquired their hostility from different sources and expressed it in different ways, to join together under a common banner for mutual assistance. On the other hand, those who found *Judengegner* of any sort threatening also adduced what seemed to them compelling reasons to lump disparate threatening acts and statements together

---

[18] See e.g. 'Antisemitische Wühlereien in Ungarn', *AZJ*, 11 July 1882, pp. 460–2; 'Der Antisemitismus', *Jeschurun*, 15 Nov. 1883, pp. 801–3.

under a single analytical heading. Doing so helped those disquieted by spreading bellicosity towards Jews to draw inferences concerning potential dangers in one part of the world from what they noticed about other threats analysed under the same rubric. In particular, observers discerned a sort of positive-feedback spiral between the public agitation of Stoecker and Treitschke in Berlin and violence against Jews in Russia: the former purportedly catalysed the latter, while the latter pointed to what the former might hope ultimately to accomplish. A May 1882 report on the Russian violence published in the *Allgemeine Zeitung des Judenthums* warned, for example, that the 'true aim' of the antisemites' agitation in Prussia was 'plundering the Jews and driving them out'—goals that the Prussian antisemites themselves had never stated in public but that appeared to the writer to lie at the bottom of what the Russian rioters hoped to accomplish.[19] In the same fashion, the newspaper warned two months later, the Hungarian resurrection of the blood libel showed that Germany could anticipate an attempt 'not only to reawaken the old, practically dormant prejudices, but even more to instil the bitterest hatred of the Jews in the populace'.[20] In short, concentration upon the gross similarities among recent events in different parts of Europe instead of on the fine details that distinguished them from one another seemed to reveal much of importance that might otherwise have remained hidden.

Calling attention to the revival of old prejudices as a potential motif in *any* activity belonging to the category suggested, moreover, that the term 'antisemitism' might also be applied to events of the past that Jews had found threatening. That suggestion, in turn, pointed Jews to useful strategies for coping with the menace that current 'antisemitic' activity was supposed to pose. A November 1883 editorial in *Jeschurun*, the organ of German Orthodoxy founded by Samson Raphael Hirsch, spoke explicitly of an 'old antisemitism' that was identical to the new variety: 'The outrages of the Middle Ages have been repeated on European soil in our day . . . murder, rape, and plunder mark the pages of contemporary Jewish history, too . . . the most absurd, disgraceful accusation, the almost forgotten unbelievable legend of a raw and stupid age, has once again been raised against the Jewish people; and fanatics continue to work to destroy the Jews' honour and respect.' However, the newspaper pointed out, during their centuries of

---

[19] 'Die Judenverfolgungen in Rußland auf ihrem Höhepunkte', *AZJ*, 9 May 1882, p. 305. The notion that the fate of Jews in Russia was determined in significant measure by hostile agitation against Jews in Germany persisted among German Jews for decades. See e.g. 'Die Ostjudenfrage', *Ost und West*, Apr.–May 1916, col. 149: 'The reversal of fortune [in Russia] was brought about by *antisemitism*, the old hatred of the Jews, which, in Berlin at the end of the 1870s, began to do mischief, taking on a new guise, giving itself a new name, and arming itself with old but newly polished arguments.'

[20] 'Der gegenwärtige Antisemitismus in seiner geschichtlichen Bedeutung', *AZJ*, 25 July 1882, pp. 489–92: 490.

exile the Jewish people had learned not only to retain their honour but to persevere as a community in the face of such assaults.[21] In similar fashion a 23-year-old fledgling journalist from Warsaw, Nahum Sokolow, showed in his 1882 catalogue of calumnies against Jews past and present, *Sinat olam le'am olam*, how patterns of Jewish thought from previous generations could help Jews cope with current events:

A cry of despair has engulfed the entire House of Israel. The hatred that has lain in wait since time immemorial for a despised and despoiled nation is rampaging forward like a storm. In every city and state where the Jewish question has appeared, the noise of quarrelling factions grows stronger and stronger . . . The ancient infectious hatred and licentiousness, which calls itself by a new name—'antisemitism'—again appears upon the brow of all the world's princes. . . . Legislators encumber us with evil and heinous decrees, while the masses open their mouths to swallow us up. In such a time of troubles we must return to the living wellspring of history and the memory of former days, so that we may bring our downcast minds back and strengthen our fallen spirit. . . . By recounting and studying past events . . . [the Jews of today] will acquire a shield . . . against the awful, thunderous blows that those who hate us bring down upon us, and they will recover their spirit and their strength.[22]

Indeed, that the new broad analytical category labelled 'antisemitism' was readily assimilable to the traditional Jewish notion of *sinat yisra'el* undoubtedly commended it to many Jews and facilitated its rapid and widespread adoption among them. Surely there was no logical reason why a category that incorporated many different perceived contemporary threats to Jewish security and well-being could not also encompass known threats from bygone eras, allowing Jews and others to draw useful inferences not only across space but across time as well. Extending the category back in time also served an additional defensive purpose. That function was suggested by the French Jewish socialist writer and future leading Dreyfusard Bernard Lazare in his 1894 survey, *L'Antisémitisme, son histoire et ses causes*, when he wrote that 'antisemitism is one of the last, though most long lived, manifestations of that old spirit of reaction and narrow conservatism, which is vainly attempting to arrest the onward movement of the Revolution'.[23] Lazare appears to have believed that those of his day who labelled themselves antisemites were keen to rationalize their perception of emancipated Jewry as a threat to their well-being; he sensed that they wanted their attitude to be perceived not as an instinctual, knee-jerk prejudice or hatred received from an earlier era but as a considered, objective response to concrete dangers, whose

[21] 'Israels Stellung zum alten und neuen Antisemitismus', *Jeschurun*, 29 Nov. 1883, p. 833.

[22] Nahum Sokolow, *Sinat olam le'am olam* [Eternal Hatred for an Eternal People] (Warsaw, 1882), pp. v–vi.

[23] Bernard Lazare, *Antisemitism: Its History and Causes* (Lincoln, Nebr., 1995), 183.

existence modern anthropology and sociology had revealed and whose severity modern political and economic arrangements had exacerbated.[24] Hence, he evidently reasoned, it made good polemical sense to expose 'the real cause of their sentiments'—'the fear of, and hatred for, the stranger', which lay 'at the bottom of anti-Judaism of the thirteenth century' no less than 'at the bottom of the antisemitism of our own days'. This 'primal, never-failing cause', he claimed, 'appears in Alexandria under the Ptolemies, in Rome during the lifetime of Cicero, in the Greek cities of Ionia, in Antioch, in Cyrenaica, in feudal Europe, and in the modern state whose soul is the spirit of nationality'.[25] Tarring the likes of Treitschke, Georg von Schoenerer, and Edmond Drumont—all of whom, he maintained, insisted upon the fundamentally rational and empirical foundations of their doctrines and programmes—with the same brush as those who had spread blood libels during the Middle Ages or depicted Jews with horns and tails, and portraying them as ignorant of their own motives, which 'may be traced back to the ancient hatred against the Jews', must have seemed like a particularly effective way both to ridicule their pretensions and to marginalize them intellectually and politically.[26]

In other words, tactical considerations on the part of both the original 'Antisemiten' and their opponents appear by the final decade of the nineteenth century to have generated a common usage according to which the word 'antisemitism' signified a broad range of utterances and actions by non-Jews that had opposed Jewish interests or threatened Jews throughout the ages. Historians have generally tended to draw their categories of analysis from the common discourse. In the case of 'antisemitism', this tendency appears to have trumped their usually vociferous insistence upon avoiding anachronism. Hence, from the appearance of Lazare's history through to the present, the thought that the term might be most profitably employed in a purely technical sense as a designation for a set of activities with strict spatial, temporal, and phenomenological bounds has found only the weakest resonance among them.[27]

*

[24] Ibid. 110–18.　　　　　　　　　　　　　　　　　　　　[25] Ibid. 175–6.

[26] Ibid. 182. Lazare employed other polemical strategies as well, most notably the argument that 'antisemitism, which everywhere is the creed of the conservative class . . . is acting, in fact, as an ally of the Revolution' (ibid.). Indeed, though Lazare proclaimed his intention to write 'an impartial study in history and sociology', he constructed the final eight chapters of the book around a point-by-point refutation of what he took to be the principal arguments of contemporaries who wrote of a purported Jewish danger, in a way that strongly suggests that he was aiming first and foremost at delegitimizing them.

[27] Some, however, have maintained that avoiding anachronism requires restricting use to the period following actual coinage of the term: Robert Chazan, *Medieval Stereotypes and Modern Antisemitism* (Berkeley, Calif., 1997), 125–9.

On the other hand, not all historians have felt comfortable ignoring distinctions among the various utterances and actions that the common label 'antisemitism' elides. As a result, from time to time some have called for a 'more precise empirical definition' of the term, one that, while encompassing a far greater range of referents than the activities of the self-described 'Antisemiten' who appeared on the political scene in Germany in the early 1880s, would nevertheless restrict its usage to a particular subset of all utterances and actions that threatened Jews' personal dignity, legal status, social standing, public image, material welfare, or physical safety in any place at any time.[28] No agreement has been reached, however, as to the specific referents that should comprise such a subset, with the result that the definition of 'antisemitism' continues to be a subject of historiographical debate.

The reasons why historians have joined such a debate in the first place but have been unable to bring it to any clear conclusion mirror an additional aspect of the process by which the label 'antisemitism' came to be employed and understood in common discourse. That process, as a result of which the set of words and deeds comprehended by the term was extended far beyond its original referents, can be understood as a social act of linguistic creativity: people tacitly agreed to combine certain features of their experience into a single mental folder, as it were, and to give the folder a specific name, in order to serve certain purposes that were important to them at the time. It thus can be said to have unfolded by dint of the semantic licence that Humpty Dumpty had offered Alice only a short time earlier. Indeed, it could not have proceeded without such warrant: those who contributed to the process had to have felt themselves masters of the word 'antisemitism', free to determine the most beneficial way for them to deploy it, not bound by any constraint that they did not impose upon themselves. Otherwise, the set of referents designated by the word would surely not have expanded nearly so rapidly or extensively as it did within a decade and a half of its initial appearance.

Ironically, though, none of the architects of the process demonstrated much self-awareness as they undertook their creative act. Instead, Alice-like, they persuaded themselves that the concept 'antisemitism' was not something that they had invented, adopted, and defined for their own purposes but was instead a tangible quality possessing an objectively true, permanent meaning inscribed in an identifiable feature of the natural world. Early evidence of such an opinion was offered by the *Allgemeine Zeitung des Judenthums* in a July 1882 editorial, in which the writer (most likely Ludwig

---

[28] Langmuir, *Toward a Definition of Antisemitism*, 16. See also, *inter alia*, Ben Halpern, 'What Is Antisemitism?', *Modern Judaism*, 1 (1981), 251–62; David Berger, 'Anti-Semitism: An Overview', in id. (ed.), *History and Hate: The Dimensions of Anti-Semitism* (Philadelphia, 1986), 3–14; Robert S. Wistrich, *Antisemitism: The Longest Hatred* (New York, 1991), pp. xv–xxvi; Albert S. Lindemann, *Anti-Semitism before the Holocaust* (London, 2000), 8–12; Dina Porat and Kenneth S. Stern, 'Defining Antisemitism', *Antisemitism Worldwide* (2003/4), 5–28.

Philippson, the newspaper's editor) ventured that he had located 'the essential element of antisemitism'.[29] That essence, he claimed, was a more or less permanent feature of human nature; it was located in 'the two-headed drive to come together and then to separate again, to construct larger and smaller communities and then to leave them . . . to join with one's own kind and to exclude others'.[30] In Christian Europe, he continued, the natural exclusionary impulse 'not only kept people of other [non-Christian] religions out of heaven on dogmatic grounds but barred them from [obtaining] civic rights [*Bürgerrecht*] for practical reasons, wherever they could not be uprooted and extirpated'.[31] That impulse to disenfranchise, expel, and annihilate, he suggested, had been transferred to the contemporary German 'Antisemiten', who in turn had passed it on to all those in Austria, Hungary, and elsewhere who now displayed 'this spirit of hostility directed against a peaceable and defenceless part of the populace'.[32]

Identifying 'antisemitism' as a timeless 'spirit' possessing an 'essence' that was a fairly permanent feature of human social behaviour implied that that spirit could exist independently of what any particular 'antisemite' said or did. Indeed, that implication was reflected in a sudden expansion not only of the word's referents but of its range of permissible linguistic usages—an expansion first evident around the time the article appeared. Since the expression had entered public discourse a bit over a year earlier, it had not taken on predicates on its own, absent a specific human agent; only individual 'Antisemiten' or groups designated as 'antisemitisch' could act, not 'Antisemitismus' itself. Instead, 'Antisemitismus' had functioned as a grammatical object only, something that 'Antisemiten' produced. The editorial in the *Allgemeine Zeitung des Judenthums*, by contrast, contained a sentence that, from a semantic point of view, does not appear to have been conceivable earlier:[33] 'Antisemitism [first] raised its head in a few parts of the Prussian state, then it jumped over to Russia, where it celebrated with frightful orgies, finally making its way, following an abortive attempt in Vienna, to Hungary, where it played its latest trump card, the blood libel.'[34] In other words, whereas initially 'antisemitism' had been understood as the product of actions undertaken by 'antisemites', now cause and effect were reversed: the actions of 'antisemites' were figured as the product of an abstract, disembodied 'antisemitism', a quality that had existed long before it had been given its current name. It thus hardly seems accidental that, beginning in mid-1882, Germany's most widely circulated

---

[29] 'Der gegenwärtige Antisemitismus', 489–91.   [30] Ibid. 491.
[31] Ibid. 490.   [32] Ibid.
[33] This is not to say that the author of the text in question was the first to employ 'der Antisemitismus' as a grammatical subject. Most likely this usage had already spread orally. Nevertheless, the text does appear to be one of its earliest written attestations.
[34] 'Der gegenwärtige Antisemitismus', 489.

Jewish newspaper began dropping the quote marks that it had routinely placed around all words derived from the stem 'antisemit-' in 1880 and 1881.[35] 'Antisemitism' was becoming reified; it was being transmuted from a word into a thing.

But what sort of thing was it? That question exercised commentators from 1882 on. In that year a Jewish medical doctor from Odessa, Leo Pinsker, located the cause of the recent so-called 'Southern Storms' in the Russian empire in a nervous condition he termed 'Judophobie', ostensibly an aberrant manifestation of another universal, eternal feature of the human psyche—fear of ghosts. That aberration, he declared, had manifested itself many times throughout the centuries after the Jewish people had lost its political independence, in 'all manner of [false] accusations', as well as in 'acts of violence, contemptuous envy, [and even] under the guise of tolerance and protection'.[36] Although Pinsker did not label these various manifest-ations 'antisemitism', his 'Judophobie' was easily assimilated to the term, to the point where the two words came quickly to designate both all manner of hostile behaviour towards Jews or Jewish interests and such behaviour's purported wellspring in the human psyche. Indeed, by the early 1890s speaking about 'antisemitism' as a type of psychopathology appears to have become quite common. An 1891 paper by a Viennese Jewish social econo-mist, Markus Ettinger, on the 'psychology and ethics of antisemitism in antiquity, the Middle Ages, and modern times', for example, characterized the 'essence' of 'this monstrous child of Ahriman' as a specific emotional dis-order, sufferers from which fail to recover from the 'unavoidable childhood illness' of 'pure animalistic egoism' and as a result never develop a proper ethical sensibility.[37]

The prospect of linking all acts and utterances threatening Jews or opposing Jewish interests to a diseased mental state (symbolized by the application of the single label 'antisemitism' to both behaviour and psycho-logical condition at once) was evidently welcomed by most who found the late nineteenth-century development of the antisemitic movement and its purported concomitants troubling. For one thing, it doubtless appealed to many on tactical grounds: being able to discredit the 'Antisemiten' and their supposed fellow travellers not only as atavistic reactionaries but as socio-paths added a potentially powerful weapon to the struggle against them. But even more, it appeared to support tactics with science. After all, if blood libels, physical attacks, restrictive legislation, social ostracism, unfavourable

[35] See above, n. 12.

[36] Leo Pinsker, *'Autoempanzipation!' Mahnruf an seine Stammesgenossen von einem russischen Juden*, 8th edn. (Berlin, 1936), 8–11.

[37] M. Ettinger, *Psychologie und Ethik des Antisemitismus im Alterthum, Mittelalter und in der Neuzeit* (Vienna, 1891), 5, 13.

literary, journalistic, or artistic portrayals, polemics against the Jewish religion, and public expressions of dissatisfaction with the role played by Jews in a country's cultural, economic, or political life were all cut from the same emotional cloth, as it were, then analysing all such phenomena under a single rubric was not merely a matter of utility; it was demanded by nature. Those who employed such an expansive analytical category could thus feel certain that they were on the right track: to their minds they had not created a folder labelled 'antisemitism' according to their own lights but had found it ready-made in the sensible universe, and as they continued to study its contents they would surely discover additional objective, essential truths about it.

By the early twentieth century, however, doubts about both the usefulness of the linkage and its accuracy began to surface with increasing frequency. For one thing, the thought that menacing behaviour towards Jews might be the product of deeply rooted psychic drives cast doubt upon the ability of liberal political arrangements to obviate such conduct. For some, that doubt played directly into the hands of the 'Antisemiten' themselves. Hence the British Jewish liberal journalist and communal leader Lucien Wolf, for one, urged in 1910 that 'anti-Semitism' be considered 'exclusively a question of European politics', whose origin lay 'not in the long struggle between Europe and Asia, or between the Church and the Synagogue ... but in the social conditions resulting from the emancipation of the Jews in the middle of the 19th century'. When seen in this light, he suggested, the way to overcome its danger was clear: pursue a liberal programme to eliminate 'weak governments and ignorant and superstitious elements in the enfranchised classes', and all manner of threat against Jews would soon cease 'to play a part in politics'.[38] Wolf offered his suggestions, moreover, at a time when British Jewry as a whole was divided regarding both the sort of political behaviour that might be considered threatening and the motivations to which such behaviour might be attributed. To what extent, for example, did advocacy of encumbrances upon the immigration of east European Jews, one of the flagship demands of the prototypical German 'Antisemiten' in the 1880s and a hotly debated issue in Britain from the 1890s on, necessarily indicate 'fear of ghosts', 'animalistic egoism', or any other psychological aberration? Wolf found a 'trace' of the German movement's influence in Britain's Aliens Act of 1905, but his assessment merely begged the question of what such influence might reveal about the emotional state of the proponents of either one.[39] In any event, much of the British Jewish

---

[38] L[ucien] W[olf], 'Anti-Semitism', *Encyclopedia Britannica*, 11th edn. (New York, 1910), ii. 134–46: 134, 145. See also Mark Levene, *War, Jews, and the New Europe: The Diplomacy of Lucien Wolf* (Oxford, 1992), 13.   [39] W[olf], 'Anti-Semitism', 145.

leadership was unwilling to equate 'anti-alienism' with 'antisemitism', let alone to detect in the former any symptom of pathology.⁴⁰

A similar difficulty in applying the concept of 'antisemitism' as it had come to be understood in common discourse surfaced in the Russian empire around the same time. In 1910 the Polish caucus in the Russian State Duma had supported a bill to establish elective municipal councils in Congress Poland with significant restrictions upon Jewish participation. The Polish delegates did so even though the bill awarded disproportionate representation to ethnic Russians and demoted the status of the Polish language; in their eyes, those defects were outweighed by the law's explicit rejection of political equality for Jews.⁴¹ In response, Vladimir Jabotinsky, writing in the Russian newspaper *Odesskie novosti*, proclaimed that 'a disease' had taken hold of 'very broad circles of the [Polish] community', one that had caused 'the antisemitism of the Poles [to] erase the Jews even from the category . . . of those who might one day be able to expect justice'.⁴² For Jabotinsky it was clear both that the Polish legislators' action belonged to the category 'antisemitism' and that it testified to a fundamental spiritual 'aberration'.⁴³ However, other Jewish observers disputed his assessment. According to his fellow Zionist from Odessa, Moshe Kleinmann, the Polish delegates had behaved in accordance with a rational assessment of their community's interests. In his words, the Poles were striving 'to create a bourgeois class *of their own* and to force us . . . to retreat from the leading ranks of this important social stratum'. That desire, in turn, stemmed in his view from 'a natural *and fundamentally just national awakening*'. Hence, he reasoned, 'this is not *antisemitism*, because it is not *hatred* of Jews that inspires such actions'.⁴⁴ Kleinmann did not deny that the Polish vote severely threatened the Jews' position in the Polish Kingdom; he asserted only that the vote had not been motivated by a desire to do Jews harm. Moreover, he reserved use of the label 'antisemitism' only for actions that *were* so motivated. In other words, he questioned the essential linkage between threatening behaviour and mental configuration that had become commonplace in critical analyses of 'antisemitism' as the term was becoming reified, and he called for restriction of the label to the subset of threatening incidents where the linkage could be clearly shown.

Such questioning and such calls increased following the First World War, in the context of violent attacks upon Jews on a historically unprecedented

⁴⁰ Eugene C. Black, *The Social Politics of Anglo-Jewry 1880–1920* (Oxford, 1988), 292–309.

⁴¹ David Engel, 'The Polish Question and the Zionist Movement: The Debate over Municipal Self-Government in Congress Poland, 1910–1911' (Heb.), *Gal-Ed*, 13 (1993), 65–72.

⁴² V. Jabotinsky, 'Polyaki i evrei', in *Polyaki i evrei: Materialy o pol'sko-evreiskom spore po povodu zakonoproekta o gorodskom samoupravlenii v Pol'she* (Odessa [1911]), 9–29: 11, 28.

⁴³ Ibid. 28.

⁴⁴ M. Kleinmann, 'Lishelat hayehudim bepolin' [On the Question of the Jews in Poland], *Hashiloah*, 24 (Mar. 1911), 199–200; emphasis in source.

scale and organized efforts in many of the new states of east-central Europe to curb purported Jewish influence. Among other things, the liberal rhetoric that surrounded the post-war peace settlements created a semantic climate in which the stem 'antisemit-' acquired pejorative overtones; few sought the mantle of the failed German political movement that had originally borne the appellation with pride. As a result, many proponents of *numerus clausus* legislation, boycotts of Jewish businesses, bans on kosher slaughtering, or incentives to Jews to migrate elsewhere—all omnipresent features of inter-war Jewish life in several east-central European countries—vigorously eschewed the 'antisemitic' label, denying any particular anti-Jewish animus by explaining, in the fashion of Polish Sejm deputy and newspaper editor Bogusław Miedziński, that 'personally I like the Danes very much, but if there were three million of them in Poland [the approximate Jewish population between the wars] I would pray to God to take them from here as soon as possible'.[45] For their part, Jewish observers regularly rose to the bait, to the point where in 1926 the Dutch Jewish journalist Fritz Bernstein complained of a 'confusion of terminology' that had 'cursed every conversation about antisemitism and antisemitic incidents with the impossibility of mutual understanding' and caused 'many serious investigations [of the subject] to fail':[46]

Scholars and laymen alike argue about what antisemitism really is in essence. . . . An ordinary person . . . can distinguish with complete confidence between a live cat and a dead one. . . . But one cannot determine with the same degree of certainty whether an incident that many people regard as unquestionably antisemitic really deserves that designation or not. By the same token, it can be said that there has not been even a single antisemitic occurrence whose antisemitic character has not been simultaneously denied with absolute conviction. And such denial does not always come from the antisemites, who often regard the term as an accusation against them and thus reject it. Jews, too, and often Jews who are injured [by the incident] often stubbornly and even vehemently reject its antisemitic character, although every bystander regards it as a clearly antisemitic episode.[47]

Bernstein believed such confusion to be a serious obstacle to 'banishing the distressing phenomenon known today as antisemitism'.[48] Especially since the Nazi rise to power his concern has been widely shared by historians, who have persuaded themselves that by pursuing their discipline with proper dispassion they could identify 'cut-off points which define *essential* antisemitism'[49] and determine thereby 'whether all of the various mani-

[45] Quoted in Władysław Pobóg-Malinowski, *Najnowsza historia polityczna Polski* (London, 1983), ii. 810.
[46] Peretz Bernstein, *Antisemitism as a Social Phenomenon* [Ha'antishemiyut ketofa'ah ḥevratit] (Tel Aviv, 1980), 42.   [47] Ibid. 33.   [48] Ibid. 31.
[49] Halpern, 'What Is Antisemitism?', 253.

festations of hatred and rejection of Jews and Judaism throughout the generations, which since the final quarter of the nineteenth century have been called antisemitism, constitute a single phenomenon, or whether [antisemitism] is merely a common label for a range of social, political, and psychological phenomena that have been lumped together for terminological convenience'.[50] For all of their efforts, however, they have been unable to produce a universally agreed algorithm for resolving Bernstein's conundrum. Many proposals have been advanced, to be sure, but they often fail to generate even the full set of behaviours that their authors designate as 'antisemitism'.[51]

The reason why eighty years of intellectual exertion have yielded such paltry results appears to be fundamentally semantic. Historians' attempts to define 'antisemitism' have generally proceeded from the premise adumbrated in the *Allgemeine Zeitung des Judenthums* in 1882—that the behaviours that properly bore the label were all a function of some recognizable state of mind. As a result, the problem of definition has commonly been understood as identifying that state—or, in semantic terms, adducing a natural basis for including some utterances and actions that Jews have found threatening within the category 'antisemitism' while excluding others. Unfortunately for all those who have tried to do so, however, decades of extensive empirical investigation of thousands of threatening utterances and actions have failed to show any consistent link between attitudes and behaviours. Indeed, what are often regarded as clear instances of 'antisemitism' were actually composite acts of plural actors who appear, to the extent that their motivations can be determined at all, to have responded to a wide variety of mental stimuli. The participants in the Dresden Congress, for example, turn out to have been a motley group who did what they did out of disparate motives and

[50] Shmuel Ettinger, *Modern Antisemitism: Studies and Essays* [Ha'antishemiyut ba'et haḥadashah] (Tel Aviv, 1978), p. ix.

[51] Robert Wistrich, for example, has defined 'antisemitism' as a 'peculiar brand of social hostility' that nonetheless differs from 'the normal, xenophobic prejudice which has prevailed between ethno-religious groups during virtually every period of history' (Wistrich, *The Longest Hatred*, p. xviii). Yet that definition hardly comports with his assertion that '37 per cent of blacks as against 20 per cent of whites [in the United States in 1990] score as antisemitic, with particular emphasis in the black community on the perceived business power of the Jews. However, this prejudice is not significantly greater than that which blacks hold towards other white groups' (ibid. 132). If, according to Wistrich, there is nothing peculiar about black attitudes regarding Jews, what justification is there for labelling them 'antisemitism' instead of 'normal, xenophobic prejudice'? Wistrich appears to have bowed to common usage, in which 'antisemitism' 'denot[es] *all* forms of hostility towards Jews and Judaism throughout history', his insistence that 'there is clearly a danger in using antisemitism in this overly generalised way' notwithstanding (ibid., p. xvi). For a similar example of incongruence between definition and referents, see Bernard Lewis, *Semites and Anti-Semites: An Inquiry into Conflict and Prejudice* (New York, 1986), 20–2, 97–8.

with disparate aims. Much the same can be said about the rioters who attacked Jewish homes and businesses in parts of France during the Dreyfus affair, the perpetrators of deadly violence against Jews in Poland following the Holocaust, and the American respondents to a 1955 survey who indicated that they would strongly object to having a Jewish neighbour.[52] 'Antisemitic' threats to Jews thus cannot be distinguished from other sorts on the basis on some purported common mental genotype.

Nor does there appear to be any other possible 'natural' basis for distinction. In the end, it seems, 'antisemitism' is indeed an invented analytical category, not a discovered one. As such, its boundaries are arbitrary: no statement about what 'antisemitism' is or is not can compel acceptance except by social agreement. Historians who are dissatisfied with the common practice of considering virtually the entire set of behaviours that Jews find threatening under a single analytical rubric thus have but one choice: to devise their own schemes for dividing the set in ways that best help them find answers to the questions that prompt their research.

*

In a sense, that is what Gavin Langmuir tried to do. First, he limited his gaze to threatening 'verbal behaviour' only, ignoring physical violence, legislation, social ostracisim, or any other actions normally counted as 'antisemitism' in common discourse. He then divided that subset further into three classes—'realistic', 'xenophobic', and 'chimerical' assertions—according to certain perceived 'formal characteristics'.[53] He also explained why he imposed this particular conceptual grid on the data that interested him instead of considering all expressions of 'hostility [towards Jews] that went beyond what [Christian] faith necessitated' as of a single piece: 'I was looking backward from Hitler . . . My conception of antisemitism depended . . . on empirical studies of various examples of prejudice by sociologists and psychologists, and on the facts of the "Final Solution".'[54] To him, the Nazi Holocaust was predicated upon chimerical assertions about Jews—'propositions that . . . attribute . . . to an outgroup and all its members characteristics that have never been empirically observed'.[55] Hence he separated all such assertions throughout history into their own analytical category, in order to determine when the particular cognitive structure that he presumed animated the Nazi war against the Jews had first appeared in time and to

---

[52] Stephen Wilson, *Ideology and Experience: Antisemitism in France at the Time of the Dreyfus Affair* (Rutherford, NJ, 1982), 106–65; David Engel, 'Patterns of Anti-Jewish Violence in Poland 1944–1946', *Yad Vashem Studies*, 26 (1998), 43–85; Charles Herbert Stember et al., *Jews in the Mind of America* (New York, 1966), 95–9.
[53] Langmuir, *Toward a Definition of Antisemitism*, 326–8.   [54] Ibid. 5.   [55] Ibid. 328.

'suggest why it had appeared then and there'.[56] To that category alone he reserved the label 'antisemitism'. 'Xenophobic' assertions about Jews were catalogued separately as 'anti-Judaism', while 'realistic' assertions (along with all threatening non-verbal behaviour) were effectively ignored.

Langmuir's Humpty Dumpty-like assertion of mastery over his professional vocabulary departed significantly from earlier discussions of his subject, which had proceeded from Alice's assumption that the meaning of 'antisemitism' cannot be a matter of individual choice. Unfortunately, instead of creating new labels of his own for his personal analytical categories, he persisted in using 'antisemitism' to designate one of them. Moreover, he represented his work not as an explanation of his idiosyncratic usage but as a statement of what 'antisemitism' *really* 'is'. Both moves created a semantic red herring that soon led him and others astray.

The effects of the red herring were evident first of all in responses that questioned the validity of the definition he proposed. One critic, evidently taken aback by the prospect that, according to Langmuir's proposal, 'Adolf Stoecker was not an anti-Semite', wondered 'how far such [a] definition . . . can deviate from accepted [common] usage before [its] usefulness is compromised'.[57] Another enquired whether 'the distinction . . . between anti-Judaism and anti-Semitism *really* hold[s]', noting that there were 'already signs of anti-Jewish persecution and hatred during . . . periods in which presumably only anti-Judaism was present'.[58] Neither reviewer understood that Langmuir had deviated from common usage and drawn his distinction not in order to provide insight into 'anti-Jewish persecution and hatred' in general but solely to answer a specific historical question: under what circumstances did a particular cognitive structure implicated in the Holocaust first appear? Langmuir's categories were created specifically to answer that question; they had no significance beyond that context. Using 'antisemitism' as a label for one of them, however, and representing the category it signified as the term's objective 'definition' deflected attention from his thesis about the ideological origins of the Final Solution and sent discussion in a direction that had spent itself long since.

Constituting 'antisemitism' as an object of study thus seriously muddled the reception of a major part of Langmuir's work. It has similarly harmed other projects and discussions as well.[59] As it happens, all of these difficulties

---

[56] Langmuir, *Toward a Definition of Antisemitism*, 3.

[57] David Berger in the *American Historical Review*, 96 (1991), 1499.

[58] Daniel Lasker in *Speculum*, 68 (1993), 827; emphasis added.

[59] Space does not permit elaboration. For more extended discussions of two problems, semantic reversal and conflation of speech and action, see David Engel, *Semantics and Politics in the Description of Polish–Jewish Relations* [Semantikah ufolitikah bete'ur hayehasim bein hapolanim layehudim] (Tel Aviv, 1990), esp. pp. 10–13; see also Engel in the *American Historical Review*, 111 (2006), 1280–1.

could have been avoided had the term 'antisemitism' been removed from the discussion and attention focused exclusively on the specific behaviour at issue.[60] Indeed, where contemporaries seeking to shield themselves from a variety of threats may have benefited at different times by lumping all threats together in a single category or dividing them according to the threateners' presumed mental state, it is not self-evident that historians will derive similar benefit from employing the same conceptual grid. On the contrary, for historians nothing *denotative* will change about the events in question if data about the 1910 vote of the Polish caucus, advocacy of immigration restrictions in Britain, or, for that matter, the riots against Jews in Alexandria in 38 CE, are grouped together with other injuries to Jewish interests and labelled 'antisemitism', grouped with alternative bits of data under a different heading, or analysed separately, each in their own right, any more than Pluto changed when it was transferred from one category of celestial bodies to another. All that will change are the historians' own subjective perceptions of the data and insights into them. Historians are free constantly to adjust their categories in ways that will enhance their insights into data and problems of interest to them at any moment. There is thus no reason why they cannot divide and redivide data that common discourse terms 'antisemitism' into ad hoc analytical categories according to their individual research agendas, or why they must retain 'antisemitism' as a label for any of them.

To put the matter another way: throughout the centuries many people have behaved violently towards Jews. Many have depicted them verbally or artistically in derogatory fashion, agitated publicly for their subjection to legal discrimination, discriminated against them socially, or privately felt varying degrees of prejudice towards or emotional revulsion from them. However, no necessary relation among particular instances of violence, hostile depiction, agitation, discrimination, and private unfriendly feeling across time and space can be assumed. Indeed, none has ever been demonstrated. Historians who, by treating some or all such instances as part of a general 'history of antisemitism' and theorizing about how the subject of that ostensible history should be defined, have nevertheless made such an assumption have done so on the basis not of empirical observation but of a socio-semantic convention created in the nineteenth century and sustained throughout the twentieth for communal and political ends, not scholarly ones. Hence eschewing 'antisemitism' as a ready-made category and seeking new frameworks for analysing its traditional constituent elements may well have a salutary effect on historical research.

[60] For an example of a study that follows this approach, see David Nirenberg, *Communities of Violence: Persecution of Minorities in the Middle Ages* (Princeton, 1996).

THREE

Does Gender Matter?

Locating Women in European Jewish History

PAULA E. HYMAN

THE EMERGENCE OF GENDER AS A
HISTORICAL TOOL

ABOUT a generation ago gender entered the lexicon of scholars of history. The feminist movement that emerged in the United States as well as in western and central Europe in the late 1960s and early 1970s led to the recognition that women's experience had been ignored in virtually all historical study. Historians had assumed either that women shared in the broad contours of historical development, and hence were subsumed in historical writing even if the overt subjects of the historical narrative were all male, or they deemed women historically insignificant because the vast majority of women had been excluded from the very stuff of history, i.e. politics and thought. The development of social history in the 1960s paved the way for the scholarly investigation of women and, later, of gender. In conferring historical significance on the activity of ordinary people and transforming them from the objects of historical forces to agents in the making of history, social history changed the parameters of historical significance so radically that women, and their traditional concerns, appeared worthy of consideration. The emergence of cultural history in the past two decades has expanded opportunities for gender analysis by highlighting the cultural discourse around persons and events.

The early efforts at recovering the historical experience of women addressed American history, and several books by historians of American women were published in the early 1970s. Gerda Lerner's *The Woman in American History*, which appeared in 1971, was among the very first.[1] By 1977 the first collection of articles on women in European history, *Becoming Visible*, had been published.[2] That book included essays from the ancient period to the twentieth century, raising issues that stimulated further scholarship. It

[1] Gerda Lerner, *The Woman in American History* (Menlo Park, Calif., 1971).
[2] Renate Bridenthal and Claudia Koonz (eds.), *Becoming Visible: Women in European History* (Boston, 1977).

was quickly followed by documentary collections and pioneering studies of women's status in modern Europe.[3] In its first years, the emerging field of women's history did not necessarily use the category of gender as an analytical tool, but as a synonym for women. Joan Wallach Scott's *Gender and the Politics of History*, which brought together a series of articles published in the early and mid-1980s, demonstrated the utility of the term 'gender' as a theoretical category for all historians—one that addressed relations of power.[4] Moreover, as a relational category gender, the socially and culturally constructed division of the sexes, cast light on men as well as women. Because Scott was widely recognized as a scholar of European history, she spoke to a broad audience of specialists in that field.

Nonetheless, gender-sensitive scholarship on the field of Jewish history has been particularly slow to make an impact. The emphasis on the study of rabbinic texts, from which women were largely excluded until the late twentieth century, as a necessity even for historians of Jews in the modern period led to a paucity of female scholars. It is no accident that women students of Jewish history were drawn to the subject of American Jewish history, itself a marginalized field, that did not privilege the knowledge of classical Jewish texts. There were some female pioneers in the study of European Jewry— Selma Stern-Täubler comes most readily to mind—but a cadre of women scholars who were most receptive to gender-sensitive scholarship was not in place until the 1980s. In this essay I will highlight the areas where gender-sensitive scholarship has recently made its mark in modern European Jewish history and suggest areas for future research.

The social-historical approach to Jewish history, which laid the groundwork for the investigation of women's roles, had emerged among Jewish historians largely in Poland in the inter-war years, when a number of practitioners of social history began their pioneering work. However, the Holocaust severed the continuity between them and a younger generation of historians trained in the United States and Israel. Moreover, with the notable exceptions of Salo Baron and Jacob Katz, scholars assumed that Jewish history was rooted virtually exclusively in intellectual history; for the most part, it explored the development of classical Jewish texts, sometimes in their contexts, as well as the ideological movements those texts represented. The

[3] See e.g. Eleanor S. Riemer and John C. Fout (eds.), *European Women: A Documentary History, 1789–1945* (New York, 1980); Priscilla Robertson, *An Experience of Women: Pattern and Change in Nineteenth-Century Europe* (Philadelphia, 1982); Patricia Labalme (ed.), *Beyond their Sex: Learned Women of the European Past* (New York, 1980); Marilyn J. Boxer and Jean H. Quataert (eds.), *Connecting Spheres: Women in the Western World, 1500 to the Present* (New York, 1987); Bonnie S. Anderson and Judith P. Zinsser, *A History of Their Own: Women in Europe from Prehistory to the Present* (New York, 1988); and Bonnie G. Smith, *Changing Lives: Women in European History Since 1700* (Lexington, Mass., 1989).

[4] Joan Wallach Scott, *Gender and the Politics of History* (New York, 1988).

texts ranged from halakhic literature, including responsa, to biblical interpretation and liturgy, but also extended to philosophical excurses and historical
and scientific writings. Communal institutions, whose *pinkasim* (minute-
books) have survived, provided the basis for the historians who investigated
how Jews governed themselves and interacted, through their leaders, with
the non-Jewish authorities. The impact of those authorities on the fate of the
Jews was duly noted. Although Jews lacked the kings and armies that peopled
the pages of world history, their central figures—the rabbis, scholars, economic elites, and communal leaders—were just as consistently male as were
the 'movers and shakers' of general history. Even the unusual women who left
written documentation, testimony, behind, such as the seventeenth-century
merchant widow Glikl of Hameln, were often dismissed as curiosities. When
in the early twentieth century the great scholar and president of the Jewish
Theological Seminary of America, Solomon Schechter, wrote an essay on
Glikl, which he included in his collections of occasional pieces, he referred
to her rather dismissively as 'a simple-minded woman,' even though he
recognized the uniqueness of her memoirs and commented on the value of
memoirs as sources.[5] He was able to see her only as a widow and mother.

The growing recognition of women's history and of the utility of gender
as an analytical tool to explore issues of power has spurred gender-sensitive
scholarship throughout the academy. Gender has now joined class and race
to form the tripartite basis of personal and group identity. Whereas references to women a generation ago were often limited in standard works of
modern European Jewish history to discussions of the salon Jewesses, as in
Jacob Katz's *Out of the Ghetto* and Michael Meyer's *The Origins of the Modern
Jew*, virtually every contemporary publication in the field pays obeisance to
the fact that women's roles and the attitudes towards women feature prominently in all periods and places.[6] Many scholars who previously did not pay
much attention to women and gender have now included them in their
research agenda. Indeed, the proliferation of research on women and gender
in both American and Israeli scholarship in Jewish history is striking. The
growing acceptance of gender as a category in Israeli scholarship was
signalled by the coining of a new word in Hebrew, *migdar*, to differentiate
gender, the socially constructed division of the sexes, from sex, the biological
distinction of male and female.[7] Scholars who specialize in social and

[5] Solomon Schechter, ' The Memoirs of a Jewess of the Seventeenth Century', *Studies in Judaism*, 2nd ser. (Philadelphia: Jewish Publication Society, 1908), 126–47: 128.
[6] Jacob Katz, *Out of the Ghetto: The Social Background of Jewish Emancipation* (Cambridge, Mass., 1973); Michael A. Meyer, *The Origins of the Modern Jew: Jewish Identity and European Culture in Germany, 1749–1824* (Detroit, 1967).
[7] Current scholarship recognizes the possibility of more than two sexual identities, and a spectrum of sexualities. See e.g. Joanne J. Meyerowitz, *How Sex Changed: A New History of Transsexuality in the United States* (Cambridge, Mass., 2002).

cultural history have foregrounded gender in much of their work, but European Jewish historians as a whole have yet to grapple with the implications of the recently published studies.

THE IMPACT OF WOMEN'S HISTORY ON JEWISH HISTORY

Gerda Lerner, the doyenne of women's history, distinguished two forms of women's history: the first stage of the recuperation of women from their invisibility in historical scholarship—compensatory history—and the second stage of contesting conventional interpretation and reshaping the paradigms of the field. It was not enough, she pointed out, to 'Add women and stir.' If I may continue her female culinary imagery, it was necessary to recalibrate the recipe.[8] Some early work did just that. Joan Kelly(-Gadol)'s essay, 'Did Women Have a Renaissance?' demonstrated that the inclusion of women in the study of the Renaissance necessitated rethinking the periodization of early modern history. Women did have a Renaissance, she concluded, just not during the period we commonly label the Renaissance. Therefore, the nature of the Renaissance as conventionally defined had to be rethought. Most scholarship on women and gender falls between Lerner's two poles, the recovery of those made invisible and the reshaping of the field; no new approach should be expected to reshape the field with every piece of scholarship. Important in the development of historiography are the adjustments, or refinements, in interpretation that new perspectives introduce, in addition to the radical transformation of historical understanding.

In the field of European Jewish history the 'discovery' of women and gender has led to a rethinking of such central categories of the modern Jewish experience as the processes of assimilation, the nature of Jewish identity-formation, and the very definition of Judaism, all of which offer the potential for paradigm shifts. More often, it has filled in gaps in our historical knowledge and suggested new subjects for study, including the subject of the social experience of women itself. So, for example, Moshe Rosman has undertaken an investigation of the roles of Jewish women in early modern Jewish society in Poland. In challenging some of the feminist conventional wisdom about women in traditional east European Jewish society, including the notion of the housewife as the central breadwinner, Rosman has approached the subject with a combination of his customary judiciousness

[8] The remark is attributed to Gerda Lerner. In essays published in the 1970s and collected in her *The Majority Finds its Past* (New York, 1979), Lerner expressed her dissatisfaction with 'compensatory history' and called for a paradigm shift (pp. 145–80).

and provocativeness.[9] In the case of the Holocaust, we are now aware of the role gender played in the experience of Jews as victims, survivors, and sometimes as collaborators, even as some critics have reacted to the new scholarship as if it were blasphemy. As Gabriel Schoenfeld, editor of *Commentary*, wrote in that journal in an assessment of academic approaches to the Holocaust, 'the worst excesses of all on today's campuses are being committed . . . by the voguish hybrid known as gender-studies'.[10] Yet, gender-sensitive scholarship in no way overturns the consensus that the ultimate determinant of Jewish fate under the Nazis was the racial antisemitism that marked every individual defined as a Jew for death. As a number of studies have demonstrated, focusing on gender allows us to identify just how their gender affected the ways Jewish men and Jewish women experienced Nazi policy, both in the camps as well as in efforts at passing and in resistance.[11] Similarly, in relation to a much earlier period, sensitivity to women and gender has enabled us better to understand the workings of Converso Judaism and the nature of the culture that Conversos transmitted within their households.[12] Given the domestic locale of much of the secret Jewish practice of Conversos, women bore the burden of performing, and also concealing Jewish ritual.

The study of the family as a historical agent as well as an object of governmental policy has expanded dramatically under the impact of gender-sensitive scholarship. To be sure, Jacob Katz had pioneered in the field with his 1944 article, 'Marriage and Sexual Life among the Jews at the End of the Middle Ages',[13] but, while granting that women were sexual beings entitled to sexual pleasure, he approached sexuality from a male perspective and was largely concerned with the discussion of male sexual issues, especially nocturnal emission, in responsa literature of the early modern period. His later sociological study, 'Family, Kinship, and Marriage among Ashkenazim in the 16th–18th Centuries',[14] analysed the structure of the Jewish family, its

[9] Moshe Rosman, 'The History of Jewish Women in Early Modern Poland: An Assessment', in ChaeRan Freeze, Paula Hyman, and Antony Polonsky (eds.), *Polin*, 18: *Jewish Women in Eastern Europe* (Oxford, 2005), 25–56.

[10] Gabriel Schoenfeld, 'Auschwitz and the Professors', *Commentary*, 105/6 (June 1998), 42–6. An abridged version of the piece was published in the *Wall Street Journal*.

[11] See Dalia Ofer and Lenore Weitzman (eds.), *Women in the Holocaust* (New Haven, 1998); Judith Tydor Baumel, *Double Jeopardy: Gender and the Holocaust* (London, 1998); and Carol Rittner and John K. Roth (eds.), *Different Voices : Women and the Holocaust* (New York, 1993). A pioneering study of women under Nazism that included a chapter on Jews is Claudia Koonz, *Mothers in the Fatherland: Women, the Family, and Nazi Politics* (New York, 1987). See also the early collection, Renate Bridenthal, Atina Grossman, and Marion Kaplan (eds.), *When Biology Became Destiny: Women in Weimar and Nazi Germany* (New York, 1984).

[12] See Renée Levine Melammed, *Heretics or Daughters of Israel? The Crypto-Jewish Women of Castile* (Oxford, 1999).

[13] (Heb.), *Zion*, 10 (1944), 21–54.   [14] *Jewish Journal of Sociology*, 1 (1959), 4–22.

method of establishment, and the constraints imposed on it by communal norms, noting also the introduction in the modern period of erotic consider-ations, for women as well as men, and autonomy in selecting a spouse. Reflecting the changes in scholarship inspired by feminist historiography, two collections of articles on the Jewish family, both products of confer-ences, raised questions about the culture of family life at different times.[15] These international conferences encouraged scholars to consider how their research contributed to our understanding of the Jewish family and how new insight into the family could illuminate other aspects of Jewish culture.

Participants in these conferences responded to the challenge. In 1981 Gershon Hundert linked the rise of hasidism to the proliferation of young people in eighteenth-century Poland, thereby adding an unexplored social and demographic dimension to the study of the beginnings of the move-ment.[16] Several years later, Immanuel Etkes presented his initial findings and thoughts on the family life of the Lithuanian rabbinic elite, the *lomedim*, demonstrating the social consequences of traditional patterns of learning. His invitation to the conference on the Jewish family held at the Jewish Theological Seminary presented him with an appropriate context to present his research.[17] In her prizewinning study of Jewish families in the Second Reich, *The Making of the Jewish Middle Class*, Marion Kaplan examined the modern German Jewish bourgeois family as the site of social change and cul-tural transmission.[18] Her focus on the family, as I will address further, led to a reconsideration of the nature of the assimilation of German Jews in the nineteenth century. She has also analysed the central role of the family as Jews responded to Nazi persecution in Germany.[19] ChaeRan Freeze's *Jewish Marriage and Divorce in Imperial Russia*[20] not only explored the dynamics of family life in a turbulent period but also illuminated the intrusion of governmental policy into the intimate lives of the masses of Russian Jews.

---

[15] Steven M. Cohen and Paula E. Hyman (eds.), *The Jewish Family: Myths and Reality* (New York, 1986), and David Kraemer (ed.), *The Jewish Family: Metaphor and Memory* (New York, 1989).

[16] Gershon David Hundert, 'Approaches to the History of the Jewish Family in Early Modern Poland–Lithuania', in Cohen and Hyman (eds.), *The Jewish Family: Myths and Reality*, 17–28.

[17] Immanuel Etkes, 'Marriage and Torah Study among the Lomdim in Lithuania in the Nineteenth Century', in Kraemer (ed.), *The Jewish Family: Metaphor and Memory*, 153–78, and *Lithuania in Jerusalem: The Learning Elite in Lithuania and the Community of the Perushim in Jerusalem in Light of the Correspondence and Writings of R. Shemuel of Kelm* [Lita beyerushalayim: ha'ilit halamdanit belita uvekehilat haperushim biyerushalayim le'or igerot ukhetavim shel r. shemuel mikelm] (Jerusalem, 1991).

[18] Marion A. Kaplan, *The Making of the Jewish Middle Class: Women, Family, and Identity in Imperial Germany* (New York, 1991).

[19] Marion A. Kaplan, *Between Dignity and Despair: Jewish Life in Nazi Germany* (New York, 1998). [20] Hanover, NH, 2002.

She showed how state policy designed with one purpose in mind, to assert tighter control over Russian Jewry by undermining traditional rabbinic authority and to foster Russification, had unanticipated negative consequences, making it more difficult for liberal forces within the Orthodox rabbinic leadership to improve the marital situation of women.

What happened within the walls of the family home was once seen as fodder for novelists and psychologists, not for historians. Yet now historians recognize the family as a critical institution mediating between the individual and the larger society. Acknowledging the centrality of the home as a historical site goes hand in hand with acknowledging the role of women as historical actors. Despite the role of the male as paterfamilias, the home was seen in both pre-modern and modern times as the sphere in which women were primarily engaged. Needless to say, gaining access to the private realm of the home and family requires ingenuity in ferreting out new sources—court records have proven quite useful—and the willingness to make greater use of such documents as personal diaries, letters, and memoirs. Although memoirs have to be read carefully and interpreted for the author's intent, it is regrettable that some historians are so quick to dismiss them as unreliable, since they are critical in the writing of women's history. However frustrating the research, investigating private life yields a great deal of new information.[21] It is impossible to understand the identity-formation of children, for example, without some knowledge of what transpires within their homes. Adults, after all, model (or perform) for children how they are expected to behave, as well as (though not intentionally) the behaviour they should avoid. For European Jews in the nineteenth and twentieth centuries, as for stigmatized minorities in other times and places, the task of adults within the family was complicated by the necessity to raise children to retain their self-esteem in a less than welcoming larger society, and also to recognize the more subtle clues of social rejection.

Within the field of German Jewish history a team of international scholars has expanded research on the family to investigate the daily lives of Jews in Germany from the early modern era through the Nazi period.[22] In the daily life approach, the activity of women is fully integrated into the narrative; women's economic roles, religious life, organizations, and experiences in universities, in addition to their domestic routines, join with men's activity to construct Jewish familial and communal life. Because of the multinational, as well as transnational, dimensions of Jewish life in modern

[21] There has been considerable scholarship on private and family life in Europe. See e.g. *A History of Private Life*, gen. eds. Philippe Ariès and Georges Duby, 5 vols. (Cambridge, Mass., 1987–91), and André Burguière, Christiane Klapisch-Zuber, Martine Segalen, and François Zonabend (eds.), *A History of the Family*, 2 vols. (Cambridge, 1996).

[22] See Marion A. Kaplan (ed.), *Jewish Daily Life in Germany, 1618–1945* (Oxford, 2005).

Europe, it would be useful to write comparative histories of Jewish daily life throughout Europe, with due attention to the experiences of women and men. Such a project would enable historians to examine how different national cultures, civil structures, and associational patterns influenced Jews as they adapted to the conditions of modernity. And it would restore the experience of the individual men and women who comprised Jewish communities to discussions of otherwise generalized sociological and historical processes.

The family has attracted the most new historical attention, but Jewish women's organizations, and the role of women in Jewish social welfare work, and thereby in politics, have also become subjects of ongoing historical investigation. In general European historiography feminist movements, the struggle for suffrage, and the role of women in political efforts to legalize birth control, restrict commercialized vice, and promote international peace have expanded our understanding of politics.[23] So too in the study of European Jews. The role of Jewish women in publicly combating what was then called 'white slavery' and criticizing Jewish involvement in the phenomenon, at a time when male-dominated communal institutions preferred to sweep the matter under the rug, has pointed out that fault lines in the definition of communal policy were not limited to Zionism or social class.[24] In addition to providing information on political activity that affected the lives of the non-elites, and on activists who often laboured with little publicity in the international socialist and Zionist movements, these studies of women's organizations also highlight different social tensions in the world of politics than emerge from a consideration of national partisan politics. In particular, they point to the struggle of women to have a voice in Jewish as well as general political discourse. They also underline the linkage of philanthropy with political activity. For women, whose public activity was typically circumscribed, philanthropy often legitimated their entry into discussions of social policy and initiated their political engagement. Although there have been books on both German and British Jewish women's organizations and articles on Jewish women's involvement in transnational European and

[23] See e.g. Leila Rupp, *Worlds of Women: The Making of an International Women's Movement* (Princeton, 1997); Linda K. Schott, *Reconstructing Women's Thoughts: The Women's International League for Peace and Freedom before World War II* (Stanford, 1997); and Christine Bard, *Les Filles de Marianne: Histoire des féminismes 1914–1940* (Paris, 1995).

[24] See Marion Kaplan, *The Jewish Feminist Movement in Germany: The Campaigns of the Jüdischer Frauenbund, 1904–1938* (Westport, Conn., 1979); Edward Bristow, *Prostitution and Prejudice: The Jewish Fight against White Slavery 1870–1919* (New York, 1983); Linda Gordon Kuzmack, *Woman's Cause: The Jewish Women's Movement in England and the United States, 1881–1933* (Columbus, Ohio, 1990); Faith Rogow, *Gone to Another Meeting: The National Council of Jewish Women, 1893–1993* (Tuscaloosa, Ala., 1993); and Paula E. Hyman, 'The Jewish Body Politic: Gendered Politics in the Early Twentieth Century', *Nashim*, 2 (1999), 37–51.

European Jewish as well as local politics,[25] the subject has yet to be integrated into considerations of Jewish politics in modern Europe.

My final example of the middle-range impact of gender-sensitive history on Jewish historiography is the way in which attitudes towards women can disclose fundamental aspects of both general and Jewish ideological movements. The issue of Enlightenment attitudes towards the Jews has recently been explored anew, with several scholars suggesting that the status of European Jews can best be understood in terms of colonialism.[26] From this perspective, the Enlightenment created Jews as internal colonials while imperialism, which appeared somewhat later, created external colonials. The inclusion of gender would enrich the discussion of this historical analogy, especially since Jewish women were often orientalized, and their status within Judaism was seen as a sign of the general oriental nature of Jewish culture and religion. Thus, the inalterable 'otherness' of the Jew in modern Western culture was based not only on religious difference but on the recognition of biological and cultural distinction. The Jew was simply a non-European, and the Jewish woman all the more so. The gendered dimension of the orientalization of Jews in modern Europe calls out for investigation.

It is art historians who have taken the lead in demonstrating that women became the focal point for the assertion of the fundamental differentness even of the assimilated Jew, even before the eruption of modern political and racial antisemitism. Thus, Carol Ockman's study of the French painter Jean Auguste Dominique Ingres's 1848 portrait of the Baronne Betty de Rothschild compares it with portraits he painted of Christian aristocratic women and suggests that the shape of her eyebrows, her crossed knees, and her pose, leaning forward, serve as visual indicators of the subject's ethnicity (or better yet, race).[27] Ockman concludes that the contemporary remarks about the portrait by a visitor to Ingres's studio, who mentioned the Baronne's 'two large eyebrows à l'orientale' along with her liveliness, 'conjure up the world of the harem rather than that of the well-bred Western home'. The commentator's 'orientalist vocabulary' indicates that he viewed the portrait as a representation of 'the quintessential Jewish woman', 'a distinctly different type' than Ingres's other female sitters.[28] Extraordinary wealth was thus no guarantor of the complete erasure of marks of difference.

[25] Kuzmack, *Woman's Cause*; Kaplan, *Jewish Feminist Movement*; Hyman, 'The Jewish Body Politic', and 'The Transnational Experience of Jewish Women in Western and Central Europe after World War I', *Michael*, 16 (2004), 21–33; Daniel Blatman, 'Women in the Jewish Labor Bund', in Ofer and Weitzman (eds.), *Women in the Holocaust*, 68–84.

[26] Jonathan Hess, *Germans, Jews, and the Claims of Modernity* (New Haven, 2002) used the term 'internal colonials'. Earlier John Efron discussed Jews as colonials in his *Defenders of the Race: Jewish Doctors and Race Science in Fin-de-Siècle Europe* (New Haven, 1994), as did Susannah Heschel in her *Abraham Geiger and the Jewish Jesus* (Chicago, 1998).

[27] Carol Ockman, 'Two Large Eyebrows à l'Orientale: Ethnic Stereotyping in Ingres's *Baronne de Rothschild*', *Art History*, 14/4 (Dec. 1991), 521–39.   [28] Ibid. 523.

Similarly, in a series of later, *fin-de-siècle* portraits of the members of a prosperous Anglo-Jewish family, at a time when antisemitism was culturally acceptable in England as elsewhere in Europe, Kathleen Adler discovers anti-Jewish stereotyping even in portraits that the family liked.[29] John Singer Sargent painted twelve portraits of Asher Wertheimer, a prosperous and acculturated British art dealer of German origin, his wife, and various of his ten children between 1898 and 1908. He had many Jews among his clients and claimed to 'prefer painting Jewish women because they had "more life and movement" than English women'.[30] Yet by comparing the portraits of the Wertheimer daughters with those of other, non-ethnic British subjects whom Sargent painted, Adler discerns elements of stereotyping and orientalism in the Wertheimer portraits. She finds that the depictions of Ena and Betty, painted together, and separately, violated the conventions of demure daughters of respectable wealthy families. Their revealing dresses suggested that they were sexually bold, and, Adler concludes, Sargent depicted them as embodying 'the fantasy of the sexual Jewess'. A portrait of Ena in male military dress challenges sexual boundaries and 'explodes the conventional expectations of society portraiture'. Finally, the youngest daughter, Almina, is painted in oriental costume, pointing to the foreignness of Jewish women and playing with the stereotype of the exotic and beautiful Jewess.[31] The orientalized Jewish woman, while attractive to her viewers, was still remarked upon as different from her peers.

In literature as well as art the assimilated Jewish woman was often orientalized. Thus, in the Palliser novels Anthony Trollope depicts Madame Max Goesler in orientalist tropes. She is exotic, mysterious, rich, sexually tempting, and a Jew.[32] He specifically describes her at one point as seated on a sofa with her feet tucked beneath her, ' as though she were seated somewhere in the East'.[33] The great novelist Honoré de Balzac, too, uses orientalist stereotypes to depict Jewish women in several volumes of *La Comédie humaine*. Describing the Jewess Pauline in the 1832–3 novel *Louis Lambert*, Balzac enthuses, 'Her features offered in its greatest purity the character of the beautiful Jewess: those oval lines so large and virginal which have je ne sais quoi of the ideal and breathe the delights of the Orient . . .'.[34] Similarly,

---

[29] Kathleen Adler, 'John Singer Sargent's Portraits of the Wertheimer Family', in Linda Nochlin and Tamar Garb (eds.), *Jew in the Text: Modernity and the Construction of Identity* (London, 1995), 83–96. The article was reprinted in Norman Kleeblatt (ed.), *John Singer Sargent: Portraits of the Wertheimer Family* (New York, 1999).

[30] Ibid. 87.   [31] Ibid. 91 (first quote), 92 (second quote).

[32] See Bryan Cheyette, *Constructions of 'the Jew' in English Literature and Society* (Cambridge, 1993), 32.

[33] Anthony Trollope, *Phineas Finn* (1869), Everyman edn. (London, 1929), 180.

[34] Balzac, *Louis Lambert* (Paris, 1832–3), 422, as cited in Ockman, 'Two Large Eyebrows', 526. See also Luce A. Klein, *Portrait de la Juive dans la littérature française* (Paris, 1970), 101–80.

in his 1860 novel *Le Voyage en Italie* Théophile Gautier imagines the Jewish girls within ghetto houses in Venice in the following terms: 'Probably if one were to enter these houses . . . one would find . . . Rebeccas and Rachels of a radiant Oriental beauty . . .'.[35] The image of the beautiful, albeit oriental-ized, 'Jewess' seems to have persisted until the beginning of the twentieth century, when negative and overtly antisemitic stereotypes of Jewish women began to predominate.

Historians have yet to explore the meaning of, and the causes for, the dis-parity between the stereotype of the Jewish male and the Jewish female in nineteenth-century European culture. Scholars of literary, cultural, and art history have long noted that Jewish women enjoyed a seductive exoticism in the popular imagination while Jewish men were perceived as repellent and dangerous. In popular literature, Jewish women were considered admirable (although they did not become potential marriage partners unless they con-verted). For much of the nineteenth century, as the image of 'la belle Juive' dominated in the visual representation of Jewish women, she had no male counterpart because gender trumped the Jewishness of the female Jew as it could not for the male Jew. As is well known, the availability of the female of a subordinated group to the powerful males of the dominant group serves to highlight their dominance. The male of the subordinated group is often per-ceived as sexually threatening in a manner from which the female is exempt. Anthropological generalizations, however, cannot take the place of careful historical research, especially because gender distinctions play a central role in the development of antisemitic imagery and discourse throughout Europe. It is critical to investigate just how important the gendering of Jewish stereotypes was to the development of the political antisemitism that arose in the last third of the nineteenth century.

The impact of gender on Jewish identities as well as on antisemitism has begun to attract attention, but largely from the vantage point of Jewish men. The subject of Jewish masculinities, as seen both by Jews and non-Jews, has emerged as a key element in the understanding of antisemitism as well as in the Jewish male's response to antisemitism in the construction of his Jewish identity.[36] The exploration of models of masculinity in European Zionism has also highlighted the impact of *fin-de-siècle* antisemitism on the Zionist construction of the New Jew. The role of women in European Zionism,

---

[35] Gautier, *Le Voyage en Italie* (Paris, 1860), 313, as cited in Klein, *Portrait de la Juive*, 108.

[36] See Sander Gilman, *Jewish Self-Hatred: Anti-Semitism and the Hidden Language of the Jews* (Baltimore, 1986); id., *The Jew's Body* (New York, 1991); id., *Freud, Race, and Gender* (Princeton, 1993); id., *Love + Marriage = Death* (Stanford, 1998); id., 'Salome, Syphilis, Sarah Bernhardt, and the "Modern Jewess"', in Nochlin and Garb (eds.), *The Jew in the Text*, 80–101; and Daniel Boyarin, *Unheroic Conduct: The Rise of Heterosexuality and the Invention of the Jewish Man* (Berkeley, Calif., 1997).

however, has yet to figure in any significant way in histories of Zionism in Europe.[37]

Most importantly, little attention has been paid to the ways in which misogyny and antisemitism intersected in the representation of the Jewish female in Europe at the start of the twentieth century, to the impact of that representation on Jewish women's construction of their identities, or to the relations between Jewish men and women.[38] Sander Gilman, Daniel Boyarin, and John Efron have all acknowledged the need to explore how Jewish women saw their Jewish identity in a hostile cultural environment, but have themselves refrained from addressing the subject in any detail. Yet the issue of Jewish identities cannot be fully understood without including the subject of women in the scholarly discourse.

Finally, integrating gender in the study of the Jewish Enlightenment movement, the Haskalah, has demonstrated the limits of the Haskalah's notion of equality. Shmuel Feiner has written two important essays that explicitly use gender as, as he calls it, 'a test case' in exploring the attitudes of the Haskalah to modernity.[39] Haskalah attitudes towards women reveal a cultural conservatism, much in line with bourgeois thought in general, that denied to women full equality in the Jewish society of the Enlightened, just as the European Enlightenment had denied full equality to (male) Jews

[37] See Michael Berkowitz, *Zionist Culture and West European Jewry before the First World War* (Cambridge, 1993); Michael Stanislawski, *Zionism and the Fin-de-Siècle: Cosmopolitanism and Nationalism from Nordau to Jabotinsky* (Berkeley, Calif., 2001); and Boyarin, *Unheroic Conduct*. My *Gender and Assimilation in Modern Jewish History: The Roles and Representation of Women* (Seattle, 1995), 79–81, 142–6, discusses the role of women in Zionism, as does Ezra Mendelsohn's *Zionism in Poland: The Formative Years, 1915–1926* (New Haven, 1981), more briefly. Puah Rakovsky reflects on women in Zionism in her memoirs, which are available in Yiddish, Hebrew, and English. For the Yiddish original, see *Zikhroynes fun a yidisher revolutsiyonerin* [Memoirs of a Jewish (Female) Revolutionary] (Buenos Aires, 1954); for the English version, see Puah Rakovsky, *My Life as a Radical Jewish Woman: Memoirs of a Zionist Feminist in Poland* (Bloomington, 2002). The Hebrew translation is entitled *Lo nikhnati*, trans. David Kalai (Tel Aviv, 1951).

[38] See Hyman, *Gender and Assimilation, passim*, but in brief, unsystematic comments. Shulamit Volkov may have been the first to point out the connections between antisemitism and misogyny. See her pioneering article, 'Antisemitism as a Cultural Code—Reflections on the History and Historiography of Antisemitism in Imperial Germany', *Leo Baeck Institute Yearbook*, 23 (1978), 25–46.

[39] Shmuel Feiner, 'The Modern Jewish Woman: A Case Study in Haskalah Attitudes towards Modernity' (Heb.), *Zion*, 58 (1993), 453–99, and 'The Pseudo-Enlightenment and the Question of Jewish Modernization', *Jewish Social Studies*, 3 (1996), 66–88. For a study focusing on Haskalah literature, see Tova Cohen, *'One Beloved, the Other Hated': Between Fiction and Reality in Haskalah Depictions of Women* [Ha'ahat ahuvah veha'ahat senuah: bein metsiut levidyon bete'urei ha'ishah besifrut hahaskalah] (Jerusalem, 2002). Cohen and Feiner have collaborated on a collection of women's writing from the period of the east European Haskalah. See their *The Voice of a Young Woman: Writings of Maskilic Women in the Nineteenth Century* [Kol almah ivriyah: kitvei nashim maskilot bame'ah hatesha esreh] (Tel Aviv, 2006).

unless they made themselves over in the model of non-Jews. (The analogy, of course, is flawed since Jews could presumably become Europeans, but women could not remake themselves into men.)

TRANSFORMING THE FIELD OF EUROPEAN JEWISH HISTORY

In addition to these important but non-transformative issues, women's and gender-sensitive history have called on European Jewish historians to rethink two fundamental assumptions of modern European Jewish history. The first is what should be subsumed in the historical study of Judaism. The development of Jewish religious thought and halakhah have rightly occupied central stage. In the past generation or two the subject of mysticism as a religious and cultural force in Jewish life has attracted a cadre of innovative, creative, and contentious scholars. The paradigm that Gershom Scholem left for understanding the development of kabbalah and hasidism has been rethought in the light of the work of, among others, Moshe Idel, Yehuda Liebes, Rachel Elior, and Immanuel Etkes in Israel and Elliot Wolfson and Arthur Green in the United States. Because of the impact of feminist scholarship, both Elliot Wolfson and Ada Rapoport-Albert have in different ways raised the subject of gendered issues in kabbalah. In *Circle in the Square*, in particular, Wolfson has demonstrated the misogyny at the heart of kabbalistic theosophy.[40] Rapoport-Albert has gone beyond kabbalistic doctrine to address the problem of the absence of female mystics within Judaism at a time when they were a presence within both Islam and Christianity. Beginning with her pioneering article on the nineteenth-century Maid of Ludmir,[41] she has asserted the inability of hasidim to include women as potential spiritual leaders. In her recent work on Shabateanism, on the other hand, she has discovered an openness to women as spiritual adepts.[42] Given the contemporary interest in kabbalah, there is more than sufficient reason to explore further the issues of women and gender in the mystical trends in modern Judaism.

[40] Elliot R. Wolfson, *Circle in the Square: Studies in the Use of Gender in Kabbalistic Symbolism* (Albany, NY, 1995). See also Moshe Idel, 'Sexual Metaphors and Praxis in the Kabbalah', in Kraemer (ed.), *The Jewish Family: Metaphor and Memory*, 197–224.

[41] 'On Women in Hasidism: S. A. Horodecky and the Maid of Ludmir Tradition', in Ada Rapoport-Albert and Steven J. Zipperstein (eds.), *Jewish History: Essays in Honor of Chimen Abramsky* (London, 1988). See also Nathaniel Deutsch, *The Maiden of Ludmir: A Jewish Holy Woman and her World* (Berkeley, Calif., 2003).

[42] 'On the Position of Women in Shabateanism' (Heb.), in Rachel Elior (ed.), *The Dream and its Interpretation: The Shabatean Movement and its Aftermath—Messianism, Shabateanism, and Frankism* [Haḥalom veshivro: hatenuah hashabeta'it usheluḥoteiha—meshiḥiyut, shabeta'ut, ufrankism] (Jerusalem, 2001), 143–327

The thorniest question raised by women's historians regarding Judaism is the nature of Jewish women's experience of Judaism and the relation of that experience to the classical texts, studied and interpreted by the rabbinic elite, that constitute Judaism for most scholars. That is, given the exclusion of women from the study of those texts and from religious leadership, what precisely was their 'lived Judaism' at different times and in different geographical settings? Chava Weissler addressed this question directly in her study of the early modern literature of *tkhines*, prayers in Yiddish written for, and sometimes by, women.[43] The question, as she recognized, is relevant when speaking of non-elite males as well as women, but exacerbated in the case of women by their exclusion as a class from most forms of learning and of synagogue leadership. Weissler pointed out that the liturgy designed specifically for women was written in a language different from the communal siddur, addressed female-specific concerns about health and family, and was recited in a female milieu. She alerted us to customs of observance, such as cemetery rituals connected to making the wicks for candles for use on Yom Kippur, that women continued to practise despite rabbinic opposition. Yet she insists that women's 'lived Judaism' was simply one of a variety of forms of Jewish expression, linked to the 'high culture' of Judaism.

What remain open for examination are the self-understanding of Jewish women along with non-elite men and the implications of their practice of Judaism for our scholarly interpretation of Judaism as a religious culture and set of rituals. More broadly, given the recognition of the marginal position of women in much of what we consider Judaism, how do we reconceptualize Judaism to include women's and non-elite men's experience?

Many historians assume that this is a question that only anthropologists can answer, and simply avoid raising it.[44] Yet the question becomes all the more pressing in studying the modern period, as the impact of the Enlightenment and the Haskalah led to the reshaping of Judaism, especially in western and central Europe. There has been some mention of the ways in which Jewish reformers, and some traditionalists, responded to the 'woman question' within Judaism, that is, the assault on Judaism as a primitive, non-Western religion because of its treatment of women. Scholars have noted that reformers included modest changes in the status of women in the marriage ceremony and in some synagogue ritual, while traditionalists developed apologetic literature on the high esteem in which Judaism has always held women. However, there has been little investigation of the religious

---

[43] Chava Weissler, *Voices of the Matriarchs: Listening to the Prayers of Early Modern Jewish Women* (Boston, 1998).

[44] For a suggestive anthropological study of Jewish women in a contemporary community, see Susan Starr Sered, *Women as Ritual Experts: The Religious Lives of Elderly Women in Jerusalem* (New York, 1992).

sensibilities of Jewish women themselves. In his magisterial history of the Reform movement, *Response to Modernity*, Michael Meyer does make brief reference to the enthusiasm of women for reform efforts both in Germany and in France throughout the nineteenth century.[45] Still, there has been no systematic study of women's role in the European synagogue, either traditional or liberal, or of women's diverse presentations of Judaism. Grace Aguilar, a nineteenth-century Anglo-Jewish writer and educator, Lily Montagu, a founder of Liberal Judaism in England, and Regina Jonas, the woman privately ordained in Germany in the 1930s, hardly exhaust the subject.[46]

Where gender-sensitive scholarship has had the greatest impact on the study of European Jewish history is in the exploration of the processes of assimilation and of the creation of modern Jewish identities. The generalizations about the assimilation of western and central European Jews based solely on public behaviour and on the pronouncements of male communal leadership have been undermined by the innovative work of Marion Kaplan in *The Making of the Jewish Middle Class*. By focusing on women and the family as the key to understanding the complex identities of German Jews at the *fin de siècle* and their creation of a bourgeois Jewish culture, Kaplan demonstrated how women both maintained and transformed customary patterns of Jewish life within the home, even while Jewish men appeared completely assimilated in the public arenas of work and politics. She also made good use of memoirs to suggest that women, because of their social position and bourgeois gender ideology, were likely to retain aspects of Jewish observance longer than men. Kaplan thereby questioned the meaning and dimensions of assimilation, or acculturation, and its pace. She also problematized the term by broadening the scope of evidence and the domains of behaviour to be examined. In doing so, she contributed mightily to a trend in contemporary Jewish scholarship to offer a more nuanced understanding of assimilated European Jews than was the case in the past. It is now hard to posit the identities of European assimilationists and Zionists as polar opposites. In

[45] See Michael A. Meyer, *Response to Modernity: A History of the Reform Movement in Judaism* (Detroit, 1995), 139–40, 210–11; on women's enthusiastic support, see pp. 55, 223. On early German reformers' attitudes towards women see especially Riv-Ellen Prell, 'The Vision of Women in Classical Reform Judaism', *Journal of the American Academy of Religion*, 50/4 (1982), 575–89, and the classic article by Abraham Geiger, 'Die Stellung des weiblichen Geschlechtes in dem Judenthum unserer Zeit', *Wissenschaftliche Zeitschrift für jüdische Theologie*, 3 (1837), 1–14.

[46] See Michael Galchinsky, *The Origin of the Modern Jewish Woman Writer: Romance and Reform in England* (Detroit, 1996); Ellen Umansky, *Lily Montagu and the Advancement of Liberal Judaism* (New York, 1983); and Elisa Klapheck, *Fräulein Rabbiner Jonas: The Story of the First Woman Rabbi*, trans. Toby Axelrod (San Francisco, 2004). Karla Goldman's *Beyond the Synagogue Gallery: Finding a Place for Women in American Judaism* (Cambridge, Mass., 2000), a history of women in the American Reform synagogue in the 19th and early 20th centuries, suggests the type of questions to pose.

part due to the incorporation of a gender-sensitive perspective, European Jewish identities in the modern period are seen as hybrid and complex.

My work added a comparative dimension to Kaplan's by contrasting Jewish societies in western and eastern Europe and the United States. I also noted that women's retention of some traditional practices was itself a form of assimilation to the bourgeois gender norms of the larger society. I was concerned as well with the way in which gender entered into the discourse of Jewish assimilation in the modern period, as some Jewish spokesmen in Europe saw assimilation as a gendered problem that they blamed on women. My own generalizations made me acutely aware of the need to contextualize assessments of gender differences both geographically and in terms of social class. We still need to explore how and why women functioned as seculariz- ers in some circumstances and as a conservative force in others and to link the structural features of society, as experienced by different groups, with choices members of those groups made. Iris Parush's *Reading Jewish Women* is a suggestive first step in exploring the cultural position of some nine- teenth-century east European Jewish women.[47]

The importance of gender in discussions of assimilation/acculturation, antisemitism, and Jewish identity-formation has been most widely accepted among those who see themselves as European historians of the Jews rather than as European Jewish historians.[48] To be sure, I am an exception, as is Steven Lowenstein, who applied the findings of gender-sensitive scholarship to his study of the rampant assimilation, and breakdown of traditional communal constraints, in late eighteenth- and early nineteenth-century Berlin. He presented a sophisticated analysis of the relationship between Enlightenment, economics, and family dynamics.[49] Much of the recent writ- ing on gender and European Jewry, however, has been produced by scholars who were trained as Europeanists and therefore often emphasize the European implications and context of the narrative about Jews that they relate.

Let me give some examples. When Deborah Hertz re-examined the phenomenon of the salon Jewesses in her *Jewish High Society in Old Regime Berlin*,[50] she was concerned with the factors in German politics and culture that fostered the development of a tolerant salon society. She provided a great deal of information about, and insight on, the Jewish *salonnières*, but

[47] Iris Parush, *Reading Jewish Women: Marginality and Modernization in Nineteenth-Century Eastern European Jewish Society*, trans. Saadya Sternberg (Waltham, Mass. and Hanover, NH, 2004).
[48] There is no hard and fast line between the two categories. Marion Kaplan, in particular, though trained as a Europeanist, has addressed questions of concern to both groups.
[49] Steven M. Lowenstein, *The Berlin Jewish Community: Enlightenment, Family, and Crisis, 1770–1830* (New York, 1994).
[50] Syracuse, NY, 2005.

the focus of her study was what the rise and fall of salon society revealed about the fragility of liberalism in Germany. The temporary integration of Jewish women into a component of enlightened society in Berlin had far more implications for the development of society and politics in Germany than for the history of Jewish women in Europe. Sander Gilman's prolific scholarship on the stereotyping of the Jewish body, mostly the male Jew's body, in western and central European culture at the *fin de siècle* has made a major contribution to understanding a specific component of European culture and to studies of European masculinities but a smaller contribution to understanding Jewish identity and responses to pervasive cultural disparagement.[51] Finally, Till van Rahden's *Juden und andere Breslauer*, perhaps the best of the proliferating recent scholarship in German on modern German Jews, incorporates gender as a matter of course as an important aspect of his exploration of the nature of Jewish integration with other Germans in Breslau, but his major goal, which he achieves, is to demonstrate how essential—for German history—is the inclusion of Jews in the German historical narrative, and not just as victims of antisemitism.[52]

These scholars from 'outside' the field of Jewish history narrowly defined, however, have been an important stimulus for research by those who define themselves as specialists in Jewish history. John Efron's *Defenders of the Race*,[53] for example, was inspired, at least in part, by Sander Gilman's work, but focuses on the ways in which Jewish doctors and race scientists employed the tools of their profession to construct an alternative reading to that widespread in their field, which presented Jews as a feeble race. He explored Jewish race science both as an entrée into the study of the acculturation of Jewish intellectuals and as a component of Jews' construction of their own identities in a generally hostile environment. Efron inserted Jews into a study of race science as actors in an intellectual and cultural milieu and not merely as the victims of a pernicious form of 'science'.

Similarly, in a provocative study of Jewish masculinity, *Unheroic Conduct*, Daniel Boyarin draws on the studies of Sander Gilman and George Mosse, and engages in dialogue with feminist and queer theorists, to assert that modern Jewish masculinity, modelled on secular European patterns, arises as part of the acculturation of Jewish males in modern times.[54] In his view, the rabbis had promoted, and Jewish men had accepted, a 'feminized' masculin-

---

[51] See the works by Gilman cited in n. 36 above.

[52] Till van Rahden, *Juden und andere Breslauer. Die Beziehungen zwischen Juden, Protestanten, und Katholiken in einer deutschen Grossstadt von 1860 bis 1925* (Göttingen, 2000).

[53] See n. 26.

[54] In addition to Gilman's many works, Boyarin was influenced by George Mosse's *Nationalism and Sexuality: Middle-Class Morality and Sexual Norms in Modern Europe* (Madison, Wis., 1985), and *The Image of Man: The Creation of Modern Masculinity* (New York, 1996). Most importantly, Boyarin is thoroughly at home in queer, feminist, and postmodernist theory.

ity until modern European culture, in which Jews participated and the approbation of whose arbiters they desperately craved, made qualities of brawn and assertiveness essential to manliness. As Hillel Kieval has pointed out, Boyarin's construction of Jewish masculinity is strikingly ahistorical.[55] However much particular assertions, or his thesis as a whole, can be challenged, he did succeed in placing the issue of the construction of masculinity within a Jewish context rather than reducing Jews to images created by members of the larger society. And he sparked a lively debate.

The study of Jewish history has been transformed in the past generation. The integration of Jews within European history as other than the object of social policy or cultural attitudes is all to the good. That Jews living in Europe functioned as citizens of their respective countries and as participants in, indeed often shapers of, the dominant culture, is necessary for a clear understanding of European history and culture. That the Jewish and European components of their identities were fused for many European Jews provides a nuanced understanding of their hybrid Jewish identities. Scholars who study both Jewish culture and Jewish social and political activity have incorporated, some hesitantly, new theoretical insights into their own work and have participated in the debates that erupt within the field of history in general. Feminist historians have been persuasive, I would assert, in arguing that engaging the questions that gender-sensitive scholarship raises is essential if historians are indeed committed to exploring every aspect of the human experience in its diverse contexts. Just as the modern German historical narrative is deeply flawed without incorporating Jews, so the modern Jewish historical narrative is equally flawed in the absence of women. And if we seek gender-sensitive scholarship on Jews that puts Jews at the centre, and draws connections chronologically and geographically, then scholars of Jewish history have to assume responsibility for writing it.

---

[55] Hillel Kieval, 'Imagining "Masculinity" in the Jewish *Fin-de-Siècle*', in Jonathan Frankel (ed.), *Jews and Gender: The Challenge to Hierarchy*, Studies in Contemporary Jewry 16 (2000), 142–55.

FOUR

Assimilation and Cultural Exchange in Modern Jewish History

MAUD MANDEL

ISTORIOGRAPHY on the modern Jewish experience has placed considerable emphasis on the distinctive paths Jews took to 'modernity'. By
analysing Jewish history from a variety of analytical perspectives and differentiating among Jews by national, regional, sexual, economic, and professional categories (to name but some of the ways Jewish modernization has
been approached), much—if not all—of the recent historical scholarship
focusing on the period from the late eighteenth to the twentieth centuries
has underscored the *multiple* routes Jews took 'out of the ghetto'. British
Jews, we have learned, differed in their emancipatory processes from
German Jews, as well as from their co-religionists in France and the United
States; the urban Jewish populations of Berlin, Paris, Vienna, and London
differed from the more rural populations in their respective countries and
from one another as well. The working class participated in ethnic mobiliza-
tion in ways distinct from their bosses and the intellectual elites. Jewish
women both in the United States and Europe modernized at a pace and in a
manner that was distinct from that of their husbands and brothers. The list
goes on. This literature has convincingly and permanently undermined the
argument that in 'western Europe . . . Jewish emancipation, in its wider
sense, occurred more or less simultaneously' and left us with a heterogeneous and nuanced picture of changing Jewish lives throughout Europe, the
Middle East, and the United States.[1]

Given this emphasis on diversity, multiplicity, and complexity, it is therefore striking to find a rather profound historiographical consensus linking
the literature on the modern Jewish experience in the Western world. That

---

[1] Jacob Katz, *Out of the Ghetto: The Social Background of Jewish Emancipation, 1770–1870*
(New York, 1973), 3. Although I am limiting this essay to a discussion of western Europe and
the United States, much of the literature on east European Jewish history and the Ottoman
Jewish experience has dealt with similar themes. See e.g. Ben Nathans, *Beyond the Pale: The
Jewish Encounter with Late Imperial Russia* (Berkeley, Calif., 2002), and Sarah Stein, *Making
Jews Modern: The Yiddish and Ladino Press in the Russian and Ottoman Empires* (Bloomington,
2004).

is to say, the scholarship on those nations in which Jewish integration proceeded most dramatically in the nineteenth and early twentieth centuries has almost universally come to the same conclusion, that whatever the process of transformation that occurred, Jews were able to maintain distinctive communities and subcultures. Or, to put it another way, wherever they lived and despite widespread acculturation, secularization, and integration, 'meaningful Jewish history . . . did not disappear'.[2] As social scientists Calvin Goldscheider and Alan Zuckerman contend, 'occupational, residential and educational change moved Jews to new locations and to greater exposure to non-Jews. But in the new order, Jews continued to interact with Jews. They concentrated in new occupations and built new communal institutions. Hence modernization created new forms of Jewish cohesion as it destroyed old forms.'[3] Although not all social scientists accept this rosy assessment of the impact of assimilation on ethnic cohesion, historians of the modernizing Jews of the nineteenth and twentieth centuries increasingly point to the dynamic ways in which various communities transformed communal structures and practices to reflect majority culture while retaining a distinctive Jewish presence.[4]

Such historiographical reassessments of assimilation emerged as a challenge to long-standing beliefs—often reflected in historical writings—that assimilation has been more perilous than antisemitism in undermining Jewish existence in the diaspora. Bolstered by Zionist ideology, which asserted that in the post-emancipatory Western world assimilation had eaten away at the Jewish national essence and ethnic cohesion, undermining creativity, spirituality, and values, earlier historiographical assessments underscored the losses incurred by Jewish life as Jews absorbed majority cultural and social mores. Seeking to dismantle the ideological limitations within which such history had been written, more recent work has successfully retheorized both the processes and the outcomes of assimilation, rewriting the field of modern Jewish history in the process.

And yet if this reconceptualization of the assimilatory process has fundamentally altered our understanding of the recent Jewish past, the analysis remains incomplete. In much of the historiography, assimilation emerges as a process by which a minority, in this case Jews, relates to the majority culture, either through imitation and absorption or, more often, through the appropriation of new forms or ideas. In other words, assimilation is conceptualized

---

[2] Pierre Birnbaum and Ira Katznelson, 'Emancipation and the Liberal Offer', in eid. (eds.), *Paths of Emancipation: Jews, States and Citizenship* (Princeton, 1995), 3–36: 19.

[3] Calvin Goldscheider and Alan Zuckerman, *The Transformation of the Jews* (Chicago, 1984), 80.

[4] For an example of a damning assessment of the link between assimilation and ethnic cohesion, see Samuel Heilman, *Portrait of American Jews: The Last Half of the 20th Century* (Seattle, 1995). For a contrary assessment, see Calvin Goldscheider, *Studying the Jewish Future* (Seattle, 2004).

largely as a one-way process in which Jews absorb, reject, or transform a static majority culture. What this perspective misses, however, is the dynamic nature of the majority society into which Jews are assimilating. It never asks the vital question: assimilating into what? Indeed, until recently, in most historical literature on Jewish integration and modernization, the surrounding culture is portrayed as homogenous and static; Jews assimilate into American or French or British culture. The culture is fixed; Jews are transformed. Little attention is paid to how that 'something' changes as a result of the assimilatory process. Recent work, however, suggests that Jews—like any minority—have been active participants in shaping the cultures in which they live. Such views encourage greater precision regarding the concept of assimilation and a more dynamic understanding of the process of cultural exchange and transformation.

How does a 'cultural exchange' model open up the field of modern Jewish history to new areas of enquiry? To answer this question, this essay will first trace how thoroughly the concept of 'assimilation' has been reconceptualized over the last three decades, focusing particularly on the case of post-revolutionary France. The goal here is to underscore both how successfully and definitively Jewish modernization has been rethought to emphasize continuity and dynamism over assimilation and loss, while also suggesting that there is more to be learned about the process of Jewish transformation than these models allow. The second part of the essay reviews three new works that have focused on the power of Jewish actors to effect change in their surrounding societies. This shift from looking at how Jews changed as a result of their inclusion into wider societies to how they helped shaped the societies in which they lived provides a challenging new paradigm for thinking about Jewish life in the West. Finally, the essay returns to twentieth-century France to look at the potential such an approach offers for rethinking modern Jewish history.

EMANCIPATION AND ASSIMILATION: A HISTORIOGRAPHICAL OVERVIEW

In May 1987, at the Jewish Theological Seminary's conference on 'The State of Jewish Studies', Paula Hyman and Todd Endelman voiced concerns that recent historiography on post-emancipation Jews had over-emphasized the 'Jewishness of assimilationist Jews'. According to Hyman, in an effort to legitimate the continuity and value of Jewish life in the diaspora, a generation of scholars had perhaps gone too far, understating the 'assimilatory pressures within nineteenth and twentieth-century European societies . . . and failing to take seriously the extent of alienation of Jews from the organized Jewish community'. Endelman seconded her concerns, noting that 'the methods they employ to study assimilation obscure the full extent to which drift and defection have weakened Western Jewry in the last two hundred years'. For Endelman, studies that have focused too narrowly on three or four decades have overlooked that 'the abandonment of Jewish attachments is a cumulative, multigenerational process, with each succeeding generation becoming progressively more distant from traditional practices and loyalties'.[5]

As these critiques suggest, by the late 1980s historians of the Western Jewish experience had already parted company with an earlier generation of nationalist historians who had used the term 'assimilation' to describe and condemn the acculturation, secularization, and integration of Jews into European and American society. Influenced by the flowering of social history in the 1960s and 1970s and by the work of American social scientists on ethnicity and inter-group relations, they rejected the previous generation's conviction that emancipation begot assimilation and 'convincingly demonstrated that a high level of Jewish consciousness and social solidarity were compatible with a high level of cultural assimilation and religious indifference'.[6]

Interestingly, both Endelman and Hyman, despite their concerns that modern Jewish historians had gone too far in stressing Jewish continuity in the post-emancipation Western world, were among the leaders of the scholarly generation that retheorized assimilation. By focusing on the acculturative *process* rather than on a pre-established end point, and by highlighting the ways in which 'ordinary Jews'—those outside the realm of political and intellectual circles—shaped the acculturative process, they—and others of their cohort—challenged work that focused on a handful of wealthy Jewish elites at the end of the nineteenth century, using them as a benchmark for judging levels of assimilation throughout the west European Jewish world. It was in 'taverns, street markets, coffee houses, theaters, [and] drawing rooms', Endelman argues, that 'acculturation and integration crystallized in countless numbers of undramatic and mostly but not entirely unrecorded acts'.[7]

This portrayal of acculturation as an ongoing, private, 'mundane' process in which the entire community was engaged not only encouraged subsequent historians to rethink the perennially elitist focus of modern Jewish historiography but also introduced important questions about the utility of the assimilation concept itself. Drawing on theories of inter-ethnic relations and majority–minority interactions, an ever-growing body of literature

---

[5] Paula Hyman, 'Modern Jewish History: The Ideological Transformation of Modern Jewish Historiography', in Shaye J. D. Cohen and Edward L. Greenstein (eds.), *The State of Jewish Studies* (Detroit, 1990), 143–57: 151, and Todd Endelman, 'Response', ibid. 158–64: 161.

[6] Endelman, 'Response', 160.

[7] Todd Endelman, *The Jews of Georgian England, 1714–1830* (Ann Arbor, 1999), p. x. Paula Hyman's *The Emancipation of the Jews of Alsace* (New Haven, 1991) documents the 'processes (rather than the end product) of social change' (p. 2) among the Jews of Alsace.

began emphasizing acculturation, secularization, economic transformation, and social integration rather than assimilation as the keys to understanding the vast changes that had influenced modern Jewish life since the Enlightenment.[8] And repeatedly sociologists and historians underscored that the adoption of cultural and social practices from the surrounding society did not necessarily undermine Jewish communal identification or group survival but rather transformed and invigorated them. Whether in Berlin, Paris, London, New York, or Vienna, it has been argued, Jews did not subsume their particularistic identities in the wider majority culture but rather transformed their institutional, religious, cultural, and economic structures to reflect dominant mores while still remaining distinctive in the process. According to Marsha Rozenblit's study of Viennese Jews, for example, 'if the urban environment facilitated cultural assimilation, it also provided the necessary demographic foundation for continued Jewish identity and the assertion of Jewish pride', allowing Jews to create 'new patterns of Jewish behavior which differed from traditional ones but were nonetheless distinctively Jewish'.[9] Deborah Dash Moore tells us that Jews in 1920s New York 'turned to existing American institutions to fashion their own moral community . . . recast[ing] available institutions into instruments of self-perpetuation'.[10] Paula Hyman writes, 'Jews struggled to find appropriate ways to maintain and legitimate their group specificity even as they expressed their wholehearted devotion to France and to the egalitarian ideals of the Revolution.' By the end of the nineteenth century, despite state-backed assimilatory pressure, Jewish populations still formed distinctive communities, recognizable by their ethnic origin, economic and urban concentration, relative social isolation, and minority religion.[11] Marion Kaplan's focus on the German Jewish family makes a similar point: 'Jews were men and women on the street and Jews at home. They displayed their Germanness while they privatized their Jewishness. Women formed the core of this process, striving for integration on the one hand and the preservation of their cultural or religious identities on the other.'[12] Granted that few historians are prepared to go quite as far as Goldscheider and Zuckerman when

[8] Much of this work drew on the sociological interpretation of assimilation by Milton Gordon in *Assimilation in American Life: The Role of Race, Religion, and National Origins* (New York, 1964).

[9] Marsha Rozenblit, *The Jews of Vienna, 1867–1914: Assimilation and Identity* (Albany, NY, 1983), 7.

[10] Deborah Dash Moore, *At Home in America: Second-Generation New York Jews* (New York, 1981), 9.   [11] Paula Hyman, *The Jews of Modern France* (Berkeley, Calif., 1998), 54, 63.

[12] Marion A. Kaplan, *The Making of the Jewish Middle Class: Women, Family and Identity in Imperial Germany* (New York, 1991), 11. For other works on Germany that stress Jewish continuity despite acculturation, see Uri Tal, *Christians and Jews in Germany: Religion, Politics, and Identity in the Second Reich, 1870–1914*, trans. Noah Jonathan Jacobs (Ithaca, NY, 1975), and David Sorkin, *The Transformation of German Jewry, 1780–1840* (New York, 1987).

they assert that 'neither political devastation nor assimilation awaits Diaspora Jews', and that 'Jewish communities changed but did not dissolve during modernization',[13] it should nonetheless also be clear that assimilation is no longer a dirty word in the field of modern Jewish history.

A closer examination of French Jewish historiography, my own field of specialization, demonstrates the profound impact of the reconceptualization of assimilation. In 1971 Michael Marrus published *The Politics of Assimilation: A Study of the French Jewish Community at the Time of the Dreyfus Affair*. As the title suggests, Marrus's text explores the politics of the Jewish community during the most challenging moment of its political existence since the 1791 emancipation. For Marrus, the Dreyfus affair stood as a stark indication of all that French Jews had lost since becoming citizens in the French state. Arguing that with the breakdown of an autonomous communal power base following the French Revolution Jewish distinctiveness had been eroded, he insisted that all bases for Jewish politics or strategies of self-defence had also been undermined. In his words: 'their community was weakened by the corrosive effects of assimilation; their politics were shaped in the image of French patriotism. . . . By the time of the Dreyfus Affair, the Jews in France had lost most sense of their sense of community.' This process, he insisted, 'undermined the basis for a distinctive Jewish existence'.[14]

Marrus's argument echoed long-standing depictions of the Jews of modern France as completely assimilated.[15] Thanks to their unprecedented full emancipation, ushered in by the French Revolution, Jews—it was held—abandoned their community, religion, and institutional structures and embraced the opportunity to become French. The universalistic definition of citizenship favoured by the new Jacobin state promoted individual liberties in the place of particularistic traditions, and undermined connections between the new Jewish French citizens and their co-religionists. As Paula Hyman points out, however, recent scholarship on the nineteenth century has demonstrated that 'such a simplistic view' has not done justice to 'the complex processes of transformation of Jewish identity occurring in the modern period'.[16] A more nuanced discussion of Jewish transformation focuses on the speed and incomplete nature of the transformation process. Over the course of the nineteenth century, as new professional, educational, and social opportunities became available to them, Jews began adopting French national cultural norms, shedding Yiddish for French, and abandoning traditional

[13] Goldscheider and Zuckerman, *The Transformation of the Jews*, 223.
[14] Michael Marrus, *The Politics of Assimilation: A Study of the French Jewish Community at the Time of the Dreyfus Affair* (Oxford, 1971), 114, 284.
[15] For another example, see Arthur Hertzberg, *The French Enlightenment and the Jews: The Origins of Modern Anti-Semitism* (New York, 1967).
[16] Hyman, *The Jews of Modern France*, 54.

apparel and practices. However, social change did not occur overnight, particularly in the more traditional communities of Alsace, and even the most acculturated generally cultivated a Franco-Jewish identity that recognized the coexistence of Jewish particularism within the universalism of their French citizenship. Even as French Jews acculturated to national norms, they remained distinctive in their educational, economic, professional, residential, and even their demographic patterns.[17]

In a variation on this argument, Michael Graetz has suggested that, although the French Revolution obliterated Jewish life as it had existed by destroying traditional Jewish governing and communal structures, new forms of Jewish cohesion paradoxically emerged. Thanks to the centralizing efforts of the new French state, the Consistoire Israélite de France emerged to take charge of Jewish religious life in France and to serve as the intermediary between the government and France's Jewish population. The result was that, throughout the nineteenth century and until the separation of church and state in 1906, Jewish group identity was both recognized and legitimized by the very legal structure supposedly committed to privatizing Jewishness and breaking down its 'national' characteristics.[18] Although citizenship of the French state may have ultimately spelled doom for the early modern autonomous Jewish communities in the sense that the ties that held Jews together were dismantled, nineteenth-century French Jewish citizens adapted to the conditions in which they found themselves by creating entirely new forms of cohesion suited to the context in which they were living.

Even more interesting in this regard was the impact of the French state's assimilatory politics on those Jews most invested in republican politics. Here I speak of the numerous nineteenth-century Jews who made careers working for the government and civil service, often in high-level posts as *préfets*, generals, magistrates, and *conseillers d'état*, or those who held seats in the Chamber of Deputies and Senate, occasionally serving as government ministers. These men, whom Pierre Birnbaum has labelled 'state Jews', carried

---

[17] See e.g. Phyllis Cohen Albert, 'Ethnicity and Jewish Solidarity in Nineteenth-Century France', in Jehuda Reinharz and Daniel Swetschinski (eds.), *Mystics, Philosophers, and Politicians: Essays in Jewish Intellectual History in Honor of Alexander Altman* (Durham, NC, 1982), 249–74; ead., 'The Right to be Different: Interpretations of the French Revolution's Promises to the Jews', *Modern Judaism*, 12 (1992), 243–57; and ead., 'L'Intégration et la persistence de l'ethnicité chez les Juifs dans la France moderne', in Pierre Birnbaum (ed.), *Histoire politique des Juifs de France: Entre universalisme et particularisme* (Paris, 1990), 221–43. See also Jay R. Berkovitz, *The Shaping of Jewish Identity in Nineteenth Century France* (Detroit, 1989); Hyman, *The Emancipation of the Jews of Alsace*; and Ronald Schechter, *Obstinate Hebrews: Representations of Jews in France, 1715–1815* (Berkeley, Calif., 2003). For an overview of the different schools in this debate, see Birnbaum, *Jewish Destinies: Citizenship, State, and Community in Modern France*, trans. Arthur Goldhammer (New York, 1999), ch. 2.

[18] Michael Graetz, *Les Juifs en France au XIXe siècle: De la Révolution française à l'Alliance Israélite Universelle* (Paris, 1989).

out their professional duties for a state committed to state-centred, assimilationist models of government.[19] As Eugene Weber's account famously demonstrated, the ever-growing centralized state continually directed its efforts, through schooling, the military, and new organs of information, to transmitting Parisian aristocratic and bourgeois elite cultural norms throughout the country.[20] Although recent work has rejected the full implications of Weber's argument, insisting persuasively that regional distinctiveness and local cultures resisted such homogenizing goals, and that ethnic, economic, and religious particularisms continued to assert broader conceptualizations of French national identity, few have questioned the state's ongoing commitment to promoting a universalistic conception of French citizenship that downplayed minority affiliations.[21]

For the 'state Jews', dedicated by profession and ideology to serving the regime, such assimilationist politics were presumably a sine qua non of their governmental participation. Indeed, Birnbaum describes these men as 'fools of the republic', by which he means less that they imprudently served the state than that they zealously absorbed the republic's ideological framework as their own, serving 'the emancipatory, rationalist Republic that was so concerned with progress with all their strength'.[22] Interestingly, however, this commitment seems to have impinged very little on the private Jewish attachments of these men, few of whom felt compelled to pull away from the Jewish community, despite hostility directed towards them for their ethnic commitments. To the contrary, the 'state Jews' kept their family names, rarely intermarried, and displayed an ongoing affiliation with Jewish life throughout their professional lives.

Here, then, at the heart of republican politics, Jewish identity continued to flourish and grow. Moreover, the French state's assimilatory doctrine began serving as a *basis* for Jewish communal politics. In fact, in the French Jewish case it was not merely the social process of assimilation but an articulated *politics* of assimilation that ironically bolstered ethnic identification and solidarity. As Lisa Moses Leff has artfully argued, the emergence of a Jewish internationalism—as embodied in the Alliance Israélite Universelle—dedicated to promoting Jewish rights, religious freedom, and tolerance, emerged

[19] Pierre Birnbaum, *Les Fous de la République: Histoire politique des Juifs d'État, de Gambetta à Vichy* (Paris, 1992).

[20] Eugene Weber, *Peasants into Frenchmen: The Modernization of Rural France, 1870–1914* (London, 1977).

[21] A number of works have challenged Weber's account. See e.g. Caroline Ford, *Creating the Nation in Provincial France: Religion and Political Identity in Brittany* (Princeton, 1993); James R. Lehning, *Peasant and French: Cultural Contact in Rural France During the Nineteenth Century* (New York, 1995); Hervé le Bras and Emmanuel Todd, *L'Invention de la France: Atlas anthropologique et politique* (Paris, 1981). Other work has echoed this criticism while still pointing to the significance of the state's universalist model. See e.g. Peter Sahlins, *Boundaries: The Making of France and Spain in the Pyrenees* (Berkeley, Calif., 1989).   [22] *Les Fous de la République*, 8.

directly from the French Jewish leadership's commitment to French universalist ideologies and imperial ambitions. As good French patriots, Adolphe
Crémieux and the other founders of the Alliance demonstrated their loyalty
both to their fellow Jews and their fellow nationals through their international solidarity movement.[23]

Leff's examination of the origins of French Jewish internationalism in the
nineteenth century provides a provocative rereading of a concept popularly
held to be an essential component of Jewish identity throughout the ages.
Leff argues, by contrast, that Jewish solidarity is a *modern* concept, born in
nineteenth-century France as an outgrowth of the political, social, and economic integration of French Jews. Beginning her analysis with the emancipation of French Jewry, she documents how rights in that nation became
linked with the anti-clerical, republican forces that took root with the revolution and gathered steam over the course of the nineteenth century. French
Jews—wary of the tenuousness of their political position—forged alliances
with those championing state secularism, believing that religious tolerance
and equal rights for all was the only way to ensure the continuity of Jewish
integration into the French state. This logic extended internationally in the
second half of the nineteenth century, when French colonial policies and liberal diplomacy sought to extend a 'civilizing' mission abroad. It was at this
point that French Jewish leaders, long committed to the nation's revolutionary traditions, began calling for an international Jewish solidarity that could
spread the civilizing mission and French universalistic values to Jewish communities suffering persecution abroad. Although Jewish communities had
traditionally extended aid to one another across territorial borders in times
of crisis, the form and content of the international solidarity that developed
at the end of the nineteenth century were new, reflecting French republican
notions of capitalism, universalism, and secular education. Indeed, as Leff
argues, Jewish internationalism as we know it could not have existed without
a conception of modern citizenship. In making this case, she demonstrates
yet again not only that French Jews did not abandon their Jewishness in
order to become integrated French citizens but that the very politics of
assimilation that Marrus condemns actually provided the basis for new forms
of Jewish cohesion. Here, then, assimilatory politics themselves invigorated
Jewish communal identity.

If the historiography of nineteenth-century French Jewish life has
successfully reconceptualized the assimilatory process, what of that of the
twentieth century? Here, certainly, the problem is thornier; the antisemitic
outpourings that accompanied the Dreyfus affair and the establishment
of the Vichy regime during the Second World War, a regime that willingly

[23] Lisa Moses Leff, *Sacred Bonds of Solidarity: The Rise of Jewish Internationalism in Nineteenth-
Century France* (Stanford, 2006).

co-operated in the Nazi's deportation of 73,000 Jews, raises challenging questions about French Jewish integration. It is perhaps no longer controversial to suggest that nineteenth-century French Jews, motivated by the progressive changes in their society and by their steadily rising economic good fortune, were able to acculturate to and benefit from the changes ushered in by state centralization, democratization, industrialization, urbanization, and capitalist development. The twentieth century, however, opened starkly for French Jews with some of the worst antisemitic outbreaks in west European history, and the period from 1940 to 1945 provided devastating evidence to many that assimilation had failed. Convinced that antisemitism had so infected French society that it would take years for it to be purged, one French rabbi proclaimed after the war that 'It is in our interests and in those of our children to reject assimilation once and for all. We will no longer allow ourselves to be deluded by vain promises; the awakening was cruel and our deception profound.' Assimilation, he insisted, was hazardous, both because it diluted Jewish life and because it had rendered Western Jews complacent and unaware of the danger around them.[24] *La Terre retrouvée*, a French Zionist paper, similarly criticized the assimilationist perspective:

numerous are those among us who believe that the pure and simple return to the pre-war status quo will suffice to end [the war] and to make us forget the nightmare through which we have lived; according to them we must simply cross our arms and wait until the complete abrogation of all anti-Jewish measures redresses the wrongs that were done. . . . However, there are those of us who believe that a return to the past, however marvellous [it] might seem amidst the infernal distress in which we currently reside, is not enough, and that it is necessary, on the contrary, to uncover in this past all the germs that could breed the illnesses from which we suffer today in order to eliminate them.[25]

Given such views and the tremendous devastation of European Jewish life wrought by the Holocaust, one should not be surprised that historiographical literature covering the twentieth century stresses the exclusions and persecutions Jews faced more than their inclusion and subsequent transformation. Indeed, in comparison to scholarship on the nineteenth century far less of the literature takes on the question of 'assimilation' as such. Thus, if scholarship on the earlier period focuses most heavily on how political emancipation influenced the pace and extent of Jewish integration, the literature on the twentieth century turns to other issues: the rise of antisemitism and its impact on Jewish politics; the interaction of native-born

[24] Sammuel René Kapel, *Au lendemain de la Shoa: Témoignage sur la naissance du Judaïsme de France et d'Afrique du Nord, 1945–1954* (Jerusalem, 1991), 10–16.
[25] 'Nos problèmes', *La Terre retrouvée*, 18 Sept. 1944. For more on assimilationist and anti-assimilationist calls in post-Second World War French Jewish life, see Maud S. Mandel, *In the Aftermath of Genocide: Armenians and Jews in Twentieth-Century France* (Durham, NC, 2003), ch. 3.

French Jews and the ever-growing numbers of east European Jewish immigrants throughout the inter-war years; the relationship of Jews to the French
state in light of its new antisemitic politics; the rise and fall of Vichy and its
impact on Jewish life, and the impact of Vichy and decolonization on Jewish
life during the second half of the twentieth century.

However, even if much of this literature does not expressly trace the
'assimilation question', the entire corpus is shaped by assertions and assumptions about the possibilities and merits of Jewish integration in twentieth-
century France and debates over the virulence and depth of French
antisemitism.[26] Take, for example, the pre-Second World War period, which
has yielded much historiographical interest, sandwiched as it is between
Dreyfus and Vichy. For some, Jews failed the challenges posed by the
Dreyfus affair precisely because the extent of their assimilation made them
misunderstand the threat they were facing.[27] By contrast, more recent scholarship has argued that many French Jews actually reaffirmed their commitment to Jewish culture and communal ties in the aftermath of the affair
while, paradoxically perhaps, vindicating their faith in the French state.
Indeed, Dreyfus's ultimate exoneration proved to many that justice would
prevail over prejudice in the republican state.[28]

A similar debate has emerged over the impact of east European Jewish
immigration on the native French Jewish establishment, with some suggesting that native French Jews, terrified by the palpable antisemitism rising
around them as the Depression-era economic crisis grew, turned against
immigrant Jews whose 'foreignness' seemingly undermined their own position in French society.[29] Others, while agreeing that all Jewish leaders

[26] For some, the exclusionary politics that emerged so clearly during the Dreyfus years and
with the rise of Vichy must be understood as an inherent part of French political life since the
Enlightenment, for ever destined to shape Jewish futures in the nation. The most extreme of
such arguments is found in Arthur Hertzberg, *The French Enlightenment and the Jews* (New
York, 1968). Others have shown, by contrast, that while antisemitism has never been absent
from French political culture, its strength and expression have shifted periodically, having
profound consequences for Jews at certain moments and playing little part in determining the
success of Jewish integration at others. See e.g. Pierre Birnbaum, *Anti-Semitism in France:
A Political History from Léon Blum to the Present*, trans. Miriam Kochan (Oxford, 1992).

[27] Marrus, *The Politics of Assimilation*.

[28] For a discussion of the renaissance in Jewish culture after the Dreyfus affair, see Nadia
Malinovich, 'Le Réveil d'Israël: Jewish Identity and Culture in France, 1900–1932', Ph.D.
diss., University of Michigan, 2000. A revised version of this text has been published as *French
and Jewish: Culture and the Politics of Identity in Early Twentieth-Century France* (Oxford, 2007).
For Jewish commitment to the French state in the same era, see Paula Hyman, *From Dreyfus to
Vichy: The Remaking of French Jewry* (New York, 1979). Philippe Landau, *Les Juifs de France et la
Grande Guerre: Un patriotisme républicain 1914–1941* (Paris, 1999), traces another example of
Jewish national loyalty.

[29] David Weinberg, *A Community on Trial: The Jews of Paris in the 1930s* (Chicago, 1977).
Hyman, *From Dreyfus to Vichy*, points out Jewish fear that the foreignness of the newcomers
would undermine the position of Jews in France, but she also underscores the impact of

believed that 'unassimilated ethnic enclaves would offend French sensibilities', have argued that there was not one native French Jewish voice on the immigrant issue, and that many Jews dedicated themselves to creating a safe refuge for their co-religionists in France.[30] Thus, despite the consensus that twentieth-century political culture posed dangerous and traumatic challenges for French Jews, recent work has continued to question assertions that they were too timid and assimilated to engage in ethnically conscious self-defence strategies.

Similar comments could be made about the literature on the Second World War and its aftermath. Indeed, one of the vexing questions regarding twentieth-century French Jewish history—a question that my own research on the post-war period has addressed at length—is how to explain the seemingly ongoing willingness of French Jews to remain 'French' after being the victims of state-sponsored exclusion and violence. As work on the war itself has shown, Vichy's anti-Jewish policies posed a fundamental challenge to French Jewish identification with the republican state, transforming Jewish citizens into national pariahs and undermining their faith in the nation to which they had given their allegiance.[31] And yet despite these challenges, in the war's aftermath, the majority 'remained *fous de la République*'.[32]

As I have previously argued after surveying communal responses to the Vichy years, most of those French Jews who survived the Holocaust remained loyal citizens following the war, neither eschewing their citizenship nor seeking to escape their ethno-religious heritage.[33] To the contrary, one of the profound continuities linking post-war French Jewish life with the pre-war period is an ongoing faith that it was possible to be both French *and* Jewish. There are many reasons why the overwhelming majority of French Jews remained loyal to the country of their birth, including the rapid abrogation of the anti-Jewish laws and the concomitant possibility of professional reintegration; the stabilization of economic life; the belief in the powerful post-war myth that the wartime atrocities had been the fault of the

interactions between native and foreign Jews on bringing out a more public Jewishness among the native Jewish establishment.

[30] Vicki Caron, *Uneasy Asylum: France and the Jewish Refugee Crisis, 1933–1942* (Stanford, 1999).

[31] As Richard Cohen and Jacques Adler have both demonstrated, it took the native Jewish leadership several years to accept their marginalized status. Initially trusting that all citizens would be protected from the worst antisemitic legislation, they were not inclined to link their fate to that of non-French Jews who had been hit first and hardest by Vichy's anti-Jewish legislation. As the war progressed, however, and anti-Jewish measures became more stringent, the native Jewish leadership became increasingly intent on preventing the complete disintegration of communal life, eventually leading them to call for united defence activities. See Richard Cohen, *The Burden of Conscience: French Jewish Leadership during the Holocaust* (Bloomington, 1987), and Jacques Adler, *The Jews of Paris and the Final Solution: Communal Response and Internal Conflicts, 1940–44* (Oxford, 1985).

[32] Birnbaum, *Jewish Destinies*, 4.   [33] Mandel, *In the Aftermath of Genocide*, 110.

Germans and the Germans alone; the aid many received from non-Jewish French citizens during the war attesting to the national bond across ethno-religious affiliations; and the difficulty of post-war migration.[34] While there were certainly those who became devoted Zionists, some even opting to relocate after 1948, and others who chose to hide their ethnic heritage by assimilating fully into French society, the overwhelming majority continued as before, identifying as French nationals, integrating into the polity, continuing to maintain distinctive ethno-religious affiliations and allegiances, and even taking part in the remodelling of Jewish institutional life around visible new cultural and religious structures. In short, even after the most challenging and devastating period in French Jewish history, a viable Jewish community emerged. As I have argued elsewhere, the Holocaust, though certainly tragic and devastating, remains an important chapter in the unfolding narrative of French Jewish history, not the end of that narrative.[35]

Analysts of the contemporary scene generally agree. Thanks in large measure to massive North African Jewish immigration as France withdrew from her colonial holdings, French Jewish life has become ever more ethnically visible. The North African Jewish population, more religiously observant and less self-conscious about expressing a publicly vocal Jewish politics than their co-religionists in France, has contributed to making French Jewish life one of the most vibrant in central and western Europe.[36] Sociological work on communal life in the 1970s and 1980s pointed repeatedly to the emergence of new forms of Jewish identification and to a great deal of ethnic identification.[37]

Certainly there are those who still proclaim that assimilation is wearing away at the fabric of communal life. In 1996, for example, Bernard Wasserstein predicted a bleak future for European Jewry. Although he held Nazism primarily to blame, Wasserstein also singled out diminishing birth rates, increasing migrations from eastern Europe, secularizing trends, and the rapid disappearance of 'authentic' Jewish culture. According to his ana-

---

[34] For the myth regarding war guilt, see Henry Rousso, *Le Syndrome de Vichy: De 1944 à nos jours* (Paris, 1990); for non-Jewish French efforts to protect native French Jews, see Susan Zuccotti, *The Holocaust, the French, and the Jews* (New York, 1993).

[35] Mandel, *In the Aftermath of Genocide*, 17. It is worth noting that Elizabeth Friedman, *Colonialism and After: An Algerian Jewish Community* (South Hadley, Mass., 1988), 90, makes a similar argument about Algerian Jews, writing that, despite the persecutions and loss of citizenship that they experienced during the war, the events 'did not undermine the certainty they felt about being French'.

[36] Claude Tapia, 'Religion et politique: Interférence dans le judaïsme français après l'immigration judéo-maghrébine', in Jean-Claude Lasry and Claude Tapia (eds.), *Les Juifs du Maghreb* (Paris, 1989), 207–23.

[37] Dominique Schnapper, *Juifs et Israélites* (Paris, 1980); Doris Bensimon and Sergio DellaPergola, *La Population juive de France: Socio-démographie et identité* (Jerusalem and Paris, 1984).

lysis, the Jews of Europe are 'slowly but surely . . . fading away'. 'Soon', he insisted, 'nothing will be left save a disembodied memory.'[38] As I hope I have demonstrated, however, this perspective has been rejected in west European Jewish historiography of late, where transformation rather than erosion has been the dominant analytical theme.

CULTURAL EXCHANGE:
MOVING BEYOND ASSIMILATION

If the category of assimilation has in fact been fully reconceptualized to focus on process rather than outcomes and on the various different kinds of transformation (cultural, social, economic, political, religious, etc.) that have shaped Jewish life, one might well ask: what next? In other words, what, if anything, is left to be said about the Jewish assimilatory process? Here it seems important to point to a variety of works that have begun to challenge the rather one-sided focus on Jewish transformation that the concept of assimilation has engendered. These works do not form a cohesive body of scholarship, nor do they self-consciously interrogate theoretical understandings of assimilation in an effort to, once again, reconceptualize the process through which change occurs. Taken together, however, they point to a more complex dynamic of cultural exchange in which Jews, as one minority in a larger sociopolitical framework, have both taken from and contributed to the wider social body. The analytical assumption behind such work, whether articulated or not, is that the majority cultures to which Jews are assimilating are themselves ever-changing, dynamic, and heterogeneous forms that both shape the parameters of minority inclusion *and* change as a result of that inclusion.[39] In the

[38] Bernard Wasserstein, *Vanishing Diaspora: Jews in Europe since 1945* (Cambridge, Mass., 1996), 290. For a different sociological assessment, see Goldscheider, *Studying the Jewish Future*, 34–41.

[39] It is worth noting that this notion of cultural exchange has long penetrated the literature on the Jews of Arab lands, generally in the language of 'symbiosis'. Thus, Shlomo Dov (Fritz) Goitein described Jewish–Muslim relations in the early centuries of Islam as characterized by 'creative symbiosis', by which he meant living together to the mutual advantage of both: see his *A Mediterranean Society: The Jewish Communities of the Arab World as Portrayed in the Documents of the Cairo Geniza*, 6 vols. (Berkeley, Calif., 1967–93). Numerous others have explored this conceptual line as well. Most famously, Bernard Lewis, in *The Jews of Islam* (Princeton, 1984), insists on a kind of symbiosis between Jews and their [Muslim] neighbors that has no parallel in the Western world between the Hellenistic and modern ages' (p. 88). Building on these works, Steven Wasserstrom, *Between Muslim and Jew: The Problem of Symbiosis under Early Islam* (Princeton, 1995), has insisted more recently that 'the debtor-creditor model of influence and borrowing must be abandoned in favor of the dialectical analysis of intercivilizational and interreligious processes' (p. 11). The overlap between this argument and the one I am making here is striking. Symbiosis has emerged as an important theme in early modern Polish Jewish history as well. See, in particular, Gershon D. Hundert, *Jews in Poland–Lithuania in the Eighteenth Century: A Genealogy of Modernity* (Berkeley, Calif., 2004).

remainder of this essay I would like to document a few examples of such work to underscore how a focus on cultural exchange, rather than assimilation, might illuminate aspects of modern Jewish history that have been under-played.

When discussing the Jewish assimilatory process in modern France, Paula Hyman notes that French Jews 'were not simply passive absorbers of bour-geois French culture; they also participated in its shaping'.[40] Although the rest of Hyman's chapter on assimilation beautifully documents how Jewish life was transformed in this period, she does not fully explore the second half of her equation—how Jews participated in the shaping of that culture. It is in attempting to address this question that a variety of new works have emerged—some more successful than others—all of which at least in part emphasize the impact of modern Jews on their surrounding societies.

Certainly the most provocative and challenging of these texts is Yuri Slezkine's *The Jewish Century*. This work, which has received both significant praise and harsh criticism, begins boldly by declaring that the 'modern age is the Jewish age' and that the modernization process itself is 'about everyone becoming Jewish'.[41] To prove this claim, Slezkine argues in his first chapter that two kinds of human grouping have dominated world history: the Apollonians and the Mercurians. The former are land-bound, establishing their wealth and success through physical labour, building armies, and root-ing themselves in the land. Mercurians, by contrast, are wanderers, whose lack of physical rootedness puts them in the position of providing goods and services to rural dwellers. Jews, among others, made up this latter group, inhabiting an insecure, transient, position in pre-modern society, which par-adoxically allowed them to foster the very characteristics and world-views central to the modern age—mobility, occupational flexibility, educational prowess, and a comfort with marginality. According to Slezkine, Jews 'arrived' in post-Enlightenment Europe with the requisite skills, values, atti-tudes, and professions that were the most relevant and valuable, establishing them as the vanguard in their urbanization, secularization, capitalism, edu-cational trajectory, and liberal professional pursuits. While he does not go so far as to argue that Jews *created* the modern age, pointing out they 'joined it late, had little to do with some of its most important episodes (such as the Scientific and Industrial Revolutions), and laboured arduously to adjust to its many demands', he stresses how well placed Jews were to prosper from

[40] Hyman, *The Jews of Modern France*, 54.
[41] Yuri Slezkine, *The Jewish Century* (Princeton, 2004), 1. For a range of the criticism, com-pare Jonathon Kahn, 'A Mythical Jewishness: Is Modernity a Jewish Creation?', *Books and Culture: A Christian Review*, 11/4 (July/Aug. 2005), 40, who describes the book as antisemitic and compares it to the Protocols of the Elders of Zion, with Sander Gilman's review in *Slavic Review*, 64/4 (Winter 2005), 892, in which he calls the book 'brilliant' (while still challenging some of its assumptions and analysis).

modernity, and how they helped pave the way for much of what has come to characterize it.[42] Not surprisingly, therefore, he links the origins of Marxism, Freudian psychoanalysis, and nationalism, among other 'isms', in this analytical framework, characterizing them as outgrowths of the Jewish historical experience.

This is not the place to debate the successes and failures of Slezkine's analysis. It is worth noting that his main focus is on Russian and Soviet Jewry, as he examines how Jews became model Soviets in the twentieth century, and there are many who are unconvinced by his sweeping characterizations and broad definitions.[43] Here I seek neither to defend nor critique the work, but rather to point out Slezkine's analytical vantage point. Although his book does not explicitly seek to challenge previous understandings of the assimilatory process, it offers a compelling reconceptualization. To Slezkine, the question of Jewish assimilation is irrelevant; if anything, he suggests that European society assimilated to the Jews, or at the very least that Jews were one of the constituent elements of European society in the twentieth century. The analytical framework rejects the perspective that minorities join and adapt to a fixed majority culture and society and instead posits (implicitly) that minorities actively participate in a shared process of cultural, economic, social, political, and intellectual production, at times even fostering the terms in which that process takes place.

Although *The Jewish Century* may be the most audacious and sweeping challenge to previous historiography on assimilation, it is by no means the only one of its kind. A second and rather different work in this vein is Andrew Heinze's *Jews and the American Soul*. In this book, Heinze traces the impact of Jewish intellectual and popular thinkers on the formation of American perspectives on the psyche and psychoanalysis. Challenging the perspective that 'modern American views of human nature are after-effects, mutations, or extenuations of Protestant modes of thought, starting with the Puritans', he argues that 'modern American ideas about human nature have Jewish as well as Christian origins'.[44] Central to his perspective is that 'Jewish values', by which he means a set of distinctive moral beliefs as articulated by both religious and secular figures, have had an enduring impact on American public conversations about the psyche. Heinze's subject is not only Sigmund Freud, his disciples and his critics, but also the popular psychologists and social commentators whose advice has filled magazines and

[42] Slezkine, *The Jewish Century*, 64.
[43] See e.g. ChaeRan Freeze, in the *Journal of World History*, 17/3 (Sept. 2006), 347–50, who takes Slezkine to task for universalizing Jewish history and for defining anyone of Jewish background as Jewish, whether affiliated in any way or not. See also Paul Lerner, 'Everyone a Jew', *Times Literary Supplement*, 4 Mar. 2005, pp. 7–8.
[44] Andrew R. Heinze, *Jews and the American Soul: Human Nature in the 20th Century* (Princeton 2004), 1–2.

self-help books, including Joyce Brothers, Ayn Rand, Betty Friedan, and many others.

Heinze's interest lies in the ways in which these individuals' Jewish background (and not simply the fact that they were Jewish) influenced their psychological perspective. He does this in two ways. First, he traces intellectual origins, examining the impact of earlier efforts 'to renovate Judaism in the hope of making it more responsive to the individual human psyche'. In Reform Judaism, ethical culture, modern Orthodoxy, the Musar movement and Habad hasidism, Heinze finds 'systems of moral reform with a strong psychological emphasis'.[45] Second, he turns to the Jewish historical experience, positing that the Jewish condition as immigrants/outsiders in both Europe and the United States led to distinctly Jewish ways of viewing the psyche. These dual perspectives fully penetrated American culture, he argues, through the work and writings of both influential professional psychologists and their popular counterparts.

Again, the point here is not to praise or critique Heinze's work, which while provocative and often fascinating at times seems to struggle with blending diverse kinds of sources and analyses in a convincing causal relationship. For example, when he argues that both Sigmund Freud and Alfred Adler, in focusing 'uniquely on the family as the critical context for understanding the moral dimension of unconscious drives', were 'follow[ing] the path of rabbinic moralists . . . and propound[ing] an ultimate moral solution for the crisis of the modern psyche',[46] his causal links seem speculative at best. More germane to this current analysis however, are Heinze's efforts both to explain the disproportionate Jewish representation in the psychological profession and to interrogate how Jewishness shaped the field, ultimately leaving a lasting imprint on the 'American psyche'. In doing so, Heinze, like Slezkine, makes an interpretative move that situates Jewish historical actors as central rather than peripheral to mainstream cultural change.

One slightly more modest example of such work helps indicate the analytical possibilities of a cultural exchange historical model for thinking through Jewish integration into Western societies. Here I return to France and to a text mentioned above, Lisa Moses Leff's *Sacred Bonds of Solidarity*. As I have noted, Leff's book traces the emergence of Jewish internationalism as an outgrowth of French republican notions of capitalism, universalism, and secular education. Unlike Slezkine and Heinze, therefore, Leff is fully indebted to previous historiographical traditions focusing on assimilation, accepting and developing the argument that the Jewish internationalists on whom she focuses were products of their environment, absorbing and transforming those national ideological values that best suited their particu-

---

[45] Heinze, *Jews and the American Soul*, 50.   [46] Ibid. 80.

laristic communal needs. However, Leff does not stop there. In documenting how Jews 'formed alliances with other liberals and republicans equally
committed to reshaping French law, foreign policy, and imperialism', she
traces how Jews 'helped shaped the terms of the struggles'.[47]

Central to her analysis is the Jewish role in the struggle for French state
secularism. In making this case, she does not suggest that Jews led the
charge. Nor does she imply that there was something 'Jewish' about the secularism that developed. Rather, she traces how the struggle to secure Jewish
rights within France influenced both domestic anti-clerical campaigns and
colonial and foreign policy: 'Throughout the nineteenth century, the proponents of a secular state championed Jews' rights in France, and later they did
so in the French colonies and around the world. . . . Activists vaunted this
support as an important sign of their movement's tolerance, high moral
standing and universality in comparison to the Catholicism they hoped to
supplant.'[48] In telling this story, Leff documents how Jews forged alliances
with such activists, promoting the secular state as their best defence against
forces of religious intolerance and exclusion. Thus, in her telling, the Jewish
historical experience was fundamental in shaping the nature of secularism in
France. Her point is not that Jews constructed French secular culture but
rather that one cannot fully understand the history of the division of church
and state and the anti-clerical movement in France without understanding
Jewish politics and placement in that society.

Perhaps it is by this point unnecessary to highlight the links between
Leff's arguments and those of Slezkine and Heinze.[49] Although all three
authors focus on different national and chronological settings, adopt different methodological approaches, and have differing degrees of success in
convincing readers of their claims, they all nevertheless point to the shift in
the conceptualization of Jewish integration that I have traced above. None
dismisses the supposition that Jews transformed and remade themselves as
they integrated into wider national, social, and political contexts. Indeed,
Leff very much reaffirms this point in her investigation of Jewish international solidarity, while Heinze and Slezkine never address the issue one
way or another. Rather, the challenge implicit in these texts is their post-
assimilatory model for thinking through Jewish history as they highlight the
intricate ways in which Jewish inclusion in a wider social body fundamentally changes the nature of that body.

The selection of these three diverse studies—and the rather critical
response that at least two of them have received—suggests that there is as yet

---

[47] Leff, *Sacred Bonds*, 6. [48] Ibid. 10.
[49] In a review essay comparing Heinze and Slezkine, Hasia Diner, 'Jews and the Making of
Modern America', *Journal of American Ethnic History*, 24/4 (Summer 2005), 100–3, also
remarks on this similarity, noting that both authors 'have breathed new life into an older and
largely discredited paradigm, that of "contributions" '.

no newly emerging consensus that the category of assimilation has outlived its explanatory power in the field of modern Jewish history. Indeed, one can understand potential discomfort with scholarship that directs readers to Jewish power and influence rather than to the dangers and compromises of the minority experience. As Ivan Kalmar and Derek Penslar have recently argued when tracing a similar reluctance to engage with the concept of 'empire', much of this hesitation is rooted in concerns over bolstering traditional antisemitic imagery. Because of the links between 'empire' and the array of supranational economic and political networks so central to antisemitic fantasies, 'scholars in Jewish studies [have been] hesitant to probe what reality might lie behind the myth'. And yet, they contend, 'scholars in Jewish studies must confront the realities of Jewish power [and] learn to distinguish between its various forms'.[50] Similarly, the texts explored above challenge us to consider the complex ways in which societies porous enough to include Jews were shaped by that inclusion. If we must be careful not to over-emphasize Jewish power and influence (indeed, *The Jewish Century* has been criticized for downplaying the vast challenges modernity created for Jews), we must not shy away from the possibilities such reconceptualizations create.

The possibilities for such analysis are quite promising. In my own area of post-Second World War French Jewish history, an examination of the *droit à la différence* campaign, which so dramatically challenged long-standing French notions of assimilation as the only answer to successful minority integration, provides a fascinating example of the ways in which Jewish inclusion helped transform French cultural life. The 'right to be different' slogan, first articulated by Richard Marienstras and the Cercle Gaston Crémieux, a French Jewish organization founded in 1967 to promote secular Jewish culture in France, became a rallying cry of numerous minority groups asserting minority culture as a basis for national affiliation in the 1980s. For Marienstras and his peers, the campaign emerged from a wider interest in 'Jewishness' in the critical years of 1967 and 1968, when the Arab–Israeli war and student uprisings in France changed the landscape of Jewish politics. Unmoved by nationalist, assimilationist, and religious articulations of Jewish identity, Marienstras sought instead to inculcate the concept of minority culture as a legitimate basis for Jewish expression in France. Arguing that French Jews should fight publicly for minority rights and cultural survival, the Cercle Gaston Crémieux worked with immigrant and provincial groups to assert the importance of providing space for cultural difference in public life. In making this case, the association rejected the assimilationist rhetoric of the French state, insisting instead on cultural survival and autonomy.

[50] Ivan Kalmar and Derek Penslar, 'Empire and the Jews', *Perspectives: The Magazine of the Association for Jewish Studies* (Fall 2005), 18–19.

Although this position repudiated the doctrines that had governed religious and minority life in France since the revolution, Marienstras was appointed by François Mitterrand to a presidential committee empowered with surveying minority cultures in 1981. The committee's report led to the establishment in 1986 of the National Council of Regional Languages and Cultures.[51] Although the government made few other permanent changes to minority policies, the Cercle played a formative role in the emerging French debate on minority particularism, a debate that in its most recent permutations—the 'headscarf' controversy and never-ending discussions about 'communitarianism'—continues to challenge French assimilatory models to this day.[52]

In this discussion of the Cercle Gaston Crémieux I do not want to over-emphasize its significance among French Jews or within the wider political landscape. Indeed, the association remained quite small and somewhat marginal to community life given the broad pro-Israel sympathies of most French Jews during the last quarter of the twentieth century. However, even if the Cercle itself only attracted a small membership, notions of the 'right to be different' animated an ever greater percentage of communal attention in the subsequent four decades, as French Jews, previously reluctant to identify publicly, grew increasingly willing to articulate a Jewish political agenda in the public arena. In this, they both mirrored a wider minority stance that was taking shape throughout France and helped shape the direction of public discourse around the issue. Or, to put it another way, the Jewish historical experience within France was central in shaping the way in which minority issues were understood and articulated in the last half of the twentieth century.

A similar argument could be made about anti-racist activities in France, which have been fundamentally shaped both by Jewish participation and the legacy of the Holocaust. In the institutional arena, Jews played the most notable role in the 1980s when many on the socialist left worked to counter the growing popularity of the right-wing National Front under the leadership of Jean-Marie Le Pen. Thus in 1984 Julien Dray, an Algerian Jew who emigrated to France following decolonization, co-founded SOS Racisme with Harlem Désir, a French Muslim. Both the activities of this organization and the concerns of the wider anti-racist movement in France have been significantly influenced by the history of Jewish inclusion and rejection in France. Indeed, some have suggested that this focus has led anti-racist forces to mistakenly conflate discrimination against Muslim immigrants in France

---

[51] For some of the backlash to these ideas see Dominique Schnapper, *L'Europe des immigrés* (Paris, 1992).

[52] See Judith Friedlander, *Vilna on the Seine: Jewish Intellectuals in France since 1968* (New Haven, 1990), 38–64, and Hyman, *The Jews of Modern France*, 206.

with that directed at Jews, thereby both misdiagnosing the problem and offering unworkable solutions.[53]

This essay is not the place to evaluate the relative success of anti-racist activities in France. Rather, I offer such campaigns and the 'right to be different' movement as further examples of how a focus on cultural exchange rather than on 'assimilation' provides a challenging new lens for investigating modern Jewish history. In both cases, Jewish participation has been instrumental in shaping the terms of the debate—in establishing the way in which minority identities can and should be articulated and the way in which racism will be conceptualized and fought. This is not to suggest, of course, that Jews are the *determining* influence on these discourses, but rather that their participation (like that of other minorities) has historical consequence. One of the benefits of such an interpretative lens is that it allows us to conceptualize French Jews as fully part of the societies they call their own, rather than as always on the periphery. A model that focuses on 'assimilation' portrays them, whether intentionally or not, as for ever on the margins—permanent outsiders working assiduously to join majority societies. And while such a framework may fit some moments in Jewish history very well, it oversimplifies the wide sweep of the modern Jewish experience. Greater attention to the ways in which both Jews and non-Jews change through encounter and interaction will make for a more dynamic understanding of the Jewish experience in the modern world.

[53] See e.g. Matti Bunzl, 'Between Anti-Semitism and Islamophobia: Some Thoughts on the New Europe', *American Ethnologist*, 32/4 (Nov. 2005), 499–508.

PART II

FROM THE MIDDLE AGES
TO MODERNITY

FIVE

Jewish Cultural History in Early Modern Europe
An Agenda for Future Study

DAVID B. RUDERMAN

I

AMONG the most dramatic explosions of interest in the study of Jewish history in the past quarter-century or more is that focused on the period usually defined as 'early modern', roughly comprising the late fifteenth to the mid-eighteenth century. When I began my graduate studies in Jewish history at the Hebrew University in the late 1960s, I was expected to master a finite canon of recent historical works on this era consisting of such authors as Israel Halperin, Hayim Hillel Ben Sasson, and Jacob Katz for central and east European Jewry; Yitzhak Baer and Haim Beinart for Spain; Shlomo Simonsohn, Moses Avigdor Shulvass, and Cecil Roth for Italy; and, of course, Gershom Scholem and Isaiah Tishby on Lurianic kabbalah and Shabateanism. This list was conspicuously weighted in favour of Israeli scholarship; almost all of it was written in Hebrew, only some in English.[1]

By the late 1970s the study of this period had been significantly enlarged by the work of a younger group of scholars, still mostly residing in Israel, as well as several prominent researchers from abroad. Yosef Yerushalmi and

---

[1] I offer only a sampling of the work of these authors in their first or early editions: Israel Halperin, *Jews and Judaism in Eastern Europe* [Yehudim veyahadut bemizraḥ eiropah] (Jerusalem, 1969–70); Hayim Hillel Ben Sasson, *Thought and Leadership* [Hagut vehanhagah] (Jerusalem, 1959); Jacob Katz, *Tradition and Crisis in Jewish Society at the End of the Middle Ages* [Masoret umashber: haḥevrah hayehudit bemotsei yemei habeinayim] (Jerusalem, 1963); Yitzhak Baer, *A History of the Jews of Christian Spain*, 2 vols. (Philadelphia, 1961–6); Haim Beinart, *Conversos before the Law of the Inquisition* [Anusim bedin ha'inquisitsiyah] (Tel Aviv, 1965); Shlomo Simonsohn, *History of the Jews in the Duchy of Mantua* (Jerusalem, 1977); Moses Avigdor Shulvass, *Jewish Life in Italy in the Epoch of the Renaissance* [Ḥayei hayehudim be'italyah bitekufat harenesans] (New York, 1955); Cecil Roth, *The History of the Jews of Italy* (Philadelphia, 1946); Gershom Scholem, *Sabbatai Sevi: The Mystical Messiah 1626–1676* (Princeton, 1973); and Isaiah Tishby, *Paths of Belief and Heresy* [Netivei emunah uminut] (Ramat Gan, 1964).

Yosef Kaplan seriously opened the study of the cultural and intellectual history of the Conversos beyond the previous focus on Benedict Spinoza and heresy.[2] Scholem's regnant reconstructions of the history of the kabbalah were now challenged by the new approaches of Moshe Idel and Yehudah Liebes.[3] Another group of young scholars, several of them trained in America and with strong interests in social and economic history, began to revive the study of Jewish history in Poland–Lithuania; these included Moshe Rosman, Gershon Hundert, and Israel Bartal.[4] Italy also received renewed attention in my own work and, especially, that of Robert Bonfil, while Joseph Hacker and Amnon Cohen opened new avenues of research on Ottoman Jewry. Richard Popkin's prestige and ability to surround himself with a talented group of researchers enhanced the study of Jewish–Christian relations, Spinozism, Converso scepticism, and millenarianism in numerous ways.[5]

The maturation of this younger cadre of scholars has produced major and fuller treatments of larger units of study. Several historians, initially attracted to the social and economic history of the 1960s, have shifted their interest to cultural history as well. They have been joined by others, still primarily Israeli-trained, but increasingly represented by North American and European scholars. In addition to the names already mentioned, we might add Elhanan Reiner and Adam Teller for eastern Europe;[6] Elliot Horowitz,

[2] Yosef H. Yerushalmi, *From Spanish Court to Italian Ghetto. Isaac Cardoso: A Study in Seventeenth-Century Marranism and Jewish Apologetics* (New York, 1971); Yosef Kaplan, *From Christianity to Judaism: The Life and Activity of the Converso Isaac Orobio de Castro* [Minatsrut leyahadut: ḥayav ufo'olo shel ha'anus yitsḥak orobio de castro] (Jerusalem, 1982).

[3] Moshe Idel, *Kabbalah: New Perspectives* (New Haven, 1988); Yehudah Liebes, *On Shabateanism and its Kabbalah: Collected Essays* [Sod ha'emunah hashabeta'it] (Jerusalem, 1995).

[4] Moshe Rosman, *The Lords' Jews: Magnate–Jewish Relations in the Polish–Lithuanian Commonwealth during the Eighteenth Century* (Cambridge, Mass., 1990); Gershon Hundert, *The Jews in a Polish Private Town: The Case of Opatów in the Eighteenth Century* (Baltimore, 1992); Israel Bartal, *The Jews of Eastern Europe: 1772–1881* (Philadelphia, 2005).

[5] David B. Ruderman, *The World of a Renaissance Jew: The Life and Thought of Abraham B. Mordecai Farissol* (Cincinnati, 1981); Robert Bonfil, *The Rabbinate in Italy in the Period of the Renaissance* [Harabanut be'italyah bitekufat harenasans] (Jerusalem, 1979); Joseph Hacker, 'The Boundaries of Jewish Autonomy: Jewish Self-Jurisdiction in the Ottoman Empire from the Sixteenth to Eighteenth Centuries' (Heb.), in Shmuel Almog et al. (eds.), *Transition and Change in Modern Jewish History: Essays Presented in Honour of Shmuel Ettinger* [Temurot bahistoriyah hayehudit haḥadashah: sefer yovel lishemu'el etinger] (Jerusalem, 1988), 349–88; Joseph Hacker, 'The Chief Rabbinate in the Ottoman Empire in the Fifteenth and Sixteenth Centuries' (Heb.), *Zion*, 49 (1984), 225–63; Amnon Cohen, *Jewish Life under Islam: Jerusalem in the Sixteenth Century* (Cambridge, Mass., 1984); and Richard Popkin, *The Third Force in Seventeenth-Century Thought* (Leiden, 1992).

[6] Elhanan Reiner, 'Transformations in the Polish and Ashkenazi Yeshivas during the Sixteenth and Seventeenth Centuries and the Dispute over *Pilpul*' (Heb.), in Israel Bartal, Ezra Mendelsohn, and Chava Turniansky (eds.), *'According to the Custom of Ashkenaz and Poland': Studies in Jewish Culture in Honour of Chone Shmeruk* [Keminhag ashkenaz upolin: sefer yovel leḥone shmeruk] (Jerusalem, 1989), 9–80; Adam Teller, *Collective Life: The Jewish Quarter in*

Joanna Weinberg, and Ariel Toaff for Italy;[7] Yosef Kaplan, Miriam Bodian, and Daniel Swetschinski for Amsterdam;[8] and Ronit Meroz, Abraham Elkayam, Matt Goldish, Jacob Barnai, and Ada Rapoport-Albert on Luria and Shabateanism, to name only a few of the increasing number of serious scholars in the field.[9]

Several areas ignored by an earlier generation have become prominent, undoubtedly the result of trends in general historical research. Elhanan Reiner, Zeev Gries, and Amnon Raz-Krakotzkin have pioneered the study of print in the formation of early modern Jewish culture.[10] Steven Burnett, Chaim Wirszubski, Matt Goldish, and many others have generated renewed interest in the study of Christian Hebraism, especially Christian kabbalah.[11] Joanna Weinberg's magisterial study of Azariah de' Rossi has significantly contributed to the study of antiquarianism and scholarship among Jews.[12] Moshe Rosman, Chava Weissler, Renée Levine Melammed, and others have opened up the study of women and gender in this period,[13] while much new

---

Poznań in the First Half of the Seventeenth Century [Ḥayim betsavta: harova hayehudi shel poznan bemaḥatsit harishonah shel hameah ha-17] (Jerusalem, 2003).

[7] Elliott Horowitz, 'The Eve of the Circumcision: A Chapter in the History of Jewish Nightlife', *Journal of Social History*, 23 (1989), 45–69; *Azariah de' Rossi's Light of the Eyes*, trans. and ed. Joanna Weinberg (New Haven, 2001); Ariel Toaff, *Love, Work, and Death: Jewish Life in Medieval Umbria* (London, 1996).

[8] Yosef Kaplan, *An Alternative Path to Modernity: The Sephardi Diaspora in Western Europe* (Leiden, 2000); Miriam Bodian, *Hebrews of the Portuguese Nation: Conversos and Community in Early Modern Amsterdam* (Bloomington, 1997); Daniel Swetschinski, *Reluctant Cosmopolitans: The Portuguese Jews of Seventeenth-Century Amsterdam* (London, 2000).

[9] Ronit Meroz, 'Redemption in the Teaching of Isaac Luria' [Ge'ulah betorat ha'ari], Ph.D. diss., Hebrew University of Jerusalem, 1988; Abraham Elkayam, 'The Secret of Belief in the Writings of Nathan of Gaza' [Sod ha'emunah bekitvei natan ha'azati], Ph.D. diss., Hebrew University of Jerusalem, 1993; Matt Goldish, *The Sabbatean Prophets* (Cambridge, Mass., 2004); Jacob Barnai, *Shabateanism: Social Aspects* [Shabeta'ut: hebetim ḥevratiyim] (Jerusalem, 2000); Ada Rapoport-Albert, 'On the Position of Women in Shabateanism' (Heb.), in Rachel Elior (ed.), *The Dream and its Interpretation: The Shabatean Movement and its Aftermath— Messianism, Shabateanism, and Frankism* [Haḥalom veshivro: hatenuah hashabeta'it usheluḥoteiha—meshiḥiyut, shabeta'ut, ufrankism], 2 vols. (Jerusalem, 2001), i. 143–328.

[10] Elhanan Reiner, 'The Ashkenazic Elite at the Beginning of the Modern Era: Manuscript versus Printed Text', in Gershon D. Hundert (ed.), *Polin*, 10: *Jews in Early Modern Poland* (London, 1997), 85–98: Zeev Gries, *Ethical Conduct Literature* [Sifrut hahanhagot] (Jerusalem, 1989); Amnon Raz-Krakotzkin, 'Censorship, Editing, and the Reshaping of Jewish Identity: The Catholic Church and Hebrew Literature in the Sixteenth Century', in Allison Coudert and Jeffrey Shoulson (eds.), *Hebraica Veritas? Christian Hebraists and the Study of Judaism in Early Modern Europe* (Philadelphia, 2004), 125–55.

[11] Steven Burnett, *From Christian Hebraism to Jewish Studies: Johannes Buxtorf (1564–1629) and Hebrew Learning in the Seventeenth Century* (Leiden, 1996); Chaim Wirszubski, *Pico della Mirandola's Encounter with Jewish Mysticism* (Cambridge, Mass., 1989); Matt Goldish, *Judaism in the Theology of Sir Isaac Newton* (Dordrecht, 1998). [12] See n. 7 above.

[13] Moshe Rosman, 'To Be a Jewish Woman in Poland–Lithuania at the Beginning of the Modern Era' (Heb.), in Israel Bartal and Israel Gutmann (eds.), *The Broken Chain: Polish Jewry through the Ages* [Kiyum veshever: yehudei polin ledorotehem], 2 vols. (Jerusalem, 2001),

work on the Conversos from a variety of researchers on three continents continues to appear. New archival work from eastern Europe, the Ottoman empire, and elsewhere has offered new vistas for reassessing Jewish cultural and social history. The ultimate result of all of this new research is an extraordinary amount of books and articles in many languages. My students now confront a body of scholarly literature they can never fully master and absorb. The finite reading list of my own student days is a thing of the past.

The publication of Jonathan Israel's *European Jewry in the Age of Mercantilism, 1550–1750* in 1985 clearly marked a significant moment in the emergence of a field increasingly referred to as 'early modern Jewish studies'.[14] For the first time a well-known historian had skilfully attempted to define what had been denied or ignored or taken for granted by most other researchers: that the period from the mid-sixteenth to the mid-eighteenth centuries, now viewed trans-regionally, needed to be distinguished from the Middle Ages on the one hand, and from the modern period on the other. Taking advantage of some of the aforementioned new writing in this field, at least that written in languages other than Hebrew, Israel constructed a new synthesis, weaving the various economic, political, and cultural strands of this period into a coherent whole. He posited the following assumption: that the principal driving forces in transforming early modern Jewish society were external factors present in European society at large, namely, mercantilism and a revolution in European thought. Regarding the first factor, he successfully demonstrated how the reintegration of the Jews into Europe by the end of the sixteenth century emerged as a result of larger socio-economic forces transforming the European continent as a whole. He was less successful in demonstrating how the second factor, the so-called intellectual crisis of the seventeenth century, primarily the secularizing tendencies precipitated by Spinozism, explained the course of Jewish cultural history in this period.

Israel's work has been widely accepted and utilized by historians of the Jewish experience in the two decades following its appearance, but there have been no serious attempts to replicate, revise, or refine its conclusions. In the absence of any other comprehensive trans-national synthesis of similar import, several historians have written useful surveys of regional centres of early modern Jewry: Bonfil for Italy; Kaplan, Swetschinski, and Bodian for the Netherlands; and Rosman and Hundert for Poland–Lithuania. Hundert's recent synthesis has even vigorously insisted on the centrality of the east European Jewish experience in defining the essence of what

i. 415–34; Chava Weissler, *Voices of the Matriarchs* (Boston, 1998); Renée Levine Melammed, *Heretics or Daughters of Israel? The Crypto-Jewish Women of Castile* (New York, 1998).

[14] The book was first published by Oxford University Press in 1985, revised in 1989, and then revised and updated in 1998 for publication by the Littman Library.

modernity means for Jewish history: a relatively insular and unchanging cultural landscape well into the twentieth century.[15]

One final development should be mentioned in closing this rapid survey of scholarly advances in recent years. David Sorkin and Shmuel Feiner, among others, have both written interpretations of the Haskalah, the Jewish Enlightenment, focusing primarily but not exclusively on developments in central Europe at the end of the eighteenth century. Both contrast the dramatic rise of a so-called republic of letters with the relatively insulated traditional societies that preceded it. Sorkin calls the earlier period a Jewish baroque, while Feiner sees the Haskalah as a real cultural revolution, viewing this era as the maskilim, the proponents of the Haskalah, apparently viewed themselves. Both scholars subsequently took cognizance of an earlier period, that is, the first half of the eighteenth century, which they designate an 'early Haskalah', but they generally ignore the seventeenth century in seeing the roots of a cultural transformation only in the later period. Jonathan Israel thus remains the lone voice among recent historians to insist that the dawn of Jewish modernity needs to be located a century earlier. As part of a larger interpretation of European culture, Israel sees the Jews as full-fledged participants in the 'radical Enlightenment', a notion he ultimately borrows from Paul Hazard and, later, Margaret Jacob.[16] Among earlier Jewish historians, his view mirrors those of Salo W. Baron, Yosef Yerushalmi, Shmuel Ettinger, and Gershom Scholem, who, each in his own way, has underscored the importance of the seventeenth century as a decisive moment in Jewish cultural development.[17]

II

With this background in mind, it is time to take account of the full import of these scholarly developments as well as their limitations in presenting an

---

[15] Robert Bonfil, *Jewish Life in Renaissance Italy* (Berkeley, Calif., 1994); the works by Kaplan, Swetschinski, and Bodian listed in n. 8 above; Moshe Rosman, 'Innovative Tradition: Jewish Culture in the Polish–Lithuanian Commonwealth', in David Biale (ed.), *Cultures of the Jews* (New York, 2002), 519–72; Gershon Hundert, *Jews in Poland–Lithuania in the Eighteenth Century* (Berkeley, Calif., 2004).

[16] Shmuel Feiner, *The Jewish Enlightenment* (Philadelphia, 2003); David Sorkin, *The Berlin Haskalah and German Religious Thought: Orphans of Knowledge* (London, 2000); Jonathan Israel, *Radical Enlightenment: Philosophy and the Making of Modernity 1650–1750* (Oxford, 2001); Paul Hazard, *The European Mind 1680–1715* (Harmondsworth, 1964); Margaret Jacob, *The Radical Enlightenment: Pantheists, Freemasons and Republicans* (London, 1981).

[17] Salo W. Baron, *A Social and Religious History of the Jews*, 3 vols. (New York, 1937), iii. 139 n. 39). Yerushalmi's position is outlined in his *From Spanish Court to Italian Ghetto*, especially the introduction, while Shmuel Ettinger's position can be found in his survey, *The History of the Jewish People from the Time of Absolutism until the Rise of the State of Israel* [Toledot am yisra'el memei ha'absolutism ad lehakamat medinat yisra'el] (Jerusalem, 1968). Scholem's view is found in his book on Shabetai Tsevi and his many other studies of Tsevi and Shabateanism.

agenda for future work in the field. Let me state at the outset that Jonathan Israel's project of attempting to define an early modern era for Jews was essentially valid. However one defines its precise chronological boundaries, there appears to be compelling evidence to posit the existence of a cultural epoch distinct from the Middle Ages and from what is generally considered the modern era. And despite the obvious regional variations and changes over the course of some two hundred years, it does seem possible now to offer a coherent interpretation of the era as a whole and to isolate those general factors that transcend specific times or places.

One might question the need for the historian to offer elaborate schemes of periodization in the first place. Any attempt at periodization invites the detailed criticisms of specialists eager to discredit facile generalizations about the past. We undoubtedly live in an age where periodization schemes have gone out of fashion since they suggest an effort to essentialize, and it is much easier and more certain to focus on the particular than to attempt the sweeping explanations of larger historical units. Most previous attempts to offer broad constructions of the past have focused on the modern period, without even recognizing a discrete early modern period. At the height of an interest in these questions, the historian Michael Meyer offered an overview of such schemes tendered by historians of the nineteenth and twentieth centuries. Historicizing these constructions, Meyer readily pointed out their subjective biases, the apparent preconceptions of these scholars in privileging one historical factor over another, and the ultimate futility of tidy formulations of when pre-modern became modern in the Jewish experience.[18]

The challenge of periodizing early modern Jewish history is certainly not made easier by the state of the field among European or world historians. As Randolph Starn has recently pointed out, early modernity represents a patent but flawed remedy for the problem of periodizing the time between medieval and modern history, touted as a kind of democratic alternative to the previously utilized terms, Renaissance and Reformation, and the high culture they appeared to suggest. This indeterminacy, he adds, confers the aura of innovation on an agenda which by now is as conventional as anything previously said about the Renaissance. He concludes: 'Early, partly, sometimes, maybe modern, early modern is a period for our period's discomfort with periodization.'[19]

In light of the risks entailed in such an endeavour, proposing the need for a bold construction of Jewish cultural history in the early modern period

[18] Michael Meyer, 'Where Does Modern Jewish History Begin?', *Judaism*, 23 (1975), 329–38. See now the insightful essay by Moshe Rosman, 'Defining the Postmodern Period in Jewish History', in Eli Lendhendler and Jack Wertheimer (eds.), *Text and Context: Essays in Modern Jewish History and Historiography in Honor of Ismar Schorsch* (New York, 2005), 95–130, which comments on both Meyer's essay and Israel's book.
[19] Randolph Starn, 'The Early Modern Muddle', *Journal of Early Modern History*, 6 (2002), 296–307.

might appear to be highly unrewarding. In presenting this agenda, nevertheless, I offer the excuse of my age and the need, after years of writing specific
monographs, to synthesize, to look at a larger picture, even beyond my own
field of specialization and expertise. It is perhaps the sense that historians, in
search of useful knowledge, are required to step back from their narrow
studies, to explore the wider and deeper meaning of an elusive historical
past, to uncover not merely a Polish Jewish history or an Italian or Ottoman
one, but a history of the Jews and their cultural legacy as a whole, that moti-
vates me to seek to identify a larger cultural epoch crossing narrow temporal
or geographical borders. There is clearly a potential danger in such an
endeavour of distorting or misconstruing the past by imposing upon it the
preoccupations of the present. Yet the project of describing a trans-national
culture in early modern Europe is useful in attempting to link in some sense
disparate communities and, more significantly, disparate historiographical
traditions rarely in contact or in conversation with each other. There
remains in the end a critical need to focus on the political, cultural, and
social features that each of the individual Jewish communities of early
modern Europe shared in common, and whether there existed any self-
consciousness on the part of a broader community of living in a distinct age,
of recognizing that some commonalities across regional Jewish cultures did
in fact exist. In the final analysis, attempting to define the early modern
period for Jewish history also helps to clarify the beginnings of Jewish
modernity in general, in tracing more meaningfully both the continuities
and discontinuities that connect and disconnect cultural trends across the
last four centuries of Jewish existence. It also might contribute, at least mod-
estly, to overcoming the 'muddle' of periodizing early modernity in general
by offering one tentative proposal on what the period might look like from
the unique vantage point of Europe's oldest minority and its peculiar development across the continent and beyond.

As I have argued, Jonathan Israel has described masterfully the political
and economic conditions that engendered the reintegration of Jews into
European society under the rubric of mercantilism. His more recent work
on Jewish trading networks among former Conversos from Recife to
Smyrna suggests a concrete social structure of trans-national co-operation
and interrelationships extending prominently across three continents.[20]
What is still required is a sweeping look at Jewish cultural formation across
these same regions populated by Converso and other Jewish merchants. In
other words, could the existence of these trading networks crossing regional
boundaries help to shape forms of trans-regional cultural production as
well? Without denying the distinctive variations among regional Jewish

---

[20] Jonathan Israel, *Diasporas within a Diaspora: Jews, Crypto-Jews, and the World of Maritime Empires* (Leiden, 2002).

cultures—central and east European, Ottoman, Italian—can a comparative and cross-cultural exploration of early modern Jewish cultures lead to a better understanding of how political and economic change affected Jewish intellectual and social life? Can such a broader perspective help us to distinguish what was, and what was not, revolutionary in the formation of Jewish culture by the late eighteenth century?

I have considered five elements which might allow me to speak about the period as a whole. Each element needs to be examined over the entire period and across regional boundaries to assess its significance as a marker of a newly emerging Jewish cultural experience. These categories overlap, but to my mind they offer us a most promising beginning in speaking about a common early modern Jewish culture. They also offer an outline for charting an agenda for future study of the field. I am hard pressed to point to any overarching epistemological or methodological reasons why I have privileged these factors over others. They represent, at best, my own intuitive sense of what was distinctive and relatively unique about this era, based on my years of studying and teaching its manifold dimensions. I would be the first to acknowledge that these markers are tentative at best, that they probably describe inadequately and incompletely the larger landscape I wish to define, and that some of the factors affected more people than others. Nevertheless, I have yet to discover a better way of characterizing the formation of a common Jewish culture in the early modern period and, for the time being, they represent for me the most meaningful rubrics for describing the historical experience of early modern Jewry.

III

The first element we might consider is that of mobility, social mixing, and hybridity. What I have in mind are both large-scale migrations like those of 1492 and 1497 and also the movement of smaller groups and even individual scholars. The notion of the refugee scholar, and the displacement, adjustment, and reorientation that being 'on the move' implies, is well known as a phenomenon of twentieth-century culture, but it is surely as critical a dimension of earlier centuries as well, especially of our period. Within Jewish culture, the expulsion of Spanish Jewry has long been viewed as a watershed in the physical dislocation and cultural transformation it engendered. Certainly for the large numbers of Jews exiting the Iberian peninsula at the end of the fifteenth century, the process of migration, of establishing new roots, of mixing with other resident Jewish populations, especially in the Ottoman empire, and the creative tensions the new environments engendered are all matters of great consequence, as they are for historians of this era. As Moshe Idel has recently argued, mobility was a key factor in the shaping of kabbalistic writing and praxis in the sixteenth century. Mobility was also a critical dimension in the lives of Converso intellectuals in the sixteenth and seventeenth centuries who migrated to Italy, southern France, Amsterdam, Hamburg, and London, even returning to Spain and Portugal when the opportunity arose. Ashkenazi Jews were similarly in motion during the same period, travelling to Italy to study medicine, migrating to southern France and Amsterdam in search of better economic conditions, or crossing the continent on their way to the land of Israel. They also moved eastward from Poland to Ukraine after its annexation in 1569. From the sixteenth century, Jewish scribes, book dealers, and itinerant preachers were constantly travelling in search of new markets and new audiences.[21]

The ultimate effect of mobility on cultural formation has not yet been systematically studied, but it is clear that it is multifaceted and includes the accelerated pace of writing in many languages, as well as the emergence of new forms of literary creativity in law, mysticism, belles-lettres, medicine, history and biography, homiletics, and more. It also includes the concentration of Jews in itinerant professions such as medicine, the performing arts, and trade; the production of custom books meant to acknowledge and to enshrine in memory regional differences liable to be forgotten; and the internal conflicts and trans-communal structures erected to address diversity and controversy, such as the printing of a universal code of Jewish law, the *Shulḥan arukh* and its accompanying *Mapah*, merging the Sephardi and Ashkenazi traditions.[22]

IV

A second element in describing early modern Jewish culture is communal cohesion accompanied by the growing laicization of communal authority. Earlier historians have long recognized the importance of powerful Jewish communal structures in the early modern period. In the Netherlands and Italy, in Germany, in the Ottoman empire, and especially in eastern Europe, Jewish communities appear to have become more elaborate and complex as agencies representing their Jewish constituencies before host governments and as providers of educational and social services to their individual

---

[21] Since this is only a sketch of an agenda, the bibliography in this section and in the ones that follow is minimal. On the 20th-century phenomenon see Lewis Coser, *Refugee Scholars in America: Their Impact and their Experiences* (New Haven, 1984); Avigdor Shinan (ed.), *Mobility and Settlement in Israel and among the Nations* [Hagirah vehityashvut beyisra'el uve'amim (Jerusalem, 1982); Yosef H. Yerushalmi, 'Exile and Expulsion in Jewish History', in Benjamin Gampel (ed.), *Crisis and Creativity in the Sephardic World 1391–1648* (New York, 1997), 3–22; Moshe Idel, 'On Mobility, Individuals and Groups: Prolegomenon for a Sociological Approach to Sixteenth-Century Kabbalah', *Kabbalah*, 3 (1998), 145–73; Sophia Menache (ed.), *Communication in the Jewish Diaspora: The Pre-Modern World* (Leiden, 1996).

[22] Printed in Cracow, 1578–80. Elhanan Reiner discusses the *Shulḥan arukh* especially in 'The Askhenazic Elite at the Beginning of the Modern Era', 97–8.

members. This powerful surge of communal development stands in sharp contrast to the decline and deterioration of communal structures in the modern period. At the same time, these elaborate communal structures did not necessarily bode well for the rabbinic leadership of a community, who often found themselves in conflict with powerful lay leaders. Jewish communities were often run by a small number of affluent families in an oligarchic and even despotic manner. In Italy, for example, despite the prominence of individual rabbis, the latter were generally beholden to the communities they served and to the wealthy families who dominated communal life, including the many confraternities that enriched the social and cultural life of the ghettos. The prominence of wealthy merchants in shaping communal affairs also marked the collective life of Amsterdam, Hamburg, and London Jewries. The governing hierarchy of these communities scrupulously controlled the management of communal affairs and demonstrated a heightened sensitivity to the projection of a proper image and to proper collective demeanour before governmental authorities. In the Ottoman empire, no chief rabbinate ever existed and the authority of the rabbis was always circumscribed by the dictates of Muslim law. Despite the growing power of the rabbis in the seventeenth century, their authority ultimately declined. Jewish communal life was weakened by the creeping penetration of merchant colonies of Conversos in Ottoman port cities such as Smyrna, and economically powerful magnates continued to hold considerable power.

The elaborate Jewish self-government of Poland–Lithuania that had emerged by the sixteenth century was strictly under lay, not rabbinic, control. Communal rules and ordinances were not enacted by halakhic authorities but by lay leaders who virtually controlled the Jewish communities. Some rabbis exercised power owing to their exceptional expertise in Jewish law and their strong personalities, but more often than not they also derived their authority from their own affluence, gained either through birth or a good marriage, thus allowing them to become part of the oligarchic power structure themselves.

The implications of this general picture seem clear. The seeds of the crisis over rabbinic authority, usually associated with the late seventeenth and the eighteenth centuries, can already be located in the sixteenth, at the very inception of powerful communal structures and at the very pinnacles of Jewish self-government and internal political life. The rabbinate was certainly not a spent institution in early modern Europe; it had not yet been drained of all its considerable legal and moral resources to direct the religious lives of the constituencies it served; and it certainly did not see itself as in crisis until the very end of this period. But its power had been eclipsed, and rabbis, reluctantly, were henceforth obliged to function within a new reality of sharing leadership with lay leaders.

V

The third and perhaps most significant element in defining an early modern Jewish culture I would call simply the 'knowledge explosion', and by this I primarily mean the impact of the printed book. Although Jews 'on the move' explain in part the possibility of a shared cultural experience between disparate Jewish communities at great physical and psychological distance from one another, books 'on the move' explain much more. Before print, no one could have conjured up the seemingly absurd merger of two legal traditions on one page, like that exemplified in the aforementioned printing of the *Shulḥan arukh*. And no one could have imagined the extraordinary layout of multiple commentaries from different eras and regions surrounding the core text of the Talmud and appearing simultaneously (on the same page) with it, or those of the rabbinic Bible, first published by the Venetian Christian printer, Daniel Bomberg, in the early decades of the sixteenth century. As Elhanan Reiner has shown, the migration of these and other Hebrew books printed in Venice into eastern Europe created a crisis for the rabbinic elites of Poland–Lithuania. The printed text soon arrested the creative and open process of a fluid scribal culture, making the text canonical and not subject to accretions and modifications. The text became the ultimate word, not the teacher, thus diminishing the authoritative capacity of the rabbi as exegete. In this new market of books originating in Venice, Amsterdam, and Constantinople, Ashkenazi readers were exposed to the classics of the Sephardi library, while eventually Sephardi readers became aware of Ashkenazi writing. Printing thus shattered the isolating hold of potent localized traditions and attitudes, as one community became increasingly aware of a conversation taking place long distances away.[23]

Another effect of the printing revolution was the emergence of secondary elites—preachers, teachers, scribes, cantors—who exploited the printing press to publish cheap books and to publicize themselves and their views. This dissemination of new publications ultimately shattered the exclusivity and hegemony of the rabbis, opening up new reading audiences. Books printed in Yiddish and Ladino, two Jewish languages that emerged in the early modern era in this new age of print, accelerated even more the wide dissemination of books and authors and the growing literacy of less educated men and women.

Besides reading and writing in Hebrew, Ladino, and Yiddish, an increasingly larger number of Jews read and wrote in Western languages as well. Jewish authors felt the need to address Christian readers beyond their

---

[23] A rich study of the published books read by east European Jews is Jacob Elbaum, *Openness and Insularity: Late Sixteenth-Century Jewish Literature in Poland and Ashkenaz* [Petihut vehistagrut: hayetsirah haruḥanit hasifrutit befolin uve'artsot ashkenaz beshalhe hame'ah hashesh esreh] (Jerusalem, 1990).

immediate community of co-religionists or Conversos, whose primary language was Spanish or Portuguese. Christians also sought out books in Hebrew, and the book revolution accelerated considerably the market of Hebraica written both by Jews and by Christians and purchased by both communities. Print also represented a critical factor in modifying the very notion of what constituted appropriate Jewish knowledge. Jewish intellectuals in dynamic cultural environments such as Mantua, Venice, Amsterdam, and Prague were bombarded with new books in print, and, like other readers, were encouraged to expand their cultural horizons, to integrate and correlate the vast range of sources and ideas now available to them with those of their own intellectual legacy.

This knowledge explosion, although primarily engendered through print, was also precipitated through the unprecedented entrance of Jews and Conversos into the university, starting with Padua in the sixteenth century. Exclusively studying medicine, the students found the university an enriching and life-transforming experience, both in the formal knowledge it enabled them to acquire and in the socializing process that inevitably emerged as Jews invaded what had previously been an almost exclusively Christian space. While print was ultimately the primary agent in bringing individual Jewish communities closer together and offering a modicum of uniformity among diverse local cultural traditions, the emerging Jewish medical community, graduates of medical schools throughout, eventually, much of Europe, also served to shape a common Jewish culture and a common Jewish identity.[24]

VI

I would call the fourth element of an early modern Jewish culture a crisis of authority, accompanied by the threat of heresy and enthusiasm, the latter term associated especially with trends prevalent across the larger European landscape during the seventeenth and eighteenth centuries. In contrast to Jonathan Israel, I would define this crisis in the Jewish world less as one precipitated by Spinozism and more as one engendered by the messianic movement of Shabetai Tsevi, called Shabateanism, although both discrete phenomena are also connected in several ways, as I shall indicate.

[24] Besides the essays by Elhanan Reiner already mentioned above, see his 'A Biography of an Agent of Change: Eleazar Altschul of Prague and his Literary Activity', in Michael Graetz (ed.), *Schoepferische Momente des europäischen Judentums* (Heidelberg, 2000), 229–47; Zeev Gries, 'Printing as a Means of Communication among Jewish Communities during the Period after the Expulsion from Spain' (Heb.), *Da'at*, 21 (1992), 5–17; Amnon Raz-Krakotzkin, 'Print and Jewish Cultural Development', *Encyclopedia of the Renaissance* (New York, 1999), v. 161–9; and Joseph Davis, 'The Reception of the *Shulhan Arukh* and the Formation of Ashkenazic Jewish Identity', *AJS Review*, 26 (2002), 251–76.

Shabetai Tsevi's declaration of his messiahship in 1665–6 engendered an enormous reaction among followers and detractors alike. He was ultimately incarcerated and converted to Islam but, nevertheless, remained the focus of messianic aspirations within the Jewish communities of the Ottoman empire and throughout Europe until well into the eighteenth century. The phenomenon of this strange messianic figure became the basis of a new antinomian and nihilistic ideology constructed especially by Nathan of Gaza and Abraham Cardoso, an ideology that challenged the very foundations of normative, rabbinic Judaism, which, as we have seen, was already in decline.

This is not the place to review the various historical reconstructions of Shabateanism, beginning with the highly influential work of Gershom Scholem and the revisions of his students and colleagues. I will stress only one recent development in the growing literature on Shabetai Tsevi and his movement: that of challenging Scholem's insistence on seeing the roots of Shabateanism as primarily an internal matter based exclusively on Lurianic kabbalah and generally isolated from the larger European context where it belongs. Several recent historians have underscored the reception of Shabetai Tsevi within the Christian world, its intertwined connections with the apocalyptic anticipations of seventeenth-century Christians, and the obvious and explicit connections between Shabateanism and Converso messianism.[25] These latter connections are most obvious in the writings of the Shabatean leader Abraham Cardoso, former Converso and leading publicist of the movement, in his attempt to portray Shabetai Tsevi as a Converso himself living with two separate identities, and constructing a syncretistic messianic ideology based on elements of both religions.

By the first decades of the eighteenth century, with the fading memory of Shabetai Tsevi, the rise of another messianic movement in Poland associated with the infamous Jacob Frank, and the decline of Shabateanism within the Ottoman orbit, the history of this movement and subsequent witch hunt to root out Shabatean iconoclasts in all corners of the European world can better be explained by recourse to the notions of enthusiasm and anti-enthusiasm. When the Shabatean prophet Nehemiah Hayon provoked unprecedented alarm among a remarkably impressive number of rabbis writing from all over Europe, the charges surrounding him had less to do with his personal connection with Shabetai Tsevi and his ideology and more to do with his pretension to understand the divine essence as expressed in a Trinitarian form, that is, to understand the Godhead exclusively through his own innate powers. Similarly, the other great internal schisms associated with Shabateanism in the eighteenth century, the accusations levelled against Moses Hayim Luzzatto and Jonathan Eybeschuetz, were primarily

---

[25] On possible Shabatean connections with prophecy and messianism in the Islamic world, see the recent summary and bibliography in Goldish, *Sabbatean Prophets*, 34–40.

concerned with their explicit or implicit challenge to the authoritative structure of the rabbinate and the anxiety they and their followers generated over this perceived diminution of its actual power. Shabateanism, then, in its later eighteenth-century dimensions, was simply a code word, a convenient label for enthusiasm, heresy, and the undermining of rabbinic authority.

Shabateanism and anti-Shabateanism and its vigilant rabbinic crusaders as pan-European phenomena underscore more than anything else the shaping of a truly early modern Jewish culture through books, emissaries, and a vast network of communication between advocates and detractors. Whatever else Shabateanism engendered among early modern Jews, it created a real sense of their relationship to each other, their need to address either positively or negatively a predicament commonly shared by all and transcending regional boundaries. The anxiety created by Shabatean heretics could even be said to have engendered a common front of 'orthodoxy' throughout the entire continent. Ironically, the Europe-wide rabbinic crusade to vilify Nehemiah Hayon and the publication of his heretical book in the early decades of the eighteenth century came to reveal not only a united front against a perceived enemy of the faith, but a common culture and a common fate. Shabateanism left no doubt in the minds of its opponents that a threat to one rabbi or community was ultimately a threat to the entire fabric of Jewish faith and institutional life.

Little evidence suggests that the contemporary Jewish community reacted to the heresy of Benedict Spinoza in the same fashion as it did to that of Shabetai Tsevi. However, the common conditions under which Shabetai Tsevi and Benedict Spinoza emerged in the second half of the seventeenth century and the common results they achieved need to be stressed. Both were patently linked to the Converso experience; Shabateanism and Spinozism in general were nurtured in Amsterdam itself; and both generated ideologies that challenged the legitimacy of rabbinic norms and rabbinic authority. In the end, both converged in interesting ways, although it is impossible to weigh them equally as factors in the collapse and deterioration of rabbinic authority, at least before the late eighteenth century. The connections between this Jewish crisis and those larger social and institutional crises of European society as a whole also appear to be quite opaque. Nevertheless, Jews and Christians living in early modern Europe, and most notably their religious and political leadership, seem to have shared a common perception of living through a genuine crisis which they could neither control nor arrest.[26]

[26] Scholem, *Sabbatai Sevi*; Liebes, *On Shabateanism and its Kabbalah*; Goldish, *Sabbatean Prophets*; Elisheva Carlebach, *The Pursuit of Heresy: Rabbi Moses Hagiz and the Sabbatean Controversies* (New York, 1990); Michael Heyd, 'The Jewish Quaker: Christian Perceptions of Sabbatai Zevi as an Enthusiast', in Coudert and Shoulson (eds.), *Hebraica Veritas?*, 234–65; Matt Goldish and Richard Popkin (eds.), *Jewish Messianism in the Early Modern World* (Dordrecht, 2001); Barnai, *Shabateanism: Social Aspects*.

VII

The fifth and final element in my scheme of a trans-national Jewish culture in early modern Europe might be called 'the blurring of religious identities' or 'mingled identities'. By this I mean not only the phenomenon of the Conversos and their conspicuous presence throughout much of Europe but also three other discrete but related groupings: individual Jewish converts to Christianity, Christian Hebraists, and Shabatean syncretists intent on forging a Jewish-Christian identity.

The religious and cultural ambiguity of Jewish self-definition first became an acute problem in early modern Europe with the reintegration of Conversos into Jewish life in Italy, northern Europe, and the Ottoman empire. For New Christians who attempted to return to Judaism in the seventeenth century, the rite of passage was neither simple nor complete. They retained, consciously or unconsciously, identifiable attitudes and associations with their distant past, both religious notions and ethnic loyalties, which, in most cases, they could not fully dislodge. For New Christians who left the Iberian peninsula but hesitated to publicly acknowledge the Jewish faith, lingering in a transitional state between Christianity and Judaism, their religious and ethnic perceptions of themselves were even more complex. For some, it was possible, even desirable, to return to Spain and Portugal if opportunity permitted.

Viewing the Converso phenomenon alongside the other aforementioned groups—individual converts, Shabateans, and Christian Hebraists—one cannot help noticing the recurrent and conspicuous boundary-crossings between Judaism and Christianity in early modern Europe, or as Richard Popkin labelled them, 'Jewish Christians' or 'Christian Jews'. When Jewish identity became a matter of choice rather than imposed communal will; when, for some, a growing secular lifestyle severely attenuated religious commitments and the time spent in either synagogue or church; when certain Christians attempted to recover their spiritual roots through the study of Judaism while certain Jews found social and intellectual relations with Christians more attractive than ever, the possibilities for Jewish-Christian syncretistic thinking and praxis seemed unlimited. Decades before the eighteenth-century Enlightenment, Jews and Christians were encountering each other in public and private places, in intellectual forums, and in radical and spiritualist movements. Certain Conversos were actually shaping a personal identity drawn simultaneously from both faith communities. Shabateanism in particular, in its Frankist and other radical forms, could easily be conjoined with radical Christian ideologies such as those of the Rosicrucians, Swedenborgians, and Freemasons.

The full history of these boundary-crossings is still to be told. We have considerable inquisitional testimonies about Conversos who could adopt and discard different religious identities either out of conviction or lack of it, or for economic motives. There is scattered evidence of Jewish collaboration with radical Christian groups; rich documentation of Jewish converts and their ambiguous identities in early modern Germany, Great Britain, and elsewhere; and the complex writings of Christian Hebraists, especially kabbalists, who appropriated esoteric Jewish notions in reconstructing their own Christian identities. This fluid and ambiguous state of religious affiliation among all of these groups, and their constantly changing combinations and collaborations, represent a central feature of early modern Jewish culture. These new expressions of religious and cultural identity surely reflect the weakened and fragile state of the Jewish and Christian communities and their religious leadership by the seventeenth century as well as the prominent search for spiritual meaning among members of both faiths in an unstable social and political climate.[27]

*

Here, then, are five factors that might allow us to describe the early modern period as a meaningful chronological unit for Jewish cultural history. Albeit with considerable variation in the number of people affected by them at different times and places, each can be located across the continent, including the Middle East. Despite these apparent differences, they still might allow us to consider how Jewish communities in early modern Europe from Cracow to Venice to Amsterdam and Smyrna were linked in fascinating ways, and how Jews living in this era were communicating with each other and were more conscious of their connections with each other—economically, socially, and religiously—than ever before. Through a thorough examination of these markers across time and space, it might be possible to grasp more fully the unique nature of the Jewish cultural experience in early modern Europe, an experience both unique to the Jewish communities across the

---

[27] See Robert Bonfil, 'Dubious Crimes in Sixteenth-Century Italy: Rethinking the Relations Between Christians, Jews, and Conversos in Pre-Modern Europe', in Moshe Lazar and Stephen Haliczer (eds.), *The Jews of Spain and the Expulsion of 1492* (Lancaster, Calif., 1997), 299–310; Kaplan, *An Alternative Path to Modernity*; Richard Popkin and Gordon Weiner (eds.), *Jewish Christians and Christian Jews* (Dordrecht, 1994); Allison Coudert, *The Impact of the Kabbalah in the Seventeenth Century* (Leiden, 1999); Elliot Wolfson, 'Messianism in the Christian Kabbalah of Johann Kemper', in Goldish and Popkin (eds.), *Jewish Messianism in the Early Modern World*, 138–87; Elisheva Carlebach, *Divided Souls: Converts from Judaism in Germany 1500–1750* (New Haven, 2001); David Graizbard, *Souls in Dispute: Converso Identities in Iberia and the Jewish Diaspora 1580–1700* (Philadelphia, 2004); and Mercedes García Arenal and Gerard Wiegers, *A Man of Three Worlds: Samuel Pallache, a Moroccan Jew in Catholic and Protestant Europe* (Baltimore, 2003).

continent and simultaneously one shared with other European peoples. Finally, through the project of describing an early modern Jewish culture, we are in a better position to understand the modern era for Jews, its continuities and discontinuities with the period that precedes it. At the very least, historians of the modern Jewish experience can no longer study their period in isolation from what immediately preceded it. Mapping early modern Jewish culture provides an invaluable context and perspective for appreciating what modernity actually entailed.

SIX

The Reformation and the Jews

MIRIAM BODIAN

THE BREAK-UP and reorganization of Western Christendom in the sixteenth and seventeenth centuries—the upheaval once called, without qualification or embarrassment, 'the Reformation'—had much to do with the emergence of modern Western social and political structures. Though its seminal thinkers may have had no such intentions, the Reformation gave impetus to phenomena that had no roots in Christian tradition—among other things, the idea of toleration as a matter of principle, radical notions of the sovereignty of the people, secularization, and individualism.[1] To be sure, there is much disagreement about how the dots should be connected between sixteenth-century events and nineteenth-century ideas and institutions. Scholars have tried to connect them in multifarious and often controversial ways. But certain basic connections seem secure.

Jews and Judaism have not been ignored in the scholarly debates over the changes that accompanied the Reformation. But they have been part of the general discussion at rather predictable junctures. Jews have been introduced into the discussion as the historical bearers (and contemporary transmitters) of important raw material for the humanist and Protestant 'return to the sources'—material which included the Hebrew text of the Old Testament as well as rabbinic works. Scholars have noted that early modern Jews became both new objects of non-Jewish scrutiny (as contemporary practitioners of ancient Hebrew rituals)[2] and targets of renewed invective, sometimes also hurled at reformers and sectarians who were reputed to be 'Judaizing'.[3] The role of the Jews as it emerges from Reformation studies

---

[1] As William Bouwsma has put it, in reference to a particularly dynamic Protestant current, 'Calvinism has been widely credited—or blamed—for much that is thought to characterize the modern world: for capitalism and modern science, for the discipline and rationalization of the complex societies of the West, for the revolutionary spirit and democracy, for secularization and social activism, for individualism, utilitarianism, and empiricism': *John Calvin: A Sixteenth-Century Portrait* (New York, 1988), 1.

[2] There was even a popular market for engravings and books on the subject of Jewish ceremony, such as Thomas Godwyn's *Moses and Aron* (1625) in the English-speaking world and Buxtorf the Elder's *Synagoga Judaica* (1603) in the German-speaking world.

[3] On the accusation of 'Judaizing' cast by Christian opponents at both Reformers and 'papists', see Salo W. Baron, *A Social and Religious History of the Jews*, 18 vols. (New York,

might be characterized thus: though essentially bystanders, they did provide important texts and linguistic services. As for Christian attitudes towards Jews, they ranged from revived hostility to awakening curiosity.

Scholars of Jewish history have most often approached the subject along different lines, emphasizing the impact of the Reformation on the conditions of Jewish life. This impact, however, was notable for its lack of coherence. Luther clearly signalled a possible threat, giving an authoritative voice to late medieval anti-Jewish sentiment while abandoning, along with other aspects of Catholic theology, the traditional Catholic protections for Jews and Judaism—protections that existed on paper, and which were sometimes enforced. (In the wake of the Holocaust, scholars—both Jewish and German—have pondered whether Luther's anti-Jewish rhetoric, with its emphasis on the antagonism between 'Jewish' and 'German', offered clues to the roots of Nazi antisemitism.[4]) Certainly from a theological point of view, the ancient logic of Christian anti-Judaism remained unchanged in both Lutheran and Calvinist camps.

Yet as people in various parts of Europe strove to deal with religious conflict among Christians—and as it became increasingly clear that these differences could not be eliminated—the novel option of *accepting* difference was given a chance. Thus in places such as sixteenth-century Poland–Lithuania, Bohemia under Maximilian II, and seventeenth-century Holland, religiously diverse societies emerged in which a Jewish minority benefited from a general attitude of accommodation. On the other hand, some regimes headed off religious dissent by adopting the time-honoured option of repression. This was the pattern in post-Tridentine Italy and Spain.

Given the seemingly contradictory trends among different regimes— some towards greater tolerance, some towards greater repression—scholars who have considered the impact of the Reformation on the conditions of Jewish existence have tended to eschew a pan-European treatment. Perhaps for this reason, the Reformation has typically surfaced as a background theme in synthetic works dealing with the Jews of early modern Europe—in

---

1952–83), xiii. 223–47; Jerome Friedman, *The Most Ancient Testimony: Sixteenth-Century Christian-Hebraica in the Age of Renaissance Nostalgia* (Athens, Ohio, 1983), 182. Friedman writes: 'As the conflict between the two Christianities increased and became more and more hostile in nature, Jews, *necessarily bystanders*, were increasingly drawn into the conflict as the polemicists' tool against the adversary' (p. 180, my emphasis). See also I. A. Rashkow, 'Hebrew Bible Translation and the Fear of Judaization', *Sixteenth Century Journal*, 21 (1990), 217–33; Heiko A. Oberman, 'Discovery of Hebrew and Discrimination against the Jews: The *Veritas Hebraica* as Double-Edged Sword in Renaissance and Reformation', in Andrew C. Fix and Susan C. Karant-Nunn (eds.), *Germania Illustrata: Essays on Early Modern Germany Presented to Gerald Strauss* (Kirksville, Mo., 1992), 19–34.

[4] Heiko A. Oberman, *Roots of Antisemitism*, trans. James Porter (Philadelphia, 1984), 94, 125 n. 1.

Jonathan Israel's *European Jewry in the Age of Mercantilism*, for example, or in David Ruderman's *Jewish Thought and Scientific Discovery in Early Modern Europe*.[5] Remarkably, no major monograph has yet been written with an explicit focus on the Reformation and the Jews.

This results in part from the fact that Jews have rarely been represented as participants in the conceptual and psychic transformations of the Reformation. Indeed, Jacob Katz has depicted them as being almost entirely unengaged. While Katz's picture, which he first formulated in 1958,[6] has not gone unchallenged, it has by no means been banished. Katz found 'the indifference of Judaism to Christianity' particularly astonishing during the Reformation, because this upheaval 'presented an opportunity for a restatement of the Jewish position *vis-à-vis* Christianity'. But, he continued,

As a matter of fact, Jewish writers of that time took very slight cognizance only of what was happening in Christianity. Luther himself did attract some attention. As is well known, he thought at first that his purification of Christianity would remove the obstacles to the conversion of the Jews. On the other hand, some Jews at first judged Luther to be a Christian rebel, on the verge of becoming a Jew himself. . . . However, even where Luther was concerned Jewish interest appears to have been essentially directed at what were taken to be signs of the coming of the messianic era—these seemed to be implied in the shock suffered by the world of 'Edom', i.e. the supreme power of the Pope—rather than at the conversion of Christians to Judaism. Once the upheaval of the Reformation had subsided, Jews ceased to interest themselves in the religious differences and controversies of the Christian world.[7]

To be sure, Katz's work was restricted to the Ashkenazi sphere, but his generalizations, as in this passage, often suggest a wider application. Throughout his work, Katz adopted the view that the social, cultural, and political trends that developed out of the Reformation—trends that had powerful consequences for Jewish communities—emerged almost entirely outside the orbit of early modern Jewish life. The European Jewish encounter with 'modernity' came only after the European Enlightenment had achieved full-blown expression, in the late eighteenth century—as Katz argued famously in his *Out of the Ghetto*.[8]

---

[5] *European Jewry in the Age of Mercantilism, 1550–1750* (Oxford, 1985; 2nd edn. 1989; 3rd edn. 1998); *Jewish Thought and Scientific Discovery in Early Modern Europe* (New Haven, 1995; 2nd edn. Detroit, 2001). The index to Israel's book refers the reader to passages on a total of twelve pages for the topic 'Reformation and the Jews', Ruderman's index to passages on a total of seven pages for the topic 'Reformation and Jewish culture'.

[6] In his *Tradition and Crisis: Jewish Society at the End of the Middle Ages*, trans. B. D. Cooperman (1st published in Hebrew, 1958; New York, 1993).

[7] Jacob Katz, *Exclusiveness and Tolerance: Studies in Jewish–Gentile Relations in Medieval and Modern Times* (West Orange, NJ, 1961), 138.

[8] See particularly Katz's criticism of Azriel Shohet: *Out of the Ghetto: The Social Background of Jewish Emancipation, 1770–1870* (New York, 1978), 34–6.

Much scholarly work has been carried out since Katz's seminal studies were published, and the picture of early modern Jewish 'detachment' from the Christian world has been modified. But, for the most part, Reformation history and Jewish history have moved on separate tracks. In this essay I would like to argue the need for a systematic history of the Jews and the Reformation, and to suggest in broad strokes how it might be written.

SALO BARON AND NEW TRENDS IN REFORMATION SCHOLARSHIP

For a long period, indeed well into the twentieth century, Reformation scholarship was very narrowly conceived—a 'confessional polemic accompanied by painstaking scholarship', as two scholars put it,[9] confined in scope to the German states in the period between 1517 and the 1550s.[10] Jewish scholars, beginning with Graetz, had their own ideological agenda, but they too tended to follow the German scholarly tradition of focusing on individual Reformation thinkers.

By the 1950s, however, when Jacob Katz was formulating his views, the time had passed when a Reformation scholar could remark that 'Luther *was* the Reformation.'[11] The field of Reformation studies had undergone fundamental transformations. Its centre of gravity had shifted from Germany to the United States and England. Scholars had broadened their canvas to include all European regions where Protestantism took root. The leading scholars were no longer dominated by confessional interests; now they tended to adopt a 'Marxist' (or at least materialist) point of view, on the one hand, or a perspective shaped by the sociology of religion, on the other.

Having been trained in sociology, Katz was well aware of these developments. But he chose a model of traditional Jewish society so insular that it rendered essentially irrelevant the religio-social dynamics of Christian society. Only in one respect did Katz feel obliged to engage with sociologists of religion. Both Max Weber and Werner Sombart perceived a relationship between Jewish economic behaviour and the rise of capitalism. According to Weber, religious conditioning promoted rational economic behaviour among Jews. (This was, however, a side issue for him; the key factor in the rise of capitalism, according to his analysis, was Calvinist religious conditioning.) For Sombart, it was not religious training but racial characteristics

---

[9] See A. G. Dickens and John Tonkin, *The Reformation in Historical Thought* (Cambridge, Mass., 1985), 181–2.

[10] See R. Po-chia Hsia, *Social Discipline in the Reformation: Central Europe, 1550–1750* (London, 1989), 1–2.

[11] Dickens and Tonkin, *The Reformation in Historical Thought*, 205. The remark was made by Joseph Lortz in *Die Reformation in Deutschland*, 2 vols. (Freiburg, 1939–40); see the translation by Ronald Walls, *The Reformation in Germany*, 2 vols. (New York 1968), i. 167.

that were at play, and Jews were given a starring role in the rise of capital-ism—in his view, a development that brought about the destruction of an idealized pre-modern *Gemeinschaft*.[12]

Responding to these hypotheses, Katz readily acknowledged Jewish involvement with Christian society in the development of a capitalist econ-omy. But though he characteristically refused to reject Sombart's analysis out of hand,[13] he ultimately declared it flawed. He wrote that 'Jews did, in fact, quickly adopt and actively promote the spread of free capitalism', but only 'once it had been developed by others'; moreover, in his view, they did so not out of any general preference (much less an innate one), but for purely instrumental reasons.[14]

Refuting simplistic and unfounded generalizations, however, did nothing to further an understanding of the complex mechanisms at work among Jews during the Reformation. In 1969 Salo Baron sketched a picture of the by then vast field of Reformation studies, and remarked: 'It is doubly astonish-ing . . . that no comprehensive study has thus far been published about the relationship between Protestantism and Judaism or about the former's impact upon Jewish history.'[15]

Though Baron did not produce such a study, his mastery of the sources (and languages) enabled him to write the story of the Jews and the Reformation in an essentially new way. It is significant that his chapter on 'Protestant Reformation' in his *A Social and Religious History of the Jews* opens with a reference to Ernst Troeltsch, in a passage that suggests the vast scope of the project as he saw it:

Ernst Troeltsch's famous definition of Protestantism merely restated an historic phenomenon characteristic of other great revolutions as well. Protestantism was, according to Troeltsch, 'in the first place, simply a modification of Catholicism, in which the Catholic formulation of the problems was retained, while a different

[12] For a recent comparison of the thinking of Weber and Sombart, see Reiner Grundmann, 'Why Is Werner Sombart Not Part of the Core of Classical Sociology?', *Journal of Classical Sociology*, 1 (2001), 257–87.
[13] For evidence of this see Jacob Katz, 'Marriage and Sexual Life among the Jews at the Close of the Middle Ages' (Heb.), *Zion*, 10 (1944–5), 21–54: 31.
[14] See Katz, *Tradition and Crisis*, 50. For a discussion of the views of Weber and Sombart on the Jews' role in the rise of capitalism, see Toni Oelsner, 'The Place of Jews in Economic History as Viewed by German Scholars', *Leo Baeck Yearbook*, 7 (1962), 183–212. See also George Mosse, *The Crisis of German Ideology: Intellectual Origins of the Third Reich* (New York, 1964), 141–2; Arthur Hertzberg, *The French Enlightenment and the Jews* (New York, 1968), 78–80; Paul Mendes-Flohr, 'Werner Sombart's *The Jews and Modern Capitalism*: An Analysis of its Ideological Premises', *Leo Baeck Yearbook*, 21 (1976), 87–107; Werner Mosse, 'Judaism, Jews and Capitalism: Weber, Sombart and Beyond', *Leo Baeck Yearbook*, 24 (1979), 3–15; Herbert Bloom, *The Economic Activities of the Jews of Amsterdam in the Seventeenth and Eighteenth Centuries* (Williamsport, 1937), pp. xi–xiii.
[15] *Social and Religious History of the Jews*, xiii. 416 n. 4.

answer was given to them. It was only gradually that out of this new answer developed consequences of radical importance for the history of religion.' Nonetheless, in the long run, the Reformation contributed to the religious diversification, and subsequently to the growing secularization, of Europe. In time, these forces were bound to affect deeply also the position of Jews in the modern world.[16]

Baron went on to analyse the long-term effects of the Reformation. First, he regarded it as 'prepar[ing] the ground for a gradual reshaping of the whole Judeo-Christian symbiosis'. Both in the revolt against corporate controls that, in his view, it triggered, and in its emphasis on individual conscience, it led to a restructuring of Jewish life. Moreover, Christian Hebraism and Protestant recourse to the text of the Old Testament 'began to build certain bridges to Judaism'. Second, he viewed the Reformation as preparing the ground for a new state and society which, despite its retention of hostile elements, 'contained forces driving toward the ultimate liberation of the Jewish people'. And third, Calvinist thinking in the realm of economics 'brought the Protestant movement much closer to the regnant ideals and realities of Jewish life'. Calvinist merchants in the Low Countries, France, and England became 'effective collaborators' of Jews. '[I]n this fashion', Baron concluded, 'Jews, Huguenots, and English dissenters became leading protagonists in the great capitalist drama which had begun to unfold in the European world.'[17]

Baron thus drew insights about the unintended modernizing trends of the Reformation into the realm of Jewish scholarship, and he depicted the Jews as active participants in an economic transformation that, in his characterization, not only lacked sinister overtones but possessed positive, even triumphalist, ones.

BEN-SASSON ON JEWISH INVOLVEMENT

By the time Haim Hillel Ben-Sasson published his pioneering work on Jews and the Reformation in the late 1960s and early 1970s,[18] many scholars had examined how this or that Protestant reformer viewed the Jews and Judaism. But no one had asked, other than superficially, an equally important question: how did early modern Jews evaluate the Protestants and the Reformation? The question was irrelevant, of course, if the Jews were indifferent to their

---

[16] Ibid. 206. Baron's quotation is from Troeltsch, *Protestantism and Progress: A Historical Study of the Relation of Protestantism and the Modern World*, trans. W. Montgomery (London, 1912), 59.   [17] *Social and Religious History of the Jews*, xiii. 291–6.

[18] Haim Hillel Ben-Sasson, 'Jewish–Christian Disputation in the Setting of Humanism and Reformation in the German Empire', *Harvard Theological Review*, 59 (1966), 369–90; 'The Reformation in Contemporary Jewish Eyes', *Proceedings of the Israel Academy of Sciences and Humanities*, 4 (Jerusalem, 1970), 239–326; 'Jews and Christian Sectarians: Existential Similarity and Dialectical Tensions in Sixteenth-Century Moravia and Poland–Lithuania', *Viator*, 4 (1973), 369–85.

Christian environment. With characteristic boldness, Ben-Sasson opened with a challenge to that view. 'Some scholars', he wrote (although he was referring to one in particular),[19] 'characterize Jewish life and thought in [the late fifteenth and early sixteenth centuries] as dominated by almost total social isolationism and strict spiritual traditionalism. According to their view, this seclusion was as much self-willed as imposed by Christian society.'[20] Ben-Sasson proceeded to argue that German Jewry was isolated neither from its Christian humanist environment nor from 'Sephardi cultural elements' which provided indirect contact with that environment.[21]

In a subsequent and more wide-ranging article, Ben-Sasson scoured six-teenth-century Jewish documents from throughout the Jewish diaspora for opinions on, or comments about, the Reformation.[22] His quotations from Jewish observers revealed these Jews' acute awareness of the changing topog-raphy of Christendom. It is impressive how many of the themes he touched on in this article would be shown to be significant by later scholars. Among other things, he showed a new awareness of the dimensions (particularly in Italy and Poland–Lithuania) of nonconformist religious beliefs that proceeded, as he put it, either 'from Christianity towards Judaism' or 'from Judaism towards Christianity',[23] beliefs that were nourished by Jewish–Christian contacts.

In a third article, Ben-Sasson sketched a set of parallels between the predicament and self-perception of radical sectarians on the one hand, and Jews on the other, in Poland–Lithuania. Both groups shared a sense of being in exile, and were proud of their voluntary and conscious separation from the majority. This situation produced severe tensions, since both groups claimed divine election, but it also created an arena for theological exchange and development. He concluded by asking a question: 'Is it to be seen as sheer coincidence, or should it be understood as evidence of the emergence of a new all-European change in relations between Jews and Christians' that members of the Converso diaspora in western Europe, like some Polish–Lithuanian Jews, were also developing polemics that were a 'mirror image' of those in their Christian environment?[24]

This somewhat cryptic rhetorical question implies that the critique of Catholic tradition that arose in radical Reformation circles, with its ques-tioning of the authenticity of historical tradition (as opposed to the revealed

[19] For a succinct account of the debate between Katz and Ben-Sasson over the degree of insularity or openness of Ashkenazi Jewry, see Ruderman, *Jewish Thought and Scientific Discovery*, 60–4.   [20] Ben-Sasson, 'Jewish–Christian Disputation', 369.
[21] Ben-Sasson's article 'Jewish–Christian Disputation' leaves much to be desired in terms of analysis of the texts on which it is based. It is not evident that the 'disputations' described in Jewish sources were public. But the passages quoted do offer evidence that learned German Jews were aware of new perspectives in humanist and Protestant circles.
[22] Ben-Sasson, 'The Reformation in Contemporary Jewish Eyes'.   [23] Ibid. 250.
[24] Ben-Sasson, 'Jews and Christian Sectarians', 385.

text of Scripture) and its validation of such criticism on the grounds of reason, was shared in certain circles among Jews and Christians. Ben-Sasson falls short of noting, however, that while Jews were using this new arsenal to defend Judaism against traditional Christianity, they were also becoming attuned to a type of criticism that could eventually be turned against rabbinic Judaism.

THE DECLINE AND FALL OF THE 'COUNTER-REFORMATION'

Ben-Sasson's intuition of Europe-wide parallels in Jewish–Christian interaction was expressed at a time when Reformation scholars were beginning to challenge the traditional sharp distinction between the 'Protestant Reformation' and the 'Catholic Counter-Reformation'. John Bossy fired the opening shot of a major reconceptualization of the period in an article published in 1970, in which he drew a striking contrast between medieval Christianity and early modern Catholicism.[25] Jean Delumeau published an important book on the heels of Bossy's article, making a similar distinction.[26] And a landmark essay by Wolfgang Reinhard in 1977 rejected the widely accepted antithesis of 'progressive Reformation' and 'reactionary Counter-Reformation'.[27]

By the 1980s Reformation scholars were adopting the term 'confessionalization' to describe a phenomenon that cut across all confessional and geographical boundaries in Europe by the late sixteenth century (some have referred to it as the 'second Reformation'). Clerical authorities of all persuasions now sought to sharpen religious commitments and identities, sensing a threat in the religious fluidity and innovative spirit characteristic of the early Reformation. They attempted to do this through measures such as the precise formulation of dogma, the imposition of discipline on members of the religious community, and educational reform.[28]

Scholars of Jewish history have been slow to ask questions about the impact of these developments on Jewish life in early modern Europe.[29] Yet

---

[25] John Bossy, 'The Counter-Reformation and the People of Catholic Europe', *Past and Present*, 47 (1970), 51–70. See further id., *Christianity in the West, 1400–1700* (Oxford, 1985).

[26] *Le Catholicisme entre Luther et Voltaire* (Paris, 1971); published in English as *Catholicism between Luther and Voltaire: A New View of the Counter-Reformation* (London, 1977).

[27] ' "Gegenreformation als Modernisierung?" Prolegomena zu einer Theorie des konfessionellen Zeitalters', *Archiv für Reformationsgeschichte*, 68 (1977), 226–52.

[28] For a concise discussion of confessionalization among Protestants and Catholics alike (as it pertains to the German states), see Hsia, *Social Discipline in the Reformation*.

[29] In a database search, the only reference I was able to find was Rotraud Ries, 'Zur Bedeutung von Reformation und Konfessionalisierung für das christlich-jüdische Verhältnis in Niedersachsen', *Aschkenas*, 6 (1996), 353–419.

work by European scholars suggests that Jews may have become subject to a new kind of control and discipline even in unexpected places—in the early modern Netherlands, for example, which has often mistakenly been depicted as a permissive society.[30] In a more obvious setting—that of post-Tridentine Italy—perceptions have already begun to shift. It is no longer sufficient to explain the new restrictions on Jewish life adopted in Italy in the 1550s—particularly the institution of ghettos and the censorship of Hebrew books—as merely the expression of anti-Jewish sentiment. Recently, Amnon Raz-Krakotzkin has argued that the censorship of Hebrew books in sixteenth-century Italy was not a specifically 'anti-Jewish' measure, but part of a wider effort to impose controls—one that accompanied the advent of printing virtually everywhere.[31] This is not to deny that anti-Jewish sentiment accompanied the imposition of new controls on Jewish communities. That would be naive. But a recognition of the wide spectrum of actions taken in Reformation Italy to impose religious conformity serves to correct the equally naive view that restrictions imposed on Jews were the simple consequence of a reactionary resurgence of antisemitism.

LAY PIETY

At about the same time that the categories of 'Reformation' and 'Counter-Reformation' were challenged, a handful of Reformation scholars turned away from traditional approaches that focused on clerically sanctioned doctrines and institutions, and focused instead on the unexplored territory of lay belief.[32]

[30] See in particular Joke Spaans, 'Religious Policies in the Seventeenth-Century Dutch Republic', in R. Po-chia Hsia and Henk van Nierop (eds.), *Calvinism and Religious Toleration in the Dutch Golden Age* (Cambridge, 2002), 72–86, where Spaans argues that there was nothing distinctively Dutch in the basic mechanism of Dutch toleration. Like other early modern confessional societies, she asserts, the Netherlanders adopted 'a disciplinary approach' to religious dissent. It was only the method of application that was distinctive. Harking back to a concept coined by S. Groenveld, Spaans suggests that the Netherlands developed a 'pillarized' structure of rigidly defined minority communities that were carefully monitored by the magistrates and strictly supervised by a board of lay elders. This resulted in a society that was 'harmonious but at the same time highly authoritarian' (p. 86). Such an argument should at least be considered when studying the pattern of behaviour of the Mahamad of the Portuguese Jewish community of Amsterdam.

[31] See Amnon Raz-Krakotzkin, *The Censor, the Editor, and the Text: The Catholic Church and the Shaping of the Jewish Canon in the Sixteenth Century*, trans. Jackie Feldman (Philadelphia, 2007); id., 'Censorship, Editing and the Reshaping of Jewish Identity: The Catholic Church and Hebrew Literature in the Sixteenth Century', in Allison Coudert and Jeffrey Shoulson (eds.), *Hebraica Veritas? Christian Hebraists and the Study of Judaism in Early Modern Europe* (Philadelphia, 2004), 125–55.

[32] On this aspect of Reformation scholarship, see the survey by Robert Scribner, 'Elements of Popular Belief', in Thomas A. Brady, Heiko A. Oberman, and James D. Tracy (eds.), *Handbook of European History 1400–1600*, 2 vols. (Leiden 1994–5), i. 231–62. See also Helen Parish and William G. Naphy (eds.), *Religion and Superstition in Reformation Europe* (Manchester, 2002).

This had the effect of blurring the once seemingly rigid boundaries between orthodoxy and nonconformity (I am thinking of the work of Keith Thomas, Natalie Davis, and Carlo Ginzburg, as well as that of Delumeau and Bossy). The turn to the study of lay piety had relatively little impact on Jewish scholarship.[33] But an increased awareness of the instability of theological boundaries in the Reformation period raises the question whether, even within the boundaries of traditional rabbinic thought, but certainly among the Jewish 'laity', echoes cannot be heard of changing European sensibilities. David Ruderman has suggested a possible instance. He has cautiously proposed that 'nominalist' currents[34] in both Protestant and Catholic Prague may have had an impact on the thinking of the Maharal of Prague, Judah Loew b. Bezalel, or at least that a parallel development appears in the Maharal's thinking.[35] '[T]he end result of the Maharal's sharp division between rabbinic truth and speculation about the natural world, his open break with Aristotelian metaphysics, his emphasis on divine will, the possibility of miracles, and the contingency of creation all suggest, at the very least, a remarkable consensus with his Protestant (and ultimately Catholic) neighbors.'[36] This kind of insight (whether or not it is sustainable; I am not qualified to judge) suggests the possibility of lively dialogic interactions with non-Jewish society that lie hidden within 'orthodox' Jewish texts. If changing perceptions spilled rather freely across the doctrinal lines separating Catholics and Protestants, surely they spilled across the Christian–Jewish divide as well.

Let me suggest the kind of echo that might be explored in my own research field. One of the less gentle institutions that promoted 'correct' belief in the Reformation period was the Spanish Inquisition. Among the messages it sought to convey to Spaniards was that extravagant belief in the miraculous and supernatural—'superstition'—lay outside the boundaries of acceptable belief. By 1607, the post-Tridentine Church had defined superstition quite precisely: 'It is superstitious to expect any effect from anything, when such an effect cannot be produced by natural causes, by divine institution, or by the ordination or approval of the Church.' By this definition, the practice of magic was clearly 'superstition'. But so, according to the routine language of Inquisition sentencing, was belief in the 'Law of Moses'. Spectators at an auto-da-fé where Judaizers were sentenced were quite likely to hear a condemnation of the 'supersticiones de los judíos'.

It is possible that the assault of the Inquisition on what it called 'superstition' prompted some educated crypto-Jews to react defensively. For them, it was self-evident that Church doctrine concerning the sacraments, particularly

---

[33] The work of Elliott Horowitz stands out as an exception.
[34] On 'nominalism' and the Reformation—a complex issue—see Alister McGrath, *The Intellectual Origins of the European Reformation* (Oxford, 1987), 69–121.
[35] Ruderman, *Jewish Thought and Scientific Discovery*, 95–9.   [36] Ibid. 98.

the Eucharist, was a form of superstition. Some crypto-Jews (and perhaps other Jews within closer range of Protestant anti-Catholic rhetoric) were impelled to 'prove' that Judaism was free of superstition. At least in educated Portuguese New Christian circles, contempt for Catholic 'superstition'—and chagrin at the charge of Jewish 'superstition'—may have contributed to the formation of a contrasting, rationalistic, 'disenchanted' notion of Judaism. Some such dynamic may have played a role, for example, in the crystallization of the highly rationalistic religious posture of Uriel da Costa.

CROSS-CONFESSIONAL DISCOURSE AMONG JEWS AND CHRISTIANS: IBERIA AND ITALY

There is one aspect of Christian–Jewish relations in the Reformation period that seems to me to be begging, at this juncture, for a pan-European treatment. I am referring to a type of theological discourse that emerged among small numbers of Jews and Christians who were able to achieve a degree of distance and detachment from traditional modes of thought. This discourse cut across confessional, cultural, and geographical boundaries, challenging from various angles the orthodoxies and modes of authority that religious elites sought to impose. Among those who engaged in it were rabbinic Jews (Ashkenazi and Sephardi), crypto-Jews, Christians of Converso background, 'Old Christian' Catholic Hebraists, Protestant Hebraists, and Christian sectarians. It was a discourse that arose directly out of the theological battles of the era, from which Jews, it is now clear, were by no means isolated. It flowered in different places at different times (though in some places, to be sure, not at all). It reflects, among other things, a psychologically crucial breakdown, in certain circles, of the taboo that Christians traditionally felt with regard to the fundamental distinguishing beliefs of Jews, and the similar taboo Jews felt about Christians. It has left its protean traces in a wide variety of sources.

Both Baron and Ben-Sasson seem to have been aware of this undercurrent in Reformation Europe. Ben-Sasson was among the first to recognize (or look for) internal responsiveness among Jews of various backgrounds to innovative lines of thinking in the Christian orbit (in particular, to the Protestant focus on the Bible, ideas about tolerance, and Reformation-related eschatological hopes). Both Baron and Ben-Sasson spotted possible Jewish contributions to heterodox Christian thinking in a variety of European contexts. But neither of them systematically analysed this cross-confessional discourse. Meanwhile, new sorts of questions have been raised that cannot easily be answered.[37] New material has been unearthed and

---

[37] Frank Manuel has pointed to one desideratum: 'As the history of the book comes to occupy its rightful place in the historical order of western culture, the vicissitudes of Hebrew printing may yield fresh insights into the network of intellectual relations among Christians

examined by, among others, Richard Popkin, Jerome Friedman, Yosef Kaplan, David Katz, and Robert Dán. Lately I have taken an interest in a set of sources from the post-Tridentine Iberian world that adds to the growing evidence.[38] Perusing the existing data, one begins to sense just how entangled the Jewish world was with the chaotic burst of individualist, literalist, rationalist, and spiritualist thinking that posed a challenge to traditional Church authority.

At least one contemporary Jew thought that Jews (of a sort) were actually responsible for the challenge to that authority. This was Samuel Usque, among the many authors cited by Ben-Sasson in his key article.[39] Usque, an ex-Converso who escaped Portugal in the first half of the sixteenth century and settled in Ferrara, suggested a seemingly bizarre causal connection between the religious disquietude of descendants of forcibly converted Jews, on the one hand, and the rise of Protestantism on the other. His brief but pointed exposition of this idea appears in two passages of his *Consolations for the Tribulations of Israel*, printed in Ferrara in 1553. According to Usque, the discontent that led to the Reformation had its roots in episodes of forced conversion of Jews in medieval Flanders and France.[40] His aim was tendentious, but the connection he drew is worth a second look.

In this way, [as a result of the conversions,] the province [of Toulouse] was sown with Jewish seed, and many of the descendants of these Jews are still uncomfortable in the faith which their ancestors accepted so reluctantly. It would not be far-fetched to assume that from these [Jewish converts in France] stem the Lutherans,[41] who have sprung up everywhere in Christendom. For since throughout Christendom Christians have forced Jews to change their religion, it seems to be divine retribution that the Jews should strike back with the weapons that were put into their hands. To punish those who compelled them to change their faith, and as a judgment upon the new faith, the Jews break out of the circle of Christian unity, and by such actions seek to re-enter the road to their faith, which they abandoned so long ago.[42]

and Jews': *The Broken Staff: Judaism through Christian Eyes* (Cambridge, Mass., 1992), 35. Raz-Krakotzkin's recently published book will perhaps stimulate some dialogue on this issue.

[38] See Miriam Bodian, *Dying in the Law of Moses: Crypto-Jewish Martyrdom in the Iberian World* (Bloomington, 2007); ead., 'In the Cross-Currents of the Reformation: Crypto-Jewish Martyrs of the Inquisition, 1570–1670', *Past and Present*, 176 (Aug. 2002), 66–104.

[39] Ben-Sasson, 'Reformation in Contemporary Jewish Eyes', 275.

[40] See Samuel Usque, *Consolação às tribulações de Israel* (Ferrara, 1553, facsimile edn. Lisbon, 1989), fos. 180ᵛ, 190ʳ. The passages appear in Martin Cohen's English translation, *Consolation for the Tribulations of Israel* (Philadelphia, 1977), 185, 193.

[41] Usque's use of the term *luteros* is not to be taken in the strict sense of the word, but in reference to dissenters from Catholicism of all kinds.

[42] I have modified Martin Cohen's translation (*Consolation*, 193). The original reads as follows: 'assi que desta maneira ficou aquella provincia semeada deste semente de que ynda agora se devem achar muitas plantas que nam sosseguem na fee que de tam ma[l] vontade aceitarom,

This idea was useful to Usque in a book that sought to depict a world on the brink of messianic transformation. The activity of the 'Lutherans', one was to infer, was a sign of both the impending fall of the Roman Church and the reunification of the Jewish people. But the idea must have been *persuasive* as well as useful. Let me try to reconstruct Usque's line of thinking.

Usque and his readers were surely aware of the accusations cast at the Reformers by their opponents that they were 'Judaizers'. They may have privately seen a certain truth in such accusations, since some Protestant criticisms of the Church coincided with deeply held views of Jews and crypto-Jews. Moreover, unlike most European Jews, Usque and his readers must also have been aware of the disproportionate involvement of New Christians in 'Protestantish' circles in sixteenth-century Spain, Portugal, and Italy.[43] These circles were at the height of their activity at the time Usque lived in the Iberian peninsula and Italy, before they were suppressed (or driven underground) by Iberian and Italian inquisitions. Usque may have reasoned something like this. Since Conversos were at the forefront of the dissemination of 'Protestantish' beliefs in Spain, Portugal, and Italy, and since persecutions and forced conversions had been perpetrated against medieval Jews in northern lands as well as in the Iberian peninsula, it stood to reason that the figures at the forefront of the Reformation in Germany were descendants of forced converts in the Franco-German region, impelled by deep ancestral inclinations.

Of course, this is a truly eccentric theory by any scholarly standard. It need hardly be said that Reformation thinking drew from an array of impulses, many of them native to late medieval Christianity. But there is also reason to believe that Conversos played a significant role. To be sure, it was a time of extraordinary theological fluidity, making it often impossible to determine who was borrowing from whom. Thus when the eminent scholar George Williams, seeking to make some order out of the Reformation in Italy, classified the Italian reformists as Lutherans, Calvinists, Anabaptists, Spiritualists, or 'Evangelical Rationalists', he hastened to qualify his taxonomy, noting that 'distinctions among these movements and phases in the

e nã serta mui disconforme presumir serem destes os luteros que pella cristandade se levantarom que pois por toda ella am forçado os judeos trocar sua ley parece justiça divina que cõ as armas que lhe puserom nas mãos, por pena da quelles que os forçarom e per juizo da fe que lhe derom os ofendam, e estes mesmos desfaçam a roda, e tornem a querer jaa entrar com estes principios no caminho que tanto tempo ha am deixado' (Usque, *Consolação*, fo. 190ʳ).

[43] The pioneering work on this topic is Marcel Bataillon, *Erasme et Espagne* (Paris, 1937); Spanish translation, *Erasmo y España*, 2nd edn., with corrections and additions (Mexico City, 1966). Important subsequent work includes Alastair Hamilton, *Heresy and Mysticism in Sixteenth-Century Spain: The Alumbrados* (Toronto, 1992); Miguel Jiménez Monteserín, 'Los hermanos Valdés y el mundo judeoconverso conquense', in *Política, religión e inquisición en la España moderna: homenaje a Joaquín Pérez Villanueva* (Madrid, 1996), 379–400; José C. Nieto, *Juan de Valdés and the Origins of the Spanish and the Italian Reformation* (Geneva, 1970).

individual careers of their leaders and followers are not so easy to keep sorted out at any one moment or in any given conventicle'.[44] In an environment of theological uncertainty and experimentation, some seekers vacillated between one circle of believers and another, or were 'serially monogamous', so to speak.[45] New Christians and crypto-Jews were without question among the players participating in Reformation thought, as George Williams has noted for Italy. He writes:

The overall impression is very strong in both Anabaptism and Evangelical Rationalism in Italy that Marranism . . . played . . . a formative role in the devolution of the doctrine of the Trinity and in the lowering of Christology up to the complete humanization of Jesus as the son of Joseph. Clearly, these theologically provocative thrusts served no soteriological or other purpose, except as they made the evangelical reformation of Catholic Christianity more acceptable precisely to those whose ancestors had been presumably forced into Christianity.[46]

There is evidence that similar processes were at work in the Iberian peninsula. As I have noted, evidence for a Converso impact on pre-Tridentine Spanish humanism has long been recognized. In recent years, however, the reach of that impact has been extended. The late Richard Popkin has argued that, at least indirectly, Conversos in Spain contributed to the emergence of antitrinitarianism, which was given full expression by two Spaniards, Miguel Servetus and Juan de Valdés, in the early 1530s.[47] Servetus, he argued, may have gained his knowledge of Jewish objections to

[44] George Williams, 'The Two Strands in Italian Anabaptism, ca. 1526–ca. 1565', in Lawrence P. Buck and Jonathan Zophy (eds.), *The Social History of the Reformation* (Columbus, Ohio, 1972), 197. The connection between Italian antitrinitarianism and 'Marranism' had already been suggested (as Williams acknowledges) by Aldo Stella in *Anabattismo e antitrinitarismo in Italia nel XVI secolo: nuove ricerche storiche* (Padua, 1969), 31, 81. On the openness of the Reformation sectarians to non-Christian theology, see George Williams, 'Sectarian Ecumenicity: Reflections on a Little Noticed Aspect of the Radical Reformation', [Baptist] *Review and Expositor*, 64/2 (1967), 141–60; id., 'Erasmus and the Reformers in Non-Christian Religions and *Salus extra Ecclesiam*', in Theodore Rabb and Jerrold Siegel (eds.), *Essays in Memory of E. Harris Harbison* (Princeton, 1969), 319–70.

[45] At least two such seekers eventually turned to rabbinic Judaism. Laureto di Buongiorno went from radical Valdesianism to Anabaptism to rabbinic Judaism (in Thessalonica), before turning himself over to the Inquisition in 1553, the year Usque's book was published. On Nicholas Antoine, who began life as a Catholic, converted to Calvinism, and sought to become a Jew, see Julien Weill, 'Nicholas Antoine', *Revue des études juives*, 37 (1898), 161–80.

[46] Williams, 'The Two Strands', 197–8, and see id., *The Radical Reformation* (Kirksville, Mo., 2000), 819 and *passim*.

[47] Richard Popkin, 'Marranos, New Christians and the Beginnings of Modern Antitrinitarianism', in Yom Tov Assis and Yosef Kaplan (eds.), *Jews and Conversos at the Time of the Expulsion* (Heb.) (Jerusalem, 1999), 143–60. Popkin goes so far as to state in this article that he wishes to show that 'after the forced conversions a special kind of marrano rejection or questioning of the Doctrine of the Trinity emerged that was to play a far-reaching role in Christendom' (p. 152).

Christian doctrine by reading conversionist, anti-Jewish texts composed by learned Jewish apostates, who in their effort to rebut Jewish objections to Christianity necessarily stated those objections. He may even have had recourse to major Jewish anti-Christian works of the fifteenth century.[48] Perhaps more unexpectedly, Sara Nalle has unearthed crypto-Jewish rhetoric in the eclectic heresy of the apparently Old Christian wool carder Bartolomé Sánchez.[49]

What has gone unnoticed is that a reverse process was also at work. That is, by a natural dialogic process (and in the absence of a rabbinic model), the 'Judaism' of crypto-Jews was sometimes shaped to conform to 'Protestantish' ideas about what constituted authentic religion, bringing their conceptualization of 'Judaism' to diverge rather starkly from the conceptualizations of most contemporary Jews. In my opinion, for example, humanist and Protestant critiques of post-Pauline Catholic tradition played a vital (if indirect) role in moulding a certain type of crypto-Jewish theology. At the core of this theology were the notions (*a*) that the self-evident truth of Scripture was accessible to anyone who could read and reason, (*b*) that true religious authority resided only in the 'Old Testament', and (*c*) that Scripture proved Catholic tradition to be false. Adherents of this sort of crypto-Judaism thus relied heavily on the foundations of Protestant anti-Catholic and anti-clerical polemics. As a consequence, they unwittingly tailored their Judaism to be immune, as it were, to their own criticisms of Catholicism: it was a belief system untouched by human inventions, one that required no tools for interpretation other than Scripture and human intelligence.

There is evidence that indicates that cross-fertilization took place between crypto-Jews and heterodox Christians in Iberian lands even after 'luterano'[50] heterodoxy had supposedly been suppressed. It is notable that two of the most celebrated 'Judaizing' martyrs of the seventeenth century had no apparent Jewish ancestry. Both of them were familiar with humanist and Protestant teachings (as they themselves testified). One of them reported theological conversations he had had with 'Portuguese' students— clearly crypto-Jews—at the University of Salamanca. Prompted by a method of enquiry inspired by humanist currents, in an environment in which basic crypto-Jewish beliefs were widely known (and indeed publicized by the Inquisition), he eventually arrived at a belief in the truth of the 'Law of Moses'.[51]

---

[48] Popkin, 'Marranos, New Christians and the Beginnings of Modern Antitrinitarianism', 148–9.

[49] Sara Nalle, *Mad for God: Bartolomé Sánchez, the Secret Messiah of Cardenete* (Charlottesville, 2001), esp. pp. 71–2.

[50] In Spain, as in Italy, this term was used rather indiscriminately to describe an inclination to any Protestant position.   [51] Bodian, *Dying in the Law of Moses*, chs. 4 and 6.

For Conversos who had been inculcated from youth with core Jewish teachings, a converse process might take place: 'Protestantish' thinking and rhetoric might lend weight and intellectual sophistication to a pre-existing interest in the 'Law of Moses'. Interestingly, we even find bonds being forged between 'Judaizing' Conversos and heterodox Old Christian Catholics, each offering to the other reciprocal validation of nonconformist expressions of religiosity. Thus, for example, the Converso martyr Luis Carvajal felt a strong kinship with the heterodox Old Christian Catholic hermit Gregorio López.[52]

To be sure, further work is needed to unravel the enigmas of clandestine heterodox thinking in Iberian lands. It has become increasingly clear that the standard categorization of heretics employed by the Inquisition—particularly, where we are concerned, the use of the terms *judaizantes*, *alumbrados*, and *luteranos*—has imposed an artificial order on a slippery reality. As John Edwards has shown, the classification of a heretic by the Inquisition as a 'crypto-Jew' or a 'blasphemer' might have to do less with the nature of his or her remarks than with his or her ancestry.[53] While much attention has been paid to the role of Catholic New Christians in the emergence of the individualistic theological current known as *alumbradismo*, a somewhat ironic corollary phenomenon—the impact of *alumbradismo* on crypto-Judaism—has not been explored. And the question of the extent to which crypto-Jewish critiques of Catholicism triggered Christian (as well as Portuguese Jewish![54]) scepticism has only begun to be explored. In any case, it would seem that the study of crypto-Judaism, *luteranismo*, and scepticism in Iberian lands in isolation from one another is no longer tenable.[55]

CROSS-CONFESSIONAL DISCOURSE AMONG JEWS AND CHRISTIANS: THE EAST

Shifting our view from heterodox Old Christians and crypto-Jews in sixteenth-century Spain to Ashkenazi Jews and sectarian Christians in

[52] On the dovetailing of crypto-Jewish and Reformation currents in Iberian lands, see Bodian, 'In the Cross-Currents of the Reformation', and ead., *Dying in the Law of Moses*.

[53] John Edwards, 'Religious Faith and Doubt in Late Medieval Spain: Soria circa 1450–1500', *Past and Present*, 120 (Aug. 1988), 3–25.

[54] For 're-Judaizing' Conversos who were committed to notions of biblical authority they had developed in the peninsula, there were obvious parallels between a fabricated Catholic tradition, as they saw it, and post-biblical rabbinic teachings.

[55] Scholars of crypto-Judaism have been more likely to study their subject without reference to *luteranismo* or Old Christian scepticism than the other way around. Yet Nicholas Griffiths, to cite but one example, has analysed popular religious scepticism in early modern Spain without even a passing mention of crypto-Judaism. See Griffiths, 'Popular Religious Skepticism and Idiosyncrasy in Post-Tridentine Cuenca', in Lesley Twomey (ed.), *Faith and Fanaticism: Religious Fervour in Early Modern Spain* (Aldershot, 1997), 95–126.

sixteenth-century Poland–Lithuania, we turn to what would seem to be an entirely different historical nexus.[56] Here there was no Converso presence to speak of. Jews lived in cohesive communities according to a rabbinic tradition that was sharply at odds with their Christian environment. Moreover, in contrast to Spain, Portugal, and Italy, that environment was not, in the mid-sixteenth century, dominated by a repressive Catholic regime. Indeed, for the most part Catholics, Lutherans, Calvinists, and sectarians in Poland–Lithuania (not to mention Armenians, Muslim Turks, and Christian Orthodox) lived together in relative peace. Poland–Lithuania became an asylum for a variety of refugee sects, including Czech Brethren from Bohemia and Anabaptists and Mennonites from the Netherlands. In this environment of religious diversity it is not surprising that there also existed a small Karaite community, of about 2,000 persons, in the mid-seventeenth century.[57] Religious boundaries remained fluid well into the seventeenth century, when the Jesuits began to reassert Catholic dominance through an intensive confessionalizing programme.[58] Yet significant Jewish–Christian theological interaction was never as intense in this region as it was in western Europe, and few educated Poles took any interest in Hebrew or, more generally, Judaism.[59]

Given this state of affairs, it may not be surprising that scholarship dealing with Jewish–Christian dialogue in the east has focused on three key figures: the Polish antitrinitarian Marcin Czechowic, the Lithuanian antitrinitarian Simon Budny, and the Karaite Jew Isaac of Troki.[60] (There were contacts between Rabbanite Jews and Christians, mainly in the towns of Raków and Lublin, of which we have traces; and there were other sectarians who took an interest in Hebrew and Judaism. But documentation on them is meagre.) Isaac of Troki, who appears to have been at home in rabbinic literature and who served in public roles for both the Karaite and Rabbanite communities,[61] engaged throughout his adult life in debates with Catholics, Lutherans, Calvinists, and antitrinitarians—'with anyone who wanted to debate with me',[62] as he put it—and was familiar with the antitrinitarian

---

[56] This section of the essay is based on secondary literature in English and German, excluding important work in Polish.

[57] Christoph Schmidt, 'Calvinisten, Täufer, Orthodoxe und Juden in der litauischen Reformation', *Zeitschrift für Religions- und Geistesgeschichte*, 52 (2000), 309–32: 328.

[58] For a complex picture of this process see Magda Teter, *Jews and Heretics in Catholic Poland: A Beleaguered Church in the Post-Reformation Era* (Cambridge, 2006).

[59] See ibid. 105–7.

[60] On Polish antitrinitarianism, see Stanislas Kot, *Socinianism in Poland: The Social and Political Antitrinitarians in the Sixteenth and Seventeenth Centuries*, trans. Earl Morse Wilbur (Boston, 1957); Williams, *The Radical Reformation*, 1135–75.

[61] See Stefan Schreiner, 'Isaac of Troki's Studies of Rabbinic Literature', in Antony Polonsky (ed.), *Polin*, 15: *Jewish Religious Life 1500–1900* (Oxford, 2002), 65–76.

[62] Isaac of Troki, *Ḥizuk emunah* (New York, 1932), 10.

works of the Lithuanian Hebraist Simon Budny as well as those of the Italian Nicholas Paruta. The antitrinitarians, for their part—most notably Simon Budny, who produced a Polish translation of the Bible—made use of Jewish exegesis to support their doctrines. It is clear, however, from surviving documentation that each side felt a strong need to distance itself from the other— the sectarians, in order to defend themselves against accusations that they were 'Judaizers'; the Jews, in order to head off possible Jewish conversions to a 'purified' form of Christianity.

Scholars seem to be in considerable disagreement about the channels of influence in these encounters. Was Isaac Troki made familiar with innovative New Testament criticism in the Christian world through his familiarity with the arguments of the antitrinitarians Nicholas Paruta, Daniel Bieliński, and Simon Budny?[63] If so, was he indirectly drawing, via the Polish antitrinitarian Jacob Paleologus (a defender of Servetus), on a discourse that had its roots in Spanish Converso circles?[64] Or did he draw on Christian antitrinitarian authors merely to add polemical weight to arguments he was actually borrowing from medieval Jewish polemics, with which he was familiar,[65] and which Paruta himself had drawn on?[66] Probably each of these possibilities is too neat. It may be that, in the swiftly flowing currents of Reformation thought, ideas were intermingled in a way that defies efforts to untangle them.

Let me illustrate with a case in which two heterodox thinkers in two apparently unconnected contexts cited the same biblical prooftext. Both of them—the sixteenth-century Lithuanian antitrinitarian Simon Budny, on the one hand, and the Portuguese Old Christian 'Judaizer' Diogo d'Assumpção (who was burned alive at the stake in Lisbon in 1603), on the other—were arguing the case for the purely human nature of Jesus. Both pointed as a prooftext to Luke 2: 52: 'And Jesus grew in wisdom and stature, and in favour with God and men.' If Jesus was God, Simon Budny argued, how could he undergo change?[67] If Jesus was God, Diogo d'Assumpção asserted, how could he have needed to grow wiser?[68] It is quite possible that this particular argument developed independently in the two contexts. But it may also be that subterranean currents, running between Poland and Italy, and between Italy and Portugal, or perhaps by other routes, connected the thinking of these vastly different heterodox figures.

[63] See Jerome Friedman, 'The Reformation and Jewish Antichristian Polemics', *Bibliothèque d'humanisme et Renaissance*, 41 (1979), 83–97; id., 'The Reformation in Alien Eyes: Jewish Perceptions of Christian Troubles', *Sixteenth Century Journal*, 14 (1983), 28–9.

[64] See Popkin, 'Marranos, New Christians and the Beginnings of Modern Antitrinitarianism'.

[65] See Schreiner, 'Isaac of Troki's Studies'.

[66] See Robert Dán, 'Isaac Troky and his "Antitrinitarian" Sources', in Robert Dán (ed.), *Occident and Orient: A Tribute to the Memory of Alexander Scheiber* (Leiden, 1988), 69–82.

[67] See Schmidt, 'Calvinisten, Täufer, Orthodoxe und Juden', 319–20.

[68] Arquivo Nacional da Torre do Tombo, Inquisição de Lisboa, no. 104, 5ᵛ.

CROSS-CONFESSIONAL DISCOURSE
AMONG JEWS AND CHRISTIANS:
THE EMERGING ATLANTIC POWERS

The picture grows in complexity when we move to France, England, and the Netherlands, where the sixteenth and seventeenth centuries witnessed Jewish–Christian boundary-crossing at an unprecedented rate, in a multitude of contexts and in ways that leave the would-be theological taxonomist bewildered. The explorations of Richard Popkin in this territory have been invaluable. It is very fitting that a volume in his honour has been entitled *Everything Connects*.[69] Popkin's work, taken up by his students, offers a rich panorama of the meeting of a multitude of original and often quirky minds, of Jews and Christians as well as of 'Jewish Christians' and 'Christian Jews'—to borrow terms from the title of a volume co-edited by Popkin.[70] We now know a great deal about how early modern savants thought about such matters as the Ten Lost Tribes, the end of days, the history of mankind, and the nature of the biblical text. Thanks to considerable advances in the study of Christian Hebraism, we are also acquainted with such enigmatic giants as Guillaume Postel and Jean Bodin, who shared a breathtaking detachment from traditional Christian thinking about both Christianity and Judaism, as well as with less stratospheric figures such as Nicolaus Serarius and Isaac La Peyrère.[71]

But Popkin and his colleagues have tended to frame their studies in the context of the history of early Enlightenment scepticism. If we want a balanced picture of 'the Reformation and the Jews' in western Europe, we need to know more about manifestations of this discourse within the boundaries of traditional revealed religion. In particular, we need to ask how literalist Protestant and sectarian Bible-reading impinged on Jewish perceptions of Christianity and on Jewish self-perception. Were the so-called 'Karaites' described by Yosef Kaplan responding in some measure to Protestant discourse?[72] How did Protestant missionizing, with its new emphases and claims, elicit new lines of defence in Jewish apologetics?

Certainly we need a thorough analysis of the most elaborate, nuanced, and learned Jewish evaluation of the Protestant world in the pre-Enlightenment

[69] James Force and David Katz (eds.), *Everything Connects. In Conference with Richard H. Popkin: Essays in his Honor* (Leiden, 1999).
[70] Richard Popkin and Gordon Weiner (eds.), *Jewish Christians and Christian Jews: From the Renaissance to the Enlightenment* (Boston, 1994).
[71] See, inter alia, Friedman, *The Most Ancient Testimony*; Frank Manuel, *The Broken Staff: Judaism through Christian Eyes* (Cambridge, Mass., 1992).
[72] See Yosef Kaplan, 'The "Karaites" of Amsterdam in the Early Eighteenth Century' (Heb.), *Zion*, 52 (1987), 279–314. Its seems particularly suggestive that some of the Sephardi 'Karaites' discussed in this article abandoned Judaism and adopted Calvinism.

period, a polemical treatise by the Amsterdam rabbi Saul Levi Mortera composed in 1659.[73] This massive treatise of more than four hundred manuscript pages sought to stake out a Jewish position with regard to Christian believers along a wide spectrum, from Catholics and Calvinists (Mortera had read Calvin's *Institutes* in Spanish translation, and quoted from it profusely) to sabbatarians and antitrinitarians.

Still, it is already abundantly clear from existing research that, by the sixteenth and seventeenth centuries, Judaism and Christianity had become inextricably entangled in European philosophical and religious discourse. Never had so many Jews and Christians penetrated so deeply into each other's religio-cultural spheres. This is not to suggest that the erosion of Christian–Jewish boundaries was an outstanding *sociological* characteristic of early modern European societies, or indeed that most Jews did not continue to live in a highly insular cultural world. But throughout Europe there were Jews who were listening to new Christian notions about religious truth, and Christians who were driven to new conclusions about the old Hebrew truth.

*

The astonishment that Salo Baron expressed in 1969 about the fact that no scholar had yet undertaken a comprehensive history of the Reformation and the Jews can only be reiterated with greater vigour today, almost forty years later. Such a project could be undertaken—though it might require a collaborative effort. It would best be carried out by adopting an organizational structure that was neither regional nor chronological, but thematic.

A chapter on the venerable topic of the impact of the Reformation on Christian attitudes to Jews and Judaism should be included. But it should eschew rigid categories that divide Europe into 'Protestant' and 'Counter-Reformation' spheres, or that label attitudes as 'antisemitic' or 'philosemitic'. It should, rather, focus on the variety of ways—some ephemeral, some lasting—in which the upheaval of the Reformation reshaped the image of Jews and Judaism in Christian eyes. A further chapter might be devoted to explicit contemporary Jewish perceptions and interpretations of the transformation taking place in their midst—the splintering of a western Christendom that had maintained its unity for centuries, and the rapid spread of innovative Christian theologies.

But the key contribution would be an integrated analysis of developments in which both Jews and Christians participated. It would include the following components: first, a discussion of a theological current we might

---

[73] The manuscript work has been published by H. P. Salomon: *Tratado da verdade da lei de Moisés* (Coimbra, 1988). Mortera was not a Portuguese Jew of Converso origin—he was apparently of mixed Italianate and Ashkenazi origin—but he had become a part of the ex-Converso diaspora quite early in his life, and devoted himself to serving its needs until his death.

call 'biblicism' (including much of what was happening among Christian Hebraists), in which orthodox Protestants, Catholics, and Jews all took part; second, an exploration of efforts in the Jewish world to come to terms theologically with scientific, economic, and political developments associated with the Reformation; third, a discussion of the speculative heterodox discourse that took place among Jews, crypto-Jews, Christians, and sceptics; and finally, a discussion of the new Christian focus on discipline, supervision, and boundary definition, which became the concern of Jewish communal leaders as well as Christian authorities (for example, in the area of censorship, in the suppression of residual Shabateanism, and in the 're-Judaizing' enterprise of the Portuguese Jews). What would emerge, I believe, is a revised picture of both the Reformation world and the Jews who inhabited it.

SEVEN

Re(de)fining Modernity in Jewish History

GERSHON DAVID HUNDERT

THE UNDERSTANDING of modernity in Jewish history demands revision. Treatments of the modern history of Jews in Europe have tended to minimize or even omit the community in Poland–Lithuania in the eighteenth century because the 'defining criteria' of modernity cannot be found there. With regard to Jewish history these criteria are most often interpreted as the progressive integration of Jews in society at large and/or the exchange of particularistic Jewish values, in varying degrees, for a more universal world-view. But, whatever the definition, the largest concentration of Jews in the world is omitted from the discussion. Since historians were and are part of the very process they describe, they tend to seek out the origins of modernity along the same continuum of Westernization in which they find themselves rather than seeking it in the considerably different experience of east European Jews. I contend that the criteria for dividing Jewish history into periods should be drawn from the Jewish experience itself, and in particular the experience of the majority of the Jewish people.

In Philip Roth's book *The Plot against America* there is a passage in which he describes his parents' generation and their Jewishness:

Their being Jews didn't issue from the rabbinate or the synagogue or from their few formal religious practices . . . Their being Jews didn't even issue from on high. To be sure, each Friday at sundown when my mother ritually . . . lit the Sabbath candles, she invoked the Almighty by his Hebrew title but otherwise no one ever made mention of 'Adonoy.' These were Jews who needed no large terms of reference, no profession of faith or doctrinal creed, in order to be Jews . . . Neither was their being Jews a mishap or a misfortune or an achievement to be 'proud' of. What they were was what they couldn't get rid of—what they couldn't even begin to want to get rid of. Their being Jews issued from their being themselves, as did their being American. It was as it was, in the nature of things, as fundamental as having arteries and veins, and they never manifested the slightest desire to change it or deny it, regardless of the consequences.[1]

---

[1] Philip Roth, *The Plot against America: A Novel* (New York, 2004), 220.

In this essay the burden of my remarks is to try to explain where the Jewishness Roth describes that 'was as it was, in the nature of things, as fundamental as having arteries and veins' came from, and to argue that the ingredients that produced this particular dish in the banquet of modernity were prepared in east-central Europe in the eighteenth century. Rather than the corporeal metaphor of arteries and veins, one might also refer to this as the 'magmatic' level of Jewish experience, which is somehow beneath or beyond cultural, religious, and political change. What Roth is talking about can be rephrased as positing a continuing positive self-evaluation as Jews, in addition to or despite other dimensions of identity.

I will advance two claims: first, that the source of this continuing and basic element of the Jewish experience is eighteenth-century east-central Europe, and second, that this, perhaps, is the most important ingredient in modern Jewish history. To make this argument it is necessary to cast aside the Germanocentric paradigm of modernity in Jewish history and to look further east to the lands where most Jews lived.

THE PRIMACY OF EAST EUROPEAN JEWRY

This first section will attempt to establish the distinctiveness and the distinctive importance of the east European Jewish experience. In the course of the eighteenth century millions of Jewish lives were lived on the lands of Poland–Lithuania. Virtually all of the heterogeneity and diversity that so many human beings are capable of was played out during that century. Fasting and feasting; perfunctory prayer and mystical intensity; chastity and licentiousness; the sadness mandated by propriety and God-intoxicated joy; vast wealth and dire poverty; orderly patriarchal solemnity and rebellious and impudent youth were all part of Jewish life. Such extremes of human experience were nevertheless bounded by commonalities and shared patterns that gave structure to a community and defined its Jewish aspect. The Jewish calendar defined the rhythm of the day, the week, and the year; the language in which life was apprehended was Yiddish—this cannot be stressed strongly enough; the commandments that were observed or transgressed were the defining categories of value. And what distinguished Polish Jewry from other Jewish communities, aside from sheer numbers, was its extraordinary vitality. This vitality expressed itself in the ramified autonomous institutions, the cultural creativity, and the singular sense of both independence and rootedness that characterized the Jewish community of Poland–Lithuania; the political hegemony to which Jews were subject did not extend meaningfully to the core elements of Jewish cultural creativity. Nevertheless, Polish Jews were deeply tied to the land in which they lived. Polish–Lithuanian Jewry inhabited a cultural universe constructed of elements that arose out of its own traditions. It was, in the Weberian sense, a 'traditional society'. The basic values and patterns of behaviour by which most Jews lived their lives were unexamined and unselfconscious.[2]

In the 1750s Stanisław Poniatowski, father of the future king Stanisław August Poniatowski, granted a privilege or charter of laws governing the Jewish community of the town of Jazłowiec. In the text he decried the fact that in other towns Jews provided their children with large dowries, they moved away, and 'consequently the town decline[d] significantly'. 'I strictly order', he went on, 'therefore, that the Jews of Jazłowiec make efforts to settle their children near them.'[3] (Here is the dream of every parent: a law forbidding their children to move away!)

This document is but one illustration of the strong contrast between the situation of Jews in the Polish–Lithuanian Commonwealth and that of Jews in German-speaking lands at the same period. In German territories in their multiple jurisdictions, there were complex rules limiting the number of Jews who could reside there and, going further, indicating that only one or none of their offspring could inherit those rights. Even though I do not think that the key emphasis in Jewish historiography should be the relations between Jews and external centres of power, we nevertheless see in this instance a dramatic difference between Polish and German lands: in one the powerful seek to encourage Jewish residence in their territories; in the other, it is severely limited.

An even more significant difference between the two regions was the difference in numbers. More than ten times as many Jews lived in the lands of the Polish–Lithuanian Commonwealth as did in the territories of the future German empire: 750,000 versus 70,000. That is, the term 'minority' is misleadingly applied to Jews in the Polish lands in the eighteenth century. The connotations of the term 'minority'—vulnerability, dependence, and marginality—can be applied to Polish–Lithuanian Jewry only with elaborate qualification. Jews, after all, made up half of the urban population of the country. And since they were concentrated in the eastern half of the Commonwealth, they often constituted an actual or effective majority of a town's population.[4]

---

[2] Gershon David Hundert, *Jews in Poland–Lithuania in the Eighteenth Century: A Genealogy of Modernity* (Berkeley, Calif., 2004).

[3] 'Na ostatku stosując się do prawa rygoru po innych miastach zachowanego, na tych, którzy w cudze państwa dzieci swoje zwyczajnie oddają, posagi onym wydają, przez co miasto znacznie upada, zaczym aby Żydzi jazłowieckie i dzieci swoje przy sobie osadzać starali się surowo przykazuję.' Jacob Goldberg, *Jewish Privileges in the Polish Commonwealth: Charters of Rights Granted to Jewish Communities in Poland–Lithuania in the Sixteenth to Eighteenth Centuries* (Jerusalem, 1985), 105.

[4] Raphael Mahler, *Jews in the Old Poland in the Light of Statistics* [Di yidn in amolikn poyln in likht fun tsifern], 2 vols. (Warsaw, 1958). Shaul Stampfer, in 'The 1764 Census of Polish Jewry', *Bar-Ilan: Annual of Bar-Ilan University*, Studies in Judaica and the Humanities 24–5 (1989), 41–147, re-examines Mahler's procedures and concludes that 'Mahler's estimates appear more reasonable than . . . any others' (p. 72).

If we are going to tell the story of Jews in this period we ought to focus on the lands where most of them lived. This has not been the case until now.

Returning for a moment to the Jazłowiec privilege, it might be said that in attempting to limit their freedom of movement the document seems to suggest a type of feudal dependence of Jews on the town owner. In fact, though, this should be read as an illustration of the limits of the lord's power—Jews could and did threaten to leave. Moreover, the threat of their leaving was the most important limitation Jews could place on the power of the owner of the town. In the towns, Jews put their commercial, industrial, and managerial expertise directly or indirectly at the service of the nobleman or governor. In return, the ruler provided peace, security, good order, and relative autonomy. The revenues produced by Jews were part of the bargain. If town owners or governors did not fulfil their obligations, Jews would demand changes, threaten to leave, or actually do so.[5]

This relative security arose substantially because of the crucial economic role played by Jews in the state in commerce and industry. Jews were a dominant element in domestic commerce and, in the second half of the eighteenth century, their role in Poland's international trade became decisive. The most dramatic and well-known expression of this is that, between 1766 and 1800, 18,609 merchants from Poland attended the fairs in Leipzig. Of these, 16,100 (over 86 per cent) were Jews.[6] As early as 1753, Jews from Brody had their own synagogue in Leipzig.[7]

Probably even more importantly in terms of their economic significance, Jews played a crucial role in turning the major agricultural product, rye, for which there was a diminishing export market, into an alcoholic beverage for sale on the domestic market. The revenues from this industry accounted for 40 per cent and more of the total revenues from the estates of the Crown and nobility, particularly in the eastern half of the country where most Jews lived. We should not forget that the lion's share of the profits went to the magnates, yet, as long as this old regime persisted, Jews had a certain secur-

[5] Eliyahu ben Yehezkel, *She'elot uteshuvot har hakarmel* [Responsa] (Frankfurt an der Oder, 1782), 'Hoshen mishpat', question 30, 24*a*–24*b*. On the relationship between Jews and Polish nobles, especially the magnates, see the following recent monographs: Adam Kaźmierczyk, *Żydzi w dobrach prywatnych w świetle sądowniczej i administracyjnej praktyki dóbr magnackich w wiekach XVI–XVIII* (Kraków, 2002); M. J. Rosman, *The Lords' Jews: Magnate–Jewish Relations in the Polish–Lithuanian Commonwealth during the Eighteenth Century* (Cambridge, Mass., 1990); Adam Teller, *Money, Power, and Influence: Jews on the Radziwiłł Holdings in Lithuania during the Eighteenth Century* [Kesef, ko'ah vehashpa'ah: hayehudim be'ahuzot beit radzivil belita bame'ah ha-18] (Jerusalem, 2006).
[6] Max Freudenthal, *Leipziger Messgäste. Die jüdischen Besucher der Leipziger Messen in den Jahren 1675 bis 1764* (Frankfurt am Main, 1928); Richard Markgraf, *Zur Geschichte der Juden auf den Messen in Leipzig von 1664–1839* (Bischofswerda, 1894); Josef Reinhold, *Polen/Litauen auf den leipziger Messen des 18. Jahrhunderts* (Weimar, 1971).
[7] Adolf Diamant, *Chronik der Juden in Leipzig* (Leipzig, 1993), 59–60, 263.

ity because they occupied important and integrated sectors of the economy of the state. I believe that this is a particular instance of the general phenomenon of Jewish integration. In private towns, for example, rabbinical office-holders were approved by the owner of the town; in Crown cities the royal official had the same prerogative. Jews frequently resorted to the court of the town owner or the governor rather than to their own rabbinic courts.

Their economic indispensability had real consequences for the security of Jews, particularly in the private towns and estates where most of them lived. In Zholkva (Żółkiew) in 1746, a Christian miller was convicted of murdering and robbing a Jewish family. He was hanged, and then beheaded, and his skull was placed on the gates of the town at the order of the court.

The subject of the relations between Jews and the Polish Church is a highly expansive one, and this is not the place to present a comprehensive analysis. Rather, I should like to draw attention to one motif in synodal legislation in the Polish–Lithuanian Commonwealth that relates to the theme I am trying to develop here: a synod in the diocese of Łuck in 1726, for example, decreed that Christians were forbidden to guard Jewish cemeteries; to light and extinguish candles on Jewish holidays; and 'to play the role of Haman in Purim comedies'.[8] A synod in 1743 in Przemyśl ordered that 'Should a Christian play the role of Haman and be led about and insulted and abused' a heavy fine would be imposed on the Jewish community.[9] These laws promulgated by Church authorities were virtually never enforced. For us they describe a remarkable situation and reflect the relative security and confidence of the Polish Jewish community in the eighteenth century. Such actions are hardly indicative of cowering and frightened

[8] Jacob Goldberg, 'Poles and Jews in the Seventeenth and Eighteenth Centuries: Rejection or Acceptance', *Jahrbücher für Geschichte Osteuropas*, NS 22 (1974), 252–7; Adam Kaźmierczyk, 'The Problem of Christian Servants as Reflected in the Legal Codes of the Polish–Lithuanian Commonwealth during the Second Half of the Seventeenth Century and in the Saxon Period', *Gal-Ed*, 15–16 (1997), 23–40; Waldemar Kowalski, 'Ludność żydowska a duchowieństwo archidiakonatu sandomierskiego w XVII–XVIII wieku', *Studia Judaica: Biuletyn Polskiego Towarzystwa Studiów Żydowskich*, 1 (1998), 177–99. For other prohibitions on playing the role of Haman, see Yehudit Kalik, *The Catholic Church and the Jews in the Polish–Lithuanian Commonwealth during the Seventeenth and Eighteenth Centuries* [Hakenesiyah hakatolit vehayehudim bemamlekhet polin-lita bame'ot ha-17–18], Ph.D. diss., the Hebrew University of Jerusalem, 1998, 67–73. In a later document, the holiday is referred to as 'Aman', and on it Jews were forbidden by the Church to dress as Germans or Poles or to fire guns: 'Na Amana abyście się nie ubierali w suknie Polskie lub Niemieckie, y w te dni nie strzelali', Franciszek Antoni Kobielski, *Światło na oświecenie narodu niewiernego to iest kazania w synagogach żydowskich miane, oraz reflexye y list odpowiadaiący na pytania synagogi brodzkiey* (Lwów, 1746), 191.

[9] Mojżesz Schorr, *Żydzi w Przemyślu do końca XVIII wieku* (Lwów, 1903; repr. Jerusalem, 1991), 41–2, 213–26; Jacek Krochmal, 'Dekret biskupa W. H. Sierakowskiego z 19 lipca 1743 roku w sprawie Żydów przemyskich', *Rocznik Przemyski*, 29–30 (1993–4), 285–99. Similar regulations were issued by the same bishop to the Jewish community of Rzeszów. Adam Kaźmierczyk, *Żydzi polscy 1648–1772: Źródła* (Kraków, 2001), 62–5.

people. The same edict in Przemyśl forbade Jews and 'bachurs' (young men) dressed like Turks and others to parade in the streets carrying torches, burn straw in triumphal fires, shoot rifles in the streets, beat drums, or make clamorous noises. On the other hand, Jews did need a bishop's permission to build a new synagogue, a requirement that was generally observed and, generally, expensive.[10] The granting of such permission, though, was contrary to the strict letter of canon law, and again bespeaks the significance of Jews to the economy, even that of the Church.

On the other hand, the growing power and influence of the Church in the eighteenth century played an important part in configuring and deepening both Polish and Jewish identity. The Church created and supported moves to increase the pressure on marginals in a society that was working to achieve religious and national conformity. Synodal and other Church legislation often reinforced boundary-drawing and discriminatory enactments. More popular forms of identity-formation such as catechisms, sermons, lessons in the schools, and contemporary literature brimmed with negative stereotypes of Jews. The constant repetition undoubtedly did have an effect on shaping Catholic attitudes to Jews. Most cruelly, trials based on the blood libel and the accusation of desecration of the Host dramatically demonstrated the distinction between Jew and Christian. The central involvement at mid-century of powerful bishops such as Dembowski, Sołtyk, and Wołłowski emphasized the determination of some in the Church hierarchy to demonize and marginalize Jews to the greatest possible extent. In fact, the involvement of these bishops in the 1740s and 1750s led to the worst period of persecution of this kind in Polish Jewish history. These developments should be seen as manifestations of the growing and inextricable linkage between the Church and the incipient emergence of Polish national identity. It was not unusual in Church documents of the eighteenth century for the term 'Polak' to be used as a synonym for (Latin) Catholic.[11]

The communal organization of Polish–Lithuanian Jewry was more diversified, extensive, and complex than that of any other community in European Jewish history. This was a result, partly, of the particular complexion of the distribution of power in the Polish Commonwealth that tolerated the autonomy of relatively powerless strata in society, including ethnic-religious groups such as Scots, Armenians, and Italians. The Jewish institutions were more elaborate and more durable than the others. And when, in the

[10] See e.g. Jacob Goldberg, 'O przywilejach biskupich dla gmin żydowskich w dawnej Rzeczypospolitej', in H. Gapski (ed.), *Christianitas et cultura Europae: Księga jubileuszowa Profesora Jerzego Kłoczowskiego* (Lublin, 1998), 625–9. The establishment or expansion of a cemetery often required similar permission. For such an edict by the archbishop of Płock to the Jews in Vitebsk see *Istoriko-yuridicheskie materialy, izvlechennye iz aktovykh knig gubernii Vitebskoi i Mogilevskoi, khranyashchikhsya v Tsentral'nom arkhive v Vitebske*, 18 (Vitebsk, 1888), 196–202.   [11] Hundert, *Jews in Poland-Lithuania*, 72–8.

eighteenth century, these institutions were weakened in order to incorporate them into the administration of the state or an individual magnate's holdings, they continued to function nevertheless, expressing Jewish separatism in an institutional form.

Polish Jews were at once insular and integrated into the society in which they lived. There were varied and sometimes intense forms of contact between Jews and Christians that were not by any means limited to instrumental commercial transactions, though these were the most common. People who live cheek by jowl inevitably begin to relate to each other in all the ways of which human beings are capable. They feud, they discuss, they gossip, they rob, they love, and they hate each other. They become familiar, more or less, with the goings-on in each other's community. The costumes of Jews mimicked those of their neighbours, Yiddish teemed with Polish words, and the architecture and decoration of synagogues betrayed their baroque origins. But this mirroring does not contradict my contention that there was little admiration on the part of Jews for much of what they saw among their Christian neighbours. The single exception here is the occasional appearance of Jewish opinions about the nobility that are not characterized by expressions of scorn. The nobility, however, was impenetrable to Jews as long as they were Jews. In the ideology of the magnates, Jews were perceived as inferior. Among Polish Jews, though, this did not lead to tortured compunctiousness like that of the Jews in Muslim Spain described by Ross Brann.[12] In their general view of culture and morality in Poland–Lithuania, Jews held themselves to be superior and their neighbours in disdain. Polish society held no attraction for Jews. Indeed, one of the hardships of the Exile itself was that Jews were thrust into the midst of the corrupt, immoral, and violent world of the gentiles.

In attempting to gain a sense of the cultural activity and preoccupations of Polish Jews in the eighteenth century, my approach was first to assemble a list of the 'best-sellers' of the period and to summarize their contents and concerns. This confirmed that, beginning in the latter decades of the seventeenth century, kabbalah altered the grammar of Jewish culture. The hasidic phenomenon was created substantially from the palette of this culture, even if on the surface it seemed similar to other contemporary movements of spiritual awakening in Europe and America. I would suggest that hasidism might be considered a form of resistance in two ways. First, it offered shelter from ways of thinking that threatened traditional beliefs, and second, it created a social organization that, unlike Jewish communal institutions, was beyond the reach of the state.

The final piece in my argument rests on the general absence from Poland–Lithuania of what I call 'the beckoning bourgeoisie'. This absence is

[12] Ross Brann, *The Compunctious Poet: Cultural Ambiguity and Hebrew Poetry in Muslim Spain* (Baltimore, 1991).

illustrated by the failure to disassemble the hierarchy of power in the Polish–Lithuanian Commonwealth even in the Constitution of 3 May 1791; that is, the nobility retained its special status in law. The critical, indispensable framework for many, if not all, of the developments associated with conventional definitions of modernity was the rise of the bourgeoisie, and the perception among Jews that it was permeable. The growth of the conviction, however illusory it might have been, of the penetrability of the middle class—that there was a place in civil society and in the nation-state for Jews—was what led to the weakening of traditional society, traditional memberships, and traditional values. Even in terms of this Germanocentric definition of modernity, the rare cases of Jews who sought to find their place in the bourgeoisie in east-central Europe prove the rule that that bourgeoisie was weak and limited to a few cities. A few Jews did, in varying degrees, seek to find their place in the bourgeoisie of Shklov, Vilna, and, especially, Warsaw. Sometimes, as in Berlin or Paris, this involved an exchange of values that led to a critique of Jewish life. Among members of the upper stratum of Jews in Warsaw a process that was somewhat analogous to what was happening further west took hold. There were a few cases of what Jacob Shatzky called 'total assimilation'.[13] The three daughters of Judyta Levi Zbytkower, who was herself the daughter of a wealthy German Jewish family and married to the richest Jew in Warsaw, eventually converted to Christianity for example.

There were also east European Jews who travelled to the west, figuratively or literally. The familiar paradigm is the story of the east European Jew who comes to Berlin and is enchanted by what he beholds and powerfully attracted to the promise of a place in civil society. My argument concerns the overwhelming majority who, with various levels of awareness, responded differently.

For the vast majority of Jews, the changes that were afoot were frightening, dangerous, and presented 'an empty void'.[14] The circumstances under which they lived created a mentality that acted as a filter through which new cultural, political, and economic currents had to pass. That mentality both buffered Jews and buttressed their defences. And when, in the nineteenth century, certain important aspects of this context broke down, these Jews, in their vast majority, were armoured against trauma and splitting—that is, psychological reversals of loyalty—by the mentality that had been formed earlier. Self-affirmation and a feeling of Jewish superiority and solidarity dominated the spectrum of self-evaluation of east European Jews.

---

[13] Jacob Shatzky, 'Alexander Kraushar and his Road to Total Assimilation', *YIVO Annual*, 7 (1953), 146–74.

[14] The reference is to Nahman of Bratslav (1772–1810), *Likutei moharan* [Collections of the Sayings of R. Nahman], ch. 64.

The combination of elements in the experience of eighteenth-century east European Jews, including their concentration in large numbers, a continuing attitude of superiority to their neighbours, their secure and even indispensable place in the economy of the region, and the general absence of a 'beckoning bourgeoisie', strengthened and deepened a positive sense of Jewish identity.

PERIODIZATION AND PREJUDICE

Periodization is not a scientific problem. The solutions proposed are not falsifiable—we can never get to QED, to an incontestable answer. It is also a problem that interests the guild of historians more than the general reader outside the academy, who tends to be more interested in new or newly retold stories of the past. Although most working historians have little interest in theory per se, they are likely to find periodization of interest because it makes them confront their own hierarchies of value and significance without descending into abstraction. The determination of the criteria distinguishing a particular period forces the historian to decide on the relative importance of various aspects of human experience, for example, whether the beginning of modernity could be identified on the basis of changes in the administration of the state, in the economy, in belief systems, or in another way. The justification of the choice made will reveal much about the chooser. The non-scientific character of the problem, therefore, does not make it less interesting.

My goal in these remarks is to try to open a debate about modernity in Jewish history and, in fact, in the discipline as a whole. As I conceived this essay, I looked up 'modernity' in the *Oxford English Dictionary*. There I found a quotation that embodies an important dimension of the topic I want to address. It is from a best-selling novel of 1904 called *The Divine Fire*. Its author, May Sinclair, turns out to have been a very interesting figure, but with no apparent connection to Jewish historiography (although the novel's main character bears the name Horace Jewdwine). Ms Sinclair's novel contains the following passage: 'My dear fellow, modernity simply means democracy. And when once democracy has been forced on us, there's no good protesting any longer.' The connection between democracy and modernity is vexed; suffice it to say for now, there is no *Masekhet demokratiyah* (tractate 'On Democracy') in the Talmud. On the subject of modernity: I would free the term from its ossified and coagulated set of associations in Jewish historiography—its being linked to particular phenomena or criteria such as Enlightenment, emancipation, urbanization, integration, and the like. In my opinion, 'modernity' should float freely, signifying only a vast set of possibilities during the past two hundred or so years.

In imperial history, the historiography of the colonized encodes the dominance of the elite. One should, I think, try to write about Jews without using the language of dominance and subjugation as if their situation were defined by their place in the state. I certainly do not question the importance of that story; of the progressive integration of Jews within the modern nation-state until the middle decades of the twentieth century, or, put another way, the joining of Jews and bourgeoisie in recent centuries. I do, however, want to shift the main focus of attention in another direction.

The experience of west European Jews has been the template for the story of modernization told by virtually every Jewish historian of the period. The features of this narrative include a small Jewish community comprising a tiny proportion of the total population of a given country and of the total number of Jews in Europe. Economically, this community was becoming progressively more integrated in the state. It chafed, however, under the contradiction between its economic integration and lack of political rights. These Jews found the culture of the majority attractive and persuaded themselves that the bourgeoisie was beckoning to them, bidding them join and take their place in civil society. That is, they persuaded themselves that the new nation-state included a place for Jews. They exchanged their values for those of the dominant culture in the hope of acceptance, politically and socially. This exchange, however, involved varying degrees of self-rejection and was, at times, traumatic. Recent literature uses terms like negotiation and hybridity rather than exchange. However, as the Chinese saying has it: when a brick and an egg collide it does not matter which was moving, the result is the same.

The configuration of this narrative along geographical lines, that is, east and west, has been contested with some justice. After all, Königsberg, an important centre of the Enlightenment and its Jewish counterpart, the Haskalah, was in East Prussia, and there were Jews in Poland–Lithuania affected by the new thinking as early as were the Jews further to the west. Nevertheless, masses of Jews, overwhelmingly from the lands east of Germany, did not conform to the master-narrative just described.

The contention that modern Jewish history should be seen in its own right is not new. Almost seventy years ago, Benzion Dinur (1884–1973), the founder of Zionist historiography, pointed out that historians have most often invoked criteria drawn from outside the realm of Jewish historical action to define the modern period in Jewish history. By action, he meant something akin to what contemporary students of postcolonial history refer to as 'agency'. Dinur rejected both the Haskalah and emancipation as beginning points of modernity because neither development reflected 'the real historical content' of the life of Jews in the modern period, nor could either be identified with the realm of Jewish 'historical activity'. For Dinur, modern Jewish history began with the *aliyah*, 'going up' to the Holy Land, of Yehudah Hasid of Szydłowiec (*c*.1660–1700) and his several hundred Shabatean followers in 1700. By this act of emigration in preparation for the return of Shabetai Tsevi (d. 1676), whom they believed to be the messiah, these Jews became agents of their own history. As Dinur explained:

There is no other event that is so interpenetrated with the historical paths of the people of Israel in modern times in all their variety. . . . This period . . . which culminated with international recognition of Jewish independence in the land of Israel . . . necessarily begins with the first *'aliyah* that saw itself as a harbinger of redemption.[15]

Dinur's analysis is obviously open to criticism as a Whiggish choice dictated by his understanding of Jewish history as leading inevitably to the establishment of the Jewish state in 1948.[16] On the other hand, the very enterprise of Jewish historiography is predicated on the assumption that Jews have *made* their own history and that they have not merely been carried along like so much flotsam and jetsam on the currents of wider trends. Gershom Scholem, the towering figure of twentieth-century Jewish studies and architect of the study of Jewish mysticism, suggested that the Shabatean messianic movement of 1665–6 marked a break in Jewish history. He argued that a new period emerged in which growing numbers of people, intoxicated by the belief that the messiah had come, freed themselves in varying degrees from the regimens of traditional Jewish society.[17] Be this as it may, surely the so-called freeing of the individual had more to do with Renaissance values and subsequent developments in European thought than it did with 'the mystical messiah'.

Whatever criteria have been used, contemporary historical literature implies that the majority of Jews, living in the largest community, eluded modernity for a century or more after it had reached western Europe. This is the approach I seek to revise. I believe there are grave distortions in the way scholars have described modernity in Jewish history. Historians have placed too much emphasis on change and ideology, too much emphasis on religious behaviour and belief, as indicators of change; too much emphasis on regions where few Jews lived and not enough on the areas where most Jews lived.

[15] Benzion Dinur, 'Modern Times in Jewish History: Their Distinctiveness, their Essence, their Image' (Heb.), in his *At the Turning Point of History* [Bemifneh hadorot] (Jerusalem, 1972), 29; the article first appeared in *Zion*, 2 (1937).

[16] Gershon David Hundert, 'Reflections on the "Whig" Interpretation of Jewish History: *Ma'asei banim siman le'avot*', in H. Joseph, J. Lightstone, and M. Oppenheim (eds.), *Truth and Compassion: Essays on Judaism and Religion in Memory of Rabbi Solomon Frank* (Waterloo, Ont., 1983), 111–19.

[17] Gershom Scholem, 'Redemption through Sin', in id., *The Messianic Idea in Judaism and Other Essays on Jewish Spirituality* (New York, 1971), 78–141 (first published in Hebrew in 1937).

History is not a train that progressively moved across Europe from west to east bringing the same developments to different countries each in its turn. Such thinking involves the twin fallacies of teleology and linearity. One problem with periodization as it has been practised is precisely its teleological quality: the sense of inevitable movement forward, or at least convergence around, piously held beliefs in tolerance, equality, enlightenment, and science. Or, as May Sinclair had it, modernity is democracy. It may be that we have now to consider all these developments as illusory. Jews in Europe responded to the developments associated with modernity—the rise of the bourgeoisie, technological change, the Enlightenment—along a continuum from total identification to utter rejection, all of which are part of modern Jewish history. The responses of many Jews in east-central Europe to the hasidic movement, for example, are an important part of the same story. There is no single goal towards which human history moves, and there is no consistent direction in which humanity has developed. Surely, our own times are teaching us that lesson yet again.

Consequently, I propose to empty the term 'modernity' of all but its chronological content and to define it merely as roughly the last two centuries. Anyone inhabiting that period was thus, by definition, 'modern'. In this way we free ourselves from the restrictive dichotomy (and coercive discourse) of 'tradition and change' and can confront the more complex, and more human, reality of the coexistence of a multitude of behaviours and outlooks that were constantly in a state of flux. The issue here is: who were the Jews at the time that they encountered the developments that until now have been associated with 'modernity'? In other words, the various aspects of the Jewish experience highlighted here formed a particular *mentalité*, a positive self-evaluation at the core of Jewish identity.

To understand the developments among Jews of recent centuries properly one must investigate the experiences of the majority of Jews in their own contexts. Because the ancestors of about 80 per cent of world Jewry lived in the Commonwealth of Poland–Lithuania in the eighteenth century, it is they who must be placed at the centre of any understanding of the Jewish experience. The lives and values of such a great number were not marginal, nor should they be subordinated to some extraneous 'progressive' model of modernity. By close reading of the past I think I have identified a magmatic level of Jewish experience, that is, the elemental continuities that persist from the early modern period almost to the present. I contend that the conventional aspects of modernity have been grafted, often imperfectly, onto those elemental continuities through adaptation, appropriation, and negotiation. The task is to reread the historical record with an eye to understanding what in the actual experience and life of east European Jewry led to this subterranean stratum that continues to underlie the modern Jewish sensibility. It may be that the tense of the last sentence is incorrect. Perhaps, that stratum of Jewish sensibility has now disappeared; I am unsure. In any case, at least in the generation of Philip Roth's parents, it 'was, in the nature of things, as fundamental as having arteries and veins'.

The terminology employed in the previous paragraph and elsewhere in this essay has the aura of essentialism about it. Indeed, terms like 'elemental continuities' and 'magmatic level of experience' are, to say the least, out of fashion in contemporary historical discourse. They are offered here as a hermeneutic device for the analysis of the east European Jewish experience and not as empirical or empirically verifiable 'facts' about the 'nature' of Jews.

I have argued here that a combination of elements in the experience of eighteenth-century east European Jews strengthened and deepened a positive sense of Jewish identity. These were the concentration of large numbers, a continuing attitude of superiority to their neighbours, the secure and even indispensable place occupied by Jews in the economy of the region, and the general absence of what I call the 'beckoning bourgeoisie'. This positive sense of identity became the central ingredient of the *mentalité* of east European Jews and constituted a kind of social-psychological translation of the concept of chosenness. My suggestion is that, in subsequent centuries, despite ideological, geographical, economic, political, and even linguistic and cultural change, and for all the exceptions that might be cited, the vast majority of east European Jews and their descendants carried this core, if transvalued, sense of chosenness with them.

PART III

ON THE EVE OF THE SPANISH EXPULSION

EIGHT

Spanish 'Judaism' and 'Christianity' in an Age of Mass Conversion

DAVID NIRENBERG

WHO IS A JEW AND WHAT IS JEWISH?

'W HO IS A JEW, and what is Jewish?' These questions have been asked countless times by diverse people, ranging from ancient prophets to modern politicians, and we know from experience that the exclusions and inclusions they precipitate are powerful. Precisely for this reason, we should not expect a simple relationship between the questions and their answers. As Horkheimer and Adorno put it in their *Dialectic of Enlightenment*, '[to] call someone a Jew amounts to an instigation to work him over until he resembles the image'.[1] Today, in some areas of Jewish history, we have become so aware of what is involved in this 'working over' that it has become difficult to talk of the 'Jewishness' of Judaism. We are increasingly exhorted to think of Judaism dialogically (that is, as developing always in relation to an ambient 'other', be it 'Hellenism', 'Christianity', or 'Islam'), and even to believe, following the recent work of Daniel Boyarin, Seth Schwartz, and Israel Yuval, that without the rise of Christianity there would be no rabbinic Judaism.

The history of Iberian Jews, converts from Judaism, and their descendants has proved remarkably resistant to this remodelling. Many scholars of Judaism in late medieval Spain (an anachronistic term but a convenient one) remain convinced that their principal task is to distinguish 'what is Jewish' and 'who is Jewish' from what and who are not. Indeed the two, 'what' and 'who', are closely related to one another. The suspected 'Jewishness' of ideas or practices is confirmed by aligning them with the 'Jewishness' of the people who express or practise them. Because the several late medieval kingdoms that made up what we now call Spain were marked by mass conversions from Judaism to Christianity, this alignment is not necessarily with an individual's confessed religion. Rather, it involves a specific kind of 'working over', in which 'Jewishness' is determined by mapping actions and

[1] Max Horkheimer and Theodor W. Adorno, *Dialectic of Enlightenment*, trans. John Cumming (New York, 1972), 186.

ideas onto genealogy. If investigation shows that an individual is descended from, married to a descendant of, or simply friendly with descendants of Jewish converts to Christianity, then they and their ideas can be characterized as 'Jewish'. This inquisitorial methodology of 'cherchez le Juif' has produced the 'Judaism' of much of Spanish culture, ranging from ideologies such as 'purity of blood' to literary genres such as the picaresque.[2] Indeed, it has even resurrected the search for the 'Jewishness' of modernity itself, a search that had for a time been discredited by its history under the Nazis.[3] In fields from philosophy to psychoanalysis, scholars today happily trace the origins of concepts believed to be constitutive of modernity and post-modernity (concepts such as irony, hybridity, and scepticism) through the flesh of Iberia's converts from Judaism and their descendants.[4]

In short, students of Spain's Judaism remain convinced that, to paraphrase Vico, the production of history is best understood in the same terms as the reproduction of the species: that is, as a genealogy. Most readers can, I am sure, think of a number of theoretical critiques of such a conviction, all of which, however, it has survived, and none of which explains its peculiar strength in Sepharad. I would simply like to suggest that the genealogical conviction is itself the product of the dialogic relationship between Christianity and Judaism that it seeks to conceal, and that it is particularly strong

[2] Some substantiation of these claims will be provided below. For more, see David Nirenberg, 'Mass Conversion and Genealogical Mentalities: Jews and Christians in Fifteenth-Century Spain', *Past and Present*, 174 (Feb. 2002), 3–41, and id., 'Figures of Thought and Figures of Flesh: "Jews" and "Judaism" in Late Medieval Spanish Poetry and Politics', *Speculum*, 81 (Jan. 2006), 398–426.

[3] On the Marranos as the 'beginning of modernization in Europe', see Richard Popkin, 'Epicureanism and Scepticism in the Early Seventeenth Century', in R. B. Palmer and R. Hamerton-Kelly (eds.), *Philomathes* (The Hague, 1971). Others see in them the cause of the 'collapse of ecclesiastical society of the Middle Ages and the rise of secularism and modernity': José Faur, *In the Shadow of History: Jews and Conversos at the Dawn of Modernity* (Albany, NY, 1992), 142. Cf. Y. Yovel on the 'special hybrid phenomenon—perhaps even sui generis' of the Marranos in his *Spinoza and Other Heretics: The Marrano of Reason* (Princeton, 1989), 23. Much more discrete are Yosef Yerushalmi's arguments about the non-normative nature of Marrano Judaism in *From Spanish Court to Italian Ghetto: Isaac Cardoso: A Study in Seventeenth-Century Marranism and Jewish Apologetics* (New York, 1971), 44. These arguments about the Converso origins of modernity nourish and are nourished by the stress on the Sephardi roots of Spinoza, Montaigne, and others. On the 'Jewishness' of Spinoza see, more generally, Manfred Walther, 'Spinoza und das Problem einer jüdischen Philosophie', in Werner Stegmaier (ed.), *Die philosophische Aktualität der jüdischen Tradition* (Frankfurt, 2000), 281–330, and, most recently, Willi Goetschel, *Spinoza's Modernity: Mendelssohn, Lessing, and Heine* (Madison, Wis., 2004).

[4] See e.g. the special issue of *Pardes*, 29 (2000), *Le Juif caché: Marranisme et modernité*, ed. Shmuel Trigano. For other arguments that find the origin and transmission of modern subjectivities in Marrano lineages see e.g. Jean-Pierre Winter, *Les Errants de la chair: Études sur l'hystérie masculine* (Paris, 1998), and Elaine Marks, *Marrano as Metaphor* (New York, 1996). A different juxtaposition of converts and modernity, although equally problematic, is Geoffrey Galt Harpham's 'So . . . What Is Enlightenment? An Inquisition into Modernity', *Critical Inquiry*, 20/3 (Spring 1994), 524–56.

in Spain because it is there that the mass conversions of Jews to Christianity gave that relationship a productive strength it had not had since the first centuries of the common era. Christianity and Judaism were in some sense reborn out of one another in Spain between 1391 and 1492, but both spent the century trying to repress the pangs of birth.

THE RUINS OF 1391: A CRISIS OF CLASSIFICATION

The fourteenth century in Sepharad drew to a close with a wave of Jewish conversions unparalleled in the Middle Ages. In the massacres of 1391, thousands or tens of thousands of Jews were killed, and a much greater number converted.[5] Reuven, son of Rabbi Nissim of Gerona and a survivor of the massacres, described the damage in words he penned in the margins of his father's Torah scroll:

Wail, holy and glorious Torah, and put on black raiment, for the expounders of your lucid words perished in the flames. For three months the conflagration spread through the holy congregations of the exile of Israel in Sepharad. The fate [of Sodom and Gomorrah] overtook the holy communities of Castile, Toledo, Seville, Mallorca, Cordoba, Valencia, Barcelona, Tàrrega, and Girona, and sixty neighbouring cities and villages. . . . The sword, slaughter, destruction, forced conversions, captivity, and spoliation were the order of the day. Many were sold as slaves to the Ishmaelites; 140,000 were unable to resist those who so barbarously forced them and gave themselves up to impurity [i.e. converted].[6]

We need not accept the accuracy of his numbers in order to recognize that these killings and conversions transformed the religious demography of the Iberian peninsula. The Jews vanished from many of the largest cities of

[5] The literature on 1391 is extensive. A beginning can be made with (for Castile) Emilio Mitre Fernandez, *Los judíos de Castilla en tiempo de Enrique III: el pogrom de 1391* (Valladolid, 1994), and (for the Crown of Aragon) the following articles by Jaume Riera i Sans: 'Los tumultos contra las juderías de la corona de Aragón en 1391', *Cuadernos de Historia*, 8 (1977), 213–25; 'Estrangers participants als avalots contra les jueríes de la Corona d'Aragó el 1391', *Anuario de Estudios Medievales*, 10 (1980), 577–83; and 'Els avalots de 1391 a Girona', *Jornades d'història dels jueus a Catalunya* (Girona, 1987), 95–159.

[6] In Abraham Hershman, *Rabbi Isaac ben Sheshet Perfet and his Times* (New York, 1943), 194–6. I have altered the translation in several places and accepted the emendations offered (along with a Catalan translation) by Jaume Riera i Sans in his 'Els avalots del 1391 a Girona', 156. See also the letter of the prominent rabbi and courtier Hasdai Crescas included in Shelomoh Ibn Verga's much later *Shevet yehudah*, in the German edition: *Das Buch Schevet Jehuda*, ed. M. Wiener (Hanover, 1924), 128. Not even contemporaries of the events attempted to determine the exact proportion of Jews killed or converted. In the case of Girona, for example, the royal chancery limited itself to stating that the majority converted, while another portion was killed ('major pars aljame sive habitantium in eadem ad fidem catholicam sunt conversi, et alii ex eis fuerunt gladio interempti'). See Archive of the Crown of Aragon, Chancery [ACA:C], 1902:16ᵛ–17ʳ (16 July 1392), cited in Riera, 'Els avalots del 1391', 135. In his 'Letter to the Community of Avignon', Hasdai Crescas wrote of Valencia that no Jews remained there except in Murviedro.

Castile, Catalonia, Valencia, and Mallorca. In their place appeared what would come to be thought of as a new religious class, that of the 'new Christians', or Conversos.

This migration of so many souls away from Israel and into the body of Christ catalysed a series of complex reactions. Doing justice to those reactions would require, at the very least, studying the emergence over time of each of the resulting communities (Jews, converts, and Old Christians, each, of course, itself very diverse), always in relation to the others, for it is this relational or dialogic element that made the reformulation of categories such as 'Jew', 'Christian', and 'convert' so dynamic. Thus far I have only been able to pursue this goal in fragmentary ways, focusing on the histories of particular topics (such as lineage and genealogy) or particular social boundaries (for example sexual intercourse) across all three communities. Here I would like to do something slightly different, and focus on just one community, the Christian, in order to give some teeth to my claim that the mass conversions precipitated a renegotiation of the relationship between Judaism and Christianity that altered the possibilities for both.

Underlying these renegotiations was a crisis of classification, one whose first symptoms became evident almost immediately.[7] King Joan of Catalonia–Aragon, for example, expressed concern in 1393. Writing to a number of his most important cities, he informed them that it had become impossible for 'natural Christians' to tell who was a convert to Christianity and who was still a Jew. Henceforth converts were to be forbidden to live, dine, or have conversation with Jews. The Jews were to be made to wear more conspicuous badges and hats, so that 'they appear to be Jews'. The king ended the letter with his most emphatic point: 'And we order and desire that if any of these said Jews are found with a Christian woman in a suspicious place, in order to have carnal copulation with her, let them both be burned without mercy.'[8]

---

[7] For an extended treatment of this crisis, see David Nirenberg, 'Conversion, Sex, and Segregation: Jews and Christians in Medieval Spain', *American Historical Review*, 107 (2002), 1065–93.

[8] ACA:C 1964:108ᵛ–109ᵛ, 18 Aug. 1393, addressed to Tortosa (= Fritz Baer, *Die Juden im christlichen Spanien, Erster Teil: Urkunden und Regesten* (Berlin, 1936), vol. i, no. 456 (pp. 716–18). Compare ACA:C 2030:136ᵛ–137ʳ, 3 Sept. 1393 (= José Hinojosa Montalvo, *The Jews of the Kingdom of Valencia* (Jerusalem, 1993), nos. 191, 440; cf. also nos. 218, 231, 235), in which the queen orders that no additional distinctions be imposed upon the Jews of Valencia, since they can already be easily recognized ('prou son senyalats'), and additional clothing regulations would lead them to abandon the city. The Tortosa letter should be viewed together with those to Barcelona (see José María Madurell Marimón, 'La cofradía de la Santa Trinidad, de los conversos de Barcelona', *Sefarad*, 18 (1958), 60–82: 72–7) and Girona (unedited, ACA:C 1960:120ᵛ–121ᵛ). A similar letter to Morvedre is dated 4 Apr. 1396 (ACA:C 1911:46ʳ⁻ᵛ, 2nd numeration). See also Riera i Sans, 'Judíos y conversos en los reinos de la corona de Aragón durante el siglo XV', in *La Expulsión de los Judíos de España: conferencias pronunciadas en el II Curso de Cultura Hispano-Judía y Sefardí de la Universidad de Castilla-la Mancha, celebrado en Toledo del 16 al 19 de sept. de 1992* (Toledo, 1993), 71–91: 83.

The letters were probably triggered by the case of Saltell Gracìa, a Jew of Barcelona who was that week being tried for 'promenading in Christian dress and under guise of that dress having sex with many Christian women'.[9] The case resonated, however, with existing concerns, which helps to explain the quite extraordinary fact that this particular king and his advisers hurried to articulate a general collapse of the normal processes of identification and classification in the wake of the mass conversions. Joan's solution to the problem was threefold. First, increase the social and physical distance between converts and Jews. Second, mark the Jews even more visibly. Third, raise vigilance towards and increase punishment of sex between Christian women and Jewish men.

Each of these reactions deserves its own history. Here, however, I only want to stress that all shared the common tendency to achieve the desired identification of Judaism, not by distinguishing the convert as a particularly 'Jewish' Christian, but by 'hypermarking' the Jews themselves. It is this same logic that, some two decades later, produced the next campaign of mass conversion under the generalship of Vincent Ferrer. In 1411 Ferrer undertook a massive project of preaching and evangelization in Castile and the Crown of Aragon. His goals were nothing less than the spiritual reform of Christians and the complete conversion of the Jews. His motivations were multiple, ranging from apocalypticism to the politics of papal schism. But what matters for us is how he sought to achieve those goals: by stressing the terrible dangers confronting Christian society because of the insufficient clarity of the distinction between Christian and Jew. Again, Ferrer did not invoke Converso heterodoxy as a justification for his anxiety, but rather the unidentifiability of the Jew. The situation was so grave, he suggested to a Castilian audience in 1412, 'that many are thought to be the children of Jews but are really Christian, and vice versa'.[10] In 1415 he told a Zaragozan audience that 'many Christian men believe their wife's children to be their own, when they are actually by Muslim and Jewish [fathers]'. If the citizens did not put a stop to such inter-faith adultery by segregating minorities, he warned, God would do so through plague. His sermon provoked a panic, and groups of Christians began to patrol the streets, on the lookout for Jews or Muslims prowling after Christian women.[11]

---

[9] 'quod ambulans in habitu christianorum et sub ipsis habitus velamine habuit rem carnalem cum pluribus mulieribus christianis': ACA:C Violant de Bar, 2030:80^{r-v}, 23 Aug. 1393.

[10] Colegio del Corpus Christi de Valencia, MS 139, fo. 113, cited in Pedro Cátedra, 'Fray Vicente Ferrer y la predicación antijudaica en la campaña castellana (1411–1412)', in Jeanne Battesti Pelegrin (ed.), *'Qu'un sang impur . . .': Les Conversos et le pouvoir en Espagne à la fin du moyen âge. Actes du 2ème colloque d'Aix-en-Provence, 18–19–20 novembre 1994* (Aix-en-Provence, 1997), 19–46: 30–1.

[11] It is thanks to his exculpatory letter to the king that we know of these events: ACA:C cartas reales [cr.] Fernando I, box 22, no. 2764, dated the last day of April [1415?], by Nicholau Burgés, procurator and syndic of Zaragoza.

Nor was this merely vulgar paranoia. It was out of a similar concern that the
king prohibited the presence of Christian women in the Jewish quarter.[12]

According to Ferrer, the problem was one of ambiguous identities. In a
formulation strikingly similar to that of King Joan two decades before,
Ferrer asserted that Jews and Muslims were living among Christians, dressing like Christians, even adopting Christian names, so that 'by their appearance they are taken and reputed by many to be Christians'.[13] Again like King
Joan, the solution he advocated was one of heightened marking and segregation. But if in 1393 such anxieties had resonated little with contemporaries,
by 1413 they proved so powerful as to convince the Pope, the kings of
Castile and of Aragon, and innumerable town councils and municipal officers to attempt one of the most extensive attempts at segregation before the
modern era.

In the interest of separating Christian from non-Christian, Jews (and to a
much lesser extent Muslims) had to be moved to totally segregated neighbourhoods and severely restricted in their market and economic activities.
Trade between Jew and Christian was forbidden, and in some towns Christians even refused to sell Jews food.[14] Entire communities found themselves
evicted, 'with boys and girls dying from exposure to the cold and the snow'.
Writing a century after these events, Abraham Zacuto called them 'the
greatest persecution that had ever occurred'. And, as in 1391, one of the consequences of this persecution was the mass conversion of thousands who
sought to avoid being barred from their trades and expelled from their
homes.[15]

---

[12] e.g. ACA:C 2416:60ᵛ–63ᵛ, 20 Mar. 1413. The fine for married women was 50 florins, and
for single women the loss of their clothes. It is worth stressing that documented cases of intercourse between Christian women and Jewish men are much rarer in the period 1391–1418
than they were in the generation before the mass conversions, at least if the vast holdings of the
Archive of the Crown of Aragon are any indication. These heightened anxieties do not, in
other words, correspond to a real increase in intercourse.

[13] 'por su aspecto son havidos e reputados por muytos seyer cristianos, senyaladament entre
qui no son conoscidos'. The quotation is from a letter written by the jurados of Zaragoza after
hearing a sermon by Ferrer, dated 28 Jan. 1415. ACA:C cr. Fernando I, box 8, no. 919. The
charge of dressing like Christians and adopting Christian names was a very old one, deriving
from the Lateran Council of 1215. It was frequently voiced in the 13th and 14th centuries,
e.g. at the Cortes of Jerez in 1268 (art. 7).

[14] Some historians have sought to minimize the impact of these policies by claiming that
they were rarely implemented, but the evidence suggests otherwise. The Archive of the Crown
of Aragon is full of details of the implementation, and of the violence and dislocation it caused.
The evidence for Castile, as with all things having to do with governance in this period, is
much sparser than that for Aragon, but what there is suggests that the decrees were enforced.
See e.g. the document from the Archivo Municipal de Alba de Tormes published in C. Carrete
Parrondo, *Fontes Iudaeorum Regni Castellae* (Salamanca, 1981), 30–1.

[15] Solomon Alami, *Igeret musar* [Ethical Epistle], ed. Adolph Jellinek (Vienna, 1872), 10b;
Abraham Zacuto, *Sefer yuḥasim hashalem* ['Book of Genealogies': a history of the development
of the Oral Law], ed. Tsevi Filipowski (Edinburgh, 1857), 225b; Heinrich Graetz, *Geschichte*

This series of mass conversions had obvious effects on how Iberian Jews thought about the question of who was a Jew. Elsewhere I have tried to follow in the footsteps of Moises Orfali, Benzion Netanyahu, and others in working through some of those developments in Jewish sources.[16] But here it is the less obvious, but equally important, question of why and how these mass conversions transformed *Christian* ideas about who was a Jew and what was Jewish that interests me. To anticipate the conclusions of the next few pages: those transformations were profound, and they were not merely the result of the ambiguous religiosity or 'Jewish' practices of the converts. (Indeed, it is striking how rarely concern about the converts' religiosity was voiced in Christian sources before the 1430s.) We are dealing instead with a much more complex phenomenon: the mass conversion's destabilization of an oppositional process of identification by which generations of Christians had defined themselves theologically and sociologically against Jews and Judaism.

THE IMPORTANCE OF JUDAISM TO CHRISTIAN SELF-DEFINITION

The theological side of this process of differentiation is well known. Christianity had since its earliest days used the Jew to represent the anti-Christian, mapping polarized dualities such as spiritual–material, allegorical–literal, sighted–blind, redemptive–damning, and good–evil onto the pairing Christian–Jew. In the perhaps over-argued formulation of Rosemary Ruether, 'It was virtually impossible for the Christian preacher or exegete to teach scripturally at all without alluding to the anti-Judaic theses. Christian scriptural teaching and preaching per se is based on a method in which anti-Judaic polemic exists as the left hand of its christological hermeneutic.'[17] This hermeneutic provided medieval theologians and their audiences with a powerful lens through which to comprehend and classify their constantly changing world. Phenomena that one wanted to characterize as dangerous

der Juden von den ältesten Zeiten bis auf die Gegenwart (Leipzig, 1890), 111. Alami blamed the disaster on the pride of rich Jews: 'Those who dwell in their venerable houses have been expelled from the palaces of delight and pleasure to live in dark caverns; the worm[?] of Jacob has embraced the rubbish heaps and the Jews have to live in hovels in summer and winter to their shame . . . For having built great houses and ample and handsome upper rooms we have been expelled and dispersed over the fields and rubbish heaps . . . Most of the great Jewish nobles and officers who stand before their kings in their castles and palaces . . . forgot their Creator and constructed palaces for themselves.' Abraham Saba of Zamora provided a similar explanation.

[16] Nirenberg, 'Mass Conversion and Genealogical Mentalities', 18–22.
[17] Rosemary Radford Ruether, *Faith and Fratricide: The Theological Roots of Anti-Semitism* (New York, 1974), 121.

were projected onto the negative pole of the Jewish–Christian opposition.[18] To take but one example from the preaching of Ferrer: 'today, nearly everything is avarice, for almost everyone commits usury, which used not to be done except by Jews. But today Christians do it too, as if they were Jews.'[19]

There is much more to be said about how medieval Christians defined themselves theologically and hermeneutically against the Jews. In Spain, at least, they did so sociologically as well. Individually and collectively Christians asserted their honour as members of God's privileged people by differentiating themselves from the dishonoured Jew.[20] In a sense this sociological practice was already encoded in St Augustine's theological principle that Jewish abjection proves the truth of the Christian faith.[21] But the daily performance of this contrast became fundamental to the representation of Christian political and social privilege. The logic of sexual privilege and sexual boundaries mentioned earlier provides one example of such differentiation,[22] but there were countless others. Community privilege, for example, could be asserted through juxtaposition with Jews, as when town councils resisted taxes by claiming that their imposition by the king made 'a Jewry out of each of his municipalities . . . and we will not give way to such a demand, for we would rather die than be made similar to Jews'.[23] And just as the erosion of corporate privilege could threaten to turn *universitas* into *juheria*, so the erosion of honour could Judaize the individual Christian. Preachers

[18] Sara Lipton, *Images of Intolerance: The Representation of Jews and Judaism in the Bible moralisée* (Berkeley, 1999), 45. Ruether, *Faith and Fratricide*, 160. Compare Theodor W. Adorno, 'What is pathological about anti-Semitism is not projective behavior as such, but the absence of reflection in it': Horkheimer and Adorno, *Dialectic of Enlightenment*, 187.

[19] St Vincent Ferrer, *Sermons*, ed. Josep Sanchis Sivera (Barcelona, 1984), v. 147. This particular projection flourished into modernity, taking secularized form even in thinkers such as Marx (*On the Jewish Question*) and Horkheimer (*The Jews and Europe*). It is only 'since Auschwitz', to quote Dan Diner, that 'common linguistic usages such as the description of phenomena from the sphere of circulation as Jewish have forfeited their dubious claim to reality' (the claim may prove unduly optimistic). Diner, 'Reason and the "Other": Horkheimer's Reflections on Anti-Semitism and Mass Annihilation', in Seyla Benhabib, Wolfgang Bonss, and John McCole (eds.), *On Max Horkheimer: New Perspectives* (Cambridge, Mass., 1993), 337.

[20] The Muslim played an important role in this process as well, but that is a subject for a different article.

[21] On this doctrine of witness, which was perhaps the chief theological justification for the continued toleration of Jews in Christian society, see most recently the chapter on Augustine in Jeremy Cohen, *Living Letters of the Law: Ideas of the Jew in Medieval Christianity* (Berkeley, Calif., 1999).

[22] A particularly important one, in that so many other distinctions were mapped onto the sexual one. For a formulation of the point derived from Lévi-Strauss see Stanley Jeyaraja Tambiah, 'Animals Are Good to Think and Good to Prohibit', in his *Culture, Thought, and Social Action: An Anthropological Perspective* (Cambridge, Mass., 1985), 169–211: 169–70.

[23] 'no és als sinó fer juheria de cascuna de ses universitats . . . a aytal demanda no darem loch, car més amam morir que ésser semblants a jueus'. Arxiu Municipal de València (AMV), Ll. M., g³ 4, 108ᵛ, 26 Oct. 1378, cited in Dolors Bramon, *Contra moros i jueus: formació i estratègia d'unes discriminacions al País Valencià* (Barcelona, 1981), 67.

often complained of Christians who believed that failure to avenge an injury 'would be a dishonour to me, for they would say of me "Oh, the madman, oh, the Jew!"'[24] According to this view, to withdraw from the economy of violence was tantamount to withdrawing from the fraternity of honourable Christian males. It was, in other words, to become 'Jewish'.

In short, Christian identity and Christian privilege in late medieval Spain were defined in large part by insisting upon their distance from the Jew. The performance of that distance could take place in countless venues: in the taking of vengeance or the paying of taxes, in the choice of foods or sexual partners, in law (as in the preferential treatment of Christian witnesses), and in ritual (as in the enclosure and stoning of Jews during Holy Week), to list but a few.[25] It is through the repeated performance of this essential distance that the symbolic capital of Christian honour and privilege was amassed.

The mass conversions of 1391 threatened the performance of Christian identity because they raised, perhaps for the first time in the Iberian Christian imagination, the possibility of a world without Jews. Many in the generation after 1391 worked to make that world a reality: a few by urging the slaughter of the unconverted;[26] others, such as the citizens of Barcelona and Valencia, by banning Jews from their cities in perpetuity; still others, like Vincent Ferrer and his supporters, by mounting a programme of evangelization intended to achieve the full conversion of the infidels.[27] These were exhilarating times for a Christian society trained to see the footprints of the messiah in the conversion of the Jews.[28] But they were also unsettling, destabilizing Christian identity in two important ways. First, the messianic

[24] Ferrer, *Sermons*, i. 42. Similar exclamations appear elsewhere in the *Sermons*: see i. 93 and 155, iii. 16, and v. 190.

[25] For an extended treatment of the Holy Week example see David Nirenberg, *Communities of Violence: Persecution of Minorities in the Middle Ages*, (Princeton, 1996), ch. 7, and id., 'Les Juifs, la violence, et le sacré', *Annales: HSS*, 50 (1995), 109–31.

[26] See for example the charges made *c.*1393 against Antoni Rieri of Lerida, who was accused, among other things, of preaching that the prophesied time had arrived 'in quo omnes iudei debant interfici, ut nullus iudeus in mundo deinceps remaneret' ('in which they all should kill the Jews, so that no Jew remain in the world henceforth'): Jaume De Puig i Oliver, 'La *Incantatio studii ilerdensis* de Nicolau Eimeric, O.P.', *Arxiu de Textos Catalans Antics*, 15 (1996), 7–108: 47. Lerida was the scene of anti-Jewish violence by Christians both old and new just a few years later: 'Segons a nostra oyda és pervengut, alcuns fills de iniquitat anelants la destrucció de la juheria d'aquexa ciutat, la qual juheria en aquella havem novellament feta e manat ésser, han cominat segons se diu alscunes vegades de la destrucció sobredita' ('It has reached our ears that some sons of iniquity, desiring the destruction of the Jewish quarter of that city, which we have newly made and commanded to be established, have several times attempted, so it is said, the aforesaid destruction'): ACA:C 2232:95ᵛ–96ʳ, 25 Oct. 1400.

[27] Ferrer's messianic inspiration is well known. See, most recently, José Guadalajara Medina, *Las profecías del anticristo en la edad media* (Madrid, 1996), 232–47.

[28] On this association in the late Middle Ages, see, most recently, Robert E. Lerner, *The Feast of Saint Abraham: Medieval Millenarians and the Jews* (Philadelphia, 2001), esp. ch. 7, on the effects of the mass conversions on Francesc Eiximenis's millenarian ideas.

'disappearance of the Jews' promised to eliminate the living representatives of a negative pole vital, as I have suggested, to the coherence of Christian theological self-understanding.[29] Second, the emergence of the converts as an intermediate class produced a rapid narrowing of the social space that had previously separated Christian from Jew, and a consequent perception of the erosion of Christian privilege.

NEW NEIGHBOURS: THE NARROWING GAP BETWEEN 'CHRISTIANS' AND 'JEWS'

This second point bears elaboration. The tens (or even hundreds) of thousands who converted over the course of this quarter-century immediately occupied a good deal of the cultural 'no man's land' that had hitherto divided Christian and Jew. On the one hand, they enjoyed all the privileges of the Christian. The convert Francesch de San Jordi (known as Astruch Rimoch before his conversion) put it a bit hyperbolically in a letter to the Jew Shaltiel Bonafos: 'Those who have emerged from the waters of baptism, from the fountains of salvation, are firmly established upon golden pedestals. They are all personages. In their courts and in their palaces there are ivories and monkeys and peacocks and dwarves; they divested themselves of their soiled attire . . . and donned the garments of salvation.'[30] Of course we know that the vast majority of converts remained poor, without peacock or dwarf, but even the lowliest Converso could now throw rocks at Jews during Holy Week, have sex with Christian prostitutes, or marry Christian women, and we know that many of them did.

Yet at the same time that these converts enjoyed the privileges of the Christian, many still lived in close social, cultural, and physical proximity to their former co-religionists. They often occupied, as they had before their conversion, houses in or near the Jewish quarter.[31] For many years (and

---

[29] I do not intend here any echo of Ruether's quite different point, in *Faith and Fratricide*, 228: 'Possibly anti-Judaism is too deeply embedded in the foundations of Christianity to be rooted out entirely without destroying the whole structure.'

[30] Quoted in Eleazar Gutwirth, 'Habitat and Ideology: The Organization of Private Space in Late Medieval *Juderías*', *Mediterranean Historical Review*, 9 (1994), 205–34: 208.

[31] The complications this might cause were recognized early, but converts were nevertheless given considerable choice in the matter. In Mallorca, for example, they were called before a notary after the riots to declare whether they wished to remain in their old homes or rent them out and move into traditionally Christian neighbourhoods. See José María Quadrado, 'La judería de la ciudad de Mallorca en 1391', *Boletín de la Real Academia de la Historia*, 9 (1886), 294–312. Shortly thereafter (on 19 August) the city would have received a letter from King Joan, ordering that Conversos should not cohabit with Jews, 'car lur conversació a present no poria esser sens perill e gran dampnatge' ('their conversation at present could not take place without great peril and great damage'): ACA:C 1994:186ᵛ–187ʳ, cited in Riera i Sans, 'Judíos y conversos', 83.

certainly throughout the period that concerns us here) their financial affairs remained hopelessly entangled with those of their earlier communities of faith. And of course they had Jewish relatives with whom they might need to communicate for any number of reasons. Some even had Jewish spouses to whom they remained legally married.[32]

Such proximity undercut the radical distinction between the two groups and thereby destabilized the foundations of Christian privilege and identity. It was this destabilization, this narrowing of the gap between Christian and Jew, which 'Old' Christians were reacting to when they complained that it was now impossible to distinguish Christian from Jew. Many converts perceived the problem as well. When a handful of Zaragozan Conversos living in a predominantly Jewish area evoked Ferrer's orders of segregation in the hope of having their Jewish neighbours evicted, they were seeking to heighten the distance upon which their new privileges depended.[33] The same logic motivated their violent invasion of the Jewish quarter.[34] Once again, the point was succinctly articulated by Ferrer: 'The Christian who is neighbour with a Jew will never be a good Christian.'[35]

The nervous energy provoked by this new 'neighbourliness' was tremendously powerful. We have already seen one outcome of that power: the segregations and mass conversions of Jews in 1411–16, which of course only increased the anxiety that they claimed to allay. But precisely because the space between Christianity and Judaism had for so long been important to many areas of Christian culture that had little to do with living Jews, the energy released by the bridging of that space proved productive in many areas of culture that had no straightforward relationship to Jews or Judaism. This productivity in turn transformed the possible uses and meanings of 'Judaism' and 'Christianity' in Spain. In other words, the intensive work to which contemporaries put the 'Judaizing' energy released by the mass conversions itself shaped the answers they found to newly pressing questions about who was a Jew and what was Jewish. If we want to understand why and how contemporaries answered these questions as they did, we cannot restrict

---

[32] For examples of these and other ambiguities of status see Nirenberg, 'Mass Conversion and Genealogical Mentalities', 13–18.

[33] The case is discussed in F. Vendrell de Millás, 'En torno a la confirmación real, en Aragón, de la pragmatica de Benedicto XIII', *Sefarad*, 20 (1960), 1–33. Less dramatic but equally meaningful are the 'distancing' actions of converts such as Gil Roiz Najarí, who successfully petitioned to have an entrance to the Jewish quarter of Teruel moved so that he would have no contact with Jews. See ACA:C 2391:102^{r-v}, 16 Mar. 1416.

[34] ACA:C 2389:111^{r-v}, 20 Nov. 1415: ACA:C 2389:110^{r-v}, 112^{r-v}, 20 Nov. 1415. Similar events occurred in other cities, such as Lerida.

[35] 'car nunqua será bon christià, lo qui és vehí de juheu': Biblioteca de Catalunya, MS 476, fos. 136^{v}–153^{v}, ed. Josep Perarnau i Espelt in 'Els quatre sermons catalans de sant Vincent Ferrer en el manuscrit 476 de la Biblioteca de Catalunya', *Arxiu de Textos Catalans Antics*, 15 (1996), 231–2.

ourselves to a search for the 'real' beliefs of converts from Judaism. We need also to pay attention to the history of the concepts through which fifteenth-century Iberian Christians articulated their concerns about 'Judaization' and put these concerns to the work of generating newly recognizable differences between 'Jewish' and 'Christian'. In this essay I will give just two examples: first (and more extensive), that of Christian poetry (which contains the earliest sustained discourse of 'Jewishness' after 1391 that I know of), and second, that of Christian politics.

PUTTING THE FEAR OF JUDAIZATION TO WORK:
THE CASE OF POETRY

The *Cancionero de Baena* is often called the 'first critical anthology' of Castilian poetry. Compiled by Juan Alfonso de Baena, it contains some 600 poems composed in the courts of four Castilian kings, ranging from before 1391 to shortly after 1430, when Baena presented it to King Juan II. The anthology is critical, in the sense that each poem is preceded by a short editorial introduction noting its merits and demerits, and the whole is prefaced with a meditation on the function of poetry and the nature of the poet's art.[36] But what is immediately striking for our purposes is that the *Cancionero's* poets, nearly all Christian, are constantly defaming one another, and the accusation of Jewishness is prominent among the charges they hurl. They accuse each other of Jewish ancestry, of having too small a foreskin or too big

[36] All citations are from the *Cancionero de Juan Alfonso de Baena*, ed. Brian Dutton and Joaquín González Cuenca (Madrid, 1993). Poems from *cancioneros* other than those in Baena's anthology are cited from Brian Dutton's *El Cancionero del Siglo XV, c.1360–1520*, 7 vols. (Salamanca, 1990–1). On the dating of Baena's work see Alberto Blecua, ' "Perdíose un quaderno . . .": sobre los cancioneros de Baena', *Anuario de Estudios Medievales*, 9 (1974–9), 229–66; Manuel Nieto Cumplido, 'Aportación histórica al Cancionero de Baena', *Historia, Instituciones, Documentos*, 6 (1979), 197–218, and id., 'Juan Alfonso de Baena y su Cancionero: nueva aportación histórica', *Boletín de la Real Academia de Córdoba*, 52 (1982), 35–57. The literature on the *Cancionero* is vast, but two recent collections may serve as a starting point: *Poetry at Court in Trastamaran Spain: From the Cancionero de Baena to the Cancionero General*, ed. E. Michael Gerli and Julian Weiss, Medieval and Renaissance Texts and Studies (Tempe, Ariz., 1998), and Jesús L. Serrano Reyes and Juan Fernández Jiménez (eds.), *Juan Alfonso de Baena y su Cancionero: actas del I Congreso Internacional sobre el Cancionero de Baena*, Baena, 16–20 Feb. 1999 (Cordoba, 2001). On attitudes towards Jews and converts in the *Cancionero* see (in addition to the works cited below) Stanley Rose, 'Anti-Semitism in the "Cancioneros" of the Fifteenth Century: The Accusation of Sexual Indiscretions', *Hispanófila*, 26 (1983), 1–11; id., 'Poesía antijudía y anticonversa en la poesía artística del siglo XV en España', Ph.D. diss., Catholic University of America, 1975; and Gregory S. Hutcheson, 'Marginality and Empowerment in Baena's Cancionero', Ph.D. diss., Harvard University, 1993. What follows is a much-compressed summary of arguments found in David Nirenberg, *Wie jüdisch war das Spanien des Mittelalters? Die Perspektive der Literatur*, Kleine Schriften des Arye Maimon-Instituts 7 (Trier, 2005), and id., 'Figures of Thought and Figures of Flesh'. Readers can refer to either of these for more of the rich bibliography on this topic.

a nose, and of heterosexual and homosexual intercourse with Jews. Indeed the collection includes many poems that insult the editor himself. His birthplace of Baena is impugned in one poem as a land where 'much good eggplant' is grown, another mocks him for having 'eyes of eggplant', and yet another accuses him of eating *adefyna* (a sabbath dish, cooked overnight), these being dishes associated with Jews. Other poets refer to his 'bath in the water of holy baptism', or to his sexual encounters with Jews both male and female (the Mariscal Íñigo de Astuñiga, for example, claims that he is stuffed full of Jewish sperm).[37]

Critics have deduced from such accusations that if a poet is attacked as Judaizing he must be a Converso. And if the attacker himself betrays knowledge of Judaism (for example, by drawing on Hebrew vocabulary, such as *meshumad* for apostate) then he too may be presumed to have a Jewish past. The result of such logic is the conviction that, as one critic put it as early as 1871, Baena's *Cancionero* is full of 'half-converted Jews'.[38] Yet in many cases where we have been able to find further, non-poetic, evidence about the poets anthologized in this volume, they turn out not to be Conversos.[39] If we insist that a poet like Baena must have been a converted Jew, it is only because we know nothing about him outside his poetry, and we cannot imagine why else he would have been insulted as one.

[37] It is entirely on the evidence of these poems that Baena's status as a Converso rests. The eggplant quotes are from poems by Diego de Estuniga (no. 424) and Juan García (no. 384). The reference to *adefyna* is by Juan de Guzmán (no. 404), and the baptismal allusion by Ferrán Manuel (no. 370). For allusions to Juan Alfonso de Baena's sexual encounters with Jewesses, see, inter alia, the same poem by Juan García. For the Mariscal's insult see no. 418. (Allusions to interfaith sexual dalliance are very common in the *Cancionero*; see e.g. no. 449.) Juan Bautista Avalle-Arce considered the possibility of a Morisco as well as a Converso background for Juan Alfonso, in 'Sobre Juan Alfonso de Baena', *Revista de Filología Hispánica*, 7 (1945), 141–7. José María Azáceta opted for Converso in his *Cancionero*, vol. i (Madrid, 1966), pp. v, 4, and accompanying notes. Dutton and Gonzalez Cuenca, the most recent editors, begin by accepting the poetic evidence of Baena's Converso status only 'provisionalmente', but end by treating it as a certainty: *Cancionero de Juan Alfonso de Baena*, pp. xv, xviii.

[38] Examples of this underlying logic are legion. In addition to the works already cited, see Francisco Cantera Burgos, 'El Cancionero de Baena: Judíos y conversos en él', *Sefarad*, 27 (1967), 71–111; Julio Rodríguez-Puértolas, *Poesía de protesta en la edad media castellana: historia y antología* (Madrid, 1968), 216–24; Cristina Arbós, 'Los cancioneros castellanos del siglo xv como fuente para la historia de los judíos españoles', in Yom Tov Assis and Yosef Kaplan (eds.), *Jews and Conversos: Studies in Society and the Inquisition* (Jerusalem, 1985), 77–8; Gregory S. Hutcheson, ' "Pinning him to the Wall": The Poetics of Self-Destruction in the Court of Juan II', *Disputatio*, 5 (2002), 87–102, esp. pp. 92–5. The quote is from Théodore de Puymaigre, *La Cour littéraire de don Juan II, roi de Castille* (Paris, 1873), 131. Cf. José Amador de los Ríos, *Estudios históricos, políticos y literarios sobre los judíos de España* (Madrid, 1848), 425 ff.

[39] As Charles Fraker conceded in his review of Wolf-Dieter Lange's *El fraile trobador. Zeit, Leben und Werk des Diego de Valencia de León (1350?–1412?)* (Frankfurt am Main, 1971), in the *Hispanic Review*, 42/3 (1974), 341–3: 'Thus one more supposed New Christian gets stricken from the canon' (p. 341).

Like so much 'Judaism' in late medieval Spain, the Judaism of these
Christian poets turns out to have as much to do with the history of Christian
thought as with their own religious 'ancestry'. In this particular case, their
insults turn out to be part of a strategic deployment of 'Judaization', developed
in order to defend secular poetry from its clerical critics. Following Plato,
Christian theologians from Augustine to Thomas Aquinas had attacked secular poetry as the most mimetic of literary genres, the one closest to the materi-
ality of nature, most tightly bound to literalism and to the flesh (both marked
as 'Jewish' in Christian discourse), and as such the most dangerously seductive
of genres. Poetic fictions, as Aquinas put it, contain no divine truth. They
'have no purpose except to signify; and such signification does not go beyond
the literal sense'.[40] Saints issued similar warnings in the Spain of Juan Alfonso
de Baena and his colleagues: both Vincent Ferrer and Alonso de Cartagena
(the Converso bishop of Burgos) preached about the dangers of poetry.[41]

Of course poetic fictions also had their late medieval defenders, most
famously Dante, Petrarch, and Boccaccio.[42] Like these Italian notables,

[40] Suspicion of poetry has deep roots in Christian aesthetics. For the case of Augustine, see
Joachim Küpper, ' "Uti" und "frui" bei Augustinus und die Problematik des Genießens in der
ästhetischen Theorie des Okzidents', in Wolfgang Klein and Ernst Müller (eds.), *Genuß und
Egoismus. Zur Kritik ihrer geschichtlichen Verknüpfung* (Berlin, 2002), 3–29; and Augustine, *De
Civitate Dei*, XI. 18 and *De Doctrina Christiana*, II. 6 (7, 8) and IV. 11 (26). For Aquinas' claim,
see his *Quodlibetal Questions*, ed. Sandra Edwards (Toronto, 1983), 7. 6. 16. Elsewhere Aquinas
attempts to distinguish between poetic fictions and other more salvific ones. See in particular
his discussion in *Summa Theologiae*, I. I. 9. See also ibid. I. II. 101 on the dependence of the ritual of the Mass on 'sensible figures'.

[41] On these themes see especially Karl Kohut, 'Zur Vorgeschichte der Diskussion um das
Verhältnis von Christentum und antiker Kultur im spanischen Humanismus. Die Rolle des
Decretum Gratiani in der Übermittlung patristischen Gedankengutes', *Archiv für Kultur-
geschichte*, 55 (1973), 80–106, and id., 'Der Beitrag der Theologie zum Literaturbegriff in der
Zeit Juans II von Kastilien: Alonso de Cartagena (1384-1456) und Alonso de Madrigal,
genannt el Tostado (1400?–1455)', *Romanische Forschungen*, 89 (1977), 183–226; see also his *Las
teorías literarias en España y Portugal durante los siglos XV y XVI* (Madrid, 1973). On Vincent
Ferrer, and on responses by *Cancionero* poets to his preaching in Castile, see Pedro Cátedra,
*Sermón, sociedad y literatura en la Edad Media: San Vicente Ferrer en Castilla (1411–1412), estudio
bibliográfico, literario y edición de los textos inéditos* (Valladolid, 1994), 251–68. For Ferrer's
Thomistic opposition to the allegorization of poetry, see Cátedra's 'La predicación castellana
de San Vicente Ferrer', *Boletín de la Real Academia de Buenas Letras de Barcelona*, 39 (1983-4),
235–309, esp. p. 278, citing Biblioteca Nacional, Madrid, MS 9,433, fos. 33ʳ-43ʳ.

[42] For a classical treatment of these issues see Ernst Robert Curtius, *European Literature and
the Latin Middle Ages*, trans. Willard R. Trask (Princeton, 1953), 214–27. But see also August
Buck, *Italienische Dichtungslehren vom Mittelalter bis zum Ausgang der Renaissance* (Tübingen,
1952), 33–53; Otfried Lieberknecht, *Allegorese und Philologie. Überlegungen zum Problem
des mehrfachen Schriftsinns in Dantes Commedia* (Stuttgart, 1999); Alastair J. Minnis, 'The
Transformation of Critical Tradition: Dante, Petrarch, and Boccaccio', in A. J. Minnis and
A. B. Scott (eds.), *Medieval Literary Theory and Criticism, c.1000–c.1375* (Oxford, 1988); and
Joachim Küpper, 'Zu einigen Aspekten der Dichtungstheorie in der Frührenaissance', in
Andreas Kablitz and Gerhard Regn (eds.), *Renaissance. Konzepte einer Epoche im Dialog der
Disziplinen* (Heidelberg, 2006), 47–71. Among the crucial texts are the following: Dante's

Baena and his colleagues were seeking to justify and enlarge the place of non-biblical poetry within Christianity.[43] They did so through a theory of 'poetic grace' much like that of Dante, a theory that is articulated in Baena's prologue to the *Cancionero* as well as in its poetry. Two lines of Latin verse scrawled at the top of the first manuscript folio capture the general theme: 'Unicuique gratia est data | Secundum Paulum relata' ('To each one grace is given | according to St Paul', a paraphrase of Ephesians 4: 7).[44] The proper use of poetic language was, our poets claimed, the product of divine grace and inspiration, and through this inspiration the lay poet, if he was a *good* poet, gained access to spiritual truth.

Without benefit of Christian exegesis it is not so clear what 'Judaism' has to do with this Pauline poetics of grace. But consider, to begin with, the way in which our lay poets made their claim that the 'infused grace of God' offered them access to divine truths that escaped the sophisticated training of the theologian.[45] The poet Ferrán Manuel de Lando, for example, reminds Friar Lope del Monte that 'God chose to reveal his secrets | to simple folk, humble, heavy, and rude, | while he left the learned nude, and hid from them his glory, | as Our Saviour makes clear | in the subtle texts of his Gospel story.'[46]

'Letter to Cangrande della Scala', in Dante Alighieri, *Tutte le opere*, ed. Luigi Blasucci (Florence, 1965), 341–52, where Dante draws a parallel between the multiple levels of meaning of biblical and non-biblical poetry; Boccaccio's *Genealogia deorum gentilium libri*, ed. Vincenzo Romano (Bari, 1951), esp. the preface and books 14–15; and, by Petrarch, *Invective contra medicum*, ed. A. Bufano, in *Opere latine di Francesco Petrarca*, vol. ii (Turin, 1975), *Familiares*, ed. Vittorio Rossi (Florence, 1997), letter 10. 4, 'De stilo Patrum et de proportione inter theologiam et poetriam', and *Collatio laureationis*, ed. C. Godi in 'La *Collatio laureationis* del Petrarca nelle due redazioni', *Studi petrarcheschi*, 5 (1988), 1–56. On the Castilian career of these texts see, inter alia, J. Piccus, 'El traductor español de *De genealogia deorum*', in *Homenaje a Rodríguez-Moñino*, 2 vols. (Madrid, 1966), 59–75, and Hernando de Talavera, 'Invectivas contra el médico rudo e parlero', ed. P. Cátedra, in *Petrarca: Obras*, vol. i, ed. Francisco Rico (Madrid, 1978), 369–410.

[43] So far as I know the only works to treat the *Cancionero de Baena* in this context are Karl Kohut, 'La teoría de la poesia cortesana en el Prologo de Juan Alfonso de Baena', *Actas del coloquio hispano-aleman Ramón Menendez Pidal* (Madrid, 1982), 120–37: 131 n. 27, and Lange, *El fraile trobador*, 101 f.

[44] *Cancionero de Juan Alfonso de Baena*, 1. The rubric is discussed in a number of poems, most notably those by Baena: no. 359 (p. 639), ll. 9–10, and Manuel de Lando, nos. 253 (pp. 451–2), ll. 17–24, and 257 (pp. 456–8), couplet 11. For a good summary and revision of the scholarly debates over the meaning of this theme of *gracia* in the *Cancionero*, see Julian Weiss, *Poet's Art: Literary Theory in Castile, c.1400–60* (Oxford, 1990), 25–40.

[45] An important example is the exchange between the poet Alfonso Álvarez de Villasandino, who prided himself on his lack of formal learning, and the theologian Fray Pedro (nos. 80–3, pp. 107–13). Pedro challenges Villasandino to explain obscurities in the Apocalypse. In no. 136 (pp. 161–2) he does the same again. Villasandino's response comes in no. 137. For the Bachellor from Salamanca, see nos. 92–3 (pp. 119–20).

[46] No. 272 (pp. 472–4), ll. 21–32: 'que Dios sus secretos quiso revelar | a párvulos simples, pesados e rudos, | e a los prudentes dexólos desnudos, escondiendo d'ellos el su resplandor, | segunt verifica Nuestro Salvador | en su Evangelio de testos agudos.' The allusion is to Matt. 11: 25.

The strategic accusation of 'Judaism' is already present here, in so far as Ferrán Manuel's verse aligns the theologian with the negative example of the seemingly learned but actually blind Pharisees in the Gospels.[47] Friar Lope's position in this debate, on the other hand, reiterates the traditional condemnation of poetry as 'literal fictions' without any hint of the divine. The poet, he says, is to be classed with those who have 'never achieved knowledge of divine deeds . . . the gentile, the Jew, and the tax collector'. In his final riposte, Friar Lope turns Lando's implicit 'Pharisaization' of theologians (that is, his accusation that those who seem clothed in learning are in reality naked and blind) on its head. 'God makes bears with furry skins, and makes the ignorant wise. | But few are the wise and truly learned, who have hairy chests and thighs.' Whatever the ontological uncertainties in this world, Lope implies, one thing is clear: in theological matters his rival Lando, a mere lay poet, ranks with Jews and beasts.[48]

Beyond such questions of the spiritual 'truth value' of poetry, the accusation of Judaizing proved generally useful for the development of a critical poetics itself. For example, the sense that bad poetry was often mistaken for good, and good poetry maligned as bad, could be powerfully expressed in terms of a 'Pharisaic poetics'. Thus the most influential of the poets in Baena's anthology, Alfonso Álvarez de Villasandino, characterizes what he calls 'metrificadores' ('metre scribblers') as 'arrendadores' (tax collectors), and mockingly describes the king rewarding them with 'ropas con señales' (clothes with badges) like those the Jews wear.[49]

Of course Baena and his colleagues did not give poetry up for lost. Instead they developed a critical framework within which to argue about its relative

[47] For the moment we are concerned only with 'Judaization' in debates about the relative value of secular poetry and theology. Accusations of Judaism are also made, however, in contests where both sides claim explicitly theological authority. In a debate (nos. 323–8) between Franciscans and Dominicans over the immaculate conception of the Virgin Mary, for example, Friar Lope accuses Diego Martínez de Medina of misreading (no. 324, l. 137: 'La palavra mal entendida | mata e non da consuelo'—'The word, when badly understood, | kills rather than consoles'—a paraphrase of 2 Cor. 3: 6), calls him a hypocritical Pharisee (ll. 209–11), and suggests that 'bueno vos será juntar | con essos de Moisén | e parientes de Cohén' ('it would be good for you to join | with the people of Moses | and the family of Cohen': no. 326, ll. 61–3).

[48] See no. 273, ll. 473–4: 'Él faze los ossos con cueros lanudos | e al que poco sabe ser grant sabidor; | pocos son los sabios de sabio valor | que tengan los pechos e lomos peludos.' Ferran responds in no. 274. Friar Lope attacks Villasandino on similar grounds in no. 117. The poem is an attack on political as well as poetic falsity, ending with a curse on those 'hypocrites' who sow discord among the magnates, and ends with the exhortation that princes 'abhor Jews' and 'honour good men' (ll. 89–96). Even here Maestro Lope may be taking aim at the poets, whose inflammatory role in royal courts seems already a literary commonplace. See for example the first lines of Diego de Valencia's poem no. 227 (pp. 266–75) on the birth of Juan II (1405), regarding the 'contiendas, roídos e daño muy farto' ('contention, noise, and great damage') that arise every day over the interpretation of figurative poetry.

[49] No. 96 (pp. 122–3), ll. 28–45. Villasandino expresses his sense of an ontological crisis of poetry most clearly in another poem with less obvious 'Pharisaic' overtones (no. 255, pp. 453–5).

merits: hence the prologue to Baena's *Cancionero*, the earliest poetic manifesto surviving in the Castilian language. I have already mentioned that the prologue presents the 'infused grace of God' as the primary prerequisite for good verse. In so far as Baena's colleagues understood the poet's state of grace as legible in the poetry itself, the poem became a literary marker of its author's place on the continuum between letter and spirit, with the bad poet, the misuser of language, understood as (among other things) a 'Jew'. Beyond divine grace there were of course other prerequisites for being a poet: knowledge of rules of metre and form; subtle inventiveness; exquisite discretion and judgement; broad reading; knowledge of a wide range of languages; familiarity with court life; nobility, or 'fydalguía', and courtesy; and always seeming to be a lover, loving whom one should, as one should, where one should. The pages of Juan Alfonso's *Cancionero* were the lists in which the mettle of each poet and each poem were put to the test and measured against this complex standard.

Juan Alfonso himself put this wittily in his poetic challenge to the poet Ferrán Manuel de Lando: 'Ferrand [*sic*] Manuel, for the public display | of your marvellous skill | in this great court of the King of Castile | Someone must give you a sting.' It is out of provocation, according to Baena, that good poetry is born. But the substance of the provocation itself should not be taken to heart: 'Ferrand Manuel, since to each | is given [poetic] grace doubled or simple, | don't let your face turn yellow | because my tongue splashes or stains you.'[50] Insult is only a picador's prod, meant to stimulate the revelation of a poet's virtues. Its 'truth claim' is not to be taken seriously.[51] In this case Ferrán responds with insults, not about Baena's 'Jewishness', but about his deficiencies as a lover. He will, he claims, have sex with Baena's girlfriend. The exchange escalates along these lines, ending with Baena's infamous assertion in *cancionero* 363 that Ferrán's asshole is full of a shepherd's sperm. In the face of this response, reports the *cancionero*, Ferrán abandons the field to Baena.[52]

[50] 'Ferrand Manuel, por que se publique | la vuestra çiençia de grant maravilla, | en esta grant cort del Rey de Castilla | conviene forçado que alguno vos pique'; 'Fernand Manuel, pues unicuique | data est graçia doblada e senzilla, non se vos torne la cara amarilla | por que mi lengua vos unte o salpique' (no. 359, p. 639, ll. 1–4, 9–12).

[51] As Baena puts it in the challenge he issued to Villasandino and Lando in 1423: 'que pierdan malenconía | e tomen plazentería, | sin enojo e sin zizaña, | ca la burla non rascaña' ('Let them lose melancholy | and gain enjoyment | without anger or faction | because mockery does not cut': no. 357, ll. 28–30). The 'truth claims' of these insults deserve to be studied in the light of Jean-Claude Milner's *De la syntaxe à l'interprétation: Quantités, insultes, exclamations* (Paris, 1978), 174–223. My thanks to Giorgio Agamben for drawing my attention to this aspect of Milner's work.

[52] See Lando to Baena, no. 360 (pp. 639–40), ll. 6–8. Baena to Lando, no. 363 (pp. 641–2). Note Baena's claim that insult is necessary for the production of poetry without defects ('sin raça e polilla': ll. 9–12). For a comment on the use of the word *raça* 'race' to signify (poetic) defect see Nirenberg, ' "Race" and "Racism" in Late Medieval Spain', in M. Greer, W. Mignolo, and M. Quilligan (eds.), *Rereading the Black Legend: The Discourses of Racial Difference in the Renaissance Empires* (Chicago, 2007), 71–87.

Here, the idiom of poetic criticism is primarily sexual. These idioms are more diverse in the contest that follows, between Baena and the most famous of the *Cancionero* poets, Alfonso Álvarez de Villasandino. Baena opens by challenging this 'rotten old man, whose ribs are made of phlegm', to a poetry contest. Villasandino, in turn, asserts that, far from being the 'fine troubador' he 'pretends' to be, Baena is a 'rustic mule' whose 'villainy' is marked on his face and in his diet of wine and garlic. He is a 'suzio cohino', a dirty Jew pig (the word plays on the proximity of Cohen and *cochino*), with the voice of a cormorant, not a poet. He knows, in short, nothing of 'this science [of poetry]', and his words are worthless.[53]

'Cohino' here is redolent with meaning, poetic and ontological, but it is no more genealogical than any of the other assertions made in the course of this contest. Baena will respond by calling Villasandino (among other things) 'swine sputum', a drunk, an apostate gambler; Villasandino by calling Baena a bastard and a pig ('tuerto chazino', 'gruniente cochino'). These claims drew their meaning and usefulness, not from the biography of their target, but from the rules of the poetic *agon* in which they were deployed, in which provocation stimulated vulgar poetry, and that poetry revealed the relative 'state of grace' of the competing poets.

This vulgarity is, in other words, the critical by-product of our poets' theology, a way of representing the lack in their rivals of any one of their multiple prerequisites for poetry. Judaism, poetic incompetence, ignorance, rudeness, sexual deviance, even animality were the negative poles of poetic virtues: divine grace, good metre and form, learning, courtesy, love, and so on. Each of these virtues was closely related to its companions, and the terms in which they were expressed were almost interchangeable. The same is true of their attendant vices. The overlapping of these variables made possible a space of play in which claims to poetic or theological 'çiençia' could be both made and criticized in a language of extreme carnality.[54] Within this system

[53] 'Señor, este vil borrico frontino, | torçino e relleno de vino e de ajos, | sus neçios afanes e locos trabajos | es porque l'tengo por trobador fino; en esto se enfinge el suzio cohino | e con muchos buenos levanta baraja; e quien reçelasse su parlar de graja | más negro sería que cuervo marino. || Quien non es capaz bastante nin dino | de aquesta çiençia de que se trabaja, | su argumentar non vale una paja, | nin un mal cogombro, tampoco un pepino.' ('Sir, this vile ass with a branded face | twisted and stuffed with wine and garlic | I consider on account of his foolish frenzy | and crazed works a fine troubador. This swells the head of the dirty Jew-pig, | he presumes to pick fights with his betters. Whoever heeds the words of this grackle | must himself be blacker than a sea-faring crow. || He who is unworthy and incapable | of this knowledge and art that we pursue, | his arguments are not worth a straw | nor a lousy cucumber, not even a gherkin.')

[54] See no. 270 (p. 470), Alfonso de Moraña against Ferrán Manuel de Lando. The latter had written a love poem that placed his beloved among the heavenly spheres, the work of the moon, Mars, and Venus. Alfonso responds by telling him that the planets and fortune are not enough to produce such beauty, that he will be loved (i.e. sodomized) only by Alfonso's Moor, and that he sins.

of thought Judaism was a key metaphor, a governing insult that carried with it a host of theological, linguistic, and physical implications. The same could be said of other idioms of opprobrium in the *Cancionero de Baena*, such as the frequent charges of homosexuality and sodomy, meant to imply of a poet that, as Villasandino put it, he had 'never served love'.[55] Indeed these idioms were often combined, as when the Franciscan monk and theologian Diego de Valencia wrote a poem whose rhyme scheme was made up almost entirely of Hebrew words, accusing Juan de Espanha of being a Jew with no testicles. Those critics who have focused on the poem's Hebrew vocabulary in order to argue that Friar Diego was a Converso have missed the point.[56] The discourse of Judaism, like those of sexuality or animality, was here as much a language of literary criticism as was the language of metre and form. As such it was separable from the genealogy and religious orthodoxy of its object. It was even possible for a real Jew to possess the qualities of a poet, as when the same Friar Diego praised the Jew Symuel Dios-Auda for his charity, his courtesy, and his 'fydalguía': 'For your word never changes or wavers | ... | these are the markers of a noble man | to say things and do them without any doubt.'[57]

The critical accusation of Judaism developed by the poets of the *Cancionero de Baena* in the years following the mass conversions was as much about language as lineage. Some of these poets may in fact have been converts, or descended from converts, but even in such cases their 'Jewishness' in poetry had no simple relationship to their 'Jewishness' in life. Nor was theirs a 'Jewish poetics', except in the sense that it was the product of a Christian theological linguistics that understood certain aspects of language

[55] No. 140, Alfonso Álvarez de Villasandino against Alfonso Ferrández Semuel: 'nunca serviste amor | nin fuste en su conpañia' ('You never served love | nor were in her company'). To this charge, Alfonso Álvarez adds that his target is an apostate Jew with a big nose, a *meshumad* (lit. 'destroyed'; the term has implications of a willing conversion from Judaism). For a suggestive study on the place of love in the production of poetry and nobility in Castile during this period see Julian Weiss, 'Alvaro de Luna, Juan de Mena and the Power of Courtly Love', *Modern Language Notes*, 106 (1991), 241–56.

[56] No. 501 (p. 343). F. Cantera Burgos is among those who move from vocabulary to sociology: 'the use he makes of his ample knowledge of Hebrew vocabulary is surprising. We would therefore not be shocked if . . . he should possess many Judaic contacts, perhaps even family': *El Cancionero de Baena*, 103. Charles F. Fraker's phrasing and conclusion are almost identical: see *Studies on the Cancionero de Baena* (Chapel Hill, NC, 1996), 9–10 n. 2. But cf. Wolf-Dieter Lange's conclusive rebuttal in *El fraile trobador*.

[57] 'ca vuestra palabra jamas non se muda | ... | Estas son señales de omne fidalgo: | dezir e fazer las cosas syn dubda' (no. 511, pp. 355–6). Of course the possibility of an ironic allusion to Jewish 'literal' understanding should not be dismissed here. Cf. however, the Marqués de Santillana's comment on the writings of Rabbi Shem Tov de Carrion: 'No vale el açor menos | por nasçer en víl nío, | ni los exemplos buenos | por los dezir iudío' ('Being born in a vile nest | does not make the hawk worth less | nor are good examples diminished | because uttered by a Jew'): 'Proemio', in *Obras completas*, ed. Angel Gómez Moreno and Maximilian P. A. M. Kerkhof (Barcelona, 1988), 451.

(ranging from letter and literalism to mimesis and hypocrisy) in terms of Judaism and Judaizing. Our poets, in short, built both their 'Jewishness' and their literary criticism out of the terms of Christian aesthetics, epistemology, and ontology.

This tendency to evaluate Christian uses of language in Jewish terms was not new. Ever since St Paul coined the verb 'to Judaize' (Ἰουδαΐζειν, Galatians 2: 14), the concept had served as a way of describing the danger of falling from the spiritual to the literal, from eternal truth to mere appearance in the world, from Christianity to Judaism. What the mass conversions produced in Spain was a new vertigo, a heightened sense of just how steep and slippery the slope was between Judaism and Christianity. Some, like Vincent Ferrer and his many supporters, reacted to this vertigo by attempting to eliminate the danger, working for the conversion or complete isolation of all Jews. Joan Alfonso de Baena and his poets, on the other hand, put the vertigo to work, exploiting the danger in the thrill-ride of a poetics that threatened everyone with Jewishness. It is important to notice, however, that neither sought to secure his Christian privilege at the expense of that of the converts by making it genealogical. For that, we must look to a slightly later period, and to politics rather than poetics.

PUTTING THE FEAR OF JUDAIZATION TO WORK: THE CASE OF POLITICS

Again, 'Judaism' was not a new charge in Christian politics. St Ambrose of Milan, for example, famously exhorted the Roman emperor Theodosius not to compel a bishop to pay for the reconstruction of a synagogue whose burning he had instigated. Ambrose presented the emperor's insistence on upholding the letter of the law as itself Judaizing, and reminded the emperor of his predecessor's unhappy fate: 'Maximus . . . hearing that a synagogue had been burnt in Rome, had sent an edict to Rome, as if he were the upholder of public order. Wherefore the Christian people said, No good is in store for him. That king has become a Jew . . .'.[58] Ambrose here implied a political 'resistance theory': monarchs who read literally, upholding the letter of the law over the demands of spirit, deserve deposition as 'Jews'.[59] The political anti-Judaism foreshadowed in this hermeneutic criticism of kings did occasionally surface in the early Middle Ages, but (for reasons we cannot

[58] 'Sancti Ambrosi Opera', in *Corpus Scriptorum Ecclesiasticorum Latinorum*, 82 pt. 3, ed. Michaela Zelzer (Vienna, 1982), 145–77, letter 40.23 (p. 173).

[59] For a fuller account of this history see David Nirenberg, 'Warum der König die Juden beschützen musste, und warum er sie verfolgen musste', in B. Jussen (ed.), *Die Macht des Königs. Herrschaft in Europa vom Frühmittelalter bis in die Neuzeit* (Munich, 2005), 226–41, and id., 'Christian Sovereignty and Jewish Flesh', in S. Nichols, J. Küpper, et al. (eds.), *The Medieval Senses* (Baltimore, forthcoming).

explore here) it became a coherent discourse in Latin Christianity only after the turn of the millennium. The frequent application of this discourse in the later Middle Ages peopled the history of medieval rebellions with 'Jew-loving' rulers. Even the 'most Catholic monarchs' of Spain, Ferdinand and Isabel, conquerors of Granada, founders of the Inquisition, expellers of the Jews, could be accused of being descended from Jews and favouring them in their policies.[60]

However old this political science of Judaizing may have been, it gained new power and utility from the increased sense of indistinction produced by the mass conversions in Spain. The 1430s was a period of fierce factionalization in Iberian politics, one that hurtled towards civil war. Within this political context, prominent factions in many town councils moved against their competitors by arguing that those who were converts or descended from converts, that is, those who where not 'Christians by nature', should be barred from holding any public office. This sharpening of the somatic limits to conversion was strongly opposed by the monarchy, and it was condemned both by the Council of Basel in 1434 and by Pope Eugenius IV in 1437. But these genealogical arguments became broadly useful during the civil wars against King Juan II of Castile and his minister Alvaro de Luna, whose attempts to strengthen the monarchy aroused fierce opposition. It was during those wars, and most explicitly during the rebellion of 1449, that the rebel government of the city of Toledo issued the first 'statute of purity of blood'. Jewish hatred of Christianity and of Christians ran indelibly in the veins of the descendants of converts, the rebels argued, and through their actions it was Judaizing society. Once these converts were barred from ever holding office or exercising power over Christians, the corruption would end and Christian society would be purified.[61]

These political arguments certainly transformed the potential meanings of 'Jew', 'convert', and 'Christian'. But neither their genealogical truth-claims nor the obvious sociopolitical consequences of the statutes they spawned bring us any closer to an unproblematic world of 'real' Converso 'Jewishness'. Scholars have devoted themselves to family trees and prosopographies, counting the number of Conversos in public office in order to uncover the sociopolitical 'realities' underlying Old Christian claims about

---

[60] On Isabel as 'protector of the Jews and daughter of a Jewess' see the account of the Polish traveller Nicolas Popplau, in Javier Liske, *Viajes de extranjeros por España y Portugal en los siglos XV, XVI, y XVII* (Madrid, 1878). On Ferdinand, see Maurice Kriegel, 'Histoire sociale et ragots: Sur l'"ascendance juive" de Ferdinand le Catholique', in *Movimientos migratorios y expulsiones en la diáspora occidental* (Pamplona, 2000), 95–100.

[61] Much of the bibliography on the Toledan revolt can conveniently be found in Benzion Netanyahu, *The Origins of the Inquisition in Fifteenth Century Spain* (New York, 1995). The events of 1434 and 1437 are discussed in Nirenberg, 'Mass Conversion and Genealogical Mentalities', 23–5.

the dangers of 'Jewish' government.[62] Such research is to my mind one-sided. There were, of course, Converso politicians, just as there were Converso poets, but their existence does not suffice to explain the rise of Converso 'Judaizing' as an explosive language of political critique. We need rather to focus, once again, on the interplay between the dizzyingly blurred religious landscape of mid-fifteenth-century Spain and the conceptual lenses of Christian culture through which that landscape could be viewed.

In the case of politics, the roots of this language of 'Judaizing' lie in the same dialectical tension discussed above in connection with poetics: the tension between the visible, carnal, and literal, on the one hand, and the invisible, spiritual, and non-literal on the other. Since I took some time to sketch the long history of this tension in poetics and hermeneutics, it is worth noting that its history in political theory is just as ancient. Aristotle articulated a key discrimination, between the corporeal politics of bare life and the higher politics of the good. As he put it in the *Nicomachean Ethics*: 'we must not follow those who advise us, being men, to think of human things, and being mortal, of mortal things, but must, so far as we can, make ourselves immortal'.[63] The 'natural' relationship of soul to body as ruler to subject provided a powerful political analogy. '[A]lthough in bad or cor-rupted natures the body will often appear to rule over the soul, because they are in an evil and unnatural condition . . . It is clear that the rule of the soul over the body . . . is natural and expedient.'[64] The reversal of these priorities, the placing of worldly gain ahead of a common and immaterial good, Aristotle presented as tyranny. Tyranny, in other words, consisted of a per-verted preference for self-interest over the commonwealth, for the mortal over the immortal, for flesh over spirit.[65]

As part of the common currency of Hellenistic political thought, these Aristotelian distinctions were converted at an early stage into Christian terms (we have already heard an echo of them in Ambrose). Moreover, the rediscovery of Aristotelian texts and commentaries in the later Middle Ages prompted their influential and self-conscious rearticulation within Christian political theology. Fifteenth-century politicians did not, there-fore, need to be readers of Aristotle (though by mid-century they could have been) in order to perceive the usefulness of the language of 'Jewish' lit-eralist and materialist tyranny for a critique of royal power, especially not in a context in which mass conversion had lent new power to the fear of Judaizing.

[62] See e.g. the many works on this topic by Francisco Márquez Villanueva, beginning with his 'Conversos y cargos concejiles en el siglo XV', *Revista de archivos, bibliotecas y museos*, 63 (1957), 503–40.
[63] *Nicomachean Ethics* 1177b; translation from *The Complete Works of Aristotle*, ed. Jonathan Barnes, 2 vols. (Princeton, NJ, 1984), ii. 1861.
[64] *Politics* 1254b: ibid. 1990.   [65] See e.g. ibid. 1279b.

It was the power of these forms of thought, as much as the Converso status of some royal officials, that made 'anti-Jewishness' such a useful political tool in mid-fifteenth-century Castile. I would go further, and claim that it was their power that underwrote the definition of Jewishness as genealogical in what are sometimes called the earliest acts of European racist legislation, the Castilian 'statutes of purity of blood'. Consider only the justifications given for the earliest of these statutes, issued in 1449, during the revolt of the city of Toledo against King Juan II of Castile.[66] The Toledan ideologues of the revolt drew a distinction between two types of governor, those who read according to the Spirit, and those who read according to the letter (for 'the letter kills, the spirit gives life'[67]), those who belong to the Church, and those who belong to the synagogue, those who are Christian humans, and those who are Jewish beasts. 'Administrators' who read like Jews, literally after the flesh, have lost the human right to participate in the *res publica*. They have become creatures of self-interest, and their power is by definition tyrannical, not sovereign.

Like many Christian political theorists before them, the Toledan rebels took Aristotle's oppositions of bare life and good life, private body and body politic, tyrant and legitimate magistrate, and grafted onto them a Pauline hermeneutic one, killing letter and life-giving spirit, animating both with the distinction between 'Jew' and Christian. They did so, not only because some of their targets were converts, but because 'Jewishness' was a well-established form for representing materialist tyranny, one that drew renewed energy from the potent confusion of bloodlines and hermeneutics produced in Castile by mass conversion and intermarriage.

Of course the existence of so many descendants of converts gave these arguments their power, and these descendants suffered the consequences of that power most acutely. But what made the arguments so explosive was their ability to threaten anyone, not only converts, with the political charge of 'Jewishness': the 'prime minister', the king, and even the pope (as one rebel theorist put it), if he ruled against the rebels. The rebels of Toledo were defeated, but their logic lost none of its utility. That utility propelled claims about the genealogical nature of the converts' Judaism to victory. Within a generation or two the Iberian body politic had produced a thick hedge of inquisition and genealogy in order to protect itself from penetration by the 'Jewish race' and its attributes.

This is obviously not the place to show how that victory was won, or to think through its many implications. Suffice it here to say that the genealogical turn

[66] These are edited in Eloy Benito Ruano, 'El memorial contra los conversos del bachiller Marcos García de Mora (Marquillos de Mazarambroz)', *Sefarad*, 17 (1957), 314–51, and 'La Sentencia-Estatuto de Pero Sarmiento contra los conversos toledanos', *Revista de la Universidad de Madrid*, 6 (1957), 277–306. The analysis that follows is based primarily on the first of these. [67] 2 Cor. 3: 6.

was taken, and that it transformed the relationship of Judaism and Christianity. We could characterize the process as an earthquake, one that jolted Christian religiosity out of its ancient Pauline course into a new channel, this one carved by nature rather than by grace. For Jews, Conversos, and Old Christians alike, the consequences of that transformation were vast (and later for Muslims, New World natives, and Europeans of the Reformation and Counter-Reformation as well, but those are other stories). Some will reproach me for not describing these transformations here. I can only plead that this essay is merely a preliminary to their history. Its goal is to make plausible the methodological claim that we cannot study the history of Jews, Christians, or converts after the mass conversions without taking seriously the ways in which each of these categories rebuilt itself in terms of the others.

Others will object that I have stressed too heavily the importance of Christian ideas in this 'rebuilding' of convert 'Jewishness', and paid too little attention to the beliefs and actions of 'real converts'. It is true that, although in a different essay I concluded otherwise,[68] in this one I have deliberately stressed the role of specific Christian intellectual traditions in the construction of convert 'Jewishness'. Such an approach runs counter to the laudable devotion of my generation of historians to uncovering the 'agency' of the minority (in this case Jews and Conversos) within a mutually constituted history of relations between Judaism and Christianity. Pushed to polemic, my approach could be forced to imply that the power of Christian forms of thought in shaping figures of Judaism was asymmetrically massive in fifteenth-century Sepharad.

This essay, however, is not meant as a polemic but as a thought experiment, one that (in good Maimonidean fashion) therapeutically inclines ingrained habits of thought towards their contraries. Scholars of Judaism in late medieval Spain have for too long adopted the inquisitorial methods invented by their subjects, assuming that the actions of anyone who can be shown to be descended from converts are in some way essentially Jewish. Exaggeration aside, my point is merely a cautionary one. The mass conversions strained to breaking point the distinctions through which Christians and Jews understood the world. Fifteenth-century Christians and Jews did succeed in re-creating differences they thought of as essential, and even in representing their classifications as continuous with crucial dichotomies of 'Christian' and 'Jew'. We should not, however, make their claims for continuity our own, nor adapt as our own methodology the tools they used to re-create their world.

[68] 'This transformation was achieved, not by the implacable migration of ideas from one culture to another, but by the jostling of countless individuals, Jew and Christian, reorienting themselves in the strangely unfamiliar religious landscape that emerged as the floodwaters of baptism receded': 'Mass Conversion and Genealogical Mentalities', 40.

NINE

The Social Context of Apostasy among Fifteenth-Century Spanish Jewry
The Dynamics of a New Religious Borderland

RAM BEN-SHALOM

THE RELATIONS BETWEEN CHRISTIANS AND JEWS

THE IMAGES of the anthropomorphized figures of Church and Synagogue that adorn the Christian art of western Europe, including that of Christian Spain, contain theological and social messages revealing the chasm that separated Christianity and Judaism. The Church, if not all of Christian society, tolerated the Jews out of respect for a distant legacy—in deference, if you will, to the symbolic and religious role played by the Jewish people in the ancient world. The lowly standing of the medieval Jew, by contrast, was precisely a result of his perceived betrayal of that historical agency. Such a view constituted the medieval foundations of those social restrictions designed to institutionalize the gulf between Jew and Christian. They were a practical expression of the symbols of the Church, Ecclesia, shown as a crowned woman, in contrast to the wretched representation of Synagoga, in several instances depicted as blindfolded—an obvious metaphor for the religious myopia of the Jews—and enveloped by a serpent symbolizing their demonic character. Could there be a more pointed illustration of the connection between the Jews and the Devil?[1]

For centuries the Jews of the Iberian world found themselves living among a Christian majority, sharing their social, economic, and cultural existence. Certain historians have referred to this common life in Christian Spain as the *Convivencia*, or coexistence.[2] This was because, alongside instances of social segregation, legal discrimination, physical (and ritual) violence, compulsory religious disputations (and trials), the obligatory attendance at sermons, and

---

[1] See Jeremy Cohen, *Living Letters of the Law: Ideas of the Jew in Medieval Christianity* (Berkeley, 1999).
[2] See Thomas F. Glick, 'Convivencia: An Introductory Note', in Vivian B. Mann, Thomas Glick, and Jerrilynn Dodds (eds.), *Convivencia: Jews, Muslims, and Christians in Medieval Spain* (New York, 1992), 1–9.

exclusion from positions of economic power, there was also a more positive aspect to the treatment of Jews. This alternative pattern of interaction included economic and professional co-operation, the open preference for Jews in certain occupations, the bestowal of privileges, the granting of a wide-ranging legal autonomy, regular social intercourse, shared scientific activity, and a thriving cultural dialogue. The symbolic gap that separated Christianity and Jewry in Spain was thus a highly fluid factor in the life of both communities. Anything but static and fixed, Christian–Jewish relations were actively shaped by a myriad of cultural, political, and religious agents. The theological and legal concepts that each side used for defining the other were open to constant negotiation and reinterpretation, a function of political and economic interests. The result was a constant fluctuation and blurring of boundaries.

The rift between Christian and Jew was not only multidimensional; it also worked in two directions. That is to say, it was not a simple function of Christian attitudes towards Jewry: differences were no less the consequence of Jewish perceptions of Christianity. Jewish restrictions on Christian participation in meals, social gatherings, and economic activities rested on the halakhic understanding of talmudic sources, and in particular those sources that address the subject of idolatry (*avodah zarah*).

The relationship of medieval Christians to the idol-worshippers of the past was a question that engaged the leading Jewish legal minds of the Middle Ages. While the tolerant views advanced by the likes of Menahem Hame'iri rejected any equation of Christianity with pagan culture, thus abolishing numerous restrictions on contact between Jews and Christians, there were others who emphasized the analogy between Christianity and the worship of other gods. This effectively limited social interaction and intensified the breach between Judaism and Christianity. What is more, the image of Christianity in the Jewish imagination spanned a spectrum that ranged from seeing it as a subversion of Judaism born of error or theological and interpretative flaws—a critique that nevertheless made it possible to recognize and even appreciate the cultural and social achievements of the Church—to seeing it as a manifestation of satanic evil in the world.[3] Such perceptions of the 'other' as demonic found expression among both Jews and Christians, serving to deepen the tendency towards mutual segregation and exclusion.

In the Middle Ages the Jewish–Christian discourse in Iberian society experienced a transformation unknown in the rest of western Europe. This was the result of the appearance of a new presence in the social fabric, the

---

[3] See Ram Ben-Shalom, *Facing Christian Culture: Historical Consciousness and Images of the Past among the Jews of Spain and Southern France during the Middle Ages* [Mul tarbut notserit: toda'ah historit vedimuyei avar bekerev yehudei sefarad uprovans biyemei habeinayim] (Jerusalem, 2006); Moshe Idel, 'The Attitude to Christianity in *Sefer ha-Meshiv*', *Immanuel*, 12 (1981), 77–95.

Conversos, or *anusim* (the coerced: the Hebrew term implies forced conversion), that is, 'New Christians'. From the time of the anti-Jewish riots in Castile and Aragon and the birth of a distinct social group of Conversos in 1391 until the expulsion of the Jews from Spain in 1492, Jewish–Christian relations evolved from a dual dynamic into a triangulated discourse practised by Jew, Converso, and Christian, one in which each side redefined its identity in relation to its two partners in Spanish life.

Christian society became divided into several schools of thought over this issue. There were those who considered the Conversos to be loyal Christians who made a significant contribution to the community. Others, however, claimed that the Conversos were subversive heretics undermining the very foundations of Hispanic culture. Still others viewed the Jewish origins of the Conversos as a source of bragging rights, a direct link to the historic people of Israel and, in particular, to the descendants of the tribe of Judah, who were related to the House of David—Jesus's dynasty. And there were some who thought that any Jewish blood constituted a genetic flaw that could not be repaired and so needed to be removed by means of far-reaching racial laws (blood-purity statutes) that distinguished between 'veteran' or Old Christians and New Christians and were intended to prevent the Conversos from introducing Judaism directly into the heart of Christian life.[4]

The rise of a Converso community in Spain likewise forced the Jews to rethink their own identity. Jewish communities became divided into Converso and observant Jewish neighbourhoods. Jewish families were divided between observant members and converts. As a result, common meals, business dealings, funerals, marriages, divorces, and social functions between members of these two groups now all required halakhic rulings as the legal authorities in the Jewish community were asked to determine if such relations were allowable or not.

In addition, old questions over the relationship between Christianity and paganism resurfaced in connection to the Conversos. Were they to be thought of as Christians in the full sense of the word? Or were they Jews who had transgressed, and were they thus to be accorded a legal status distinct from that of the Christian?

And so we find that the concerns of Hispanic Christians regarding the religious and social identity of the Conversos were shared in equal measure by Spain's Jews. The nature of that identity, of course, would determine

---

[4] David Nirenberg, 'Das Konzept von Rasse in der Forschung über mittelalterlichen iberischen Antijudaismus', in Christoph Cluse et al. (eds.), *Jüdische Gemeinden und ihr christlicher Kontext in kulturräumlich vergleichender Betrachtung* (Hanover, 2003), 49–72; id., 'Mass Conversion and Genealogical Mentalities: Jews and Christians in Fifteenth-Century Spain', *Past and Present*, 174 (Feb. 2002), 3–41.

Christian and Jewish attitudes towards and acceptance of the Conversos into their respective communities. At the same time, daily interaction between the groups in the social, occupational, and cultural spheres had a crucial influence on how each perceived the other.

This was the context for the changing nature of the division between Jew and Christian over the course of the fifteenth century. Did the Conversos function as a social bridge that connected majority and minority cultures in Spain? Were they a conduit through which ideas, customs, and collective memories flowed in both directions, effectively restructuring the differences that traditionally divided Jew and Christian? Or was the appearance of the Converso a provocation, one that then forced both camps to recast their own collective identities?

It is clear that questions concerning the relationship between Judaism and Christianity in fifteenth-century Spain cannot be discussed without understanding this new socio-religious force that had now appeared on the historical stage. If, for instance, we are to accept the view advanced by some scholars and embraced in particular by Benzion Netanyahu,[5] namely, that the majority of the Conversos were loyal Christians who maintained no conscious connection to Judaism, then the Jewish attitude towards them, and Jewish perceptions of the social and cultural relations between the two groups, become important in understanding the general nature of Jewish–Christian relations. But if Netanyahu's interpretation is mistaken, and numerous Conversos actually made an effort to preserve a relationship with Judaism, then we find ourselves asking if this liminal constituency did not constitute a new common ground between Judaism and Christianity. For, as we will see below, it was evident to the Jews that the Conversos, if only on the basis of their outward behaviour, had embraced at least some aspects of Christianity. This meant that Jewish engagement with the Conversos was an indication of a strategy of openness towards those same features of Christianity that the Conversos represented.

A NEW SOCIAL TRIANGLE

Netanyahu's thesis will serve as a starting point for testing one element in these triangular relations, namely, the Jewish position regarding the Converso. Once that relationship is better understood, we can begin to examine the division between Judaism and Christianity and to address the possibility that this division was narrowed in the fifteenth century, when each of these groups was forced to understand itself in relation to the other.

[5] In *The Marranos of Spain: From the Late Fourteenth to the Early Sixteenth Century According to Contemporary Hebrew Sources* (Ithaca, NY, 1999).

In his study of Conversos, Netanyahu analyses the responsa of the Spanish rabbis who emigrated to northern Africa following the violent persecutions of 1391. He focuses on those halakhic rulings that pertain to the Conversos and which were formulated in response to issues raised by Spanish Jews. He finds for instance that Isaac bar Sheshet (Ribash, 1326–1408), a member of this generation, gave expression to a growing recognition of the non-Jewish character of the Conversos. In addition, according to Netanyahu, members of the Duran family, who succeeded Isaac bar Sheshet as the leading rabbinic authorities in northern Africa in the fifteenth century, exhibited a similar attitude. According to this reading, each important rabbinical figure initially demonstrated an open, tolerant position towards the Conversos in his halakhic rulings. This liberality then underwent a transformation, ultimately evolving into a severe denunciation of the Conversos once the actual extent of their Christian identity became apparent.[6]

In contrast to Netanyahu's interpretation of the responsa, which rests on his clustering all rabbinical opinions regarding the identity of the Conversos into a single corpus, I propose that we read these documents in a different way. Instead of focusing on the formal position delineated by halakhic rulings, we should first attempt to reconstruct the nature of the social relations that actually prevailed between Jew and Converso, relations that were clearly reflected in the queries presented to the rabbis for consideration. This

---

[6] While Netanyahu's scholarship in *The Marranos of Spain* raises several methodological issues that cast doubt on his conclusion, this is not the place to explore them in any detail. See e.g. Gerson D. Cohen's review of the book in *Jewish Social Studies*, 29 (1967), 178–84; Albert A. Sicroff, 'The Marranos: Forced Converts or Apostates?', *Midstream*, 12 (1966), 71–5, esp. p. 74; Benzion Netanyahu, 'On the Historical Meaning of the Hebrew Sources Related to the Marranos', in *Hispania Judaica*, ed. Josep M. Solà-Solé, Samuel G. Armistead, and Joseph H. Silverman, 1 (1980), 79–102; Yosef H. Yerushalmi, *From Spanish Court to Italian Ghetto. Isaac Cardoso: A Study in Seventeenth-Century Marranism and Jewish Apologetics*, 2nd edn. (Seattle, 1981), 21–42; Shaul Regev, 'The Attitude towards the Conversos in 15th–16th-Century Jewish Thought', *Revue des études juives*, 156 (1997), 117–34; Eleazer Gutwirth, 'Elementos étnicos e históricos en las relaciones judeo-conversas en Segovia', in Yosef Kaplan (ed.), *Jews and Conversos: Studies in Society and the Inquisition* (Jerusalem, 1985), 83–102; Moisés Orfali Leví, *Los conversos españoles en la literatura rabínica: problemas jurídicos y opiniones legales durante los siglos XII–XVI* (Salamanca, 1982). The rabbinic responsa that have been collected in both printed and manuscript editions are not dated. Netanyahu usually determines their date on the basis of the respondent's method and approach. A more tolerant, liberal approach is necessarily an indication of his early years while a more severe policy is invariably assigned a later date. This appears to me to be nothing more than speculation. It is more likely that the justifications (for either a tolerant or a strict approach) cited in these rabbinic opinions are connected to the specific halakhic issue in question. Likewise, at least three of the rabbinic authorities studied by Netanyahu were members of the same Duran family (father, son, and grandson) and it seems likely that the two offspring may well have been influenced by the family elder, who had sat for a long time in the rabbinical court, enabling the younger family members to accumulate personal experience in cases of this type.

approach will be much more effective if we want to understand popular opinion within Jewish society in relation to the Conversos, and will even give us a glimpse of Christian perceptions of them, not to mention the Conversos' own sense of themselves. Only then can we properly interpret the efforts of Jewish communities and rabbinical authorities to sort these complications out.

The same responsa that seem to anchor Netanyahu's thesis lead us to rather different conclusions, among them the impression that Jewish life in fifteenth-century Spain exhibited a wide range of opinions regarding the Conversos, opinions that largely diverge from those described by Netanyahu.[7] Rather than finding a growing Jewish recognition of the Conversos as Christians, we find a widespread sense of mutuality, familiarity, and ongoing dialogue between the two populations. Here I will present a small sampling of the responsa, mostly from the period following 1391 and continuing through the first half of the fifteenth century. Netanyahu has observed that large segments of the Converso population were 'pushed' back towards Judaism in the 1480s, in the wake of the Inquisition and as a result of their rejection by Hispanic society. He consequently views this decade as a turning point in the creation of a Converso identity and in the Converso dialogue with Judaism. For this reason I have chosen to focus my analysis on the years prior to these events.

The queries raised by the Jewish community with the rabbis about the first generation of converts clearly show that social intercourse between Jews and Conversos had not ceased. Conversos were, for example, active in Jewish wine production, either in the employ of Jews or as independent producers of wine which they claimed to be entirely kosher and so suitable for sale to Jews, both at home and abroad. The wine business was a highly delicate matter since Jewish law forbids non-Jewish contact with wine during its production if it is to be considered kosher. It was thus essential to adopt a clear stand regarding the religious identity of the Conversos and to determine how far they could be trusted to oversee the wine and ensure that it did not come into contact with non-Jews. Conversos also invited Jews to dine, offering them meals which they claimed had been prepared according to Jewish dietary laws,[8] and we also find Jewish widows who had no sons of their own relying, whether or not by choice, on the Converso population to satisfy halakhic demands for levirate marriage and *ḥalitsah*.[9] Divorces took

[7] I am aware of the methodological difficulties that these questions raise, which do not always reflect an accurate picture of reality. See Haym Soloveitchik, 'Can Halakhic Texts Talk History?', *AJS Review*, 3 (1978), 153–96.

[8] Isaac bar Sheshet, *She'elot uteshuvot* [responsa] (Jerusalem, 1975), nos. 4 (p. 1*a*) and 11 (p. 3*b*).

[9] Ibid., no. 1 (p. 1*a*). If a man dies with no issue, his brother is obliged by biblical law to marry the widow in order to raise up children in the dead man's name; this institution is known as *yibum*, levirate marriage. However, if either party does not wish to marry the other, a 'release' ceremony (*ḥalitsah*) is conducted in front of a court, after which the widow is free to marry anyone she wishes.

place within the Converso community according to Jewish law.[10] The behavioural partition some Conversos observed between a public Christianity and a private Judaism was accepted by Jews as entirely natural given the circumstances. Thus, for instance, it was said of two Conversos who served as witnesses in divorce proceedings that they 'were considered kosher by the people of God, and the opposite by the *goyim* [Christians]'.[11] That is to say, while the Christians considered them to be Christian, the Jews had no doubts about their Judaism. Even the growing number of halakhic rulings during this period that were connected to the kosher status of Converso wine points, in my opinion, to the generally prevalent belief among the Jews who sent these questions to their rabbis on the Converso's Jewish credentials.

A similar picture takes shape when one reads the responses of Shimon ben Tsemah Duran (Rashbats, 1361–1444) to the next generation's requests for rabbinical guidance. Duran had succeeded Isaac bar Sheshet as the leader of North African Jewry, and in his day too the production, distribution, and sale of wine constituted one of the principal concerns of both Jews and Conversos. Netanyahu is right in this context to distinguish between Duran's attitude towards the Conversos in the period around 1391 and the situation that developed after 1414 in the wake of the mass conversions brought about by the preaching of Vincent Ferrer and the religious dispute of Tortosa. Duran saw no reason to doubt the *kashrut* of the wine of the first Conversos, who were considered to be Jews in every respect unless they had consciously violated the law.[12] But he later changed his view as he sought to adapt his rulings to an increasingly complex reality in which Conversos had less and less opportunity to live openly as Jews and to fulfil the biblical commandments. That is to say, Duran distinguished between those instances in which Conversos truly behaved as Jews and those instances where their Judaism became suspect.

Thus, for example, when one of the Conversos of Majorca testified in support of the *kashrut* of a wine that had been kept in the storeroom of a Christian woman, Duran concluded that, while the convert's testimony was not to be automatically disqualified (in contrast to the testimony of a

[10] Ibid., no. 11 (p. *3a*).　　　　　　　　　　　　　　　　　　　　　　　[11] Ibid.

[12] Shimon ben Tsemah Duran, *Sefer hatashbets* [responsa] (Lemberg, 1851), vol. i, no. 63 (p. 23*a*). 'These are *anusim* who are considered to be kosher . . . unless it became apparent to us that this kosher status was diminished because they are not careful in relation to forbidden things; but if there is no evidence of this then we should not cast them out. And so it certainly follows that if they are credible witnesses regarding the prohibitions in the Torah, and certainly regarding the rabbinic prohibitions on matters such as wine, *then they are considered to be of the people of Israel*' (emphasis added). This concerned the *anusim* living in Majorca, and Duran explicitly takes note (p. 22*b*), 'Because it came in the first days of the coercion [*haonsin—* time of persecutions].' All translations keep as closely as possible to the demanding, obscure style of the original medieval Hebrew, with a minimum of stylistic changes.

Christian, which was not permissible under Jewish law),[13] there was a distinct possibility of it being influenced by unrelated considerations, namely, the Converso's fear that if he tried to prevent Christians from touching the wine he would betray his underlying Jewish values, and thus lead the woman to inform on him to the authorities.[14] And so it appears that Duran's dismissal of the Converso's testimony was based on the specific circumstances surrounding this case rather than being a wholesale denial of the legitimacy of Converso testimony in general. Here, too, the relationship between query and response reveals that there was a segment of the Jewish public in Majorca that disagreed with Duran's position, preferring to accept the deposition of a Converso rather than that of a Jewish witness who also testified in the case.[15] And in fact when an investigation of the Christian woman's storeroom was carried out the Converso's claims rather than those of this Jewish witness were found to be true, although Duran had preferred the latter's testimony. Nonetheless, as I have observed, he was careful not to disqualify the testimony of all Conversos in the rabbinical courts out of hand, or even to raise questions about its legitimacy.

This query, which was posed by Mordechai Nagar of Majorca, together with Duran's response, gives us a glimpse into the complex relationships between Majorca's Jews and Conversos in the important matter of wine. As we have seen, the Conversos produced wine themselves with the intention of selling it to Jews, purchased wine from Jewish producers for resale to other Jews, and often laboured at wine presses belonging to Jews. In all such activities they were considered by the Jews to be entirely trustworthy, and there were no fears that the wine had been contaminated by contact with Christians. By contrast, many Jews of Majorca had little faith in Conversos who were assigned to guard wine stored with Christians: they knew that the Conversos were often too anxious about their indefinite status in society, and too worried that they would be suspected of being observant Jews, to keep the Christians away from the wine.[16] This distinction testifies to the practi-

---

[13] *Sefer hatashbets*, vol. i, no. 66 (p. 24*b*).

[14] Ibid. 'As you see from their interests and their accustomed manner of interacting with idolaters [Christians], this is the forced one [*ba'anus*] here. Because he is presumed to be an idolater in the eyes of the non-Jewish woman he would certainly obey her; for were he to stand up to her, she would say to him: you are still a Jew and your views are closer to those of the Jews than the idolaters. For this reason he is not to be trusted with guarding [the wine].'

[15] See ibid., p. 24*a*.

[16] Ibid. 'And with regard to the loyalty of the *anusim*, [the Jews] say that, although they are considered by them to be faithful when they say that they bought this wine from a certain Jew, or when they make it themselves, with regard to watching over the wine it is not the custom to put faith in them. Because of their forced conversion they are not able to prevent the idolaters from touching their wine and they are not careful regarding this contact by idolaters. It is commonly known that they are not to be trusted to guard the wine; even though they press the wine together with the Jews, it is the custom to keep the wine with the Jews and not the *anusim*.'

cal approach adopted by the Jews in their relations with Conversos: while recognizing them as sharing a common Jewish origin, their specifically *religious* identity was complicated by their also being part of the Christian community.

The Conversos of Majorca also imported wine from Jewish sources in Aragon (for instance, from Murviedro in the kingdom of Valencia) and marketed it in northern Africa. This was the context of another query posed to the rabbinical authorities regarding the *kashrut* of wine. Since plain written testimony from the Jewish winemaker was not available, Duran was asked whether one could rely on the word of the Converso middleman to authenticate the wine's *kashrut*. Duran, like Isaac bar Sheshet before him,[17] denied the Converso the authority to determine whether the wine was kosher or not. But he also confidently declared that there was no reason to harbour suspicions regarding the wine. He initially thought to issue a general ruling that would legalize all wine imported by Conversos from Murviedro, but he said that, because there was a small group of Conversos who regularly violated Jewish law, he would validate the wine only if the Jewish purchaser affirmed that he put complete trust in the Converso with whom he was dealing. I should emphasize that we are examining a case here in which there was no written evidence from Murviedro regarding the *kashrut* of the wine. If written authorization could be produced, or if the Converso pledged to send such proof in the future, then no legal doubts would arise.[18] The Converso was thus allowed to serve as a broker in the wine trade. It seems that a similar level of trust regarding the production and sale of wine was not to be found outside Majorca in this period. In addition, Duran was adamant in prohibiting anyone from drinking wine that had been made by Conversos.[19] In these instances as well, however, we can discern a certain sensitivity on the part of Duran towards the developing conditions of life in the fifteenth century, namely, a world in which the members of a Converso population that identified itself in many respects with the Jewish people found themselves living as Christians and thus having to maintain a delicate relationship with the Christian community. Given the circumstances it is no surprise that the rabbinical authorities found it necessary to issue halakhic guidelines.

[17] *She'elot uteshuvot*, no. 12 (p. 3*b*). See Mark D. Meyerson, *A Jewish Renaissance in Fifteenth-Century Spain* (Princeton, 2004), 112–19.

[18] *Sefer hatashbets*, vol. ii, no. 60 (p. 10*b*): 'The *anusim* are certainly not to be trusted with regard to the *kashrut* of the wine . . . it [might have been] possible to accept all the wine coming from Murviedro to these lands [North Africa] brought by the *anusim* . . . but because one must be aware that a few of the *anusim* may have transgressed in their actions . . . I will not allow it for any of them. And as I usually say to one who has received wine, if you trust the sender drink it in your home and take care not to sell it to a Jew who does not know the sender. But in this case it should be allowed to all because this *anus* who has sent the wine [wrote] to the Jew to whom it was sent that he would soon send him papers of a Jew that would clear it [the wine].'

[19] Ibid., vol. iii, no. 312 (p. 47*a*).

The divorces (*gitin*) of the Conversos also adhered to Jewish law. The Jewish leadership of Majorca considered this perfectly natural, recognizing the legality of divorce documents without any hesitation. Isaac bar Sheshet and Duran, however, insisted that each case be closely examined on its own merits. In one instance when the scribe (*sofer*) was identified as an apostate, that is, as a voluntary rather than a forced convert, Duran overturned the decision of community leaders in Majorca to recognize his divorce.[20] In another case from Majorca, however, which involved a scribe identified as a forced convert who secretly continued to practise Judaism, Duran accepted the documents.[21] Duran consistently demanded that an informed investigation be carried out each time to determine what kind of Converso the divorce witness was: whether he belonged to the legitimate converts who sought to maintain their Judaism, or whether he was one of those who voluntarily violated the Torah's commandments, and even took part in the persecution of Jews.[22]

The general confidence felt by Majorca's Jews regarding the Conversos led Duran to raise a number of questions before the community. In contrast to the homogeneous conditions that had held sway in the immediate aftermath of the 1391 conversion, the second generation of converts in Majorca was composed of several types. Some lived as Christians in every respect. Most of those who secretly maintained their Jewish identity nevertheless violated aspects of Jewish law in public, for example not observing the sanctity of the sabbath. Many could have left Majorca and migrated to northern Africa where it would have been possible to return to Judaism openly. However, they stayed in Majorca out of considerations of convenience and comfort. Others did leave, but later returned. In view of this situation Duran asked the Jews in Majorca not to view the Converso community as monolithic. Rather, they should make a point of examining each specific case or situation in order to determine to which sub-group a particular Converso belonged.[23]

The *Convivencia* that characterized the intercourse between Jews and Conversos in Majorca led Duran to issue a demand (sometime before 1435) that Converso dignitaries should not be brought into the Jewish community's social disputes. He even demanded that this prohibition be instituted as a special ordinance bearing the penalty of excommunication.[24] His remarks in this instance are revealing of the extensive involvement of the Conversos in community life and of the desire on the part of the Jews to turn to them

---

[20] *Sefer hatashbets*, vol. iii, no. 40 (p. 10*b*).   [21] Ibid., no. 43 (pp. 10*b*–11*a*).

[22] Ibid., no. 10 (p. 3*a*–*b*).   [23] Ibid., vol. i, no. 66 (p. 25*a*–*b*).

[24] Ibid., vol. iii, no. 227 (p. 36*a*–*b*). 'What is this confidence you have in pointless hatred amongst you, because of which your words are heard by the notables among the *anusim* . . . Create a boundary here by means of excommunication and a ban so that no one will involve one of these *anusim* in his interpersonal disputes.'

for assistance during moments of crisis. Duran now sought to establish social and political boundaries between the two communities at a time when such boundaries seemed to be losing their importance in Majorca.

Duran's responsa also shed light on marital practices. Conversos married other Conversos according to Jewish law, under a canopy while reciting the traditional vows;[25] they then married again in a Christian ceremony. This practice raised halakhic problems if one spouse left Spain, as that spouse's status as a Jew had to be freshly verified in the receiving community. Duran said that he considered a marriage valid in these circumstances on condition that the witnesses to the Jewish ceremony had been Jews and not Conversos. At the same time, if the witnesses were converts who secretly still adhered to Judaism and the wedding ceremony had taken place in a city with a Jewish population then the marriage was considered valid for the reason that its consummation was a form of sanctification.[26] As he remarked:

Even more so, these *anusim* are the 'worm Jacob' (Isaiah 41: 14) and men of Judah [and therefore still to be considered as within the Jewish community], so that if one of them sanctifies the woman by marriage then his marriage is binding; and as for an uncircumcised child of these converts, he too is legitimate if the mother is an *anusah* and the father an idolater [a Christian] . . . and how much the more so if the father and the mother are both *anusim*.[27]

One of Duran's decisions reveals something of Christian views of Majorca's Conversos, as Duran perceived them. According to him, the Conversos lived a generally comfortable existence. True, they had to worry about accusations of having returned to the Jewish fold. But no one compelled them to practise Christian ritual and they were free to leave Majorca at any time and emigrate to countries where they could live openly as Jews. Duran thought, then, that the Conversos were perceived by Christians as Jews in every respect save for the sacrament of baptism, which kept them from becoming fully Jewish again. It followed that the only Christian aspect of the Conversos' lives was their Christianized names, and certainly not their way of life or their ritual practices.[28]

[25] The three halakhically valid forms of marriage are by purchase or gift (*kinyan*), by deed (i.e. contract) (*shetar*), and by consummation (*bi'ah*); the standard form of marriage includes all three.   [26] Ibid., vol. iii, no. 47 (pp. 11*b*–12*a*).   [27] Ibid., p. 11*a*.

[28] Ibid., vol. i, no. 66 (p. 25*b*). 'But in these persecutions and especially in that place [Majorca] they [the Christians] ease their attitude towards the *anusim* so that they may act as they wish and no one forces them to worship idols, and they are almost considered to be Jews by them to the point where they are given permission to leave as they desire, and if an idolater [a Christian] wanted to leave that place and convert to the faith of Moses, even if he was to pay all the treasure in the world, they would not let him. Quite the opposite, they would kill him. And so we see that they are considered by them to be fully Jews except that their religion requires that whoever converted, even by force, cannot return to Judaism, and because of this they do not keep an eye on them. And so the only thing they have from their conversion is their idolatrous [Christian] name.'

If we accept Duran's view as a reliable reflection of life in fifteenth-century Majorca it won't surprise us to discover that Converso behaviour provoked grave suspicions in some sections of Hispanic society. If a Jewish leader such as Duran considered the names of the Conversos to be their only Christian characteristic—and it does not really matter if this was the case or not, or whether it was in the process of changing—then this view could easily find its way into Christian circles. We should thus consider it an authentic opinion of the times, exposing popular fears of Jewish penetration into the heart of Christian Spain.

A CHRISTIAN VIEW OF THE CONVERSOS

I will now turn to a brief examination of the nature of Christian Hispanic identity as it took shape during the fifteenth century, influenced as it was by the impression—whether real or imagined—that Jewish converts were effectively narrowing the gap that divided Judaism and Christianity. I will look at this redefinition of Christian identity in the first half of the fifteenth century through a close reading of two central texts: the *Cancionero de Juan Alfonso de Baena*, an anthology of courtly poetry from Castile from the late fourteenth century to approximately 1430,[29] and the *Memorial* (November 1449) of Marcos García de Mora, who was the ideologue and principal spokesman of the revolt in Toledo, which also targeted the Converso population. The *Memorial* was addressed to Pope Nicholas V, King Juan II of Castile, and all the kings and princes of Christendom, both spiritual and temporal. I will also look at two supplementary texts: a petition of 2 May 1449 addressed to Juan II by the city of Toledo, which listed the citizens' demands and presented an ultimatum to the king, and the general directive, the *Sentencia-Estatutu*, of 5 June 1449, issued against the Conversos in Toledo by Pero Sarmiento, who was the leader of the rebellion. Together, these last three documents represent the motives, sentiments, doctrines, attitudes, and convictions of the anti-Converso party in Toledo.[30]

The *Cancionero* anthology presents an interesting reflection of the social life of the period, containing numerous examples of 'Jewish' penetration into Christian Hispanic culture through the mediation of Converso poets. The common scholarly view here is of Conversos functioning as a cultural bridge. Such a view emphasizes their role in introducing Jewish ideas into the heart of Hispanic cultural discourse, consequently seeing Hispanic identity as reshaped by its interaction with a novel and vital world-view

---

[29] *Cancionero de Juan Alfonso de Baena*, ed. Brian Dutton and Joaquín González Cuenca (Madrid, 1993).

[30] See Eloy B. Ruano, *Los orígenes del problema converso* (Barcelona, 1976), 102–32, 191–6; Benzion Netanyahu, *The Origins of the Inquisition in Fifteenth Century Spain* (New York, 1995), 351–84, 486–516.

introduced by the 'New Christians'.[31] But the question arises as to whether this poetic phenomenon had a different meaning. Should we understand the numerous allegations hurled by these courtly poets at each other—attacks that mobilized accusations of Judaization and the supposed embrace of Jewish customs and of a Jewish *mentalité* by rivals—as a reflection of the fact that the poets still fundamentally identified each other as Jewish? Or rather, are we witness here to a new version of an old hermeneutic-theological model whose roots are to be found in Pauline thought, and through which Christianity has always, from its beginnings, constructed its identity: the use of the concept of the Jew as a means of defining a negative 'other' in contrast to which a world of positive Christian concepts can be constructed?[32]

It seems to me that this latter view separates the text (in this instance, the court poetry) from its historical context. It is true that accusations of Judaization in the Middle Ages are no indication of the presence of an actual Jew, or Converso, in the intellectual, religious, or cultural dialogue. However, can we divorce a text that addresses the subject of Judaization in Castile in the early fifteenth century from a historical reality in which a sizeable public of Conversos had recently entered Christian Hispanic society and its centres of power en masse? Even if we were to assume that the motivation for adopting such anti-Jewish rhetoric by the poets of the *Cancionero de Baena* rested on the old Pauline model dividing flesh and spirit, the historical context of mass conversion in Castile now gave this model a new and entirely different meaning. The concept of the Jew could not be such a general and vague one; it could not represent a negative value in and of its own right. That is, in fifteenth-century Castile it was an entirely contemporary concept, representative of real Jews and Conversos (even if, in this or that instance, the subject of the specific affront is not actually a Converso).

What is more, new elements are to be discerned in the poets' mutual recriminations that had not been part of the older model. I refer principally to an example from a poem by Alfonso Álvarez de Villasandino, who noted that 'the target of his poem was an apostate Jew with a prominent nose, a *meshumad*'.[33] Would the designation *meshumad* have been used in the framework of the old model? Would Paul or his immediate successors have considered 'Converso' or *meshumad* to be negative labels? Only the threatening historical reality of an actual Converso wielding power (such as, for instance,

[31] See Francisco Cantera Burgos, 'El *Cancionero* de Baena: Judíos y conversos en él', *Sefarad*, 27 (1967), 71–111; Fernando Díaz Esteban, 'Jewish Literary Creation in Spanish', in Haim Beinart (ed.), *Moreshet Sepharad: The Sephardi Legacy* (Jerusalem, 1992), i. 411–51.

[32] See David Nirenberg, 'Figures of Thought and Figures of Flesh; "Jews" and "Judaism" in Late Medieval Spanish Poetry and Politics', *Speculum*, 81 (2006), 398–426, as well as Chapter 8 in the present volume.

[33] See *cancionero* 140 (pp. 164–5). The term *meshumad* has implications of a willing convert from Judaism.

the 'Jewish' Pope Anacletus II (1130–8) in the dispute over the papacy in the twelfth century[34]) or of a group of Conversos enjoying political and social authority could change the discourse on Judaism to a discourse on *meshumadut*. One has to also remember that the adoption of Hebrew terms and the depiction of Jewish customs and rites—for example kosher cuisine, the rite of circumcision, and observance of the sabbath or of holy days and festivals such as Yom Kippur and Sukkot—was far more frequent in the poetic discourse of the fifteenth century than in the years prior to mass conversion.[35] In a poem by Diego de Valencia, for example, directed against the Converso Juan de España of León, numerous Hebrew-related words appear, including 'adonay' (God), 'cohenim' (priests), 'sofar' (ram's horn), and 'mila' (circumcision),[36] and Álvarez de Villasandino, in his poem attacking Alfonso Ferrandes Semuel, makes use of 'meshumad' (convert), 'ssamaz' (*shamash*—beadle), 'homaz' (*ḥumash*—the Pentateuch), 'cedaqua' (*tsedakah*—charity), and 'tefyla' (prayer).[37] All testify, in my opinion, to a growing familiarity with Jewish neighbours and to the social context of mass conversion.

The same can be said of the 'purity of blood' regulations published by García de Mora, Sarmiento, and the rebels in Toledo in 1449. One can suggest that the Judaism under attack in these texts is not especially connected to Jews or Conversos but belongs, rather, to a language of political criticism in which Judaism represents the ruler (in particular, Alvaro de Luna). The Conversos who were actually to be found in Toledo, according to this reading, did no more than give symbolic force to García de Mora and Sarmiento's rhetoric. But this assumption again divorces the text from its historical context, a context in which Sarmiento's first act was to burn down the home of the tax collector, the Converso Alonso Cota, after which he went on to encourage the riots against the Conversos of Toledo, began an investigation of several Converso notables, and subsequently sentenced them to be burned after their confession of Judaization. If we were to read the Jewish references in these texts as a solely symbolic language, are we not actually falling victim ourselves to Sarmiento's hidden political strategy? Did he not actually fear the Jewish penetration of Christianity by means of the increasingly central place of the Conversos in Christian society? Did Sarmiento just use the Conversos for his own political ends? Why should we not accept the possibility that the actual aim of García de Mora and Sarmiento was to thwart the economic and social gains of the Conversos in Toledo, and that in order to accomplish this they mobilized the Inquisition

[34] See Aryeh Grabois, 'From "Theological" Jew-Hatred to "Racial" Jew-Hatred: The Controversy over the "Jewish" Pope in the Twelfth Century' (Heb.), *Zion*, 47 (1982), 1–16.
[35] See Cristina Arbós, 'Los cancioneros castellanos del siglo xv como fuente para la historia de los judíos españoles', in Kaplan, *Jews and Conversos*, 78–9.
[36] See Cantera Burgos, 'El *Cancionero* de Baena', 97–101.
[37] See Arbós, 'Los cancioneros', 80.

model that focused on the Judaism lurking in Converso society, a Judaism based on the original meaning of obeying Jewish biblical commandments, that is, the Torah?

In fact, this is the picture of events revealed in the *Sentencia-Estatutu*: the Conversos continued to observe the laws of Moses, believing that Jesus was not a divine being but a Jew who had been crucified, and holding a Passover *seder* of their own in which they performed a symbolic sacrifice rather than worshipping the body of the saviour at the church altar.[38] In his *Memorial*, García de Mora reiterates the charges brought by the *Sentencia-Estatutu* in regard to the religious crimes of the Conversos. He describes their 'infidelity', their refusal to accept the dogmas of Christianity, and their violation of specific Christian laws and rites.[39] Why should we presume that these texts do not express any actual apprehensions on the part of Sarmiento and his circle? Even if their fears were largely groundless—and one can make the argument that the Conversos were altogether faithful Christians—can we so cavalierly dismiss the existence of the fear itself? The truth is, as we have seen above, that there were those in the Jewish community who shared the views expressed by García de Mora, Sarmiento, and their circle regarding the Judaism of the Conversos and their authentic attempt to create a religious-cultural identity of their own, distinct from Catholicism.

A JEWISH VIEW OF THE CONVERSOS

An example of the Jewish view of Conversos can be found in the writings of Isaac Nathan regarding the group of Jews who converted to Christianity as a result of the missionary efforts of Vincent Ferrer, Benedict XIII, and the convert Joshua Halorki. Nathan lived in Arles in the fifteenth century, born into a family which was one of Provence's most significant Jewish dynasties and whose social and cultural activities spanned two centuries, from the thirteenth to the fifteenth. He was the wealthiest Jew in the city: a merchant, draper, and financier whose business activities were at times the equal of those of the Italian merchants in Avignon. He was also a social leader, the official Procurator of the Jewish community in Provence. He was well known in Spain too, as a result of his role in theological disputes with Christian thinkers. Among the Jews of Provence he was referred to as *me'or galutenu*—'luminary of our exile'—an appellation awarded only to those of the highest social and intellectual stature. He was also a busy literary figure,

[38] See Yitzhak Baer, *A History of the Jews in Christian Spain*, 2 vols. (Philadelphia, 1961), ii. 277–80; Netanyahu, *Origins of the Inquisition*, 351–84.

[39] See Netanyahu, *Origins of the Inquisition*, 486–511; Dayle Seidenspinner-Nuñez, 'Prelude to the Inquisition: The Discourse of Persecution, the Toledan Rebellion of 1449, and the Contest for Orthodoxy', in Wout J. van Bekkum and Paul M. Cobb (eds.), *Strategies of Medieval Communal Identity: Judaism, Christianity and Islam* (Leuven, 2004), 54–6.

best known as the author of the first Hebrew concordance to the Bible, *Me'ir nativ*. Most prominently, Nathan was associated with the polemics and debate of his day as he directed most of his energy to refutations of the Christian mission and to a sharpening of the Jewish position.[40]

In his ethical work *Me'amets ko'aḥ* (which exists only in manuscript form), Nathan provides us with a description of the mass conversions of the early fifteenth century, coming as they did in the wake of the campaign by Vincent Ferrer and the anti-Jewish laws enacted after the Tortosa disputation.[41] According to Nathan, Ferrer's sermons and the new legislation were directed at Converso society and meant to instil in it a proper Christian spirit. It is interesting to note that Nathan depicts Ferrer's efforts at shaping the Christian identity of the Conversos as resting on an unmitigated racially based disqualification of Jewish life. However, we are not talking here about the general type of accusations characteristic of the Pauline model of flesh and spirit. Rather, this is a detailed account of Jewish crimes, entirely consistent with the antisemitic view of Judaism that had been developing since the twelfth century:

There came the day of their Passover when the preacher [Ferrer] rose as was his habit and spoke about the death of Jesus and amazed them with the story, [telling it] in its length and its breadth and called out from his throat in a great voice that the revenge of his crucified god [brought] the eternal punishment of the Jews, upon whose brows there remains a sign and an example of the pointless crime they committed, and that one day of every month of the year worms will be found in their mouths and they will urinate blood in exchange for the blood which they spilled, and while the Jews think that in order to atone for the blood they will steal a small Christian child and slaughter him on Passover and sacrifice his blood to their god and thus think that this will heal their sores.[42]

The effeminate, murderous, and racialized figure of the Jew in this fictitious sermon seeks to rehabilitate the fundamental dogmas of Christology by portraying a mirror image: the Jewish male's menstruation is the divine punishment for the spilling of Jesus's blood; the ritual murder of Christian children

[40] See Louis Stouff, 'Isaac Nathan et les siens: Une famille juive d'Arles des XIVe et XVe siècles', *Provence historique*, 37 (1987), 499–512; id., 'Activités et professions dans une communauté juive de Provence au bas moyen-âge: La Juiverie d'Arles 1400–1450', in *Minorités, techniques et métiers: Actes de la table ronde du Groupement d'intérêt scientifique, sciences humaines sur l'aire Méditerranéenne*, Abbaye de Sénanque, Oct. 1978 (Aix-en-Provence, 1980), 61, 64, 66, 69, 73, 77; id., *Arles à la fin du moyen âge*, 2 vols. (Aix-en-Provence, 1986), i. 289, 309, 313–18, 334, 345, 356; Ram Ben-Shalom, 'Concerning the Question of the Author of the First Hebrew Concordance *Me'ir nativ*' (Heb.), *Kiryat sefer*, 64 (1992–3), 754–60; id., 'The Tortosa Disputation, Vincent Ferrer, and the Problem of the Conversos According to the Testimony of Isaac Nathan' (Heb.), *Zion*, 56 (1991), 21–54.

[41] See Ben-Shalom, 'The Tortosa Disputation', 21–45.

[42] Ibid. 44, citing Isaac Nathan, *Me'amets ko'aḥ*.

is a Jewish attempt to bring about self-redemption and ritual cleansing, which essentially corroborates the confession and self-recognition by the Jews of their sinful role in the murder of Christ.

An examination of the sermons actually delivered by Ferrer in Castile and Aragon does not match the rhetoric attributed to him by Nathan.[43] One might possibly discern in some of Ferrer's sermons the Pauline-Augustinian image of the Jew, the view of fleshly Judaism whose theological role was to confirm the victory of spiritual Christianity. At the same time, we are working here in the sphere of literary invention, and as far as Isaac Nathan and fifteenth-century Jewry was concerned Vincent Ferrer was a symbolic representative of Christianity and its mission. As such, the Jews saw Ferrer using his sermons to attack Judaism, mobilizing a literary and oral arsenal that was developed in the late Middle Ages: theologically based racism, demonization, and blood libels. This new phenomenon, which, among other things, gave birth to the Converso society of Spain, required an immediate response, and also forced the Jews to redefine their collective identity in order to mark the boundaries of their existence, to clearly define the border between Jew and Christian, and to determine whether the Conversos belonged to the religious-cultural entity known as the Jewish people. The question for the Jews, in other words, was whether to draw the line separating Judaism and Christianity as running between themselves and the established Christian population, or between them and the Conversos. Or perhaps they saw it as a no man's land, a borderland, best left without definitive boundaries.

Answers to the questions concerning a new collective identity were offered in a variety of spheres: in halakhic works and responsa (as shown above), in moral thought, in philosophy and poetry, in daily relationships, and in social and economic intercourse.[44]

Let us take a closer look at Isaac Nathan's view of the situation. The text quoted above continues by describing the response of the Conversos to Ferrer's racist sermon:

When the converts heard these three lies and truly understood that this was nothing, that they themselves were their [own] witnesses, the plague of heresy grew up in them and in their faith and some of them escaped to the wide tracts of the earth.

Those that grew and became rich and were plentiful in number and could not escape cleverly decided to become a fraternity, and they became a united one, and they undertook to obey the commandment [*mitsvah*] to give half a shekel to each person every week, and they made a charity fund and did an even greater deed of charity, fraternity, and amicability in supporting the poor and marrying off young women [i.e. helping young women find husbands by providing them with

---

[43] See Pedro M. Cátedra García, *Sermón, sociedad y literatura en la Edad Media: San Vicente Ferrer en Castilla (1411–1412), estudio bibliográfico, literario y edición de los textos inéditos* (Valladolid, 1994), 241–51.   [44] See n. 6.

dowries]. And they built for themselves a shrine and they chose some of their men
to serve in that shrine and to worship there, and they enlisted from amongst themselves preachers who would sermonize to them, in emulation of the other gentiles,
about the roots of their faith which they had come to as a shelter, but did not
[repeat] the deceptions and lies and imagined miracles as other preachers did, and
thus their practice has continued until this day, and they are all men of grace, men
of action, men of truth, who do good deeds, notables who find more grace and
honour than the people of those districts, they worship their God and do not
become haughty or follow false gods.

   From out of [Vincent Ferrer's] lies the opposite came and instead of what he
sought to shape as the new faith in their heart, in what they converted to, he led
them to deny and doubt that which was correct and true [according to the tenets of
their new faith].[45]

   In contrast to the ambivalent and critical attitude of other Jews towards
the Conversos, Isaac Nathan offers numerous superlatives in describing
their new life. It seems that he draws the boundary of Jewish collective identity far beyond the formal lines of separation between Jewish and Christian
communities. But it is also important to note what Nathan does not say here.
He does not mention the Conversos' observance of the sabbath or any other
attempt on their part to observe the principal Jewish commandments. He
does emphasize their *mitsvah* of charity, but this also finds expression in
Christianity. Likewise, the description of charity associations in Converso
society (which, according to Haim Beinart, existed in Aragon and Castile,
principally in the first half of the fifteenth century[46]) does not depict a
distinctly Jewish phenomenon. The Jewish identity of the Conversos is
revealed here by the belief in one God ('their God') and the thorough rejection of the Christian belief in the Trinity.[47] In Nathan's eyes, observing the
mitsvot does not constitute a condition for being defined as a Jew. It is
enough to have a common social life that includes sermons addressing
questions of faith whose contents are fundamentally distinct from Christian
sermons. We are speaking about a collective identity that took shape while
distancing itself from the other.

   Yet one has to be precise, to read between the lines, and attempt to recognize the subtle contours which Nathan gives to the Christian other. Did he,
like Ferrer, try to create a demonic, threatening other, or a ridiculous other,
one whose negative characteristics were exaggerated so that, the more vulgar
and profane it appeared to be the easier it was to offer an antithetical charac-

   [45] Isaac Nathan, *Me'amets ko'aḥ*, cited in Ben-Shalom, 'The Tortosa Disputation', 44–5.
   [46] See Beinart, *Conversos on Trial by the Inquisition* [Anusim bedin ha'inkvisitsiyah] (Tel Aviv,
1965), 49–50.
   [47] The Hebrew expression *rehavim vesatei khazav* (Ps. 40: 5) was commonly used by polemicists to denote idolatry and Christian belief in the Trinity.

terization of lofty Jewish spirituality? This would then make it possible to sharpen the picture of a collective Jewish identity. It seems to me that the answer to this question is negative. In terms of faith, Nathan presents the reader with the classic dichotomy between a single God and a divine Trinity, between one and many, while, of course, rejecting out of hand the Christian mission and its antisemitic, racist content. And yet he concludes his remarks with this sentence: 'From out of [Vincent Ferrer's] lies the opposite came and instead of what he sought to shape as the new faith in their heart, in what they converted to, he led them to deny and doubt that which was correct and true [in their new faith].' That is to say, Ferrer's racist moralizing and prevarication regarding the Jewish other failed, and not just because they pushed the Conversos towards a collective existence as a fraternity of grace that rejected the Trinity. Ferrer's project was a colossal failure in that it alienated the Conversos from the positive religious aspects of Christianity, from 'that which was correct and true'. Nathan does not provide details of what was correct and true in Christianity, but from other sections of his work it is clear that he referred to important moral-theological views that were based in the Christian tradition and that were absent from Jewish intellectual discourse.[48] It appears that Nathan sought to draw the boundaries of Jewish identity to their maximum extent, far beyond the borderlands.

A NEW GRAMMAR FOR CONVERSION

I would now like to comment on another aspect of Isaac Nathan's text, one that sheds light on new practices to be discerned in the discourse of conversion in the fifteenth century.

Nathan attempted to justify the existence of the Conversos, who preferred to live as Christians rather than escape and live as Jews, as many others chose to do. He thought it likely that considerations of wealth and property would keep the Conversos from leaving Spain. He does not entertain the possibility that a person would prefer to sacrifice his wealth in order to live openly as a propertyless Jew. At first glance, this might seem like an unorthodox view, informed by Nathan's own bourgeois standing and great wealth, which also gave him high status in non-Jewish society. But we can find similar views to those expressed by him among the most prominent halakhic figures of his generation. Material considerations were integral to the conversion discourse. Of particular interest in this context is the position taken by Duran immediately after 1391, which supported a continued life of religious coercion in spite of the real possibility of escaping Spain and returning to Judaism, all in order to protect one's property: 'that even if the *anusim* were themselves to say that the main reason for them to stay there [in Majorca] is none other but that

[48] I intend to elaborate on this topic in a forthcoming article.

their property will not be taken from them, they are not to be called intentional worshippers of another god'.[49] With regard to another instance, when a Jew had escaped from Majorca in fear of his life while his wife was forced to convert, and when later the woman herself fled to North Africa in order to escape Christian coercion and return to Judaism, Duran writes:

And as to his losing all that he owned in his taverns because of her rush to leave, it would seem that she is responsible for this loss, because it is not in the conditions of the marriage contract [*ketubah*] that she would sanctify the name of the Lord by leaving Majorca, and if she did sanctify the name of the Lord and lost his property by her sanctification, we did not find that the woman will be exempted from this . . . and so it is simple that the husband is released from her marriage contract since the kingdom took it . . . and so I have made a judgement here, putting theory into practice.[50]

That is to say, Duran justified the claim of the husband against his wife for rushing too quickly to escape religious coercion in Majorca and sacrificing the family's considerable property there in order to do so. It would seem that he thought she should have first made responsible arrangements for the property while living as a convert and only then should she have returned to Judaism.

Isaac Abravanel, a prominent Jewish leader in Castile at the end of the fifteenth century, sheds additional light on the central place of questions of property and wealth in the discourse over conversion. While he expresses understanding of the inner repentance experienced by Conversos and sympathizes with their inability to carry out the Jewish commandments while living on Christian soil, he also emphasizes that during the messianic period all Conversos will be obliged to perform all the commandments of the Torah. At the same time, he demonstrates considerable sensitivity to the difficulties involved in such future repentance. He therefore stresses:

Let them [the Conversos] not think that, as they will be obliged to depart from the path of the gentiles in this issue of observing the commandments, they will also have to depart from other material goods and property which they purchased while sitting among the gentiles, as well as the children who will be born of gentile daughters. This will not be this [way] because the Blessed One will let them [have] the fruit of their womb and the fruit of their animals and land, and all their handiwork for good . . . Let them not think that they will have to leave their capital and depart from wife and children and dwell in lonely poverty, want, and physical asceticism.[51]

Abravanel then promises the Conversos a 'light' and comfortable redemption. The only visible change in their position will be a religious one. Socially

---

[49] *Sefer hatashbets*, vol. i, no. 63 (p. 22*b*).   [50] Ibid., vol. ii, no. 176 (p. 28*a*).
[51] Isaac Abravanel, *Mashmia yeshuah* [The Announcer of Salvation] (Königsberg, 1860), 4*b*.

and economically, the Converso population will not have to suffer any great change. They will continue to be wealthy people, as they are now, and their 'Christian' offspring will be able to remain with them and become faithful Jews as well. This view as propounded by Abravanel can perhaps be understood as a realistic insight, that is, a combination of a profound analysis of the socio-economic situation of the Conversos together with an attempt to reinforce the messianic hopes nurtured by them.

I would also like to address the other side of the coin, that is, the economic aspects of Spanish Christian views of the conversion discourse, as expressed, for instance, in the writings of Pero Sarmiento and Marcos García de Mora and in numerous other texts. I refer to the accusation commonly levelled against the Conversos that their conversion was not genuine but was designed to help them accumulate property and push established Christians out of positions of economic power. I do not mean to suggest that there was any kind of symmetry between the anti-Converso claims of the Christian camp in Castile and the slightly different Jewish views regarding the need to hold on to one's wealth and property as a justification for living a life under religious coercion. This might be an example of the antisemitic distortion of legitimate Jewish concerns. Still, it does seem to me that this discourse points to a narrowing of the conceptual gap, and to the existence of a shared language that grew up in the inter-religious borderlands. Property and wealth were a very important element in the discourse of conversion, and each side in that discourse apparently redefined its position regarding the relationship between conversion and property. We can then point to a new perspective, ostensibly shared by Jews and Christians, that was taking shape in the borderlands. It is likewise possible to discern a common terminology and shared ideas that might have grown out of traditional models, but which had changed direction and were adapted to the new historical context.

In this context it is worth emphasizing the notion of the subversive Converso, given a prominent place in the text of Pero Sarmiento and in numerous other works written in the second half of the fifteenth century, all of which anticipated the ideology of the Spanish Inquisition that took shape in the last decade of the century.[52] The perception of the Conversos as a danger to Christian society was prevalent among several groups in Spain. It was manifest in the 1449 revolt in Toledo, in the sermonizing of Alonso de Espina, and in the *Libro llamado el alborayque*, an anonymous satire written in the 1450s or 1460s. Here the Conversos are portrayed as conspirators who reap large profits and continually repress the poor. They do not adhere to the Catholic faith except for practices surrounding birth and death. They succeed in acquiring high public office, which they do in order to enhance

---

[52] This section is based on the arguments in Ram Ben-Shalom, 'The Converso as Subversive: Jewish Traditions or Christian Libel?', *Journal of Jewish Studies*, 50 (1999), 259–83.

their income and provoke the Christians to kill one another. They are allowed to become priests, a position that they then exploit in order to uncover, by means of the rite of confession, the secrets of Christianity. They are allowed to serve as physicians and surgeons, under which guise they murder Christians, take their women, inherit their positions, and contaminate their blood.[53]

A pointed expression of such anti-Converso ideology is found in the reputed correspondence between the Jewish communities of Spain and Constantinople. These letters, since discovered to be forgeries, portray Spanish Jews soliciting their Turkish brethren about the recommended course of action to take in response to the Spanish king's decision to convert them and seize their property. They are advised that they have no choice but to accept the royal decree and convert. With regard to their property, they are advised to raise their sons to be merchants in order to reacquire what was theirs. Regarding the intention to murder them, they are told to raise their sons to become doctors and pharmacists in order to assassinate the Christians. In response to the destruction of their synagogues, they are advised to teach their sons to be priests and theologians and so be in a position to destroy Christian places of worship. In addition, the Jews should make every effort to ensure that the next generation will become lawyers, administrators, notaries, and advisers in order to be involved in affairs of state. Thus they would be able to rule the country and exact revenge.[54] Obviously, this text was designed to portray the Converso as a subversive and a revolutionary and to encourage the popular opinion that all possible measures should be taken to expel him from Spanish society.

It is interesting to discover that this view of the Converso found expression within the Jewish and Converso milieu as well. One such example is provided by Isaac Abravanel, who assigns the Conversos a central role in the Redemption.[55] He certainly considers many of those who converted in

---

[53] See Baer, *History of the Jews in Christian Spain*, ii. 280–2, 394–8; Hiram Pflaum, 'Une ancienne satire espagnole contre les Marranes', *Revue des études juives*, 86 (1928), 131–50; Haim Beinart, 'The Great Conversion and the Converso Problem', in id. (ed.), *Moreshet Sepharad*, i. 366; Moshe Lazar, 'Anti-Jewish and Anti-Converso Propaganda: *Confutatio libri talmud* and *Alboraique*', in Moshe Lazar and Stephen Haliczer (eds.), *The Jews of Spain and the Expulsion* (Lancaster, 1997), esp. pp. 163–8; Angus Mackay, 'The Hispanic-Converso Predicament', *Transactions of the Royal Historical Society*, 5th ser., 35 (1985), 159–79: 168.

[54] See Isidore Loeb, 'La Correspondance des Juifs d'Espagne avec ceux de Constantinople', *Revue des études juives*, 15 (1887), 262–76; Heinrich Graetz, 'But réel de la correspondance échangée vers la fin du XVe siècle, entre les Juifs espagnols et provençaux et les Juifs de Constantinople', *Revue des études juives*, 19 (1889), 106–14; Aaron Z. Aescoly, 'The Correspondence Between the Jews of Spain and Provence and the Jews of Constantinople and the History of the *Anusim* of Provence' (Heb.), *Zion*, 10 (1945), 102–39.

[55] See Isaac Abravanel's commentary on Obadiah 1: 20 in *Perush al nevi'im ukhetuvim* [Commentary on the Prophets] (Tel Aviv, 1960), 117.

response to the sufferings of exile to be an integral part of the Jewish people, and destined to play an important role in the messianic age.[56] Since most of the Jews had been banished from the lands of Edom (the Christian world) after 1492, they could not directly obey the scriptural stipulations for Redemption. By contrast, the mass of Conversos, large communities of whom remained in Edom, could satisfy those requirements. Their reconversion, already begun in Abravanel's day, was thus to be a central event in the messianic age. Abravanel distinguishes between two kinds of Converso: those loyal to the Christian faith and those who repudiated it. However, he understood that the Inquisition made no such distinction, burning both types at the stake.[57] Abravanel also takes note of a third group, the Averroistic Conversos, who had no positivist religion, referring to them as 'the heretics'.[58]

Religious heresy was commonplace among Jews and Conversos in fifteenth-century Spain. Abravanel addresses the issue of the Conversos in considering this religious nihilism, seeing them as actors in a historical-theological process predetermined by God. Human civilization is constantly moving towards a true universal understanding of God, who, for his part, does not expressly or definitively repudiate false religions through such events as convulsions and miracles. Rather, he works by accommodation, adapting himself to historical reality and to this or that stage of humanity's moral development.[59] As part of a global heresy that included a corrupted Catholic priesthood and millenarian movements in Islam, the Conversos prepared the world for Redemption.[60]

---

[56] See Regev, 'The Attitude towards the Conversos', 121–8.

[57] Isaac Abravanel, *Ma'ayenei hayeshuah* [Wells of Salvation] (Stettin, 1860), ch. 12: 6 (p. 57*b*).

[58] Isaac Abravanel, *Yeshuot meshiḥo* [Salvations of his Anointed] (Königsberg, 1861), p. 34*a*. 'As a consequence of the persecutions, many of our people rejected their religion and this means heresy [*minut*]. Because of the malfeasance of the gentiles and their use of force, many Jews left God, and because they left their law and did not adopt another religion [the talmudic scholar Rabbi Isaac] used the word heresy.' See J. Faur, 'Four Classes of Conversos: A Typological Study', *Revue des études juives*, 149 (1990), 122.

[59] See Amos Funkenstein, ' "Scripture Speaks the Language of Man": The Uses and Abuses of the Medieval Principle of Accommodation', *Philosophes médiévaux*, 26 (1986), 92–101.

[60] Abravanel, *Yeshuot meshiḥo*, 34*a*. 'The perfect one [Rabbi Isaac, BT *San.* 97*a*] said that [the messiah would not come] until the entire kingdom was afflicted with heresy, meaning all the nations of the world, in general, and, in particular, the wicked kingdom. He is possibly speaking of Rome [all of Christianity], where the number of heretics will increase, as we see happening today in the kingdom of Spain [Sepharad] where the heretics and apostates in their various countries have increased, and where they are burned in the many thousands because of their heresy, and when all the priests and archbishops of Rome seek to enrich themselves and take bribes, and are not concerned with the fate of their religion for they too are branded with heresy. It is also possible that he actually meant here the Ishmaelite nation, for as their prophet Muhammad wrote and announced to them, his faith and religion would not endure ten centuries . . . and who knows that when the time of judgement arrives, the Ishmaelite nations will be without religion, and the entire kingdom will be afflicted with heresy.' On radicalism,

The question arises of how the Averroistic movement and global heresy in general could actually advance civilization. Was the former considered to be a stage of religious development, further advanced than Christianity or Islam? As Abravanel writes, 'When a man subscribes to no faith, when he is void of any religion, he will more easily accept the true religion than will someone else who follows a rival faith. Thus, it was God's wisdom that before the arrival of the messiah and the revelation of God's faith, the entire Kingdom will be afflicted with heresy.'[61]

For Abravanel, the Averroistic movement was no better than Christian or Muslim monotheism. He had no doubt that faith in a positivist God was preferable to an absence of faith founded on philosophy. Nevertheless, God's programme is to advance humanity towards Jewish monotheism. When the time came, it would be harder to convince zealous believers in rival religions to accept an alternative positivist faith than it would be to win over the followers of Averroës. And so it was the latter who helped pave the way for Jewish monotheism.

The role Abravanel assigns to the Conversos recalls their own view of forced conversion as a heavenly mission. They even cited biblical precedent for this view, Queen Esther,[62] who, like the Conversos, hid her real identity and sustained her faith in God while living in an alien environment.[63] The Conversos considered their fate to be tied to the messianic ambitions of Judaism. Some even saw themselves as fulfilling an essential need in the process of Redemption. Thus, it was said, the Converso Fernando de Madrid told a Jew some time around the year 1481 that the messiah could not appear until the Conversos atoned for their conversion to Christianity, and that when the messiah did come it would be in Seville.[64] This view is related to Christian theology, which tied Jesus' return (the Second Coming) to the conversion of the Jews. In Jewish messianic propaganda, too, forced conversion and the burning of the converts by the Inquisition was an essential stage in the apocalyptic process, because these events were considered to be atonement for the ancient sins that had brought about the destruction of the Temple.[65]

scepticism, and religious materialism in Spain and the rest of western Europe see John Edwards, 'Religious Faith and Doubt in Late Medieval Spain: Soria circa 1450–1500', *Past and Present*, 120 (1988), 15; id., 'Male and Female Religious Experience among Spanish New Christians, 1400–1500', in Raymond B. Waddington and Arthur H. Williamson (eds.), *The Expulsion of the Jews, 1492 and After* (New York, 1994), 43, 47; George H. Williams, *The Radical Reformation* (Philadelphia, 1962), esp. pp. 20–6.

  [61] *Yeshuot meshiḥo*, 34*b*.

  [62] See Hirsch Z. Zimmels, *Die Marranen in der Rabbinischen Literatur* (Berlin, 1932), 79–80; Baer, *History of the Jews in Christian Spain*, ii. 238–9.

  [63] See Cecil Roth, *A History of the Marranos* (Philadelphia, 1932), 186–8.

  [64] See Baer, *History of the Jews in Christian Spain*, ii. 352.

  [65] See Isaiah Tishby, *Messianism in the Time of the Expulsion from Spain and Portugal* [Meshiḥiyut bedor gerushei sefarad uportugal] (Jerusalem, 1985), 18–19.

The notion of heavenly mission was particularly noticeable in the Converso phenomenon. Other evidence of attitudes towards Conversos among the Jewish community can be found in a dispute among the Jews of Aragon during the first decade of the fifteenth century. The subject of debate was whether to use the skills and abilities of several prominent Conversos who held high positions in the royal court for the benefit of the community. Some considered this to be an act of *mitsvah haba'ah be'averah*— fulfilling a commandment through transgression—and therefore argued against any contact with the Conversos. Others, including the leaders of the community in Saragossa, contended that it would not contravene religious precepts. They exhibited sensitivity to the double life that the Conversos were forced to lead, and even justified the Conversos' need to live according to Christian beliefs in public, which, as they explained to Jewish audiences, 'does no harm and does no damage but [is done] to adorn oneself'.[66] They ascribed to such Conversos the role of 'restoring to their [the Christians'] hearts the love for us [the Jews] and not to strengthen the reach of that one who touches us [in a manner which is] not according to the law'[67]—i.e. that the presence of influential Conversos in the royal court could encourage the Christian rulers to look more favourably upon the Jewish community and possibly prevent any hostile measures being taken against it.

Such observations allow us to re-examine the correspondence between the Jews of Spain and Constantinople. There is no question that these letters were a Christian forgery. As such, we can assume that the forger adopted an extreme interpretation of the Converso. In fact, while certainly representative of a venomous anti-Jewish perspective, they simultaneously reflected the apologia of Jews and Conversos. The Jewish and Converso view of the convert as a secret emissary was analogous to the view of the Inquisition and of certain circles within Spanish society after the 1449 revolt in Toledo, where the same vision of the convert as subversive emissary developed. The Jewish view was meant to justify conversion away from Judaism—considered a very grave sin in Jewish law—and to support those who were living a life of coerced identity. This was not an organized and aggressive ideology as depicted by Inquisition circles, but a defensive approach that drew its inspiration from the realm of mythology, polemic, and apocalypse.

The view of the Inquisition and earlier groups regarding the converts served as the basis for an anti-Converso ideology in Spain. It justified purging converts from high positions in Spanish society. This view, in contrast to that of the Jews, was indeed acted upon and was used to achieve political and economic aims. However, one can certainly see how these two perspectives could reinforce each other. On one hand, the image of the Converso as

---

[66] See the epistle of the Jewish community of Saragossa in Fritz Baer, *Die Juden im christlichen Spanien* (Berlin, 1929), i, doc. 471, pp. 757–8. [67] Ibid.

subversive, which was devised and encouraged among Christians, was inverted by the Converso into a justification for living a Christian life. On the other hand, the self-perception of the Conversos as heavenly emissaries and the attitude of Jews towards the Conversos as subversives reinforced in a similar way Christian fears about the presence of the New Christians.

In the light of all these examples, one may conclude that conversion in the first half of the fifteenth century significantly obscured the polarity between Judaism and Christianity and revealed such boundaries as only seemingly unambiguous and enduring. A new dynamic was born in this inter-religious borderland, a dynamic that sowed the seeds of a new collective identity. I don't think that we can properly call this a rebirth. Rather, we are witness to the emergence of conditions capable of nurturing a new collective culture that would be far more complex and far less bounded. Jewish practice— whether real or imagined—caused Spanish society to develop a racist form of thought and search for pure Christian roots. At the same time, this society experienced literary innovation and intellectual and religious ferment. For its part, Jewish cultural and social life was busy re-examining its own boundaries and creating a different, more pluralistic perspective of Christianity while accepting the Converso community, Christianized as it may have been, as an integral part of the collective Jewish identity.

PART IV

FROM EUROPE TO
AMERICA AND BACK

TEN

Transnationalism and Mutual Influence

American and East European Jewries in the 1920s and 1930s

DANIEL SOYER

T HE HISTORIES of American and European Jewries were very much intertwined in the 1920s and 1930s. The American community was, of course, largely the product of migration from the communities of central and eastern Europe in the nineteenth and early twentieth centuries, but by 1920 it had come to overshadow its source communities in a number of ways. In terms of population, American Jewry had become the largest in the world, having grown from 250,000 in 1880 to over 3.5 million, nearly a quarter of world Jewry, forty years later. Perhaps as importantly, American Jews by that time far outstripped their east European brothers and sisters in terms of wealth and power, a contrast further sharpened by the destruction that the First World War had visited on European Jewish communities. Given this tremendous disparity of material resources, the American community inevitably had a significant impact whenever it engaged with its communities of origin. And given that eastern Europe was the source of most of American Jewry, and remained an important presence in the American Jewish imagination, it would have been surprising had it not continued to influence American Jewish culture even after the era of mass migration had come to an end. In fact, the two communities did continue to interact, as this essay shows.

There are a number of reasons why the continued interaction and mutual influence of American and east European Jews on each other might be overlooked. Unproductive in terms of traditional forms of Jewish cultural creativity, American Jewry has also seemed unstable, always on the verge of

Portions of this chapter appeared in different form in Daniel Soyer, 'Soviet Travel and the Making of an American Jewish Communist: Moissaye Olgin's Trip to Russia in 1920–1921', *American Communist History*, 4/1 (June 2005), 1–20.

assimilation and therefore, to many, destined to be short-lived. On the other hand, American immigration history, including American Jewish history, has focused on Americanization—the process by which immigrants become American—whether this was through the coercion of authorities outside the immigrant communities or enthusiastically engaged in by the immigrants themselves. Not that there haven't been controversies over the extent of acculturation and its erosion of ethnic culture and identity. In the late 1960s and the 1970s scholars began to emphasize continuity and cultural retention, which was often seen as a form of resistance to an oppressive Anglo-American cultural and political-economic hegemony. In the 1990s historians borrowed the notion of 'invention' from literary theorists, promoting a de-essentialized view of ethnic identity and insisting that immigrants and their descendants retained a great deal of agency in the ongoing construction of ethnic American identities different from both those of the Anglo-American mainstream and the old-country tradition. Despite their often contentious differences, however, all of these schools of thought shared the original prime concern, which was how people become American and adopt an American identity.[1]

If anything, Jews seemed eager to Americanize, exhibiting a much lower rate of return to their old homes than did many of the other sizeable immigrant groups of the late nineteenth and early twentieth centuries to which they were compared. They struck roots, acquiring property and opening businesses, at a relatively quick pace. They embraced the American ideologies of democracy, freedom, voluntarism, and equality, applying them eagerly to their own communal institutions, and taking full advantage of public institutions, such as schools. And they pioneered emerging modern American cultural forms—in film, publishing, and the visual arts, for example. Jews fitted very well with the paradigm of one-way Americanization.[2]

The concept of 'transnationalism', however, which historians have begun to adopt from the social scientists who originated it, challenges the centrality of Americanization. Not to be confused with the simple retention of ethnic cultures that historians have long recognized, transnationalism refers to 'the

---

[1] See John Bodnar, *The Transplanted: A History of Immigrants in Urban America* (Bloomington, 1985); Russell A. Kazal, 'Revisiting Assimilation: The Rise, Fall, and Reappraisal of a Concept in American Ethnic History', *American Historical Review*, 100 (Apr. 1995), 437–71; Gary Gerstle, 'Liberty, Coercion and the Making of Americans', *Journal of American History*, 84/2 (1997), 524–58; Kathleen Neils Conzen et al., 'The Invention of Ethnicity: A Perspective from the U.S.A.', *Journal of American Ethnic History*, 12/1 (Fall 1992), 3–41.

[2] See e.g. Hasia Diner, 'From Covenant to Constitution: The Americanization of Judaism', in M. L. Bradbury and James B. Gilbert (eds.), *Transforming Faith: The Sacred and Secular in Modern American History* (New York, 1989); Andrew Heinze, *Adapting to Abundance: Jewish Immigrants, Mass Consumption and the Search for American Identity* (New York, 1990); Daniel Soyer, *Jewish Immigrant Associations and American Identity in New York, 1880–1939* (Cambridge, Mass., 1997).

processes by which immigrants build social fields that link together their country of origin and their country of settlement'.[3] Transnationalism might thus include the involvement of emigrants in homeland politics, business ventures that cross state boundaries, the sending of private and communal aid, travel back and forth between the home country and country of settlement, family structures and personal relationships that remain intact despite distance, communication between those who have left and those who remain behind, and any other social patterns that cross national boundaries and bind immigrants to compatriots still in their country of origin (as well as to those who emigrated to other countries of settlement) in an ongoing and active way. Transnational migrants, it can be said, participate in two societies in two geographical locations at once, even if they spend most or all of their time in only one of them. A transnational perspective focuses on the ways in which migrants negotiate complex interactions across borders and develop an identity that transcends those of both host and home society. It thus complicates any picture of Americanization that implies that immigrants lost all connection to their original community once they left home.[4]

But by no means are transnationalism and Americanization mutually exclusive. Indeed, the two processes often coexist—what historian David Gerber has called 'dual incorporation'. The Jewish case makes this especially clear. American Jewish travellers to eastern Europe, for example, often found that their transnational forays paradoxically strengthened their sense of American identity even as they renewed ties with families and communities in the 'old home'. Not only did American Jewish relief missions bring American dollars to Jewish communities in eastern Europe, but their emissaries also brought a very American sensibility to their work in their needy home towns. Moreover, transnational commitments to homeland struggles sometimes draw immigrants into American politics, ironically enmeshing them further in American social life.[5] Ultimately, Americanization may indeed be corrosive of transnationalism, but for the immigrant generation

[3] Nina Glick Schiller, Linda Basch, and Christina Blanc-Szanton, 'Transnationalism: A New Analytic Framework for Understanding Migration', *Annals of the New York Academy of Sciences*, 645 (1992), 1–24: 26. For related definitions, see Ewa Morawska, 'Immigrants, Transnationalism, and Ethnicization: A Comparison of this Great Wave and the Last', in Gary Gerstle and John Mollenkopf (eds.), *E Pluribus Unum? Contemporary and Historical Perspectives on Immigrant Political Incorporation* (New York, 2001), 175–6; Robert Smith, 'How Durable and New Is Transnational Life? Historical Retrieval through Local Comparison', *Diaspora*, 9/2 (2000), 203–33: 203–4.

[4] For overviews of transnationalism see also Steven Vertovec and Robin Cohen's introduction to their *Migration, Diaspora and Transnationalism* (Cheltenham, UK, 1999), pp. xxiii–xxiv; Peter Kivisto, 'Theorizing Transnational Immigration: A Critical Review of Current Efforts', *Ethnic and Racial Studies*, 24/4 (July 2001), 549–97.

[5] David Gerber, 'Internationalization and Transnationalization', in Reed Ueda (ed.), *A Companion to American Immigration* (Oxford, 2006), 225–54. See also Kivisto, 'Theorizing Transnational Immigration'.

and many of their children ties to the home community often remain alive even as American roots are sunk.

If transnationalism challenges the perception of American Jews as enthusiastic and thorough Americanizers, it also challenges European Jewish historians to reintegrate the large and wealthy American Jewish community into the narrative of European Jewish history. Indeed, European Jewish historians should have no trouble recognizing that Jews have a long history of transnationalism. Not only did the Jews of eastern Europe already possess a stronger consciousness of peoplehood than did many of the European peasant peoples who crossed the ocean at the same time as they did, but this consciousness spanned state borders while they were living in the 'old country' as much as it did after migration.[6] There is therefore no need for the marginalization of American Jewry in Jewish historiography. Neither greater distance nor the presence of a vast ocean severed the connection between the emigrants and their home communities. Rather, the Jews' transnational consciousness survived the journey and American Jews continued to identify closely with Jews in other places. Transnational consciousness led to much concrete transnational activity in the decades immediately following the mass migration, despite the openness of American society and the pressure to Americanize.[7]

The period after the First World War was an important transnational moment for the east European Jews in America. As anthropologist Robert Smith has argued, transnationalism should not be viewed as an absolute condition.[8] It is not the case that one group or one individual is either transnational or not. Rather, transnationalism is an aspect of immigrant life. It may wax and wane according to conditions in either the country of origin or the country of settlement, or according to the resources of time and money

[6] Morawska differentiates between two different types of transnationalism: (1) the 'shift beyond or, as it were, vertically over (rather than horizontally across) the accustomed territorial state-level memberships, state-bound national identities, and civic-political claims' (such as the European Union); (2) the 'combination of civic-political memberships, economic involvements, social networks, and cultural identities that links people and institutions in two or more nation states in diverse, multilayered patterns'. Morawska, 'Immigrants, Transnationalism, and Ethnicization', 175–6. The present essay largely concerns transnationalism of the latter sort. Even in Europe, Jewish transnationalism was that of a population that spilled 'horizontally across' state borders rather than transcending or superseding them in any formal sense. The Jews were not different in that respect than, say, Mexicans in the US southwest—a community formed by a combination of border shifts and cross-border migrations whose consciousness and activities spanned the border in question.

[7] Though perhaps less than on the part of some other contemporary immigrant groups. See Nancy Foner, *From Ellis Island to JFK: New York's Two Great Waves of Immigration* (New Haven, 2000), 171–6; Ewa Morawska, 'Changing Images of the Old Country in the Development of Ethnic Identity among East European Immigrants, 1880s–1930s: A Comparison of Jewish and Slavic Representations', *YIVO Annual*, 21 (1993), 273–341.

[8] Smith, 'How Durable and New Is Transnational Life?'.

available to the migrant community. There is also a spectrum of trans-national activities and commitments: some individuals may lead intensely transnational lives, travelling back and forth frequently and consciously engaging at a high level in communal affairs in both places. Others may limit their commitment to sending money to family members left behind (work-ing in one country to support a family in another country is a classic form of transnational activity). Still others in a given community might not be transnational in orientation at all.

Smith also argues that transnationalism must be measured not only by the effect that it has on the immigrant community, but also by its impact on the community of origin. This essay will suggest that American Jewish interven-tion in east European Jewish communities following the First World War did have an impact on local social and political arrangements.[9] It will also begin to address the challenge to American Jewish historians by examining how continued contact with Europe influenced developments in the American Jewish community.

AMERICAN JEWISH AID AND EAST EUROPEAN JEWRY AFTER THE FIRST WORLD WAR

The First World War devastated the Jewish communities of eastern Europe. During this war, and the smaller wars that followed, hundreds of thousands were killed, and hundreds of thousands more were uprooted. Property losses amounted to hundreds of millions of dollars. Largely unaffected by the war, American Jews mobilized in a number of ways to aid European Jewry. Following the religious, political, and social fault lines that ran through the Jewish population, various sectors of the community organized to raise money for their unfortunate counterparts overseas. Orthodox elements, for example, formed the Central Committee for the Relief of Jews Suffering through the War (known as the CRC), while the wealthy Americanized establishment set up the American Jewish Relief Committee (AJRC), and socialist and labour elements organized the People's Relief Committee (PRC). Significantly, these groups overcame their differences in an effort to deliver aid in a professional and efficient manner, creating the American Jewish Joint Distribution Committee (JDC) to disburse the funds they had collected.[10]

At the same time, thousands of *landsmanshaftn*, mutual aid societies formed by immigrants from the same town in Europe, often several to each

[9] Ibid. 209.
[10] On the JDC and its constituent groups, see Oscar Handlin, *A Continuing Task: The American Jewish Joint Distribution Committee, 1914–1964* (New York, 1964), 19–47; Yehuda Bauer, *My Brother's Keeper: A History of the American Jewish Joint Distribution Committee, 1929–1939* (Philadelphia, 1974), 3–18.

town, established their own united relief committees to aid their home towns. During, and especially after, the war, they sent millions of dollars to their compatriots back home. They sent much of this assistance through the offices of the JDC, the Hebrew Sheltering and Immigrant Aid Society (known as the HIAS), the Red Cross, and other agencies that established operations in Poland and other countries of eastern Europe. But while the professional relief agencies sought to distribute aid in a dispassionate, professional, and efficient way, the *landsmanshaft* relief committees had a more emotional and personal approach. Relations were therefore often tense.

Dissatisfied with the work of the professional social workers, the relief committees began to send their own 'delegates' overseas. Hundreds of these delegates went to Europe between 1919 and 1921, each carrying tens of thousands of dollars in personal remittances and general aid. The feverish activity spanned national boundaries as American relief workers, professional and amateur, departed from New York and travelled through Paris and Warsaw on their way to their home towns. In doing so they entered a transnational space that involved them intensively in the affairs of their home communities. Their involvement, in turn, had an impact on the communal structure of both the home town and the immigrant communities in the United States.

Despite their differences, the professional social workers of the JDC and the amateur activists of the *landsmanshaftn* shared certain characteristics. Chief among these was the desire to maintain a non-partisan, non-ideological stance in carrying out the relief work Both the JDC and the united *landsmanshaft* relief committees had overcome political divisions within the immigrant community—the JDC by uniting the Orthodox CRC, the socialist PRC, and the establishment AJRC; the united *landsmanshaft* relief committees by combining the efforts of home-town societies that had earlier splintered along political, religious, generational, and other lines. (One small European town could be represented in New York by several different societies—a religious one, a radical one, and so on) They attempted to impose this non-partisan ethos on the highly factionalized, partisan, and ideologically charged east European Jewish communities.

Indeed, the preference for non-partisan expertise became something of a hallmark of American intervention in local Jewish affairs. In Poland, for example, as historian Rachel Rojanski has shown, the JDC at first channelled funds through pre-existing local groups, but soon decided that it would have to intervene more directly in Polish Jewish communal affairs in order to ensure a fair and efficient distribution of resources. The JDC thereafter played an instrumental role in the formation of non-partisan social welfare agencies, credit unions, co-operatives, and other institutions, often with the co-operation of local committees appointed at least in part by the JDC itself. Although it frequently worked with rabbis and other traditional authority figures, it seems to have favoured doctors, engineers, nurses, architects, and other members of the modern technical intelligentsia. It also used its financial clout to force mergers, or at least co-operation, between co-operatives, credit unions, and other institutions affiliated to rival political groups.[11]

Of course, this technocratic intervention was itself highly political in its effect. JDC officials inserted themselves into local communal affairs, wielding their hundreds of thousands of dollars and sophisticated organizational network as weapons. As JDC operative Baruch Zuckerman put it, all JDC representatives strove to abide by the organization's non-political principle, but 'they almost never succeeded'.[12] Moreover, this political intervention was transnational in that decisions concerning Polish Jewry's communal structure were made in New York.

The JDC professionals and *landsmanshaft* amateurs faced the same sort of dangers on their missions. Zuckerman himself was arrested at least once in Romania, and conditions in Poland were especially bad during the 1920 Soviet–Polish war. Harry Berger, for example, travelled to his home city of Minsk, then controlled by Poland, in 1920, representing a coalition of Minsker societies in the United States.[13] Berger and a colleague first learned the value of bribes in Paris, and when they stepped off the train in Minsk, then in the Polish–Soviet war zone, with $20,000 in cash and some 24 million Polish marks ($120,000) in a Polish bank account, they were thus not surprised to be immediately detained by drunken officers of the gendarmerie, who accused them of carrying Bolshevik propaganda and funds, confiscated private letters they were carrying—and demanded a bribe. Berger was later arrested again by officials who hoped to extort more money from him, but he bought their good will with a contribution to the Polish Red Cross.

The situation that Berger found in Minsk reveals the extent to which American Jews and non-Jews intervened in local affairs. Even under such trying conditions, Berger and his friend were not alone. Significantly, there were 'several' other American Jewish *landsmanshaft* delegates in Minsk at the time, representing immigrants from nearby towns. Some were purely 'private entrepreneurs' hoping to make money by manipulating exchange rates, but others were legitimate.[14] In addition, 'uniformed representatives' of the American Young Men's Christian Association were on hand to help Berger resolve a problem with his bank. Berger reported being 'besieged by hundreds and thousands of people who were supposed to receive money from their American relatives, and also by those who only hoped to receive

---

[11] Rachel Rojanski, 'American Jewry's Influence on the Establishment of the Jewish Welfare Apparatus in Poland, 1920–1929' (Heb.), *Gal-Ed*, 11 (1989), 59–86.

[12] Baruch Zuckerman, *On the Road* [Afn veg] (New York, 1956), 383.

[13] Harry Berger, 'Journey through Hell' (Yiddish), in *From Friends to a Friend: A Gift for Harry Berger on his Fiftieth Birthday* [Fun fraynt tsu a fraynt: a matone heri berger'n tsu zayn 5oten geburtstog] (Philadelphia, 1936), 101–48.   [14] Ibid. 114.

money'.[15] The presence of these emissaries went far not only in ameliorating the physical needs of the local inhabitants, Berger concluded, but also in boosting their spirits. Those who received assistance from their families knew that they were not forgotten. In addition, communal aid from abroad bolstered several important institutions.

It is difficult to assess how personal aid from relatives abroad might have affected the local Jewish and non-Jewish economies, altered class alignments, and the like. It is easier to demonstrate that American money helped support certain public bodies. Indeed, during their stay the delegates wielded tremendous power as a direct result of their control over discretionary funds. Most of the money that Berger brought to Minsk, for example, was in the form of personal remittances sent by American Jews to their families in Europe. But the Minsker delegate had tens of thousands of dollars to distribute as he saw fit. Some of this money he gave to needy individuals whose relatives had not sent them anything. But he also contributed large sums to such institutions as the Jewish hospital and the children's colony, whose work impressed him as he investigated local conditions. The delegates also provided a number of patronage jobs, though, as Berger reports, not as many as the locals hoped or expected.[16]

The case of Brisk illustrates even more clearly the ways in which the Americans intervened in local affairs, and the potential significance of that intervention on their impoverished European home towns. As Smith has argued, emigrant intervention in local affairs can have the effect of upsetting traditional hierarchies of power, but only if challenges to those hierarchies are already under way. In Jewish eastern Europe, of course, such challenges had begun decades before, mounted first by the nineteenth-century Haskalah and later by the socialist and Zionist movements. The First World War further disrupted traditional hierarchies of authority. During the war, as Steven Zipperstein has demonstrated, relief agencies, often staffed by young radicals, became a new centre of authority in the Jewish community.[17] The Americans furthered this transition, sometimes adding a dose of American pragmatism and social work professionalism to the mix.

The state of Brisk relief demonstrates the degree to which American Jews overcame partisan divisions within their own ranks. The United Brisker Relief included *landsmanshaftn* from across the political and religious spectrum. While the Brisker branch of the labour Zionist Jewish National Workers' Alliance and the anti-Zionist Brisker Bundist Fareyn took the lead in forming a united relief committee, they were soon joined by the Brisker

[15] Berger, 'Journey through Hell', 109.   [16] Ibid. 135, 139–40.
[17] Steven J. Zipperstein, 'The Politics of Relief: The Transformation of Russian Jewish Communal Life During the First World War', *Studies in Contemporary Jewry*, 4 (1988), 22–36.

Branch 286, Workmen's Circle; Brisker Shul Tifereth Israel; Brisker Ladies' Society; Brisker Young Men's (*sic*); Brisker Lodge 337, Independent Order B'rith Sholom; Brisker Lodge 682, Independent Order Brith Abraham; the Semiatsher Society; Rabbi Zuberstein Lodge; Brisker Untershtitsung Fareyn; and the Brisker Zelbstbildung Klub.[18]

Like other similar committees, the United Brisker Relief initiated a discourse of relief that rhetorically closed the gap between the emigrants and those left behind. It emphasized its constituency's close relationship with the people who had remained in Europe and called on the American *landslayt* to accept responsibility for supporting the unfortunate war-torn inhabitants of Brisk. 'We, the fortunate Briskers, who are here in this free country', it insisted, must take an interest in 'our Briskers' and 'our brothers and sisters' suffering from the war. It criticized the American *landslayt*—'well-fed, well-dressed, and cheerful'—for not doing enough for their relatives overseas, and tried to entice people to its meetings by promising them news from home received through special channels.[19]

The United Brisker Relief accomplished little during the war, but in 1920, in response to appeals from Brisk, a revived committee sent former chairman Philip Rabinowitch overseas with some $80,000. Like Berger and Zuckerman, he too faced danger, nearly turning back from fear of antisemitic bands operating near the city. But the transnational Brisker network was pressed into service to keep the delegate on track. After Rabinowitch wrote of his hesitation to Jacob Finkelstein in New York, Finkelstein dispatched Brisker landsman and journalist Pesach Novick, who had lived for a time in New York and was then in Vilna, to encourage Rabinowitch and help him carry out his mission. Once in Brisk, Rabinowitch found crowds of desperate *landslayt* grateful for the assistance from America.[20] The success of Rabinowitch's mission, and renewed appeals from Brisk, prompted the United Brisker Relief to send another delegation, consisting of Jacob Finkelstein and H. Kleinberg, in 1921, this time with $110,000 for their beleaguered home town, including $15,000 in general relief funds in addition to $95,000 in personal

[18] Jacob Finkelstein, 'The *Landsmanshaft* Societies and the History of the United Brisker Relief' (Yiddish), in *Encyclopedia of the Diaspora: Brisk-Litovsk* [Entsiklopedye fun di goleslender: brisk d'lite] (Jerusalem, 1955), 612–15; id., '50 Years of United Brisker Relief', in *50th Anniversary of United Brisker Relief, 1915–1965* (New York, 1965), 3.

[19] 'To All Briskers' (Yiddish), in *Brisker Relief for the War Sufferers* (New York, 1917), unpaginated.

[20] Letters from Beril Farber and L. Muliar to Jacob Finkelstein, 25 July 1919; R. Isaac Ze'ev Soloveichik to Nisn Liberman, 2 Heshvan 5680 (26 Oct. 1919); Kooperatywa to Corn [*sic*] Relief Committee, 8 Apr. 1920; Philip Rabinowitch to Jacob Finkelstein, 28 June [1920], all in folder 2, Records of United Brisker Relief (RUBR); 'A grus fun brisk' [A Greeting from Brisk], 15 June 1920, in scrapbook, folder 3, RUBR; Jacob Finkelstein, 'Geshikhte fun fareyniktn brisker relif' [History of the United Brisker Relief], folder 12, RUBR, 15–16; id., 'The *Landsmanshaft* Societies' (Yiddish), 619–20, 623.

remittances.[21] They distributed monies to the Talmud Torah, the old-age home, the Jewish hospital, the pharmacy and clinic, the orphanage, the Great Synagogue, several smaller study houses, the schools of the Young Zion movement, and the Workers' Relief Committee.[22]

In Brisk, as in other receiving communities, the *landsmanshaft* delegates entered into a highly politicized and factionalized environment. Conservative traditionalists and radical labour elements clashed over the proper priorities for the distribution of relief funds. The Brisker rabbi, for example, pointed out to the Americans that many 'respectable' (*balebatishe*) individuals had been ruined by the war. They needed help, which the rabbi felt should take the form of discreet individual payments, since such people were reluctant to take advantage of aid provided by general public agencies. But the radicals argued that such assistance would be doled out unequally between the fallen bourgeoisie and proletarian poor, and would only serve to rebuild the wealth and authority of the former. Radical elements condemned charitable aid to individuals and called for funds for institutions that they believed would treat all segments of the population equally and perhaps effect structural change in the communal hierarchy. They thus favoured public kitchens, schools, and clinics.[23]

In some places, the JDC and the *landsmanshaftn* co-operated with local rabbis and kehilahs. But the American agencies often appointed their own 'American relief committees' to represent them on the local level, bypassing the traditional communal authorities. When JDC representative Baruch Zuckerman (a Labour Zionist) came to Brisk in 1919, he inserted himself into the struggle between the 'young' radicals and the 'old' members of the traditional establishment. After meeting with members of various parties, from the Bund to the Mizrachi, Zuckerman decided to bypass the local kehilah and set up a new relief committee that included representatives of the new parties of right and left, as well as 'non-partisan' representatives of the established kehilah. He also mandated that a specified amount of aid money should go to the radicals' favoured institutions. As one letter-writer reported, the traditional leaders 'had to do this against their will, because

[21] Letters from Levengard et al. to Jacob Finkelstein, 8 Nov. 1920, and Sol Weiss to Jacob Finkelstein, 17 Jan. 1921, folder 6, RUBR; 'Hilf oyf peysakh durkh di brisker shloykhim' [Pesach Aid through the Brisker Delegates], folder 6, RUBR; financial summary for 'Yor 1921', folder 1, RUBR; letter of credit, Bank of the United States to United Brisker Relief, 9 Mar. 1921, in scrapbook, folder 3, RUBR; 'Brisker relif komitet' [Relief Committee of Brisk], unidentified, undated clipping, folder 82, Archives of the American Jewish Joint Distribution Committee (AAJJDC), 1919–1921.
[22] See receipts from various organizations to the delegates of the United Brisker Relief, April–May 1921, folder 2, RUBR.
[23] Farber and Mulier to Finkelstein, 25 July 1919; Soloveichik to Liberman, 2 Heshvan 5680 (26 Oct. 1919), folder 2, RUBR.

Mr. Zuckerman said so'. But now that he had left the scene, the 'reactionaries [*shvartse*]' were 'exploiting' his absence to reassert themselves.[24]

Sometimes, the Americans threw their weight behind 'workers' relief committees' representing youthful radical forces in the towns, but often they sought to impose an American spirit of pragmatism and non-partisanship on a highly ideologically charged and fractious situation. When delegates Finkelstein and Kleinberg arrived in Brisk two years after Zuckerman, they met with a wide spectrum of communal leaders, from the chief rabbi to the leaders of radical factions. Despite their own radical inclinations, they strove to be studiously non-partisan in their distribution of the $15,000 entrusted to them for general communal aid. Using the power that their control over such large sums of money gave them, the Americans attempted to force the locals to create a united relief committee representing all factions. While they had limited success in getting Zuckerman's relief committee to work with the rabbi and the kehilah, they did manage to bring feuding radical factions into a 'united workers' committee', on which the New York relief committee was to have representation.[25]

Especially in the years after the First World War, then, American Jews used their enormous resources to reshape east European Jewry in an American image. As Rachel Rojanski has suggested, this was true even—perhaps especially—when organizations like the JDC sought to encourage locally run agencies to take over the tasks of direct relief. The Americans sought particularly to overcome the highly charged ideological atmosphere in Poland and to stimulate the growth of an indigenous technocratic professional communal leadership. There were limits to their success, of course, and Jewish life in eastern Europe remained heavily politicized throughout the inter-war period. But while the limits are clear, the extent of the Americans' influence remains uncertain and requires more research.

THE CONTINUED INFLUENCE OF EAST EUROPEAN JEWRY ON AMERICA

If the influence of American aid on European communities was great, the impact of European events on the American community was also significant.

[24] *The People's Relief of America: Facts and Documents, 1915–1924* [Pipels relif fun amerika: faktn un documentn, 1915–1924] (New York, 1924); Farber and Mulier to Finkelstein, 25 July 1919, folder 2, RUBR. See also Samuel Kassow, 'Community and Identity in the Interwar Shtetl', in Israel Gutman, Ezra Mendelsohn, and Chone Shmeruk (eds.), *The Jews of Poland between Two World Wars* (Hanover, NH, 1989), 202–3, 213–14.

[25] Finkelstein, 'Geshikhte fun fareyniktn brisker relif', 18; id., 'The *Landsmanshaft* Societies' (Yiddish), 624–5; Petition of Jewish Artisans' Union, 2 May 1921, folder 2, RUBR; 'Reglamin

Europe was the source of the American community, and therefore of its culture. But the influence of European Jewish developments on American Jewry continued even after the end of mass migration. Sometimes the effects of this influence were paradoxical, as when closer contact between the two communities helped American Jewry define its distinctiveness. Sometimes events in Europe exerted their own countervailing influence on Jewish American life, as when travellers brought Soviet ideologies home to the United States.

The need to mobilize for overseas aid can itself be seen as an indirect European influence on the development of the American Jewish community. Relief activities stimulated communal activity, calling into being a new set of organizations, some of which—like the JDC—still exist today. Underlying these organizational efforts was a new consciousness on the part of American Jews that their central role in the Jewish world was to provide material and technical assistance to less fortunate communities in other countries.

At the same time, paradoxically, given that the discourse of relief stressed kinship between givers and receivers, the relief effort brought home to American Jews just how different they were from their *landslayt* still in the old home. One member of the United Horodyszczer Relief Organizations expressed it thus: 'We look at things and people a little differently than they do. They don't understand our way of thinking. Their psychology is very different.'[26] In civic terms, the material and political security of Jews in the United States contrasted so starkly with the hostility, poverty, and instability encountered by Jews in eastern Europe that transnational activity often hastened the process of Americanization, as even the most transnationally inclined immigrants came to identify themselves as Americans. This can be seen in the reactions of the *landsmanshaft* delegates and other travellers to their old home towns. Even as they engaged in a deeply transnational enterprise, travelling personally across borders to deliver aid and help reorganize communities, they indicated that the standards by which they measured the world had shifted: despite his emotional commitment to the Jews of Minsk, for example, Harry Berger could not help seeing the Belarusian metropolis through the eyes of a Westerner. He compared his native city to the larger and richer cosmopolitan cities through which he had travelled: 'Coming from New York, and having travelled through such gigantic cities as London, Paris, and Warsaw, I felt, as I travelled through the streets of Minsk as if I had fallen into a cellar. The houses, which I thought I knew so well from before, now looked to me to be strangely small, low, and insignificant.'[27] His sensibilities

fun a.h.k. in brisk' [By-laws of the A[merican] R[elief] C[ommittee] in Brisk], folder 14/9–10, RUBR; Memo, JDC Warsaw to Landsmannschaft Department, New York, 23 June 1921, folder 123, AAJJDC, 1919–1921.

[26] *The Mountain of Horodyszcze* [Horodishcher barg] (New York, 1920), 21.
[27] Berger, 'A Journey' (Yiddish), 106.

were thus no longer those of a Minsker Jew, but those of the Philadelphian he had become. In inter-war Jewish life, then, transnationalism was not at all incompatible with Americanization.

Further, a visit to the old home could also convince the visitor that her or his true home was the new one. Some accounts demonstrate a shift in identity during the course of a trip. Sidney Herbst, for example, kept a diary during his 1935 journey to Sędziszów on behalf of the First Sędziszów Galician Society. As he leaves Warsaw for his town of origin, he expresses his happiness at heading 'for home'. But the tone shifts very quickly after the arrival at his destination, which he perceives as cold, shabby, horrible, and altogether wretched. Within days, he writes, 'Can't wait 'til I leave. Counting days like in a prison.' The only time he feels 'sort of at home' in Poland is at the American consulate in Warsaw![28] Similarly, when Rose Schoenfeld returned 'home' to New York from a private trip to her home town of Drohobycz in 1932, she 'thanked God properly for the first time for leading me on the right path to America, the land of freedom, where I could make decent people of my children'.[29] Her transnational venture thus confirmed for her that she had made the right decision in emigrating and committing herself and her children to America.

Moreover, although they were ostensibly in their home towns as *landslayt* bringing aid to their friends and relations, the delegates often found it necessary or expedient to emphasize their American identity. As Berger explained to officials who were demanding to see a list of aid recipients during one of his detentions, 'We had been elected by a huge number of American citizens in order to carry out our relief mission here, our work had also been authorized officially by the American government, which had issued us special relief passports, and we considered our relief mission to be a confidential and private matter, according to the American custom.'[30] Berger thus managed to invoke his status and values as an American three times in one sentence, concluding with a demand to be allowed to contact the US ambassador.

The experiences of travellers also filtered through to American Jewish politics, and here the influence was more direct. Soviet Russia, in particular, held a special fascination for American Jews, many of whom had either come from the old Russian empire themselves or had parents who had. This fascinating country of origin, remade by the revolution, was highly problematic of course, and disputes over the nature of the revolution and the resulting regime, and their significance for Jews, were a staple of Jewish political debates in the inter-war years. Encouraged by the Soviet authorities, many

[28] Diary of Sidney Herbst, entries for 14, 15, and 23 Jan. 1935, Herbst family file, Collection on Family History and Genealogy, RG 126, YIVO Archives.
[29] Rose Schoenfeld, autobiography no. 110, p. 30, Collection of American Jewish Autobiographies, RG 102, YIVO Archives.   [30] Berger, 'A Journey' (Yiddish), 118.

American Jews—both private individuals and public figures—travelled to Russia to see the Jewish past and the socialist future for themselves. When they returned to America they discussed their impressions in a variety of public forums, including mass rallies, organizational meetings, the Yiddish press, books, and radio programmes.

Travellers to Russia did in fact find eager audiences awaiting them upon their return to the United States, and these audiences used the travellers' reports to help them make up their minds about the Soviet experiment. Thus, when garment worker Meyer Kushner challenged a glowing report given by a pro-Soviet official of his union around 1936, he did so by citing another eyewitness account, that of a personal friend. The official, in turn, urged Kushner to go to Russia and see for himself.[31] Given the difficulties of disentangling such radically different perceptions, how much influence did these reports really exercise? The evidence is inconclusive, but all sides certainly thought them effective.[32] One publication of the Profintern, the Moscow-based international federation of pro-Soviet trade unions, noted in 1932 that workers considered delegates returning to America from Soviet trips to be 'authoritative' and that their 'social role and influence on the masses are very great'.[33] Emma Goldman agreed, conceding to her dismay that such tourists were the 'traveling salesmen of the Russian revolution . . . more responsible than the Bolsheviks themselves for the lies and dissipations about Russia'.[34] A variety of contemporaries, from settlement house leader Lillian Wald to knitted goods worker Joe Rapoport, recalled being influenced by the lectures of returning travellers before making their own trips.[35]

Indeed, the Jewish immigrant community in America seems to have had a nearly insatiable appetite for travelogues of the Soviet Union. Abraham Cahan, legendary for his ability to pander to the masses, clearly saw this. The

[31] Meyer Kushner, *The Life and Struggles of a Cloak-Maker* [Lebn un kamf fun a kloukmakher] (New York, 1960), 261.
[32] Lewis S. Feuer has argued that published travellers' reports 'affected the American political consciousness more deeply . . . than any other foreign influence in its history': 'American Travelers to the Soviet Union 1917–1932: The Formation of a Component of New Deal Ideology', *American Quarterly*, 14/2 (Summer 1962), 119–49.
[33] Sylvia Margulies, *The Pilgrimage to Russia: The Soviet Union and the Treatment of Foreigners, 1924–1937* (Madison, Wis., 1968), 25. The Comintern also kept tabs on published accounts. See Harvey Klehr, John Earl Haynes, and Kyrill M. Anderson, *The Soviet World of American Communism* (New Haven, 1998), 217, 315.
[34] Quoted in Zosa Szajkowski, *Jews, Wars, and Communism*, 2 vols. (New York, 1972), i. 408.
[35] Feuer, 'American Travelers to the Soviet Union', 128; Kenneth Kann, *Joe Rapoport: The Life of a Jewish Radical* (Philadelphia, 1981), 72. A settlement house was a kind of community centre providing educational and social services to a slum neighbourhood. It was distinguished from other centres by the fact that its staff of middle-class reformers actually lived in the house in order to share in the experiences of their needy neighbours, the better to identify with them. Often, settlement workers went beyond the provision of social services to become involved in political reform.

Forward covered its editor's journey in great detail, often on the first page, from the time he arrived in Russia in July 1927 to his return to New York in October of that year. The paper continued to serialize long Soviet travelogues intermittently throughout the late 1920s and the 1930s: staffers and correspondents such as Mendl Osherowitch, Harry Lang, Boruch Charney Vladeck, and Israel Joshua Singer wrote some of them, and outsiders (including British trade union chief Sir Walter Citrine) contributed others.

The first major eyewitness account of Soviet life that the *Forward* published was written by Moissaye (Moyshe) Olgin, a *Forward* staffer and former Bundist who returned to Russia in 1920. Olgin's trip to Russia was clearly an important moment in a number of ways. On a personal level, the visit reawakened his faith in the possibility of socialist transformation, which had been shaken by the collapse of the Second International during the First World War. It also turned him from a sceptic into an enthusiastic supporter of the Soviet regime, setting him on his course to communism.[36] On a political level, it helped pave the way for the split of the Jewish Socialist Federation from the Socialist Party in September 1921 and its alliance with the Communist Party to form the Workers Party that December. On his return to New York in April, Olgin was welcomed home at a mass rally attended by 'thousands of people', according to *Forward*, 'who came to hear the truth' about Russia.[37] His series of articles in the paper, which ran for nearly six months, along with Olgin's lectures at the Socialist Party's Rand School and other venues around the country, made a deep impression on the radical Yiddish-speaking public.[38] One sympathetic critic later placed him in the tradition of John Reed as one who bore witness to the revolution from

[36] David Prudson, 'Communism and the Jewish Labour Movement in the US, 1919–1929' [Hakomunism utenu'at hapo'alim hayehudit be'aretsot habrit, 1919–1929], Ph.D. dissertation, University of Tel Aviv, 1985, 27–8; Olgin, untitled questionnaire, no date, Russian State Archive of Social and Political History (Rossiiskii gosudarstvennyi arkhiv sotsial'no-politicheskoi istorii; RGASPI), Moscow, Comintern Records (*fond* 495), series 261, folder 449.

[37] Other speakers at the rally, at which Olgin spoke for an hour and a half, included Abraham Cahan, Vladimir Medem, Baruch Vladeck, J. B. Salutsky, and Morris Winchevsky. The Workmen's Circle mandolin orchestra provided entertainment. See the following articles in the *Forward*: 'Kaboles ponem far m. olgin' [Reception for M. Olgin] (advertisement), 5 Apr. 1921; 'Ale greytn zikh tsu heren genose olgin's grus fun soveten-rusland' [Everyone Getting Ready to Hear Comrade Olgin's Greetings from the Soviet Union], 8 Apr. 1921; 'Olgin oyfgenumen mit groys bagaysterung fun toyzender menshen' [Olgin Received with Great Enthusiasm by Thousands of People], 11 Apr. 1921.

[38] See the following in the *Forward*: 'Haynt gen. olgin's ershte lektshur in rend skuhl' [Today Comrade Olgin's First Lecture at Rand School], 15 Apr. 1921; 'Kumt hern gen. olgin vegen rusland morgen in bronzvil' [Come Hear Comrade Olgin on Russia Tomorrow in Brownsville] (advertisement), 19 Apr. 1921; 'Zuntog baytog in di bronks' [Sunday in the Bronx] (advertisement), 20 Apr. 1921; 'Bronzvil! Harlem! M. Olgin' [Brownsville! Harlem! M. Olgin!] (advertisement), 14 May 1921; 'Haynt lektshurt olgin in harlem' [Today Olgin Lectures in Harlem], 18 May 1921. Prudson, 'Communism and the Jewish Labour

first-hand experience.[39] The most consistent supporter of unity with the communists, Olgin rallied the left within the Federation and pushed first for the split and then for the merger.

Olgin was abroad for ten months, about six of them in Soviet Russia, from August or September 1920 to February 1921.[40] He passed through Petrograd, and spent extended periods of time in Moscow and Nizhny Novgorod (Russia proper) in Kazan (Tatar Republic), and in Minsk (Belarus, in the former Pale of Settlement), with short side trips to smaller locations. Plans to travel to his native Ukraine fell through when he came down with pneumonia towards the end of his trip. He visited peasant villages, military bases, large factories, schools, synagogues, government offices, theatres, and hospitals, and attended meetings of all sorts of official and quasi-official bodies. He spoke with high government officials, including Trotsky, Bukharin, and foreign minister Georgy Chicherin, with opposition leaders, including Menshevik leader Yuly Martov, and with anonymous workers and peasants.

Those who influenced him the most on his journey were his former comrades in the Bund and in the Jewish socialist circles of New York—some of whom now played an important role in the regime and some of whom had become its opponents. As the *Forward* reported:

Speaking of the activity of our comrades in Russia, Comrade Olgin explained . . . that someone who was once active in the socialist movement in Russia would not feel foreign there now, even if he had been away for several years. You meet acquaintances everywhere you go, not only in party circles, but also in the highest levels of government. The Jewish comrades occupy a very eminent position in the government.[41]

Movement', 28; Simon Solomon, 'Derinerungen fun der yidisher arbeter bavegung, pt. II: klivland, 1917–1922' [Memoirs of the Jewish Workers' Movement, pt. II: Cleveland, 1917–1922], 241, Manuscripts Collection (RG 108), fo. 56.3, YIVO Archives; Melech Epstein, *The Jew and Communism, 1919–1941* (New York, n.d.), 383–4.

[39] Moyshe Katz, 'Olgin's bukh "sovetn-farband" [Olgin's Book, 'Soviet Union'], *Freiheit*, 5 Nov. 1944, p. 6.

[40] It is difficult to date Olgin's trip exactly since the dates of his arrival and departure are never mentioned explicitly in his account. According to Prudson ('Communism and the Jewish Labour Movement', 28), Olgin left New York on 29 May 1920 and returned on 4 April 1921. But according to the *Forward*, which agrees on the return date, he was away for eight months. See 'Genose olgin brengt a bagaystertn grus fun sovet rusland' [Comrade Olgin Brings Enthusiastic Greetings from Soviet Russia], *Forward*, 5 Apr. 1921. Olgin indicates that he arrived in Russia in the Jewish month of Elul, corresponding in 1920 to August/September; the *Forward* notes that he left Russia for Germany during February 1921: Olgin, 'Genose olgin's ershter artikl vegn soviet-rusland' [Comrade Olgin's First Article about Soviet Russia], *Forward*, 31 Mar. 1921; 'Bald—olgin's beshraybungen fun soviet rusland farn "forverts"' [Soon—Olgin's Sketches from Soviet Russia for 'Forward'], *Forward*, 25 Feb. 1921.

[41] 'Genose olgin brengt a bagaystertn grus fun sovet Rusland', 16. See also, Olgin, 'Vos tut zikh oyf an arbayter-konferents in rusland' [What Goes On at a Workers' Conference in Russia?], *Forward*, 3 Apr. 1921.

The Bundist influence could cut both ways, since the Bund had split between supporters and opponents of the Bolsheviks. He spent considerable time with Rafael Abramovitch the prominent Bundist and left-wing Menshevik leader, whom Olgin later recalled as a 'close and intimate friend' of fifteen years' standing.[42] But Abramovitch did not leave a good impression. On the contrary, he seems to have served as the model for Olgin's critique of Mensheviks and intellectuals, two categories that he tended to conflate. He was probably speaking about Abramovitch when he described the following scene:

I spent an evening in the home of a former friend of mine, a Menshevik, who now served in a Soviet office. On his table I found real tea, and sugar, and butter, and cookies, and cheese, and white bread, and sausage. He certainly lived better than a communist, and much better than ten commissars. But he complained. He cursed the communists. His wife cursed the communists. His wife's sister cursed the communists. They heaped scorn [*shvebl un pekh*, literally 'sulphur and pitch'] on the communists for so long, that a small boy, my friend's son, about six years old, called out, 'Yes. I wish an emperor would come and hang all the communists.'[43]

Olgin contrasted the Mensheviks' defeatist griping with the enthusiastic self-sacrifice of the communists, who willingly offered extra labour, put themselves in physical danger, and endured material hardship for the sake of the revolution. The implication was clear: while the self-sacrificing communists were building socialism, the Mensheviks were living high and doing nothing but complain.

Olgin also met Mark Liber at Abramovitch's house. Liber, another Bundist, was a leader of the right-wing Mensheviks, who called openly for the overthrow of the Soviets. If anything, Liber made an even worse impression than Abramovitch. Again, unlike the cheerful and purposeful communists, Olgin found Liber to be 'embittered' and morose. 'Not a single smile touched his lips', reported Olgin, adding, 'True, he had just got out of gaol, where the Cheka had held him for a couple of months.'[44] But this was hardly an excuse for Liber's refusal to share in the joy of the revolution.

A contact who apparently impressed Olgin much more favourably was General Petrovsky, also known as David Lipets and Dr Max Goldfarb. As Goldfarb, this former Bundist had been a member of the Jewish Socialist Federation in New York and labour editor of the *Forward*. Now, as Petrovsky, he headed all of the officer training schools for the Red Army. Olgin was especially taken with the broad education offered to officer candidates drawn

[42] M. Olgin, *Soviet Union* [Sovetn-farband] (New York, 1944), 144.
[43] Olgin, 'Farvos men zidlt in rusland di komunisten' [Why the Communists Are Cursed in Russia], *Forward*, 18 May 1921.
[44] Olgin, 'Vos vilen di menshevikes in rusland?' [What Do the Mensheviks Want in Russia?], *Forward*, 3 June 1921.

from the peasantry and the working class, and he wrote several articles about the system. He noted that Goldfarb was now Petrovsky, that Trotsky had nothing but praise for the former New Yorker, and that he had attended an imposing graduation ceremony for the cadets in Red Square. But other than that, he had little to say about his encounter with the general.[45]

But Yiddish literary critic Daniel Charney, who attended the parade with Olgin, remembered that the sight of a former tsarist general dismounting from his horse in deference to Petrovsky's higher rank had made a deep impression on Olgin:

It is possible that the grandeur of his friend Dr Max Goldfarb awakened in Olgin the 'passion' [*yeyster hore*, literally 'evil inclination'] for Bolshevism. It is very pleasant, after all, to 'ride the horse', even when you don't know how to ride. . . . When several days later I saw M. Olgin in a magnificent automobile, which had been put at his disposal by Lipets-Petrovsky, it became clear to me that Olgin was already learning to 'ride'.[46]

Charney thus questioned Olgin's integrity by suggesting that his conversion to communism was simply the result of being impressed by the trappings of power in the hands of someone similar to himself (a common criticism of Olgin's character among his political opponents was that he was unduly deferential to those with power).[47] Abramovitch also claimed that Petrovsky had influenced Olgin.

In Minsk, Olgin dropped in at the office of *Der Veker*, formerly the organ of the Bund and now the publication of the Komfarband (Komunistisher Farband, Communist Federation), a short-lived organization of pro-communist Bundists soon to be absorbed by the Communist Party proper. 'Here', he wrote, 'I was sure that I would find acquaintances, and I was not mistaken. Within half an hour I met Rakhmiel [Arn Vaynshteyn] and Ester [Maria Frumkin], whom I had not seen in eight years.'[48] The fact that several of his comrades were serving in the Belarusian government was not lost on him. Neither was the pressure being exerted on them as friends of the Soviet regime to liquidate their independent Jewish party and merge fully with the mainstream communists. While some of Olgin's old friends—like Abramovitch and Charney—ridiculed Olgin for his willingness to defer to

[45] Olgin, 'A parad fun royte soldatn in moskve' [A Parade of Red Soldiers in Moscow], *Forward*, 2 June 1921; id., 'Vi azoy men makht in rusland ofitsiren fun proste soldaten un poyerim?' [How Officers Are Made of Simple Soldiers and Peasants in Russia], *Forward*, 23 June 1921.

[46] Doniel Charney, *What a Decade (1914–1924): Memoirs* [A yortsendlik aza (1914–1924), memuarn] (New York, 1943), 291–3; Abramovitch, *In Two Revolutions: The Story of a Generation* [In tsvey revolutsies: di geshikhte fun a dor] (New York, 1944), 148.

[47] See e.g. A. Liessin, 'Un er hot dokh nit oysgehaltn', [And He Did Not Endure], *Tsukunft* (Aug. 1928), 492–5.   [48] Olgin, 'In Minsk', *Forward*, 31 July 1921.

power, there was a political logic to Olgin's perception of the state of affairs in Russia and to the direction of his politics. As the middle ground gave way, he chose to cast his lot with the workers, with the revolution, with socialism, and, therefore, with the communists.

Olgin's conversion had more than just a personal meaning. Influenced by his own encounter with Soviet Russia, he returned to the United States to help steer a section of the Jewish left towards the communists. When the Jewish Socialist Federation split from the Socialist Party and entered merger negotiations with the communists, Olgin was consistently the most pro-Bolshevik of the ostensibly non-communist negotiators. When many of his Jewish Federation comrades in the Workers Party tired of the communists and returned to the socialists, Olgin remained as the Workers Party and the Communist Party became more and more synonymous. Soon, he emerged as one of the most orthodox of the American Bolsheviks. Through Olgin, then, Russian Jewish developments influenced not only the American Jewish left, but the general American left as well.

*

The post-First World War era brought the end of mass migration, but not the end of mutual contact and influence between the sending and receiving communities. The activities that allowed American Jews to intervene in east European Jewish communal affairs are clear, but their impact is less so. After the war, both community-wide Jewish relief agencies and individual *landsmanshaftn* carried out a massive relief campaign that pumped millions of dollars into the east European, especially Polish, Jewish economy. These relief funds were supplemented by private remittances to families from relatives in the United States. American dollars thus sustained both individual households and communal institutions.

The Americans consciously sought to influence the communities they supported. Representatives of *landsmanshaftn* and other organizations carried much of this money personally on missions to the old home towns. These 'delegates' entered most obviously into 'transnational space', but they were backed up by thousands of donors who provided funds, listened to reports, and sometimes met in committees in New York to decide how communities in Poland should be run. American relief groups, both communal and *landsmanshaft*, attempted to impose a model of American non-ideological pragmatism and professionalism on the highly politicized local communities in their home towns. Beyond this, the extent of American cultural and political influence remains to be discovered, as does the degree to which American aid actually impacted on the Jewish economy.

Conversely, eastern Europe continued to exert influence on American Jews throughout the inter-war period. Concern for European Jewry,

ironically, drew American Jews further into the American political system
and led to new forms of communal organization that became mainstays of
American Jewish life (the American Jewish Congress, for example, or the
Joint Distribution Committee). Direct influence also came, surprisingly,
from Russia, which at least some American Jews came to see in a positive
light after the revolutions of 1917.

The personal connections that many American Jews had with Russia magnified its influence not only on the Jewish left, but on the American left as a
whole. These personal connections were especially intense in the case of a
few former Russian Jewish revolutionaries, like Olgin, who ventured back to
Russia to meet old comrades and see at first hand how their dreams were
being realized. But their reports and articles drew many more Jews into a
transnational network and magnified the European influence on American
Jewish politics.

The influence thus flowed in both directions: from the United States to
eastern Europe along with American visitors and money, and from Europe
to America, as returning travellers brought back the ideas and experience of
the revolution. Additional examples could no doubt be provided: traditional-
ist American Jews sending their sons to east European yeshivas, for example,
or European Jewish intellectuals reading the American Yiddish press. How
and to what degree American influences transformed European Jewish society remains an open question. At the very least, the Americans furthered the
ongoing revolution in Jewish communal authority. On the American side,
intervention in east European Jewish affairs paradoxically helped American
Jewry define its own distinct identity. At the same time, European political
developments continued to shape American Jewish political alignments even
after mass immigration had slowed to a trickle.

The Holocaust all but obliterated the east European Jewish heartland
outside the Soviet Union, and the Cold War and Soviet antisemitism
dimmed any attraction Russia had for most Jews. Moreover, in the post-war
period, Israel replaced Europe as the focus of transnational Jewish concern
and mutual influence. All of these developments, together with the passing
of the immigrant generation, obscure the degree to which the largely immigrant American Jewish community maintained ties with its east European
source community in the inter-war period.

ELEVEN

Transplanting the Heart Back East
Returning Jewish Musical Culture from the United States to Europe

JUDAH M. COHEN

ANNE THOMPSON, the Associated Press reporter who followed Cantor Rebecca Garfein to Berlin in 1998, framed the visit in triumphant terms. Her article, 'Liberal Judaism Reborn in Germany',[1] appeared in English-language newspapers across the world, and chronicled the voyage of an American female cantor from the Riverdale section of the Bronx, New York, to the German capital. Garfein went to Berlin at the invitation of a local Jewish community leader, with plans to lead a religious service and perform in a concert as part of the city's Jüdische Kulturtage (Jewish cultural festival). Yet her visit had far greater symbolic importance: Garfein, noted the reporter, was to become the first female cantor ever to lead a Jewish religious service in Berlin. The previous year, in 1997, she had gained the distinction of becoming the first female cantor to give a concert of synagogue music in that city. Her return to participate in the community's religious life in 1998 therefore led both the reporter and many of the people interviewed for the article to portray her as successfully restoring Liberal Judaism to its European roots, and bringing 'home' a musical and liturgical tradition obliterated by the Holocaust.

Garfein's story is one of several from the 1990s and 2000s in which musical artists reportedly 'returned' European Jewish cultural practices to their lands of origin. While each event had its own unique story, the chronicles of these tours tended to follow a certain metanarrative and fulfil a remarkably similar set of criteria. They frequently involved American musicians; they tended to frame the 'reimported' practices as continuous with European Jewish musical traditions from the early twentieth century; they invariably

I wish to express my gratitude to Rebecca Garfein, Ken Richmond, and Joshua Jacobson for providing invaluable comments on drafts of this essay, and to Larry Sandberg, Miriam Shazeer, and Michelle Levin for their encouragement and help in obtaining graphics permissions.

[1] Associated Press, 21 Nov. 1998.

cited the Holocaust as a point of rupture or 'loss' for these traditions; they implied the role of the United States as a surrogate home for European Jewish musical practices that nurtured the music in European Jewry's absence; and they often celebrated the 'repatriation' of such musical practices as a symbolic public event, making it worthy of commodification and distribution through various media outlets. The individual artists participating in these trips, moreover, would frequently describe their role as both tourists and cultural ambassadors. On the one hand they served publicly as vessels of musical migration and respected voices of musical authenticity; on the other, they often found time between performances to explore personal agendas of individual and communal Jewish history, typically as Americans coming to terms with the Holocaust or seeking information on relatives who fell victim to the Nazi regime.

A closer look at this phenomenon, however, reveals a far more complex set of processes taking place, one that both illustrates how people construct concepts of tradition and illuminates ways of understanding and theorizing cultural transmission through such constructs. It is important to note, for example, that these acts of musical 'return' almost always involved European societies that on the whole willingly accepted the underlying structures and ideologies of return established by outside artists. Ruth Gruber has explored the recent European interest in promoting and performing an ostensibly romanticized Jewish culture (often independent of any local Jewish presence), and Mark Slobin and others have discussed the emerging transnational nature of the genre called 'klezmer music' as it flows between Europe, the United States, and Israel.[2] Yet while both authors acknowledge the importance of outside artists to the revival of European Jewish cultural life, neither discusses in any detail what it means for the process of reverse transatlantic musical transmission actually to take place, or how it figures within broader historical questions of cultural migration. The question of how these tourist-ambassadors nurtured such a level of cultural significance within the realms of Jewish perception on both sides of the Atlantic has remained unexplored.

I will attempt to address this question here by briefly analysing three instances of musical 'repatriation' effected from west to east: Cantor Rebecca Garfein's aforementioned Berlin concerts in 1997 and 1998; the summer 2000 tour of the Klezmaniacs, a high-school klezmer band from Massachusetts, through Poland, Ukraine, and Israel; and the Zamir Chorale of Boston's two-week tour of central and east European sites in 1999. Each of these trips received significant media coverage (often initiated by the participants themselves), and the perceived cultural importance of their

---

[2] Ruth Ellen Gruber, *Virtually Jewish* (Berkeley, 2002); Mark Slobin, *Fiddler on the Move: Exploring the Klezmer World* (New York, 2000).

activities, often framed within American discourses of Holocaust memory, led to the production of three compact discs, two feature-length documentaries, and several newspaper articles and press releases. The three cases I highlight here, moreover, offer perspectives on an entire genre of Jewish musical return to Europe, which includes acts by more mainstream performers such as Shlomo Carlebach and Itzhak Perlman, as well as other figures with a more specialized appeal.

I will argue, however, that these tours did not merely transplant Jewish music back to its 'homeland'. Rather, the liturgical, klezmer, and choral labels used by these groups respectively served a double purpose as 'heritage musics' (to use Barbara Kirshenblatt-Gimblett's term) representing versions of authentic east European culture[3] and as vessels for American Jewish cultural practices to move eastward and take root. The performers who carried the music across the Atlantic negotiated a balance in this process: they served alternately as culture-bearers who brought 'lost' musical genres back into currency and as visitors who deeply valued their own role in the narrative of post-Holocaust return.

A LAND OF MANY HISTORIES: TRACING THE TRAJECTORIES OF JEWISH MUSICAL PRACTICE

The case studies I focus on here provide a commentary on the role that sound plays in constructing historical narrative and its practical impact in shaping contemporary social and cultural activities. Following suggestions fostered by new historicist schools of thought, I will view history as a deeply subjective understanding of the past that constantly competes with other historical understandings, all using the forms at their disposal to vie for their own sense of legitimacy.[4] Within this approach, different social groups (which may claim communal identity under the rubric of class, occupation, nationality, geographical location, and so forth) often create their own specific voices of historical discourse, developing them through internal debates about which parameters of history are most relevant, which historical moments are most defining, which interpretations best serve current agendas, and which interpreters are most socially relevant. Academic historians, while often claiming the formal training and cultural capital to fashion the most informed narrative of history, represent only one of these voices, and one particularly prone to bemoaning 'popular' perceptions of history as naive, simplistic, or politically or commercially motivated. Yet in order to

[3] See Barbara Kirshenblatt-Gimblett, 'Sounds of Sensibility', in Mark Slobin (ed.), *American Klezmer: Its Roots and Offshoots* (Berkeley, 2002), 129–73: 133–4.

[4] Joel Fineman, 'The History of the Anecdote: Fiction and Fiction', in H. Aram Veeser (ed.) *The New Historicism* (New York, 1989), 49–76.

understand the case studies presented here such 'popular' views of history need to receive a full hearing—as active interpretations of the past, and as perceptions that themselves shape historical events and future historical thinking. By taking a broad ethnographic approach that explores how these various historical discourses interact, by focusing on the medium of sound (which often seems elusive in conventional retellings of history), and by examining how individuals bring together issues of interpretation in the context of real movements and events, I therefore enter a rich yet ambiguous realm that links story, history, and historiography. While I will present historical 'facts' here, I also acknowledge that facts, together with historical frameworks and concepts, are necessarily selective in even the most painstaking studies, and often illustrate a tie with the present as much as an understanding of the past. For the musicians and audiences I introduce here, the use and production of sound constitutes a similar strategy for linking historical discourses on many levels to produce meaning. To them, the experience of music can serve at once as a pleasurable sensation, a means of bringing the past to life, a form of erudition, a qualitative argument for historical authority, an indicator of essential Jewish 'qualities', a mode of healing social conflict or historical rupture, and a public means for imbuing a moment with symbolic importance.

These multilayered constructions of history, as represented by the musicians and others who employ them, come at a crucial point within the framework of a centuries-old historical trajectory that includes an important American detour. In order to gain a more nuanced understanding of that trajectory, I will begin by providing some background on the three 'traditions' of musical expression these artists illustrate in their performances: synagogue music (epitomized by the cantor or *ḥazan*), klezmer music, and choral music for concert performance.

From the mid-nineteenth to the early twentieth centuries, the mass migration of central and east European Jews to the United States caused a cultural shift in American Jewish practice. As described by Hasia Diner, Jonathan Sarna, Daniel Soyer, Michael Weisser, and many other scholars of American Jewish history, the arrivals found themselves enmeshed in a dialogue of negotiation between Jewish practices which they felt epitomized their land of origin, and those that reflected the ethos of their new home.[5] Immigrants would often try to re-create aspects of religious and communal life in Europe by establishing synagogues, mutual aid societies (*landsmanshaftn*), and other institutions as places for developing forms of Jewish discourse appropriate to their new surroundings. Music, a crucial element of

[5] See e.g. Hasia Diner, *The Jews of the United States* (Berkeley, Calif., 2004), 1–3; Jonathan Sarna, *American Judaism: A History* (New Haven, 2004), 136–207; Michael Weisser, *A Brotherhood of Memory: Jewish Landsmanshaftn in the New World* (New York, 1985).

religious and communal activity, served as a significant barometer of these discussions during what Soyer has called the 'complex and ongoing series of adjustments' that characterized the move westward.[6]

The figure of the *ḥazan*, identified at the time as a synagogue musical leader, provides an important paradigm for understanding how such negotiations proceeded. As early as the mid-nineteenth century, eastern Europe began to gain broad recognition as the breeding ground for a particularly heightened form of religious musical performance, propagated by a well-developed and hierarchical training complex of choirs and cantorial positions. Even Germany and Austria modelled this 'east European' aesthetic in their nineteenth-century cantorial training schools (or *Lehrerseminare*), and instructors seem to have been more likely to praise the skills of students born and trained in the east.[7] After 1880 transatlantic immigration, combined with the emergence of the recording industry, brought the east European cantor to a new level of international acclaim. The most celebrated practitioners, such as Josef (Yossele) Rosenblatt, toured concert halls on both sides of the Atlantic, sold numerous recordings of their performances, earned comparisons with opera stars, and gained great celebrity. In the United States, moreover, the large numbers of east European Jewish immigrants helped the cantorial idiom dominate both the perception and performance of Jewish religious sound, and the cantor's American dilemma of how to practise his art amid the lures of the jazz age gained its own place in history as the plot for the first feature film with synchronized sound, *The Jazz Singer* (1927).

Similar kinds of migration and transformation took place among the Jewish musicians often called *klezmorim*. Performing at Jewish life-cycle rituals and *landsmanshaftn* gatherings, they served simultaneously as representatives of some form of aural 'tradition' and as a reflection of their new American environment. As Walter Z. Feldman has pointed out, the trip westward resulted in numerous changes to what at that point comprised a wide range of practices and styles: musical genres and dance types were consolidated; the clarinet began to overtake the violin as the dominant leading melodic instrument (perhaps because it produced a louder sound); and the *klezmorim* themselves began to experiment by establishing their first labour unions in the hope of ensuring equitable employment and fair pay.[8]

[6] Daniel Soyer, *Jewish Immigrant Associations and American Identity in New York, 1880–1939* (Cambridge, Mass., 1997), 3.

[7] Geoffrey Goldberg, 'Maier Levi of Esslingen, Germany: A Small-Town *Hazzan* in the Time of the Emancipation and his Cantorial Compendium', Ph.D. diss., Hebrew University of Jerusalem, 2000, 32.

[8] Walter Z. Feldman, 'Bulgărească/Bulgarish/Bulgar: The Transformation of a Klezmer Dance Genre', in Slobin (ed.), *American Klezmer*, 84–124; James Loeffler, 'Di Rusishe Progresiv Muzikal Yunyon No. 1 fun Amerike: The First Klezmer Union in America', in Slobin (ed.), *American Klezmer*, 35–51. Mark Slobin's collection provides the most comprehensive discussion and presentation of American klezmer music to date.

Jewish choral societies also appear to have begun in central and eastern Europe. According to Marion Jacobson, the first Yiddish choruses likely grew out of late nineteenth-century European Zionist, labour, and progressive organizations, and may have taken their cue from contemporary German workers' singing societies.[9] Particularly influential among these early groups was Hazomir ('The Nightingale'), a society founded in Łódź, which established choral groups in several European cities and enjoyed direction by accomplished musicians such as Joseph Rumshinsky (who would later conduct similar groups in the United States). American Jewish institutions made attempts to support amateur choral groups from the first decade of the twentieth century; but it was not until in the mid-1910s that sustainable choruses, established by Yiddish-speaking émigrés, gained popularity in the United States. Groups such as New York's Workmen's Circle Chorus and Chicago's Freiheit Gezang Farein (both founded in 1914) began as collectives of amateurs but eventually developed into polished choral performers and social clubs, sometimes counting hundreds of members in their ranks. In 1924 these and other left-wing musical groups formed the Jewish Music Alliance, which continued to promote community music-making in what they considered to be a Yiddish idiom.[10]

From the sanctuary to the wedding hall to the concert hall, these three musical forms addressed different needs in American Jewish life while at the same time effecting a real transnational dialogue with central and eastern Europe. Particularly important in each case was eastern Europe's continued status as a place of perceived musical authority, a cultural centre of the Jewish world that maintained its musical training structures and consequently conferred an aura of authenticity upon its exported practitioners. Though conditions in the US increasingly shifted American Jewish musical practice away from its European origins, the continued possibility for musicians and their recordings to travel relatively fluidly from one region to another kept eastern and central Europe as a real and present part of the American Jewish sonic experience.

Each of these musical traditions experienced significant ruptures during the twentieth century, as the Holocaust destroyed what many saw as the 'source' of such musical practices, leaving American Jewry to set its own agenda for musical self-expression. Hebrew Union College, for example, established the nation's first cantorial school in 1948 both to remember and to re-create the east European *ḥazan* in America; the Jewish Theological

[9] Marion Jacobson, 'With Song to the Struggle: An Ethnographic and Historical Study of the Yiddish Folk Chorus', Ph.D. diss., New York University, 2004, 54, 61.

[10] Ibid. 84 ff. See also the essays collected in Mordecai Yardeini (ed.), *50 Years of Yiddish Song in America* (New York, 1964).

Seminary and Yeshiva University followed suit shortly after.[11] Transforming what their creators perceived as an orally transmitted, apprenticeship-based tradition into a multi-year, curriculum-based course of study, these schools recast the cantor as an academically trained figure able to serve as the musical authority in America's synagogues. Such institutions also renewed the cantorial repertoire, fashioning their own canons from published collections and laying a fertile centre ground for the creation and dissemination of new liturgical compositions. The post-war period was also a low point for *klezmorim*: with a new, mainly American-born generation of Jews gaining prominence, the instrumental styles associated with eastern Europe gave way in the 1950s and 1960s to new modes of musical expression, often more closely associated with American and Israeli idioms. Such choices often relegated east European-born musicians and their music to 'Old World' enclaves such as Catskill resorts and New York's hasidic scene, while other artists viewed the style as a source for parody.[12] Choirs also experienced a significant shift away from mainstream Jewish musical production as the Yiddish left-wing heyday of the early twentieth century began to fade in the 1950s, falling into political disfavour and associated with an ageing populace.[13] With weakening ties to a no longer thriving European Jewish society, these forms of expression found themselves struggling for attention wholly within the context of the United States (though with an occasional nod towards the emerging state of Israel), and engaging in various attempts to maintain their relevance to a reoriented Jewish population.

In the 1960s, however, many young Jews began to 'rediscover' the cultural traditions they saw as belonging to their parents and grandparents during the searches for their 'own' culture that were common among American youth at the time. Younger musicians and music enthusiasts began to express renewed interest in the three forms of musical expression described here (among others), and recontextualized their sounds within counter-cultural philosophies to represent some aspect of essential Jewishness. The material once played by *klezmorim*, for example, gained a reinvigorated and consolidated identity as 'klezmer music' at this time, with the first groups attempting to research and re-create a symbolically 'Jewish' music of the past.[14] The young Stanley Sperber co-founded the Massad Choral Group in 1960 as an extension of the vocal ensemble at his Zionist summer camp of the same name. As the camp's director was concerned about their use of Massad's name in a different context the group eventually changed it to the Zamir

[11] Judah M. Cohen, 'Becoming a Reform Jewish Cantor: A Study in Cultural Investment', Ph.D. diss, Harvard University, 2002, 86–117.

[12] Hankus Netsky, 'American Klezmer: A Brief History', in Slobin (ed.), *American Klezmer*, 13–23: 19–20.   [13] Jacobson, 'With Song to the Struggle', 135 ff.

[14] See e.g. *A Jumpin' Night in the Garden of Eden*, dir. Michal Goldman (First Run Features, 1988).

Chorale. And in 1971 Hebrew Union College admitted its first female cantorial student, whose graduation four years later marked the start of a significant gender shift within the profession. Each of these events manifested new forms of Jewish identity, and provided a new generation of people with a sense of a rooted, transnational musical past, even as that past was itself mostly couched in contemporary ideologies.

By the late 1990s the klezmer genre, the Zamir Chorale (and its sister organization, the Zamir Chorale of Boston), and the female cantor had all found places on the map of—and perhaps had become emblematic of—American Jewish culture. Seen by both practitioners and listeners as iconic markers in a long-standing Jewish cultural history, these musical styles essentially represented an invented continuity, and a uniquely American dialogue with Jewish identity and tradition. At the same time, their claims to a European lineage enabled them to be presented as authentic Jewish musical practices from the past, thus facilitating their entry back into central and eastern Europe as 'returned' genres.

RETURNING LIBERAL JUDAISM THROUGH THE FEMALE VOICE

Cantor Rebecca Garfein (Figure 1) embodied this dual role of tradition-bearer and culture broker particularly strongly.[15] As a 1993 graduate of New York's Hebrew Union College School of Sacred Music, she received an education steeped in the recitatives and choral works of the great central and east European cantors, as chosen and framed by her instructors; she trained with contemporary cantorial authorities who inspired deep respect from students for their direct lineage back to the traditions and practices of eastern Europe; and she gained extensive experience learning and presenting music written by American Jewish composers who defined themselves in terms of the cantorial tradition. As a woman, her voice fell into a different range from the voices of her male predecessors, but, after over twenty years of female cantorial education at Hebrew Union College that included the addition of female faculty members, the development of techniques for 'adapting' classic cantorial repertoire to the female voice, and classes that tended to enrol more women than men, her range was no longer unusual.

To Dr Andreas Nachama, however, the recently appointed president of the Berlin Jewish community and assistant artistic director of the city's annual Jüdische Kulturtage, a female cantor was ideal for sending a statement about Progressive Judaism to Berlin's Jewish population. This statement was the subtext in Nachama's invitation to Garfein to give a concert at

---

[15] I take this phrase from Mellonee Burnim, 'Culture Bearer and Tradition Bearer: An Ethnomusicologist's Research on Gospel Music', *Ethnomusicology*, 29/3 (1985), 432–47.

FIGURE 1. Headshot of Cantor Rebecca Garfein used to publicize her 1997 Berlin concert; the photo also appears twice on the CD release of the concert. *Used with permission*

the Centrum Judaicum as part of the 1997 festival. The festival's theme that year—the Jews of New York City—paved the way for her arrival, but in addition to the concert itself Nachama also saw Garfein's visit as an opportunity to introduce and model a new musical repertoire from American composers in a manner that might broaden the Liberal Jewish community's prayer aesthetic. Garfein's trip would thus serve multiple purposes.

The organization of the concert, however, required some negotiation and adjustment of expectations, particularly with regard to musical content. After receiving the invitation, Garfein attempted to assemble a repertoire that reflected her idea of the Berlin Jewish community's musical legacy: having learned during her cantorial training that nineteenth-century Berlin gave rise to a high point in Jewish musical history, she considered a programme featuring the works of Berlin composer Louis Lewandowski (1821–94) and his contemporaries. For Nachama, however, the concert appeared to involve a different kind of return, one that would renew the liturgy of the Liberal synagogue through a sound that broke from the past:

I was preparing for the concert, and I assumed incorrectly that [Nachama] would want to hear German-Jewish music. And his comment to me was 'No, we *do* that. We know that already. We want you to prepare a concert of music that is popular in the United States. . . . We don't want to hear our music; we want to hear *your* music.' So that was basically where the idea of the concert came from.[16]

Thus, at Nachama's request, Garfein prepared a programme of mainly American Jewish liturgical compositions by twentieth-century synagogue composers such as Max Helfman (1901–63), Lazar Weiner (1897–1982),

---

[16] Interview with Cantor Rebecca Garfein, 22 Dec. 2004.

Meir Finkelstein (b. 1951),[17] and Rachelle Nelson (b. 1956). She sent copies
of the music in advance to the choir of the Pestalozzi Strasse Synagogue, a
mixed-gender group that normally sang at religious services in a sanctuary a
short walk away from the anticipated performance space. When she arrived
in Berlin (where she found her face gracing the cover of the festival programme in one newspaper), she held one rehearsal with the choir and then
performed in the evening. The concert, in what had been the women's
gallery of the partially reconstructed Oranienburger Strasse Synagogue
(now the Centrum Judaicum), was by all accounts a success: Garfein and the
choir performed to a packed and enthusiastic room. As per Nachama's intentions, moreover, the city's Liberal egalitarian congregation used the event as
an opportunity to begin incorporating selections from the concert into their
weekly worship, presumably in the hope of broadening their repertoire to
include American composers.

Garfein received a second invitation the following year to lead an egalitarian service (as noted, another first), and to give a separate concert with
Estrongo Nachama—a Holocaust survivor, the local *Oberkantor*, and the
father of Andreas. The Friday night service that resulted from this invitation
became a signal event, highlighted by the Associated Press as symbolizing
the return of Liberal Judaism to Berlin. To the Berlin Liberal Jewish community, moreover, the event was seen as another opportunity to import
American Reform Jewish music into its religious practice. In preparing for
the service, Garfein noted, 'they wanted a lot of the music that I do here [in
New York], not necessarily what they do there'.[18] The service thus gave the
congregation an ethnographic opportunity to experience the sound of
American Reform Judaism in action, perhaps with the expectation that it
would reinvigorate Liberal Judaism in Berlin. Garfein's concert with
Estrongo Nachama, meanwhile, followed the Jüdische Kulturtage theme for
that year of Vienna, and thus featured musical selections by Gustav Mahler,
Arnold Schoenberg, and Salomon Sulzer among others. Although involving
a more conventional European repertoire, this event, too, had symbolic
importance, bringing together two cantors from different continents, generations, and genders. In so doing, it projected an evocative image of continuity among Jewish singers of sacred music, providing the audience with
historical narratives of both revival and transformation.

Garfein's visits to Berlin in 1997 and 1998 had lasting repercussions on the
city's Liberal congregation that went beyond new repertoire alone. Shortly

[17] Though born in Israel and trained in the United Kingdom before emigrating to the United
States in 1974 (and, as of October 2007, working at a synagogue in Toronto), Finkelstein is
generally described by his contemporaries as an American composer. See, for example, his biography at the Milken Archive of American Jewish Music. <http://www.milkenarchive.
org/artists/artists.taf?artistid=286> (accessed 16 Oct. 2007).
[18] Interview with Cantor Rebecca Garfein, 22 Dec. 2004.

after the second concert, one of the female choristers began to take a regular role as the Berlin congregation's cantorial soloist, singing selections Garfein had brought over and actively seeking out additional repertoire and training in the United States. Garfein's visits thus appear to have created an opportunity for women to assume positions of liturgical leadership in Berlin as part of its Liberal 'renaissance', while at the same time opening up a connection with American resources. Both she and Andreas Nachama later spent additional time studying cantorial and rabbinic material (respectively) in the American Jewish Renewal movement: Nachama received his *semikhah* (ordination) from Renewal rabbi and spiritual figurehead Zalman Shachter-Shalomi in 2000 and the chorister began using the title of *Kantorin* around the same time to describe her role in the Berlin Liberal Jewish community.[19]

Before Garfein's first trip to Germany her husband had insisted on making arrangements to record the concert, arguing that it could have historic significance. His expectations proved correct: with the encouragement of Andreas Nachama and the Jüdische Kulturtage, the tape from the concert became Cantor Garfein's first commercial recording, *Sacred Chants of the Contemporary Synagogue* (Figure 2).[20] As portrayed on the CD, Garfein's visit unequivocally aligned with the history of Progressive Judaism in Germany: Nachama's liner notes placed it on a level of importance equal to that of the first international conference of the World Union of Progressive Judaism, held in Berlin in August 1928, thereby linking the two events as the 'birth' and 'revival' of the movement.[21] The marketing strategy for the CD reflected this narrative as well: Garfein released the recording at the 1998 Jüdische Kulturtage in Berlin during a special press event, and the following January, in a gathering held at New York City's German Consulate, she officially released the CD in the United States.[22] Thus did an American singer of Jewish music become a symbol of (if not the publicized catalyst for) the reawakening spirit of Progressive Judaism in Berlin—and, by extension, Germany.

[19] <http://www.nachama.de/an1_frames.htm> (accessed 29 June 2005).

[20] According to Garfein (interview, 22 Dec. 2004), the music on the CD was the same as that given at the concert, with two exceptions. First, she eliminated one of the encores—a repeat of Robbie Solomon's 'Yismeḥu'. More significantly, however, she and her husband added 'reverb' (hall sound) to the recording in order to give it 'more of a feeling of being in a [concert] hall'. This change, a reaction to the 'dryness' of the performance space, brought it more into line with audience expectations of the sound music in a synagogue (and a vocal performance space in general) should have. It is worth considering whether the modification reflected a greater sense of the synagogue which had stood in that spot, rather than of the reconstructed space.

[21] Andreas Nachama, 'Reflections from Berlin'. Liner notes to Rebecca Garfein, *Sacred Chants of the Contemporary Synagogue* (New York: Bari Productions, 1998), 4–5.

[22] ' "Sacred Chants of the Contemporary Synagogue" Features Mezzo-Soprano Cantor Rebecca Garfein in Historic Berlin Concert Recording', PR Newswire, 19 Jan. 1998. ProQuest.

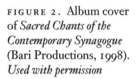

FIGURE 2. Album cover
of *Sacred Chants of the
Contemporary Synagogue*
(Bari Productions, 1998).
Used with permission

Garfein's trips to Germany also incorporated a personal mission: her grandparents had escaped from Germany in 1938, and, like others who embarked on 'roots' tours, she wished to discover more about her relatives' lives before the Second World War. During her first visit, she attempted unsuccessfully to locate her great-grandparents' gravesites in nearby Potsdam. According to Garfein, however, a local archivist contacted her four hours before her concert, claiming he had information about her family; then, in a symbolic gesture, he mysteriously delivered a packet of information to Garfein backstage at the concert, between encores. This material reinforced Garfein's ties to the Jewish past in Germany, while also affording her the personal catharsis often seen as an important part of the post-Holocaust Jewish roots tour narrative.[23] The following year she returned with her parents, and, when not performing, she took the time to explore places and names of importance to her family history based on the papers she had received.

While the leaders of Berlin's Jewish community framed Garfein's visits as key moments for reinvigorating Liberal Jewish practice in Germany, they were neither the first nor the only ones to employ such a strategy. In November 1996, a year before Garfein's first concert, American cantors Steven and Elizabeth Berke, who were affiliated to the Conservative movement in the US, received a similar invitation to perform in Munich—an appearance later publicized on the resulting CD, subtitled 'A Concert in

[23] This narrative has become an important part of documentary films such as *The Last Days* (dir. James Moll, 1998), novels such as Jonathan Safran Foer's *Everything is Illuminated* (New York, 2002), and other experiences as recounted here.

Honor of the Re-establishment of Liberal Judaism in Germany'.[24] In a comparable merging of histories forged through a mediation process between the Berkes and the concert organizers, the musical programme traced a trajectory from European Jewish synagogue music (starting with Louis Lewandowski), across the Atlantic to America (with compositions the German organizers requested for their 'more lively' nature). The performance itself, moreover, was only one of several activities celebrating Liberal Judaism during the weekend, including a conference on the fortieth anniversary of the death of Leo Baeck, a Saturday morning service also led by the Berkes, the introduction of a new German Liberal Jewish prayer book, and the installation of a Liberal German *Oberrabbiner*. According to materials produced by the participants, the weekend left a lasting legacy, not only because of the new prayer book and *Oberrabbiner*, but also in the enduring enthusiasm of those who had attended (particularly the non-Jewish madrigal choir, from the local Hochschule für Musik, that accompanied the Berkes in performance and in the service, and who afterwards expressed their desire to continue singing the repertoire).[25]

In both Berlin and Munich, cantors and local organizers collaborated to create a seamless history of synagogue music between Europe and the United States. To the performers and many of the listeners, this history provided an important symbolic narrative of return that referenced the Holocaust as a place of disappearance and offered new opportunities for personal investigation and reflection on Jewish life in Germany. Within the context of the German Jewish Liberal congregants who invited these cantors, however, the narrative provided an additional agenda: by 're-establishing' Liberal Judaism through vessels of American Liberal Jewish musical authority, the concerts and surrounding events provided an opportunity for small, young congregations to challenge both the dominance and historicity of German Orthodox Jewish practice. More than just sentimentally acknowledging the past, these communities used the narrative of German Jewish Liberal continuity to gain momentum as they struggled to heighten public awareness of their practice and legacy within an environment that they perceived as unsympathetic.

THE KLEZMANIACS: YOUTH MEETING MEMORIES

While Rebecca Garfein helped Berlin's Liberal Jewish community to herald a new era of communal and musical memory, the Klezmaniacs presented a different kind of cultural return. Founded in 1995 by accomplished klezmer

---

[24] Steven C. Berke and Elizabeth S. Berke, *Jewish Masterworks of the Synagogue Liturgy* (Deutsche Harmonia Mundi, 1996).

[25] Elizabeth and Steven C. Berke, 'Alive and Well in Munich', *Journal of Synagogue Music*, 25/2 (1998), 8–17. (This article erroneously attributes authorship to Daniel S. Katz.)

violinist and then cantorial soloist Ken Richmond, the Klezmaniacs comprised a collective of high-school-age musicians based in North Shore Massachusetts. After several years of rehearsals, local performances, attendance at klezmer gatherings (including the annual KlezKamp conference), and master classes with accomplished klezmer musicians, the Klezmaniacs marked their progress by embarking upon a tour of Poland, Ukraine, and Israel over three weeks in the summer of 2000. The trip, some time in the planning, gained a significant amount of local publicity and financial support, and for many players it represented the first visit to what they saw as the lands that originated the music they played. Their experience would thus serve as both youthful adventure and multifaceted heritage tour.

The well-documented klezmer craze in eastern Europe at the time—and the level of authenticity that craze afforded visiting Jewish musicians—endowed the American group with a certain aura of privilege as cultural ambassadors, and served as a means for the whole entourage to transmit (or 'return') not just the music per se, but also a somewhat more complex American Jewish youth culture. As dedicated amateur klezmer musicians they came as much to learn as to perform, with the implication that their experiences in the 'old country' would enhance both their playing and their cultural capital as klezmer musicians in the United States; but the trip also came with all the trappings of a teen tour, complete with chaperones, spontaneous (though mild) adolescent behaviour, and an interest in youth-based social and cultural activities. Klezmaniacs lead singer Shira Shazeer summarized their mission at one concert: 'We're coming to the places where our music came from and bringing our own sort of special version of it.'[26] As devotees of klezmer music, the group aimed to fulfil the genre's expectations; but the members also recognized that their ages, backgrounds, geographical origins, experiences, tastes, and ideologies would imbue the group with a unique voice and personality that might differ from what they saw as an 'authentic' klezmer sound and mentality.

The Klezmaniacs' 'special version' of klezmer music, viewed in hindsight, manifested itself in three different kinds of event, each of which addressed a particular aspect of the musical repatriation experience. First and most conventional were the group's eighteen scheduled performances, most of which took place in standard venues such as concert halls, art galleries, restaurants (including one called Klezmer Hois), and designated outdoor spaces. Such locations, sanctioned by society as appropriate for the production of klezmer music, provided the basis for what Ruth Finnegan has described as 'a complex of expected roles and opportunities for music'.[27] As places where

---

[26] *Klezmer on Fish Street*, dir. Yale Strom (New York: Castle Hill Productions, 2004). I am grateful to Andrew Ingall and the New York Jewish Museum for making their copy of the film available on my research schedule.

[27] Ruth Finnegan, *The Hidden Musicians: Music-Making in an English Town* (New York, 1989), 193.

numerous other American and European klezmer ensembles had performed before, these sites provided the clearest conditions for cultural contact: a physical and behavioural differentiation between performer and listener, a prescribed norm for interaction between those producing the sound and those listening to it, and accepted behaviours for appreciation or recognition. The Klezmaniacs' regular use of these spaces on their trip thus placed the group in a pool with other klezmer ensembles, giving legitimacy to the performers' efforts.

The second kind of event, performed either as part of a prearranged concert or spontaneously, involved the act of 'reclaiming' a space and the restoration of its previous perceived historical meaning through a process of musical re-encoding. Using specific formulations of sound as transient yet transformative media, the high-school musicians fashioned themselves as a sanctifying force for Jewish eastern Europe, singing and playing their music to reinscribe Judaism into select locations. This act, important in all three case studies discussed here, received particularly dramatic illustration during a *motsei shabat* (end of the sabbath) celebration in Kazimierz, the Jewish quarter of Kraków (which by the time of the Klezmaniacs' visit housed almost no Jews). As Ken Richmond recalled afterwards on the group's website:

At the close of our first Shabbat in Krakow, we began to perform for Havdalah in Kasmierz [*sic*], the old Jewish quarter. We had been invited to lead a small group of Jewish American teenagers in music and dancing. As the sound of our music echoed off the old synagogues, hundreds of teenagers, on other youth tours, poured out of the streets and restaurants to join the revelry. What a sight it was to see hundreds of Jewish youth reclaiming Kasmierz! But as our music carried through the square, aided by the voices of our zealous young comrades, today's residents of Kazmierz called the police. The police quelled our celebration, invoking a city ordinance prohibiting noise after 10 p.m. Some of the youth refused to stop singing. After leading the throng in a mellow rendition of 'Eliyahu Hanavi' [Elijah the Prophet] we exited quickly before anyone got arrested.[28]

For Yale Strom, the filmmaker documenting the Klezmaniacs' journey, the scene appeared to hold such resonance that he used it as both a framing and a transitional device for the resulting documentary.

The act of reclaiming sites through music also played itself out in ways that went beyond the klezmer genre and into other forms of 'Jewish music'. Frequently performing at places of historical importance, the young people (led by Richmond) reinscribed a sense of Jewish presence by performing music that invoked a communal sense of identity. When the group visited

[28] <http://web.archive.org/web/20060505223827/www.klezmaniacs.org/tourpage.html> (originally accessed 30 Dec. 2004). Students also sang Shlomo Carlebach's 'Am yisra'el chai' ('The Nation of Israel Lives') that evening, again emphasizing the confrontational nature of their activity (*Klezmer on Fish Street*).

Auschwitz, for example, Richmond switched to a cantorial mode to sing
'El male raḥamim' ('God full of mercy', the traditional prayer invoking
God's mercy for the deceased) in front of the other members;[29] on the bus to
Treblinka, he led them in singing the Rav's Nigun;[30] they also sang at the
Gerer Rebbe's grave in Warsaw.[31] Through such performances, Richmond
and the Klezmaniacs created their own musical 'map' of the region—one
that both acknowledged and provided commentary on the meaning of the
places they visited.

The last type of event involved the Klezmaniacs in their capacity as
American Jewish musicians, reinforcing and complementing other forms of
American Jewish culture brought over to east European Jewry. In the
Klezmaniacs' case, this process involved a visit to a Polish summer camp for
Jewish youth jointly run by Poles and North Americans (and at least partly
funded by the American Jewish Joint Distribution Committee) south of
Warsaw.[32] Appearing as role models to the young people, most of whom
seemed to have little experience with the kind of lived Judaism promoted by
the camp, the Klezmaniacs carried an aura of celebrity. In honour of the
group's visit campers created posters that depicted klezmer musicians
dressed in hasidic garb playing stringed instruments (balalaika, guitar, violin). They showed great interest in the players' musical instruments, and
they danced and clapped along with their scheduled performance. Yet the
interaction between the Klezmaniacs and the campers went well beyond
the prescribed behaviours of a klezmer concert, as group members also
joined campers in their daily recreational activities, playing ping-pong with
them and giving piggy-back rides. The music was thus a springboard for
giving the campers a greater understanding of American Jewish life. The
Klezmaniacs, initially seen as an emblem of Jewish activity, thus contextualized their music within a broader Jewish consciousness—one the campers
could observe as a living example of the Judaism encouraged by the camp's
organizers.

As with several other instances of American klezmer musicians travelling
to eastern Europe, the Klezmaniacs' tour offered a ripe opportunity for
documenting the narrative of return, especially since the culture-bearers
were young people, and they were accompanied by a Holocaust survivor

[29] *Klezmer on Fish Street.*
[30] Ibid. The Rav's Nigun is considered one of the holiest *nigunim* in Habad Lubavitch,
believed to be written by the movement's founder, Shneur Zalman of Lyady, and listed first in
the group's three-volume *Sefer hanigunim*. Ellen Koskoff, *Music in Lubavitcher Life* (Urbana,
2001), 88–90; *Sefer hanigunim*, vol. i, ed. Samuel Zalmanoff (New York, 1948), 1.
[31] <http://web.archive.org/web/20060519032441/klezmaniacs.org/photo/warsaw.html>
(originally accessed 21 June 2005).
[32] <http://web.archive.org/web/20001209104400/http://www.jewish.org.pl/english/
foundati/TSKZ.html > (site reflects the page as of 9 December 2000).

FIGURE 3. Cover art for the Klezmaniacs' album *Sveet Like Herring Vit Potatoes*. Design by Michelle Levin. *Used with permission*

grandmother pursuing her own return narrative. To mark the occasion both symbolically and personally, the group made digital recordings of its performances, and soon after its return to the United States, its leaders compiled the best live tracks with recorded dialogue from the trip to create the album *Sveet Like Herring Vit Potatoes: Live from the Old Country* (2001; Figure 3). The group's activities also received attention from Yale Strom, who filmed the Klezmaniacs' tour and featured them in his 2004 film *Klezmer on Fish Street*.[33] Pictures from the trip posted on the group's website, moreover, suggested a level of comfort with this pervasively documentary approach: photographs of the group routinely included members of the camera crew in-frame, and occasionally even in the process of recording (Figure 4). Thus, paralleling Garfein's visit, the importance of the Klezmaniacs' trip became apparent as much through its derivative products as in its actual occurrence. In this manner it continued to supplement projects such as Itzhak Perlman's 'In the Fiddler's House' series (which led to two CDs and one concert/documentary) and the 2004 film *Klezmer Musicians Travel 'Home' to Krakow* in its intense framing of the 'returning' European klezmer scene.[34]

The Klezmaniacs, like many of the American klezmer ensembles performing in Europe, situated the rationale for their trip in both real and

[33] This film, incidentally, derived its name from the street in Będzin, Poland, where the accompanying grandmother grew up; the Klezmaniacs gave a spontaneous performance on her return to her old home.

[34] Itzhak Perlman, *In the Fiddler's House*, CD, Angel 55555 (1995); id., *Live in the Fiddler's House*, CD, Angel 56209 (1996); *Itzhak Perlman: In the Fiddler's House*, dir. Glenn DuBose and Don Lenzer (Emd/Capitol, 1995); *Klezmer Musicians Travel 'Home' to Krakow*, dir. Curt Fissel (JEM/GLO Productions, 2004).

FIGURE 4. The Klezmaniacs filmed and photographed while playing in a square in Kraków. Photograph by Miriam Shazeer. *Used with permission*

imagined history: real in the sense of being based on a documented musical past associated with particular places and individuals in Europe, and imagined in that this past had to be reconceived and reframed away from its historical source in order to gain relevance to the performers and their tour. Though the Klezmaniacs' appearance in eastern Europe did not gain publicity as a 'first', as Garfein's concert did, the excursion did mark another opportunity for east European populations to acknowledge American Jewish artists as 'guardians' of an absent European Jewish culture, and therefore recognize them as particularly qualified to bring that culture back.

REVIVING THE ECHOES: THE ZAMIR CHORALE OF BOSTON

Similar forces went into operation when the Zamir Chorale of Boston embarked on its tour of Poland and central Europe in 1999. Boston Zamir, as the group is known familiarly, situates itself historically as an extension of what its founder Joshua Jacobson describes as the 'Zamir Movement',[35] a phrase that refers to a tradition of Zionist choral singing Jacobson traces back to 1899 in Łódź. As he contextualizes the movement in his publica-

---

[35] Joshua Jacobson, email communication, 16 June 2004.

tions, choral societies devoted to presenting Jewish music sprang up throughout Europe in the late nineteenth and early twentieth centuries, and eventually took root in the United States as well, but most had died out by the 1950s.[36] In 1960, he continues, several teenagers from New York's Zionist Camp Massad, inspired by their summer choral experiences, created an ensemble they called the Massad Choral Group. A couple of years later, as the choir grew to exist as an independent, New York City-based, year-round entity, it changed its name to the Zamir Chorale.[37] While not involved in the group's early years, Jacobson began singing and working with Zamir's founder, Stanley Sperber, at New Hampshire's Camp Yavneh in the mid-1960s. Motivated (in part, he notes, by Sperber's encouragement) to create his own incarnation of the ensemble, Jacobson received permission from Sperber to use the Zamir name, and started the Zamir Chorale of Boston in 1969.[38] Several years into the group's existence he learned about the organization he would cast as Zamir's east European antecedent, Hazomir.[39]

[36] Joshua Jacobson, 'Some Preliminary Notes on the Study of the Jewish Choral Movement', *Journal of Synagogue Music*, 16/2 (1986), 59–62; id., 'From Ha-Zomir to Zamir: 100 Years of the Jewish Choral Movement', *Jewish Heritage Online Magazine*, <http://jhom.com/topics/choir/zamir.htm>; posted in 2000, an abridged version of Jacobson, 'Some Preliminary Notes'. Note that Marion Jacobson, 'With Song to the Struggle', suggests that Yiddish choirs were alive and well in the post-war period, though fulfilling a significantly different role than they did before the war.

[37] See also Stanley Sperber, 'Reminiscences on the Origins of Zamir Chorale in America', *Notes from Zamir* (May 2005), <http://www.zamir.org/Notes/NFZ-Spring05.shtml> (accessed 22 June 2005).

[38] Rachel King, 'Joshua Jacobson: Growing Up with Zamir', *Notes from Zamir* (May 2005). <http://www.zamir.org/Notes/NFZ-Spring05.shtml> (accessed 22 June 2005). I presume this article to have a high degree of accuracy (at least in portraying the story Jacobson wanted to portray), since it appears on the organization's website. Scott Sokol, however, goes further, to note that Boston Zamir may have come about out of a request from a local music luminary to have 'a group of young singers at one of her acclaimed musical events': Scott M. Sokol, 'Jewish Voices Return to Europe: A Travelog', *Journal of Synagogue Music*, 28/1 (2001), 66–73: 67.

[39] In an interview with Sheryl Kaskowitz, Jacobson recalls possibly first learning about Hazomir by reading Macy Nulman's *Concise Encyclopedia of Jewish Music* (New York, 1975): see Sheryl Kaskowitz, 'Revival, Rediscovery and Continuity: The Construction of Narratives in the History of an American Jewish Choir', unpublished presentation for Music 206, Harvard University, 20 Dec. 2004. Interestingly, retrospective accounts vary regarding the level of awareness that the Zamir choir founders had of Hazomir. Although Jacobson has never claimed to have had knowledge about the Polish Hazomir society when he founded Boston Zamir, he does occasionally include references to the 1899 group in his post-1960 Zamir Movement narrative. In a 2003 interview, for example, he stated that, in the early 1960s, Moshe Avital, who served as director of Camp Yavneh while Jacobson was attending it, 'suggested that [the founders of the Zamir Chorale of Boston] rename their choir after the old Zamir choirs that had existed in Europe in the early part of the century': 'The Beginnings of the Zamir Chorale of Boston: Camp Yavneh, 1960s', <http://www.jhom.com/topics/choir/jacobson.htm> (accessed 23 June 2005). This knowledge appears to have become a part of the group's oral history (see e.g. Sokol, 'Jewish Voices Return to Europe', 67), and provides a 'missing link' between the two organizations.

Jacobson's discovery appears to have deepened the significance of the Zamir Chorale's existence for both its singers and its audiences, and allowed Boston Zamir to lay claim to a history and context mirroring those of other forms of European Jewish culture—originating in the east, and migrating west. More importantly for this discussion, the extended narrative of Zamir's history became a crucial rationale for the group's trip to central and eastern Europe in June and July 1999.

Boston Zamir's six-city tour, entitled 'The Songs Live On', publicly celebrated a double milestone: the thirtieth year of the Zamir Chorale of Boston, and the hundredth anniversary of the founding of the Łódź Hazomir society.[40] The itinerary of the trip and the language used to describe its aims made it clear that the choir intended to conflate these two events through strategies of continuity, embodiment, evocation, and activism. 'Zamir Returns to Roots in Eastern Europe', began the group's own press release shortly after the tour ended, implying a meaningful experience that strengthened its sense of history and its affinity with the earlier Hazomir ensemble.[41] Further references in the press release to the singers as 'ambassadors' and 'pilgrims' reinforced on other levels the ensemble's historical mission of 'bringing back' Jewish choral singing to Europe. Implicit throughout the press release and other publicity material was the centrality of the Holocaust to this narrative: as much as the tour aimed to honour the memory of the Jewish choral singers seen as the progenitors of Zamir, it also needed to commemorate the events that caused Jewish choral singing in Europe to 'fall silent' until its renascence in the late 1990s.[42]

With this rationale, the Zamir Chorale of Boston prepared a broad and eclectic programme of music representing the tastes of the modern Jewish choral world, from arrangements of Israeli pioneer songs to George Gershwin's 'I Got Rhythm', from local European folksongs to Israeli art music compositions, from prayer settings by seventeenth-century Italian composer Salamone Rossi to settings by twentieth-century American Jewish composers Max Janowski and Meir Finkelstein. Other selections emphasized the group's specific connections to an interrupted past, most notably a series of choral settings by Viktor Ullmann—composed for performance in the Terezín concentration camp[43]—and 'Hazomir', a piece by Warsaw Hazomir conductor Leo Low that served as an early anthem for the Zamir

---

[40] Richard Higgins, 'Dual Anniversary', *Boston Globe*, 13 June 1999, 2; Chana Shavelson, 'Continuing with Tradition: Zamir Chorale of Boston to Tour Europe', *Jewish Advocate* (Boston), 24 June 1999, 17.

[41] <http://www.zamir.org/pr/releases/release.cgi?date=19990815> (accessed 22 June 2005).

[42] Ibid.

[43] For more on Ullmann, see Joža Karas, *Music in Terezín 1941–1945* (New York, 1985), 111–20; Verena Naegele, *Viktor Ullmann. Komponieren in verlorener Zeit* (Cologne, 2002), esp. pp. 324–52 (in Terezín).

Chorale (thus enhancing the story of how the two groups shared a spiritual affinity even before their historical connection became known). Taken as a whole, this material appeared to embody a varied representation of Judaism, as well as a varied précis of 'Jewish music', to offer to the overwhelmingly non-Jewish audiences that attended their concerts.

The same themes as those traced in the previous two case studies were evident in Boston Zamir's trip, though there seemed to be a particular emphasis among the chorale members on using song to reclaim and recast a symbolic landscape. Of course, the cities and (occasionally) the venues in which the group sang were constructed as sites of great significance to Jewish choral singing and to European Jewry in general: Warsaw, Łódź, Vienna, surviving synagogues in Kraków and Prague, and Terezín's House of Culture. Yet the group's geographical re-encoding of these spaces through the use of song extended well beyond the concert hall. Jacobson and others highlighted these activities in a resulting documentary, accompanied by footage and music from the trip illustrating the process:

Every place we went we sang 'Halleluyah' [Psalm 146] by Salamone Rossi, the earliest known Jewish choral music. [With Jacobson directing, Boston Zamir begins to sing the piece spontaneously in front of the Nozyk Synagogue in Warsaw.] It seemed especially appropriate when we visited the only synagogue in Warsaw that survived World War II. [Group continues singing. With sound of choir still in background, cut to shot of another choir member interviewed during a visit to a Jewish cemetery.]

[Chorale member Larry Sandberg:] We're reaffirming that . . . the Nazis did not succeed. We are still here. [Cut to ceiling shot of the Spanish Synagogue in Prague; the singing continues. The camera pans down to reveal Boston Zamir singing the selection in a concert, with full concert regalia. The group finishes the piece, and the audience applauds.][44]

Upon arriving outside the Łódź building where the original Hazomir group rehearsed, Boston Zamir broke into an arrangement of 'Havah nagilah'. During an unscheduled visit to the Łódź Jewish cemetery, the group sang 'Makh tsi di eygelekh' ('Close Your Eyes'), a song attributed to the conductor of Hazomir in the Łódź ghetto. And when they visited Auschwitz, the chorus members sang Salamone Rossi's setting of 'Al naharot bavel' (Psalm 137) after Jacobson exhorted the ensemble to 'pray in the way we do best'.[45] Just as with the Klezmaniacs, the Zamir Chorale of Boston transformed its journey into a form of reclamation through sound, translating the group's experience into a public form of expression wherever it went.

The visit also brought with it a sense that Boston Zamir's activities would inspire others to resuscitate Hazomir's spirit in eastern Europe: the group

---

[44] *Zamir: Jewish Voices Return to Poland*, dir. Rob Cooper and Eric Stange, videocassette (Spy Pond Productions, 2000), about 24 minutes into the film.   [45] Ibid.

gave several of its CDs as a gift to the Polish choir that had opened for them in Łódź, for example. When the Poles also asked Boston Zamir for sheet music of its repertoire, Jacobson, in response, announced his intention to send it, adding publicly: 'how wonderful to know that Zamir's music will continue in this way'.[46] Thus, once again the narrative of post-Holocaust return became a form of cultural migration: similar in name, but exceedingly different in substance.[47]

Just as importantly, the tour manifested a search for personal and spiritual connections between Boston Zamir of 1969 and Hazomir of 1899. Among the highlights of the trip, as described after the event, was the group's opportunity to make contact with two surviving former members of European Hazomir ensembles; these members' interactions with Boston Zamir, presented within the framework of a common mission, cemented in terms of spiritual relationships anything the historical relationship between the two entities lacked. For the singers, moreover, learning about the activities of Łódź Hazomir became tantamount to learning about their 'musical ancestors' (a term Jacobson used specifically). On other levels as well, participants made efforts to draw connections between the two ensembles. In the resulting documentary of the tour, for example, Jacobson's narration highlighted the importance of religious pluralism to the early Hazomir group, and projected a clear connection to values he also attributed to Boston Zamir. Occasionally the comparison went even further, to the extent that the singers, once in Europe, began to see themselves as replacements for, or even embodiments of, the earlier ensembles. When welcomed to Łódź by the city's mayor, Jacobson responded by averring in front of the group: 'I feel I speak for everyone when I say that at this moment, we feel that we are the Zamir Chorale of Łódź.'[48] Such moments, illustrating the intensity and intimacy of the Zamir experience for both singers and audiences, exemplify the extent to which a historical conflation of the two groups served a crucial role in determining the tour's effectiveness. According to Sheryl Kaskowitz, who conducted interviews with several members of Boston Zamir who went on the trip, the east European tour also served to deepen members' relationships with and commitment to the group.[49] By performing in the cities and on the stages where the first Hazomir ensemble reportedly sang, and by speaking with former members of the society, the singers could take away tangible experiences necessary for stitching together a single history

---

[46] *Zamir*, about 55 minutes into the film.
[47] Though not directly related to the Zamir Chorale of Boston's tour, a Jewish choir called 'Clil/Tslil' took root in Łódź in March 2003: <http://www.clil.pl/eng/main1024.htm> (accessed 29 June 2005). I am grateful to Joshua Jacobson for alerting me to this development, which, especially in the timeline presented by Boston Zamir's visit, has great symbolic significance.
[48] *Zamir*, about 8 minutes into the film.
[49] Sheryl Kaskowitz, email communication, 29 Dec. 2004. I am grateful to Sheryl for sharing her thoughts and research on the Zamir Chorale of Boston.

FIGURE 5. Cover art for the Zamir Chorale of Boston's CD *The Songs Live On* (2000; <www.zamir.org>). Design by Florette Kupfer. *Used with permission*

from two separate organizations. Coming to see themselves as heirs to a long-standing Jewish choral tradition, the Boston Zamir members gained the cultural integrity to claim their role as post-Holocaust musical emissaries, simultaneously restoring the memory of the original Hazomir, and reinscribing the idea of the Jewish choral society in Europe through its distinctly American lens.

As with my other two examples, the perceived importance of this cultural excursion attracted significant media attention: in addition to press coverage in Boston newspapers, the trip became the subject of a 'Live' album of performances from the tour and an hour-long documentary—both initiated and arranged by Boston Zamir. Here, too, specific choices emphasized the Zamir narrative of post-Holocaust return. The album, entitled *The Songs Live On: The Centennial Tour*, once again placed the American group within the context of the Polish group's history, unified by name and by a common participation in the 'Zamir movement'; on the CD cover, the names of the tour cities complemented a large, central white outline of a nightingale with the Hebrew word *hazamir* displayed conspicuously above its wing (Figure 5). The documentary, meanwhile, carried the title *Zamir: Jewish Voices Return to Poland*, foregrounding the site of the Holocaust's greatest Jewish losses even as the tour covered by the film included performances in Austria and the Czech Republic. On the front of the VHS slipcase, moreover, the graphic designers placed a 1941 portrait of the Łódź Hazomir performers; those who wished to see the 1999 group would need to watch the film itself, which included additional photographs of Hazomir ensembles interspersed with

Boston Zamir's performances and experiences. The resulting association between those singers who had been 'silenced since the Holocaust' and the American singers who seemingly toured in their stead ('return[ing] home [to Europe] for a triumphant song-filled celebration') thus appeared to develop, by design, into an intimate relationship.[50] As Boston Zamir openly attributed the formation of its identity to the pre-war Hazomir, so did the group style itself a living embodiment of Hazomir's values, succeeding in spite of the horrors of the Holocaust.

*

In this essay I have attempted to come to terms with a particular form of cultural migration, one that seems to intend a permanent transfer of cultural practice through human experiences that fall more along the lines of tourism than migration. Trained in 'heritage musics' in the United States, and travelling into an emotionally charged landscape, the musicians I have described here arrived in Europe as recognized practitioners and guardians of 'Jewish' musical forms believed lost during the Holocaust. Their mission to bring the music, and by association the cultural practices the music symbolized, 'back' to its place of origin thus fulfilled a multivalent relationship with history. To both musicians and audience members, each performance seemed to effect a convergence of once disparate and ruptured narratives into a continuous story of flight, destruction, and rebirth: in each case a local rethinking of European Jewish history. The recordings, writings, and films that emerged from these experiences, moreover, provided an important means for conveying such narratives to a wider (primarily English-speaking) public. Yet at the same time, in each of these cases the musical genre transported under such narrative pretences had undergone significant transformation in the United States, largely through revivals that reflected American cultural norms. The very privileging of these transformed genres speaks to America's status as the veritable second homeland for European Jewish culture, and source of authority for what Ruth Gruber would call 'things Jewish'.[51] Travel from the United States 'back' to central and eastern Europe thus completed a circuit of tradition to those involved, refashioning history in order to create it anew.

In this way did the music of pre-war European Jewry find its way back home. Or perhaps it is better to say: thus did late twentieth-century American Jewry use sound to build bridges across the Atlantic, from west to east.

---

[51] Gruber, *Virtually Jewish*.

Contributors

RAM BEN-SHALOM is Senior Lecturer in the Department of History, Philosophy, and Judaic Studies at the Open University of Israel.

MIRIAM BODIAN is Professor of Jewish History in the Graduate School of Jewish Studies, Touro College, New York.

JEREMY COHEN is Abraham and Edita Spiegel Family Foundation Professor of European Jewish History at Tel Aviv University.

JUDAH M. COHEN is Lou and Sybil Mervis Professor of Jewish Culture and Assistant Professor of Folklore and Ethnomusicology at Indiana University.

DAVID ENGEL is Greenberg Professor of Holocaust Studies, Professor of Hebrew and Judaic Studies, and Professor of History at New York University, and a Fellow of the Goldstein-Goren Diaspora Research Center, Tel Aviv University.

GERSHON DAVID HUNDERT is Professor of History and Leanor Segal Professor of Jewish Studies at McGill University.

PAULA E. HYMAN is Lucy G. Moses Professor of Modern Jewish History at Yale University.

MAUD MANDEL is Associate Professor of History and Judaic Studies at Brown University.

DAVID NIRENBERG is Professor in the Committee on Social Thought and Department of History at the University of Chicago.

MOSHE ROSMAN is Professor of Jewish History at Bar-Ilan University.

DAVID B. RUDERMAN is Joseph Meyerhoff Professor of Modern Jewish History and Ella Darivoff Director in the Center for Advanced Judaic Studies, University of Pennsylvania.

DANIEL SOYER is Associate Professor of History at Fordham University, New York.

Index

new approaches to 66, 96
in Poland–Lithuania 139
Kalmar, Ivan 90
Kaplan, Marion A. 59, 68, 69, 76
Kaplan, Yosef 16, 27, 96, 97, 98, 123, 130
Karaites 130
Kaskowitz, Sheryl 242
Katz, David 123
Katz, Jacob 9, 26, 55, 56, 58–9, 95, 114, 115, 116
kehilahs 210, 211
kelal yisrael 5
Kelly(-Gadol), Joan 57
Kieval, Hillel 71
Kirshenblatt-Gimblett, Barbara 223
Kleinberg, H. 209, 211
Kleinmann, Moshe 48
Klezmaniacs 12, 222, 233–8, 241
klezmer music 222, 227, 233–8
Klezmer Musicians Travel 'Home' to Krakow (film documentary) 237
klezmorim 225, 227
knowledge 9, 105
Komfarband (Komunistisher Farband, Communist Federation) 218
Königsberg 142
Koonz, Claudia 54–5
Kraków 241
Kushner, Meyer 214

L
La Peyrère, Isaac 130
La Terre retrouvée 81
labour groups 205, 208, 210, 226
Ladino 105
laity 9, 103–4, 120–2
landslayt 209, 213
landsmanshaftn 205–6, 207, 208, 210, 212, 219, 224
Lang, Harry 215
Langmuir, Gavin 7, 30, 51–2
language 32–3, 34, 103
see also Hebrew; Yiddish
law, Jewish:
autonomy of 174
and Conversos 182
and early modern mobility 103
see also halakhah
law, Muslim 104
law, non-Jewish 24, 51
anti-Jewish 188
and antisemitism 35, 36, 46, 53

discriminatory 173
and French Jews 78
and Jazłowiec privilege 135, 136
numerus clausus 49
Lazare, Bernard 42–3
Le Pen, Jean-Marie 91
Leff, Lisa Moses 79–80, 88–9
Leipzig trade fairs 25, 136
Leipzig University, 'Reconsidering the Borderlines' conference 16
Lerner, Gerda 8, 54, 57
letters 60
Lewandowski, Louis 229, 233
Lewis, Bernard 85 n.
Liber, Mark 217
Liberal Judaism 68, 230, 231, 232, 233
liberalism 40, 47, 49, 70
Libro llamado el alborayque 193
Liebes, Yehuda 66, 96
Łódź 226, 238, 242
lomedim 59
London:
assimilation in 76
and early modern mobility 103
emancipation in 72
merchants in 104
and post-war relief 212
Low, Leo, 'Hazomir' 240–1
Low Countries 117
Lowenstein, Steven 69
Lublin 128
Łuck 137
Luna, Alvaro de 169
Luria, Isaac 97, 107
Luther, Martin 113, 114, 115
Lutherans 123, 124–5, 128
Luzzatto, Moses Hayim 107

M
Madrid, Fernando de 196
magic 121
Maharal of Prague 121
Mahler, Gustav 230
Maid of Ludmir 66
Maimon, Solomon 23
Majorca 179, 180, 182, 183
majority culture 3, 74–5, 85, 87
see also culture, Jewish
'Makh tsi di eygelekh' ('Close Your Eyes') (song) 241
Mallorca 152, 158 n.
Mandel, Maud 8

Printed and bound by CPI Group (UK) Ltd, Croydon, CR0 4YY

09/06/2025

14685793-0003